NIRVANA

17- 17 99

6 95

NIRVANA

THE CHOSEN REJECTS

KURT ST. THOMAS *with* **TROY SMITH**

 St. Martin's Griffin ⚏ New York

www.stmartins.com

Title page: Krist Novoselic, Kurt Cobain, Dave Grohl, and Kurt St. Thomas, September 1991. Photo by Julie Kramer.

Library of Congress Cataloging-in-Publication Data

St. Thomas, Kurt.
    Nirvana : the chosen rejects / Kurt St. Thomas with Troy Smith.
      p. cm.
Discography: p. 233.
Includes bibliographical references (p. 277).
    ISBN 0-312-20663-1
    EAN 978-0312-20663-5
  1. Nirvana (Musical group)   2. Rock musicians—United States—Biography.
I. Smith, Troy. II. Title.
    ML421.N57S7 2004
    782.42166'092'2—dc21   99-015933

10 9 8 7 6 5 4

We were the chosen rejects. We chose not to be a part of the popular crowd. I mean, I can remember a lot of times the more popular people, the "jock type" of people who were into sports, and staying clean, and brushing their teeth all the time, and doing what their parents were asking them to do, they always asked me if I wanted to join their little club, and I decided not to, you know, I would rather hang out with the people who didn't get picked for the baseball team, you know, who smoke cigarettes and listen to rock 'n' roll music.

KURT COBAIN
1967–1994

Author's Note

Many of the quotes and much of the information that appear in *Nirvana: The Chosen Rejects* were taken from three separate interviews I conducted with Kurt Cobain, Krist Novoselic, and Dave Grohl in 1992. These sessions spawned the creation of the Geffen/DGC-released promotional compact disc *Nevermind It's an Interview*. Other quotes and relevant information were gleaned from interviews conducted by many interviewers with the band members over the course of their brief history together. All quotes have been identified by source notes at the end of this book.

Kurt Cobain was known to use different spellings of his name (i.e., Kurt Cobain, Kurt Kobain, Curtis D. Cohbaine) during the time in which this story takes place. Chris Novoselic changed the spelling of his name to "Krist" in 1993 to reflect his Croatian heritage. For consistency, I have chosen to refer to the two musicians as "Kurt" and "Krist."

NIRVANA

One

We don't like to think of ourselves as a political band
because you tend to become too anal . . . We just ask people
to be aware a bit, and I think the songs kinda reflect that.

—KURT COBAIN

It was more than just a concert, it was an awakening, a new venture into a new world for the thousands of people who lined the street behind Boston's famed Fenway Park, desperate for a chance to see Nirvana play inside an eight-hundred-person club called Axis. It was September 23, 1991, the night before *Nevermind* was released to retail stores throughout the United States. A month and a half of hype and radio station airplay of "Smells Like Teen Spirit" had driven people from their warm and cozy homes onto a chilly street for the slimmest of hopes to see the band that was on the verge of becoming the most popular group in alternative music and, eventually, mainstream rock 'n' roll. The line, which extended beyond the horizon of the quarter-mile-long street, was an extraordinary sight to behold, considering that just over a year before, in a tiny club a couple of miles away in Cambridge, less than 150 people had even shown the slightest interest in seeing this then-unknown band play live.

By now, Nirvana occupied a unique place in alternative culture. Playing sold-out concerts like this one had become the norm for them in 1991, as it would for the next two years. "Smells Like Teen Spirit" was alternative music's first true smash hit to cross into the mainstream, and it created a new cult of fans from all walks of life who might not otherwise have explored the world of punk rock. On this night, that collective consciousness was waiting in line for a concert already sold out as a result of on-air promotion and support by WFNX-FM, which invited Nirvana and fifteen other bands to play an AIDS benefit concert that filled the stages of four nightclubs on Lansdowne Street. For me, as music director of the station, the night was a culmination of months of hard work needed to put together a show of such magnitude. It was my responsibility to book all sixteen acts for the concert, but when I first heard the *Nevermind* demo in early 1991, it was very clear who would be the first band I would try to secure to play the gig itself.

It's hard to argue the point that the album, *Nevermind*, shifted the world of rock music to the hard left, but Nirvana really began changing the landscape of music and mainstream radio programming nearly two years before *Nevermind*'s release. It was in the winter of 1989 when many of us first heard Nirvana's first single, "Love Buzz," and once I got a copy of their debut album, *Bleach*, I listened to nothing else for three months. Musically, *Bleach* reminded me of a cross-section of my favorite bands from a number of different eras. It churned out the heavy grind of Black Sabbath, Led Zeppelin, and Aerosmith; it fostered the punk attitude of Black Flag and the Dead Kennedys; and it followed the simple pop melodies of John Lennon and the Beatles. It reflected an uncanny mix of sounds and rhythms of the classic rock bands I grew up with and the underground bands that I was introduced to in college. *Bleach* was fresh and innovative and sounded unlike anything that was being played in the alternative music scene at the time.

I'm sure my friends thought I was nuts, spending most of the next year constantly talking about a band that few people had ever heard of; in the summer of 1991, I even told the new local promotions guy for the David Geffen Company (DGC), Nirvana's label, how lucky he was to be able to promote the new Nirvana record that was due out later that fall. When "Smells Like Teen Spirit" finally arrived at the radio station in early August, it was put on the airwaves during my evening show as soon as I ripped it out of the envelope in which it had arrived. "This is the world premiere of Nirvana's 'Smells Like Teen Spirit,'" I announced to all who were tuned in, "and this song will change the way we think about music." That same DGC local guy, Ted Volk, heard what I said and jumped all over me about it. "What are you, insane?" was all he could say to me. Perhaps, but all I know is the minute I played the song, our telephones rang off the wall. In the two decades of being a disc jockey, I have never seen, before or since, the phone lines light up they way they did when we first played "Smells Like Teen Spirit."

Most of the time when we played the song, our listeners weren't really listening at all. They were reacting. "Who does this song?" "What song is this?" "Who are these guys?" were the most common questions at first, and they were followed by "Can you play the mosquito song?" and "I wanna hear that mulatto song." It didn't matter that they didn't know the name of the song or the group. And it definitely wasn't just Kurt Cobain's hard-to-understand lyrics that were driving them to the phones. It was the energy of Dave Grohl's concussive drumming, of Krist Novoselic's throbbing bass, and of Kurt's gut-wrenching screams that made them absolutely stop what they were doing and clog up our request lines for hours. Playing "Teen Spirit" on the air wasn't the first time we'd ever played Nirvana—"Here She Comes Now" actually received some exposure earlier in 1991, and our nighttime disc jockey regularly defied the format orders of our program director by playing *Bleach*, sometimes in its entirety, during the overnight hours. But neither generated the response and reaction that "Teen Spirit" inspired that August.

It was the keen insight of people like Mark Kates, the head of alternative promotion at DGC Records, that stoked the fire of Nirvana's marketing machine for the support of *Nevermind*. His undying passion for antiestablishment was one of the reasons both Sonic Youth and Nirvana joined DGC's roster of artists, but his tenacity for recognizing talent in its incubation stage began much earlier when he was a regular fixture in the burgeoning Boston underground music scene. Working for the local independent record label Ace of Hearts allowed Kates to form a relationship with Mission of Burma, the seminal punk group whose impact on alternative music made it possible for bands like Nirvana to be heard in the mainstream. This well-earned credibility helped push "Smells Like Teen Spirit" to the level of American radio airplay it needed to reach the masses, and Kates, along with DGC's head of college promotion, John Rosenfelder, was very instrumental in bringing Nirvana to Boston to play our benefit concert.

By the time the show rolled around in September, I was thoroughly prepared for an in-depth and insightful conversation with Nirvana just prior to their noteworthy performance. The night before, I had dinner with them at an upscale restaurant in town, where the other patrons gave us all the "who the hell are these guys?" look as we entered wearing jeans with holes in them, T-shirts hanging out of our pants, and sneakers untied. It was a relaxed and casual time, and Krist and Kurt and I talked about how I'd first met them at a Nirvana show in Cambridge almost a year and a half before. After dinner, we bid our good-byes and good wishes and the group headed over a few blocks to see their friends the Melvins play the celebrated Boston underground club the Rat. It was a great night, and I was looking forward to transferring the vibe onto the airwaves for all of Boston to hear the following evening.

But somehow, none of this mattered by the time the trio from the tiny town of Aberdeen, Washington, got behind the mic with me the night of the concert to conduct one of their few American radio interviews. Kurt and Krist weren't exactly excited about doing the interview, and Dave was pissed off because I hadn't introduced him as a member of the band (he was late arriving for the start of it). The live discussion was absolutely terrible—because of the complexity of the huge concert, bands were constantly being shoved in and out of the interview area, creating a hectic scene that bordered on chaos. By the time they got behind the radio mic, Nirvana wasn't paying attention, and the proximity of the wasted crowd caused distractions at every turn. What a contrast compared to the serenity of the interview session I would conduct with the band just a few months later after their first appearance on *Saturday Night Live*.

MTV was in town to cover this multiband, multigenre concert, about which Krist commented, "Variety is a wonderful thing, There's something for everybody." MTV initially showed little interest in covering the event until they found out Nirvana was playing. For reasons still unknown, their marketing team had set up a game of Twister in a nightclub next door that included the use of Crisco shortening, and Krist did not hesitate to put his six-foot-seven-inch frame into the center of the action. In an attempt to get some of the Crisco off his pants, Krist grabbed a nearby American flag and wiped his ass with it, in clear view of a jarheadlike creature who undoubtedly took offense to this seemingly innocent gesture. It ignited a fight with several testosterone-filled individuals who were watching the game, and the sudden increase in the room's energy level ignited the band, who by now were undoubtedly primed for a sonic assault unlike any other that had graced the Axis stage.

The club was packed as soon as the doors opened. The local fire marshal almost shut it down for packing so many people into the place, but after much pleading and begging, the show was allowed to go on as planned. The then up-and-coming Smashing Pumpkins underground trailblazers and local punk favorites Bullet LaVolta lit the fuse and fanned the flames for the overheated and overstimulated audience that filled the room that night. Their adoration for Nirvana had reached astonishing levels due to the sudden and surprising growth of the band's popularity, and the principal object of their affection was a lanky, impish guitar player who, because of writing "Teen Spirit," was placed in the unexpectedly difficult position of being hailed as the new spokesman for their generation.

It was my privilege to introduce Nirvana to the raucous and sweaty crowd. As I was standing next to the stage, I looked at Kurt, and I thanked him for playing the concert. Kurt didn't speak a lot, but when he did, he was able to sum up thoughts of a thousand words in a very short but concise way. He looked at me and smiled. "Thanks for promoting this," was all he said. In another time, that comment would have taken on another, more sarcastic, interpretation, confirming the never-ending and unpredictable contradiction of Kurt Cobain. His comments always presented a unique duality—I don't really want to be a rock star, I'm really glad I'm a rock star. But for this show he seemed very sincere in his appreciation, and he was genuinely blown away by the joy of the crowd and their enthusiasm for the band. Hard-core punks wedged against the front of the stage were giving me the middle finger as I ran onstage and screamed into the house mic, "Would you please welcome the greatest fucking band in the world, Nirvana!" The roar from the crowd immediately clashed with explosive feedback from "Aneurysm," and the room exploded into a sea of moshing bodies never before experienced. The long road of anonymity traveled by Nirvana was finally over, and by the time the threesome awoke from sleep the next afternoon, they would never again be known as just another rock band from the Pacific Northwest.

Two

Leave It to Beaver is probably the most classic
TV show ever. There's something so wholesome about it.
It's a well-written show. It's really good.

—KURT COBAIN

The town of Aberdeen is located midway up the Pacific coast of Washington State, 108 miles southwest of Seattle and seventy-six miles from Tacoma. The name "Aberdeen" means "where two rivers merge" (in this case the Wynoochee and Wishkah), and though it is barely four miles wide and three miles long, Aberdeen is a powerfully murky, dark, and foggy place, with an average rainfall of eighty inches a year and a serious history of suicide among its residents. The main industry is logging, but near the end of the twentieth century automation in the logging industry had hurt the already poverty-stricken town, leaving many longtime workers suddenly jobless.

Aberdeen's economy was once fueled by several whorehouses, serving sailors who made frequent port stops and lonely lumberjacks who were a long way from home. Today the town is separated into two main divisions: One lies on the top of several steep hills, where most of the lumber mill owners live, while the other, below the hills, is reserved for those with minimal paychecks and limited social influence. As you drive into Aberdeen on Route 12, it's hard to miss its resemblance to low-income communities all over America: lots of fast-food stores, a strip mall here and there, and not much else. "It's totally secluded from any culture at all," said Kurt about the place where he spent his formative years. "Nothing but rednecks and guns and booze." Entering Aberdeen, you pass through the Flats, a poor section of town whose most notable contribution to Aberdeen society is its collection of gun shops and liquor stores.

Kurt Donald Cobain was born in Hoquiam, Washington, on February 20, 1967, just a couple of miles from Aberdeen. He was the first child born to Donald Leland Cobain and the former Wendy Elizabeth Fradenburg, who were married on July 31, 1965. When Kurt was six months old, the Cobains moved to Aberdeen and bought a house at 1210 East First Street. Don, an auto mechanic, got a job a couple of blocks from the house at the local Chevron station. He also picked up a second job at Mayr Brothers Logging company, where he worked for most of Kurt's childhood. Wendy held down several different jobs, including office secretary for the county commissioner; from 1976 to 1978, she was a saleswoman at Pearson's department store.

Kurt's relationships with his mother and father were like night and day. Even during his most difficult periods of growing up, he always had good things to say about his mom, whom he loved dearly. "My mother was a fantastic, attentive, and compassionate mother throughout my childhood," Kurt said, "until I started becoming incorrigible and rebellious. She was from a completely different era . . . You'd go to the prom, find your high school love, have your child, and devote your life to them. She was eighteen or twenty when she had me and she did a really great job."

Michael Azerrad, in his Nirvana book *Come as You Are*, recorded Kurt's childhood memories. "My mom was always physically affectionate with me. We always kissed good-bye and hugged . . . I'm surprised to find out that so many families aren't that way. Those were pretty blissful times." Kurt's mother echoed the same feelings. "There's nothing like your first-born, nothing," said Wendy. "No child even comes close to that. I was totaled out on [Kurt]. My every waking hour was for him."

The two Cobain men, on the other hand, had nothing in common. "He wanted me to be in sports and I didn't like sports," said Kurt. "I was artistic and he just didn't appreciate that type of thing, so I just always felt ashamed . . . [My parents] weren't artistic and I was. I liked music and they didn't. Subconsciously, maybe I thought I was adopted."

Kurt's full sister, Kimberly, was born in 1970. (He later had a half-sister named Brianne through Wendy's second marriage, to Pat O'Connor.) Shortly after, three-year-old Kurt was diagnosed as "hyperactive" by doctors, who were unable to control the unruly preschooler. He was given regular doses of Ritalin, the amphetamine-based drug used to sedate hyperactive children, to curb his rambunctious behavior. The drug often kept Kurt awake well into the early morning hours, and he was given sedatives to counter those side effects.

In spite of the uneasiness he felt as a result of the medicine, Kurt maintained a very happy childhood. His mother recalled him as "enthusiastic," an eager-minded child who must have been hard to keep up with, and Kurt himself remembered his early years as a wildly active and joyful period.

When Kurt's artistic ability began to surface, his appreciation for his own talent was slow to follow. "After a while . . . every present [we gave him] was a paintbrush or an easel," said Wendy. "We kind of almost killed [his artistic interest] for him. He would never be happy about his art. He would never be satisfied with it." When a drawing Kurt had done in school made the cover of the school newspaper, he didn't think it was very good, although everyone else did.

When Kurt was seven, his love of art began transforming into a love of music. This came as no surprise to anyone in the family, since several members had diverse musical backgrounds. His mother's uncle, Delbert Fradenburg, was a musician. Fradenburg, who used the stage name Dale Arden, had moved to California to become a singer and made several records in the late 1940s and early 1950s. Another uncle, Chuck Fradenburg, was in a number of rock bands; Kurt's aunt, Mari Earl (formerly Fradenburg) made a respectable living singing in country and lounge bands around Aberdeen. Mari was a huge musical influence on Kurt, buying him his first Beatles and Monkees records. After a while, Kurt became interested in drumming and started taking lessons. One of his first influences was Ringo Starr.

"Ever since I can remember, since I was a little kid, I wanted to be Ringo Starr," Kurt reminisced, "but I wanted to be John Lennon playing drums." Kurt's aspirations were apparent at an early age. "When I was . . . around seven years old, I thought for sure I could be a rock star . . . I knew I could be the president if I wanted to, but that was a stupid idea. I'd rather be a rock star."

Kurt's early childhood was uplifting, but everything changed in 1975, when his parents divorced. He moved with his father to the neighboring town of Montesano, just a few miles east of Aberdeen. The divorce devastated Kurt. "I just remember all of a sudden not being the same person, feeling like I wasn't worthy anymore. I didn't feel like I deserved to be hanging out with other kids, because they had parents [who lived together] and I didn't anymore." Kurt expressed his unhappiness in his own unique way, sketching rude caricatures of his parents on his bedroom walls, captioning them "Dad sucks, Mom sucks," and "I hate Mom, I hate Dad, Dad hates Mom, Mom hates Dad, it simply wants to make you sad."

Don Cobain remarried shortly after the divorce, and it was a difficult adjustment for the whole Cobain family. In an effort to get closer to his son, Don thought Kurt would enjoy the time-honored father-son tradition of hunting. But Kurt wanted nothing to do with it. "Now that I look back on it," Kurt said, "I know I had the sense that killing animals is wrong, especially for sport. I didn't understand that at the time. I just knew that I didn't want to be there."

Don agreed that his relationship with Kurt had taken an awful turn for the worse, that Kurt had come to the conclusion that only his mother had his best interests at heart. He has also admitted to having a bad temper, and remembered hitting his son. "I do probably blow up before I think. And I hurt people's feelings and, I get over it, I forget about it, and nobody else does," said Don. "My dad beat me with a belt, gave me a black eye. I spanked [Kurt] with a belt, yes."

Ignoring his son's protests, Don pushed Kurt into playing sports; the teenager even won a medal in wrestling in junior high. But Kurt hated every moment of it. He once blew a big wrestling match by allowing his opponent to pin him, just to piss off his father who, after witnessing Kurt's stunt, walked out of the gym in disgust.

Kurt's attitude toward his parents and its effects on his life carried over into his days at school. "I felt alienated. Right around the age of nine, I started feeling more confused. I couldn't understand at the time why I really didn't want to hang out with the kids at school. Years later I realized why: I obviously didn't relate to them, because they didn't appreciate anything artistic or cultural . . . It was their bread to become loggers. That's it. I think the fact that

I'm physically small—I was a really small kid—had a lot to do with why I didn't want to go into the logging industry."

Like many kids his age in the early 1970s, Kurt worshiped Evel Knievel. The daredevil life became such an obsession that Kurt rigged and performed his own stunts at the house. "Oh heck yeah . . . Evel Knievel was a big influence," Cobain said in *Nevermind It's an Interview*. "I'd jump my bike and I took all my bedding and pillows out of our house and put it on the deck, and got up on top of the roof and would jump off. And I took a thin piece of metal one time and duct-taped it to my chest and put a bunch of firecrackers on it and lit 'em on fire!"

In an attempt to find his own identity, Kurt started hanging out with the social outcasts, people on whom he could take out his frustrations. "My mom thought that I was better than those kids," said Kurt, "so I picked on them every once in a while—the scummy kids, the dirty kids. I just remember there were a couple of kids that stunk like pee all the time and I would bully them around and get into fights with them. By the fourth grade I realized that these kids are probably cooler than the higher-class children, more down to earth, down to the dirt." Kurt's inability to find other kids interested in art or music pushed him into further isolation. "I never had a friend in my life the whole time I was living in Aberdeen," he said openly, "and at the time I didn't know why. I thought I was different. I thought I must be gay or something because I didn't identify with any of the guys at all . . . They just wanted to fight . . . It gave me this real hatred for the average American macho male."

In junior high school, one of the few people Kurt did make friends with was Scott Cokeley. He and Scott were both in the school band and ran together on the track team. Scott thought Kurt was one of the cooler kids in school. "He played drums, and I remember he was really good," said Cokeley about Kurt in 1994. "He could be really quiet sometimes and sometimes he'd come around and do something funny. The girls in our class liked him a lot, so he had people that cared about him, even then."

If he had friends who cared about him, Kurt was not aware of it. Unable to handle living with his father or deal with the pressures that resulted from it, and after months of crying and begging and pleading with his mother, Kurt moved back in with her and transferred to Aberdeen High School.

The teenage rednecks of Aberdeen were in abundance and in full bloom by the time Kurt returned to try and finish high school. Withdrawing into his own realm seemed to be the only way to deal with the world around him. "I was chased around a lot by rednecks in four-by-fours because I wore a trench coat and had spiked hair," said Kurt. "I remember . . . being beaten up by [a] neighbor in a hickory shirt and tractor hat because he didn't like me, my friends, or the way we looked. He held me down for, like, an hour and a half with his nostrils flared, his breath stinking, playing out this total power trip. Things like that gave me a real intense hatred for rednecks and macho men in general."

It was a prejudice that was deeply ingrained in Kurt's heart, and he certainly took no excuse for their behavior toward him. "I don't feel sorry for them or feel that they're particularly misguided," he said. "I just feel that they're un-educated dickheads. There's a lot of them. They aren't just in Aberdeen, they're everywhere. I was really surprised to find them in New York City, which is supposed to be this really cultured place. I thought it was only in logging communities that those people existed."

People who hate one another usually do so because they hate themselves for what they are and what they have become. "[In Aberdeen] there was no kind of social outlet . . . Everyone was so negative and macho all the time . . . We hated all that we were," Kurt confirmed. "[So we just stayed] in our rooms all the time playing guitar. It's very hard to deal with these social cliques, you're always expected to be in a certain social category for different walks of life."

Kurt's disdain for the world of Aberdeen began to consume him, and with it came a burgeoning sense of rebellion against authority. "I became anti-social and I started to understand the reality of my surroundings, which didn't have a lot to offer . . . I felt so different and so crazy that [the kids in Aberdeen] just left me alone. They were afraid! I always felt that they would vote me 'Most Likely to Kill Everyone at a High School Dance' . . . I'd got to the point where I'd fantasized about it, but I'd have always opted for killing myself first."

Kurt's self-imposed isolation from his peers and society occasioned a sense of confusion about his own sexuality. Even explaining it proved tricky. "See, I've always wanted male friends that I could be real intimate with and talk about important things with and be as affectionate with . . . as I would be with a girl," Kurt told *The Advocate* in 1993. "Throughout my life I've always been really close with girls and made friends with girls. And I've always been a really sickly, feminine person anyhow, so I thought I was gay for a while because I didn't find any of the girls in my high school attractive at all. They had really awful haircuts and fucked-up attitudes . . . But I'm really glad that I found a few gay friends, because it totally saved me from becoming a monk or something."

Kurt remarked later that year, "Women are totally oppressed in small towns like Aberdeen. The words 'bitch' and 'cunt' were totally common; I mean, you'd hear [men use them] all the time. It took me years to realize that these were the things that were bothering me."

Kurt finally met the kind of friend he'd wished he'd come across earlier in his life. Jesse Reed was in Kurt's advanced art class during his junior year at Aberdeen High. The two became instant friends, sharing everything, including empathetic stories of severe stomach pains. "We called it 'witch stomach,' " said Reed about their shared aliments. "All through my childhood, I had an upset stomach, peptic ulcer. My stomach got better, but [Kurt's] was worse." As their friendship deepened Jesse nicknamed Kurt "Slow-brain," a play on his last name, because of Kurt's attitude toward school. Reed noticed that even as Kurt gave every sign of being a loner, he spent plenty of time coming up with schemes and practical jokes to confuse the Aberdeen community. "One of his ideas," Reed said, "was to make a bunch of flyers up with [this phony] band's name on it, *Organized Confusion*, print millions of 'em, and then plaster 'em all over Aberdeen.

"Then he started getting into sick stuff. One Halloween, we had the cops come up to our door and tell us to take down this life-sized baby doll that we had in the window with a noose around its neck. They thought we were Satan worshippers and stuff, and that's the whole reason Kurt wanted to do it anyway." When some of Kurt's notions didn't pan out the way he wanted, he started pulling off random acts of vandalism, including spray-painting *God Is Gay* on buildings, cars, and trucks.

"That was a lot of fun," Kurt said, though presumably aware of its perversity. "The funnest thing about that was not actually the act but the next morning. I'd get up early in the morning to walk through the neighborhood that I'd terrorized to see the aftermath. *[God Is Gay]* was the worst thing I could have spray-painted on their cars. Nothing would have been more effective.

"Aberdeen was depressing, and there were a lot of negative things about it, but it was really fun to fuck with people all the time. I loved to go to parties—jock keggers—and just run around drunk and obnoxious, smoking cigars and spitting on the backs of these big redneck jocks . . . By the end of the evening . . . I'd end up offending a girl, and she'd get her boyfriend to come beat me up." Jesse Reed added, laughing, "My dad thought [Kurt] was maladjusted, but I always believed in him."

Kurt's taunting got to the point where he would go out of his way to provoke high school classmates. "I used to pretend I was gay just to fuck with people. I've had the reputation of being a homosexual ever since I was fourteen . . . I [even] found a couple of gay friends in Aberdeen—which is almost impossible . . . I got beat up a lot, of course, because of my association with them. People just thought I was weird at first, just some fucked-up kid. But once I got the gay guy tag, it gave me the freedom to be able to be a freak and let people know that they should just stay away from me . . . 'I'm gay, so I can't even be touched.' It made for quite a few scary experiences in alleys walking home from school, though."

Kurt never actually had sex with a man, but the opinion of his classmates remained unchanged. After gym class, they "felt threatened because they were naked and I was supposedly gay," Kurt said, "so they either better cover up their penises or punch me. Or both. Every day after school, this one kid would hold me down in the snow and sit on my head. After that, I started being proud of the fact that I was gay even though I wasn't. I really enjoyed the conflict. It was pretty exciting, because I almost found my identity. I was a *special* geek. I wasn't quite the punk rocker I was looking for, but at least it was better than being the *average* geek."

But his excitement was short-lived. "My mother wouldn't allow me to be friends with [this guy] any more, because she's homophobic," Kurt recalled. "It was devastating, because finally I'd found a male friend who I actually hugged and was affectionate to. I was putting the pieces of the puzzle together, and he played a big role."

Kurt's struggle for identity spilled over into the classroom as well. "The biggest reason I flunked out of certain classes was because I hated the teachers so much. There was this one guy who was a religious fanatic, an apocalyptic racist. He taught social sciences and he would do nothing but waste our time by incorporating [the Book of] Revelations into history . . . Son of a bitch . . . I used to fantasize how I'd kill him in front of the class. Because the rest of the class were completely buying it . . . Totally swallowing this garbage . . . I couldn't believe so many people were just taking it."

Unable to adjust to living with his mother and dealing with the Aberdeen educational system at the same time, Kurt got kicked out of Wendy's house in 1984. Cold and hungry from living on the streets and in the homes of various friends, Kurt ultimately called his father for help. Don, who had a new family and problems of his own, told Kurt he could come and stay with him, but only on a trial basis. With nowhere to go, Kurt agreed to his dad's terms. "When I did, he had me take the test for the navy, and he had me pawn my guitar," Kurt recalled. "He had the recruiter come to the house two nights in a row. I was really trying to better myself and do what my parents wanted me to do. But I smoked some pot and magically came to the realization that I didn't belong there—especially not in the navy. So I just packed up my stuff and left, walking past the recruiting officer, and I said, 'See ya.' " Kurt sought refuge at Jesse Reed's house, but it didn't last long. Unhappy over the fact that he could not play his guitar there, Kurt kicked out a window. The Reeds threw him out.

Like many of rock's legendary stories, the one about how Kurt got his first guitar travels many strange paths. That fact that Kurt loved to make up stories while he was being interviewed didn't help. Kurt explained, "I was fifteen when I got my first guitar. My mother had just gotten married . . . My step-father went out on her and she got so irate that she took all [of his] guns, various guns, pistols, rifles, and stuff and walked down to the river, and threw them in. And then I hired this kid to fish a couple of them out and I sold them and then I got my first guitar with the money. I took lessons for a week. I learned how to play 'Back in Black' by AC/DC. It's pretty much the 'Louie Louie' chords, so that's all I needed to know. I never did pay the guitar teacher for that week either. I still owe him money. [Then] I just started writing songs on my own. Once you know power chords you don't need to know anything else."

Kurt told Katherine Turman in *Rip* magazine, "When I first started . . . I was heavily into Led Zeppelin. It eventually turned into what I thought was my own style, but it turned out to be punk rock."

The man who allegedly taught Kurt how to play was Warren Mason, a Rosevear's music store employee. According to Mason (who also taught Krist Novoselic a few chords), Kurt's Uncle Chuck approached him; he paid for the lessons in an effort to help get Kurt interested in something constructive. It apparently worked for a short period of time. Kurt started to write material on his own. Learning the Zeppelin classic "Stairway to Heaven" was his goal, but as Mason recalled, "We never even got to that. He got taken out of lessons before that. Then his mom made him quit, because he wasn't doing his homework. He was just playing his guitar."

In a 1991 interview, Kurt reflected back to those days. "I don't understand anything technical about music at all. I don't understand any of it, and I've never had the patience to learn. Besides 'Back in Black,' 'My Best Friend's Girlfriend,' and 'Louie, Louie,' I don't think I ever finished learning how to play anyone else's song in its entirety." The teacher-student relationship lasted three months, and after Kurt quit the lessons, Mason lost contact with him. However, the student had left an impression on the teacher. "He was from a broken home, and depressed," said Mason. "I never really saw the depressed side of him, because he was always sparkling and real happy about things— maybe because he was around something he liked."

Playing guitar meant everything to Kurt. It was his only escape from the world around him. Jesse Reed recalled one evening when Kurt came home from his dishwashing job, his hand wrapped in a bloodstained rag. "He was washing dishes, and something broke, and it damn near cut his finger off. And he told me, 'If I lose my fingers, I'm going to kill myself if I can't play my guitar.' And I believed him. I had no reason not to."

Playing guitar brought great joy to Kurt, but true happiness was still very far from his life. He was becoming more and more self-reliant, and he trusted few. He was increasingly aware of his surroundings, and of the social walls around him. "I started watching the news and realizing that [even among adults], the older kids were beating up on the younger kids and there's a lot of violence going on in the world . . . In high school . . . it was like the icing on the cake. I just couldn't deal with social situations, people, and social cliques, stuff like that. So I just started an aggressive band and started listening to punk rock."

The second British Invasion of America was well under way when Kurt discovered the euphoria of punk music. "It was like listening to something from a different planet," he said. "It took me a few days to accept it. I sensed that it was speaking more clearly and more realistically than the average rock and roll lyric." Once he got his feet wet in the cool punk mud, there was no turning back. "The Sex Pistols, the Buzzcocks, any 'seventy-seven punk rock band was totally influential to our music. But it was almost impossible to get exposed to English punk. We only had one radio station, a soft rock AM station. I remember being about fourteen and having a subscription to *Creem* magazine and I would read about the Sex Pistols, but I never got to hear anything . . . I decided to create my own punk rock with my electric guitar."

For Kurt, playing punk rock music was the tonic he needed. "It was definitely a good release," he said. "I thought of it as a job. It was my mission. I knew I had to practice. As soon as I got my guitar, I just became so obsessed with it."

It was a chance meeting with Buzz Osborne, a seminal Aberdeen punk and founder of the legendary Melvins, that put the seal of approval on punk rock for Kurt. Kurt said he was "instantly converted" after listening to one of Osborne's punk rock compilation tapes. "That was the day I shaved my head and bought combat boots.

"We grew up in the hardcore generation of the early 'eighties and were subjected to a lot of . . . I suppose I should say '*bullshit* underground' music . . . At the time when everybody was pretending to be punk rockers we were listening to anti-hardcore bands like the Butthole Surfers."

Osborne and the Melvins had their own scene that was already going on by the time Kurt was in high school, but Osborne remembered his early encounters with an eager Cobain. "I used to see Kurt in some classes and with my younger brother. When Kurt played junior league baseball. We all used to jam together." Kurt was heavily influenced by Osborne, who took him to see his first Black Flag show "He just had a really awesome attitude toward the average redneck," Kurt recalled. "I was really inspired by his attitude. It was 'Fuck with them as much as you can get away with.' We would go to jock parties and follow the big muscle men around and spit on their backs. And write dirty sayings on the walls of their houses and take the eggs out of the refrigerator and put them in the host's bed. Just try to get away with as much damage as we could."

It was a combination of that life of despair in Aberdeen and the degenerate inspiration of punk that temporarily saved Kurt from lapsing into apathy. "Becoming a punk rocker fed into my low self-esteem because it helped me realize that I don't need to become a rock star," he said. "I was fighting this thin line—I was always on the left or right side of not caring and not wanting to and not being able to, yet kind of wanting to at the same time. Still wanting to prove myself to people. It's kind of confusing. I'm so glad that I got into punk rock . . . It gave me these few years that I needed to grow up and put my values in perspective and realize what kind of person I am . . . It was really a godsend."

In 1985, faced with repeating his junior year because of unexcused absences, Kurt dropped out of school. "I knew I was better than anyone in my school," Kurt said in his own defense. "I quit school in the last month [of the school year]. I also didn't want to go to college in Texas or New York, it was too frightening for me. And I realized I liked music a lot more."

Out of school and out of options, Kurt got a job as a janitor at the place he despised the most—Aberdeen High School.

Three

People think that you sold out 'cause you made money,
you know? I think if you make money and start voting
Republican, because you get tax breaks . . . and they're the party
of the rich, I mean, that's sold out.

—KRIST NOVOSELIC

Krist Anthony Novoselic was born in Compton, California, on May 16, 1965, the son of Croatian immigrants Maria and Krist Novoselic. Novoselic, which roughly translates as "newcomer," is a common Croatian name.

Krist should know; he's gone back to Croatia many times, and has acquired a broad knowledge of his heritage. "Both of my parents were born and raised in Croatia. Our family comes from the small island of Iz, two hours by boat from the town of Zadar. The Novoselics' roots there trace back to the mid-1700s." Krist's newlywed parents lived up to their family name, transplanting to the United States in 1963 and setting up a new home for Krist, his brother, Robert, and his sister, Diana. By 1979, the Novoselics were newcomers again, this time living in gloomy Aberdeen.

Unlike most residents who move to Aberdeen, Krist's family did not come to work in the logging industry. Krist's dad, a machinist, relocated there simply because work was available. For the Novoselic children, life in their dreary new surroundings was a far cry from their sunshine-filled neighborhood in Compton, which gave Krist, a lanky, gentle teenager, an almost sympathetic vision of Aberdeen. "It's isolated. It's a wood-industry town, you know. They've been through a lot of hard times. When the economy goes down, less homes are being built, there's less lumber going out. Things work in cycles: three-four years good times, three-four years bad times . . . It's like the edge . . . No ideas are going through. There's like a collective [unconsciousness] there. Just people in their houses, rained out, drinking a lot. A lot of drugs. There's no white-collar, just a few bankers downtown and lawyers. Public defenders and prosecutors. That's the legal system. Maybe a few private lawyers doing divorce cases."

Having barely adjusted to high school life in Compton, Krist now faced the new challenge of meeting the kids of Aberdeen. As with any American high school, being the tall kid brought taunts and leers at Aberdeen High, which made Krist feel isolated and alone. Though he tried, he just couldn't find a common ground to get along with any of his peers, and everyone, from the heads to the jocks, treated him badly. He was different, and the kids at Aberdeen High made sure he knew that.

"It was a big culture shock for him," said Kurt about his friend moving up to the county of Gray's Harbor, " 'cause he was listening to [new wave music like] Devo at the time."

Krist also dug his own style of personal attire, which he wore proudly. The logger-type attire—big, flared, high-water pants, suspenders, and Pendletons—favored by many of the Aberdeen kids was a complete turnoff to Krist, who was used to wearing the hip California fashion like straight-leg jeans. Eventually, the trends that Krist and a few others like him introduced to the logging town caught up with the "in crowd" at Aberdeen, and by the time he graduated, it seemed everyone was wearing the clothes Krist first wore as a freshman. It was almost as if he had suffered their mockery for nothing.

The impending divorce of his parents along with a nasty brush with reconstructive facial surgery meant even more angst and suffering for Krist. To fix an underbite, doctors cut a section of bone out of his jaw to allow them to move some teeth forward, leaving Krist to feed and breathe through a ghastly tangle of wire holding his jaw together. "I looked like Jay Leno," Krist recalled.

"He'd go out and get all fucked up [on alcohol] and he'd be puking and it would be draining through his wires," recalled his high school friend Matt Lukin. "He said he never did have to cut them, but all the food was like milkshakes anyway, no solid food. Still, it was somewhat reckless of him [to get drunk in that condition]."

"I've always been a big drinker," Krist has said. "When I drink, I just don't stop. I like to drink because you're in some weird cartoon land where anything goes. Your vision is blurry and nothing and everything makes sense. It's crazy."

Dale Crover, drummer for the Melvins, and Matt Lukin, founder of Mudhoney, were two of a small number of people Krist trusted and befriended during his years at Aberdeen High School. Drunkenness can just as easily repel potential friends as lure them, but Krist's new friends treated him like the big man on campus. "You'd go to parties and people would be like 'Hey Novie!' " said Lukin. Kurt became friends with Lukin and Crover in 1983 and first met Krist around the same time. Kurt, a loner in high school, was instantly attracted to Krist's offbeat look at life. "He was a hilarious person who obviously had a different sense of humor," Kurt recalled. "Everyone was just laughing *at* him but I was laughing *with* him, because he was basically making fools out of everybody else. He was just a really clever, funny, loudmouth person. He was taller than anybody in school. He was *huge!* It was too bad I never got to hang out with him [then], because I really needed a friend during high school."

Krist remembered meeting Kurt when the two were hanging out with the Melvins. "I think [we were] in some social situation . . . I remember having more and more of a rap with him . . . just getting more and more aquainted. Then . . . a little social group came together and we just kinda hung out, you know, talked about things," said Krist. Their conversations drew Krist closer to Kurt's eccentricities about life, and the lanky teenager became absorbed with his new friend's enlightened humor and unusual artistic perspectives. To Krist, Kurt was a bohemian in every sense of the word.

When Krist graduated from high school in the spring of 1983, there wasn't much of a music scene in Aberdeen. There were only a few places where a rock band could play live, let alone congregate in a social setting to exchange ideas with other musicians, but still there was one small community of musicians hanging out and playing together with regularity. It centered around Buzz Osborne, the same guy who introduced Kurt and Krist to each other, Kurt to Dale Crover, and Kurt to his girlfriend, Tracy Marander. And it was Osborne who tipped off Dave Grohl years later to call Kurt and Krist when they were looking for a new drummer. Osborne was revered in those early Aberdeen circles, so much that Krist credits Osborne and Lukin with introducing him and his friends to the punk lifestyle. "I was a KISS fan [growing up]," Krist said. "When I was really young, like ten years old, I had all their posters and stuff. And then, when I got older, I got into punk rock. I saw a lot of cool shows, like Hüsker Dü."

Hours spent in Seattle's hip mom-and-pop used record stores and in the city's thriving rock club scene deepened Osborne's appreciation of punk rock, and it rubbed off instantly on the impressionable Krist. "I remember meeting Buzz, he played guitar and I go 'Yeah man, I play guitar' and he goes 'Well hey let's get together . . . I'm really into punk rock' and he goes 'Have you ever heard of this band The Butthole Surfers?' 'No.' 'Have you ever heard of this band The Dead Kennedys?' 'Oh yeah, I've heard of them.' There was stuff like Flipper and a lot of hardcore; Minor Threat and Black Flag. I didn't really have a grasp on any of that stuff. I heard it, and I was listening to it for a few days, and I was like 'Wow, this stuff's really raw and wild.' I was used to hearing all this really produced stuff like the Sex Pistols and Ramones. This was all just low-budget, no-budget stuff, and it sounded live to me, and then I borrowed the record *Generic Flipper* and I listened to it and it was like a revelation. It was like 'wow,' it was just heavy. It was art. I was affected, and I've never been the same since. It was like a breakthrough."

Four

The Melvins are really raw emotionally, their music
is really gut level, gut appealing music. I think that's one
of the most important things in music.

—KRIST NOVOSELIC

The seeds that would sprout into the abundant flower bed called Nirvana were being planted by mid-1985 in the unsuspecting mind of Kurt Cobain. In fact, the idea may have had its roots in a show with the Melvins and Poison Idea that Kurt and Jesse Reed attended that summer in Seattle. "We were like, 'Wow, look at all these great people!' " Reed remembered. "Everybody was cool. Even though they had Mohawks, no one was 'Billy Bad Ass.' What I thought was so phenomenal was slam dancing! It was just great, controlled rage." Kurt and Jesse had finally found their niche, and it inspired a musical freedom that had already been fueled in Kurt by the bands he grew up listening to. The combination of classic, kick-ass heavy metal fused with the Melvins' brand of punk rock laid the foundation for what would become the bloodline of Kurt's songwriting. "We just started accepting the fact that we liked the music that we grew up on: Alice Cooper, the MC5, KISS," said Kurt. "It was almost taboo to admit something like that in 'eighty-five, but we grew our hair long and said, 'Fuck what everybody else thinks, we're going to do what we want.' It's mainly just an homage—we're paying homage to all the music we loved as kids, and we haven't denied the punk-rock energy that inspired us as teenagers."

That motivation helped Kurt form his first band, Fecal Matter. He recruited drummer Dale Crover to play bass and they got together with drummer Greg Hokanson. By the end of 1985, they had recorded their first demo, made on a four-track tape deck owned by Kurt's country-singing aunt, Mari Fradenburg.

"They were just some really cool songs," said Lukin, one of the first people to hear the demo tape, "especially for somebody in Aberdeen who played guitar at that point that was our age—most guys just wanted to play Judas Priest. We found it kind of odd that some kid was writing his own songs and would rather play that than Mötley Crüe." The demo consisted of songs that included: "Spank Thru," "If You Must," "Pen Cap Chew," "Bambi Slaughter," "Sound of Dentage," "Laminated Effect," and "Downer." Crover's bass parts and Kurt's guitar licks were recorded together directly onto the tape, while Hokanson's drumming was done separately.

Thrown together on a whim, Fecal Matter actually landed a gig, opening for the Melvins at the Spot Tavern, a beach bar in the remote little town of Moclips on the Washington coast. Kurt and Crover then ditched Hokanson, and the two began rehearsing day and night in preparation for recording another demo tape. Crover eventually dropped out before the tape could be made, and Kurt rehearsed the songs with Buzz Osborne on bass and the Melvins' Mike Dillard on drums. Then, as soon as it had begun, the whole project evaporated; Dillard lost interest and Osborne wouldn't buy a bass rig. His lack of interest pissed off Kurt severely.

A year after Kurt started recording the Fecal Matter demo, Krist Novoselic listened to the tape. Up to that point, Kurt had tried several times to get an uninterested Krist to check out several versions of the demo. This time Krist liked what he heard. "One of the songs was 'Spank Thru' and I really liked it. It got me excited, so I go, 'Hey man, let's start a band.'"

The ever-suspicious Kurt, though he liked Krist, was reluctant to commit to Krist's suggestion, but he certainly did want to see what Krist could offer. When they finally got together to jam, they both played guitar, and Jesse Reed played bass. "Krist and Kurt automatically hit it off," recalled Reed, who noticed the immediate bond Kurt and Krist developed during the first sessions. "I felt so inferior around them, so I just handed the bass to Krist, and Krist started picking out what Kurt was playing." The sessions were a huge success; Krist was ready to start a band with Kurt. "I played guitar," Krist said, but he knew that in a band with Kurt he'd have to give up the slot. "But I go, 'Hey man, I know where I can get a bass and an amp.' And we scrounged up a drummer and we started practicing; took it very seriously too."

By the fall of 1986, the friendship between Krist and Kurt was cemented. Krist's girlfriend, Shelli Dilly, had been friends with Kurt since high school, and she often offered Kurt the backseat of Krist's Volkswagen van whenever he needed a place to crash. It was about this same time that Kurt met his first true love, Tracy Marander.

He'd actually met her a few years earlier, a passing glance outside a punk club in Seattle. Tracy was well known in the punk community, attending more shows than anyone could count, and she knew plenty about music. The two had more in common than they could imagine; they both even had pet rats with names. Tracy was not only a girlfriend, but a real friend whom Kurt could trust, and she was a big supporter of his new band, which by now was in need of a rehearsal space.

Krist's mother, Maria, allowed him and the band to practice in the empty apartment above her beauty shop. But she wasn't crazy about the idea, and certainly wasn't crazy about her son's selection of friends. "Fuck, she hated my guts," said Kurt. "She called me trash . . . I always heard her talking to Krist, saying he should find other friends, always putting him down and calling him a loser, calling all his friends losers." But Krist fought through his mom's prejudices, especially when they were directed at Kurt, and because of his efforts a solid friendship between the two guitarists began to take root.

In the early months of 1987 Krist and Kurt found a new drummer, Aaron Burckhard. A friend of the Melvins who always seemed to be hanging around the band whenever they went, Burckhard lived down the street from Kurt in Aberdeen. Completely focused on communing with the established Melvins— occasionally he got to sit behind Dale Crover's drum set and jam with the band—Burckhard was caught off guard by the invitation to join Kurt and Krist. "We all used to hang out in this alley where the Melvins practiced," he said. "I used to hang out there and watch 'em practice. I knew Krist but didn't know Kurt. They showed up [at the Melvins' practice and said] they were gonna start a band. They asked me join." The invitation was genuine. Kurt thought Burckhard was an upbeat, happy guy who could be a bit loud at times, but never reached a level of obnoxiousness that would cause a rift in their friendship.

Without a name or any immediate plans other than to rehearse, the band began a series of sessions in the apartment above the beauty shop. When Krist's parents eventually divorced, Maria moved into the space, forcing the band to move its rehearsals to Kurt's shack. "I had the apartment decorated in typical punk rock fashion with baby dolls hanging by their necks with blood all over them," said Kurt, describing the layout. "There was beer and puke and blood all over the carpet, garbage stacked up for months. I never did do the dishes. Jesse [Reed] and I cooked food for about a week and then put all our greasy hamburger dishes in the sink and filled it up full of water and it sat there for the entire five months I was there." In the living room, Kurt kept a bathtub full of turtles. He had a few pet rats, too, that had complete run-of-the-house privileges.

The trio tried to practice as much as possible, but Burckhard and Krist didn't share Kurt's zeal for rehearsal. Often Krist would miss practice for one reason or another, and it was almost impossible to keep Burckhard interested, especially on the first of every month. That was the day when his live-in girlfriend's welfare check came in. Burckhard would end up blowing most of it at the local tavern, like the rest of Aberdeen's residents, who viewed the first as if it were a holiday.

"There really wasn't much [to do]," Burckhard said without apology, "except sit around, drink beer, smoke pot, and practice. Kurt practiced. He was a diehard. Every night we'd do our set three or four times." In time Krist began to appreciate Kurt's enthusiasm, dedicating himself to practicing even harder. Some sessions were so intense that the slightest mistake would set them off. "I'd get all pissed off if we had a bad rehearsal: 'God, it's gotta be good, it's gotta be rock, it's gotta be fucking fun,' " said Krist. In time their hard work and determination paid off. They grew more confident in their abilities and their set list, and they landed a few gigs to test out their material on a live audience.

Their first gig really wasn't a performance at all. Scheduled to play a party in Olympia, Washington, they loaded up Krist's VW, arrived at the house to find the party had already been broken up, turned around, and drove home.

The first time they actually played out was at a house party in Raymond, Washington. The crowd wasn't expecting anything like the trio and their dates, so Krist and Kurt seized the opportunity to educate them all on the finer points of the punk aesthetic. Krist started the ball rolling, running past all of the startled guests, who were gathered in and around the house, screaming and jumping through an open window. The fake vampire blood he wore on his face and hands ended up on everything he touched. "We were out there and partied, tore the place [up], and scared the hell out of everybody," Burckhard recalled. "Krist was drunk, running, jumping through the window, coming [back in] through the back door. Krist's old lady, Shelli, and Kurt's girlfriend, Tracy [Marander], started making out. That really freaked everybody out. [The crowd] were yuppie-type people, all huddled in the kitchen. They didn't know what to think. Kurt was climbing all over the furniture, pouring beer down the couch."

By the time they got behind their instruments to play, no one was there to listen. "We had everyone so scared of us that they were in the kitchen hiding from us," said Kurt. "We had the run of the entire living room and the rest of the house." The band's set list that night included original songs like "Hairspray Queen," "Spank Thru," "Anorexorcist," "Raunchola," "Aero Zeppelin," "Beeswax," and "Floyd the Barber," and covers of Cher's "Gypsies, Tramps and Thieves" that featured Krist on lead vocal, "Love Buzz" (an obscure song from the Dutch band Shocking Blue, known for their hit "Venus"), "White Lace and Strange" (first recorded by the unknown 1960s band Thunder and Roses), and Flipper's raucous punk classic "Sex Bomb." Kurt's signature gut-wrenching style was beginning to take form, and the punk rock spirit he and Krist picked up from Osborne was starting to develop in earnest.

The trio's first big live test came in the spring of 1987, at the closing night of Gescco Hall in Olympia. A very small crowd showed, but no doubt appreciated what they heard; reports of people tearing down protective plastic sheeting on the walls and rolling on the floor in them quickly spread around town. The still-unnamed trio's next show was at the Community World Theater in Tacoma. The Circle Jerks and the Melvins had played the theater in the past, and the owner, Jim May, a friend of Kurt's girlfriend Tracy, needed to put a name on the marquee. Kurt blurted out, "Skid Row," and the name went up in lights that night.

That April they played a set at Evergreen State College's KAOS studio in Olympia. John Goodmanson and Donna Dresch, who played in the band Danger Mouse, brought the trio up to the station, where, in a midnight session, Skid Row played six to nine songs, including "Love Buzz," "Floyd the Barber," "Downer," "Mexican Seafood," "Spank Thru," and "Hairspray Queen." "We got a lot of phone calls," Burckhard said. "People just loved the music."

In the fall of 1987, faced with eviction from his shack, Kurt moved into Tracy's nearby apartment in Olympia, a hip college town. Krist and Shelli also relocated, to Tacoma. The move was a welcome change for Kurt. "Living [in Olympia] taught me a lot," he later acknowledged. "It was great, a really nice place to live." To everyone's surprise, the move domesticated Kurt. "I'm a good chef, I'm a totally good cook," he said proudly one day. Krist, overhearing the comment, agreed wholeheartedly. "We'll all vouch for that," he said. Even Jesse Reed, who by now had joined the navy and visited Kurt on leaves, began to notice some startling changes in his old friend's personality. "[When] I went to Olympia [to visit Kurt]," Reed recalled, "he [even] had his driver's license. It's like, 'Wow, Kurt's finally getting a little responsibility.' "

While it seemed that the band was getting off to a good start, Kurt and Krist were growing tired of Burckhard's approach to rehearsal. They were never sure whether he would show up to play or not. Unable to keep in touch with Burckhard, Kurt placed an ad in the *Seattle Rocket* in October looking for a drummer: "Serious drummer wanted. Underground attitude, Black Flag, Melvins, Zeppelin, Scratch Acid, Ethel Merman. Versatile as heck. Kurdt 352-0992." They eventually recruited Dave Foster to play drums.

He was a good drummer who liked to play Kurt and Krist's music, but Foster's bullying attitude rubbed the budding pacifists the wrong way. Foster was a really straight guy, and Kurt and Krist's counterculture lifestyle intimidated him. "He also had a problem," said Krist. "He had to go to anger counseling. He'd get in fights and beat the hell out of people. One time we saw him and he was with this friend in his trick truck and the guy spat on his truck, and he kicked the guy in the head."

Kurt, Krist, and Foster started jamming together, and even though the sessions went well, Foster recognized how uneasy Kurt and Krist were around him. "I think they were . . . uncomfortable, being around what they thought was probably a redneck or something," Foster said. "When all my friends came around, I think that I made them uncomfortable. Because they weren't the type of people [Kurt and Krist] hung out with."

As the trio began to think seriously about establishing themselves as a permanent band, they fumbled around with a succession of different names: Skid Row, Ted Ed Fred, Bliss, Throat Oyster, Pen Cap Chew, and Windowpane. Eventually they settled on a suggestion of Kurt's: Nirvana. "I wanted a name that was kind of beautiful or nice and pretty instead of a mean, raunchy punk-rock name like the Angry Samoans. I wanted to have something different."

When Krist and Kurt finally finished and mixed the Aunt Mari demo tape, copies were made and sent out to the major indie labels and scenesters. There was no response except for one guy in Seattle who was producing some of Seattle's up-and-coming alternative bands. And he just happened to be good friends with the owners of Sub Pop Records.

Five

The way I see Nirvana, it's just a name, you know, a name for
our band, really. I don't have any kind of philosophical application
towards the band regarding the name.

—KRIST NOVOSELIC

Much has been written about the beginning stages of what we know today as "alternative music." In the early 1980s, while bands like U2 and R.E.M. introduced the world to one version of the alternative sound, in the Pacific Northwest, bands like Malfunkshun, Green River, and the Schemps (founded by Soundgarden's Kim Thayil and Chris Cornell) were playing what would become known as the "Seattle Sound," or more commonly as "grunge." In pot-smoke-filled rehearsal spaces throughout the Emerald City, long-haired youth in SST T-shirts created the new Seattle underground scene. Nightclubs like the Showbox and the Gorilla Room/Gardens were the proving grounds for all of Seattle's newest alternative talent.

The band that many believe began the whole Seattle alternative movement was the U-Men. Until their inception, Seattle's music legacy was that of being the home of Jimi Hendrix. Local music remained stale and stagnant. The U-Men were a breath of fresh air, and the once bored and disgruntled youth of the city were suddenly invigorated.

The musical landscape in the Pacific Northwest portrayed the popular and cool U-Men in a unique light that they were never willing to convert to commercial success. In spite of the apparent demand, the band never hit the road to play their songs; they considered touring to be more of a vacation than an opportunity for people to hear their sound and buy their records. As a result, 1985 saw the U-Men fade into obscurity just when the alternative melting pot began to boil.

The Melvins and the newly formed Soundgarden picked up the baton the U-Men dropped and ran with a fury, often touring and selling out shows together, even sharing the same stage with underground pioneers Hüsker Dü. Named after the area where a local serial killer struck repeatedly, Green River (whose members eventually split up to form Mudhoney and Pearl Jam) toured to support a new album they released on Homestead Records. Suddenly the popularity of the Seattle sound began to grow nationwide. Unable to properly label the music "heavy metal" or "hard rock," Mudhoney's lead singer, Mark Arm, coined the term "grunge." It applied to just about any band coming out of the Seattle area that had exceptionally long hair and wore flannel shirts. Before alternative was co-opted by the mainstream, one record label seized the opportunity to call this newest underground sensation its own.

Sub Pop Records was founded by Bruce Pavitt and Jonathan Poneman in 1986. It began as a fanzine, *Sub Pop LTD*, created by Pavitt when he attended Evergreen State College in Olympia, Washington. Pavitt, a Chicago native, then began making compilation tapes that focused on local and regional music scenes in the United States and eventually centered on the Seattle scene. "Music is most interesting when looked at from a regional perspective," Pavitt explained. "All sorts of visual artists, writers, and musicians are going to be collaborating within the same community." Kim Thayil of Soundgarden introduced Pavitt to Poneman, who was a radio disc jockey at KCMU and a local punk-rock promoter. In July 1987, Pavitt and Poneman's Sub Pop released Green River's eight-song album, *Dry as a Bone*. The duo then released a Soundgarden promotional EP entitled *Fopp*. In 1988, Sub Pop debuted Soundgarden's first commercial EP, *The Screaming Life/Fopp*.

Pavitt and Poneman were hip to the successes and failures of a number of national indie record labels. They were savvy enough to produce artwork for record sleeves of Sub Pop releases with images that focused more on mosh pit audiences than the bands themselves. They didn't sign bands to contracts in those early days. Legend has it that one night Krist went over to Pavitt's house and demanded that Nirvana be signed to a contract. Pavitt relented, and Nirvana became the label's first official signee. Independent label and band relationships were often started this way: "Hey, we love that song. Wanna make a record?" It was that simple philosophy and arrangement that brought Nirvana into the Sub Pop family.

The Sub Pop founders were friends with Jack Endino, a member of the band Skin Yard, and the producer of Green River, Soundgarden, and Mudhoney. Along with Chris Hanszek (producer of the *Deep Six* compilation), Endino founded Reciprocal Recording. True to the punk ethic of avoiding the spotlight, Endino liked to list himself on liner notes as an engineer only, and not as a producer.

Endino explained why people consider him to be the chief architect of the Seattle grunge sound. "It was a combination of my style as a producer/engineer and Sub Pop's choice of what bands to sign and to send to me," he said. "After 1989, the so-called 'Seattle sound' became pretty diluted and unrecognizable, but prior to that, Sub Pop was definitely signing a certain kind of band, putting out a certain kind of record, and generating a lot of publicity for that particular sound."

The approach to producing that sound didn't exactly require a degree in music harmonics. Endino was known for his affinity for using excessive amounts of distortion, and he wasn't crazy about using reverb that could muddy the mix of a band's songs. What he did dig was the classic early-1970s method of recording big guitar sound. In the simplest of terms, it meant mixing one guitar to the left speaker and one to the right, so that it produced a quasi-stereo effect. It's an old but effective trick that gave bands like Nirvana the roomy, warm guitar resonance Endino loved to create.

This effortless appreciation for raw feedback drew Endino to Kurt's music. When Kurt and Crover first met Endino in 1987 and played him the Aunt Mari demo, Endino couldn't wait to tell Poneman about the band's "embryonic ingenuity." Poneman then met Kurt at the Broadway Espresso in Seattle. "Kurt was pretty laid back," said Poneman. "Obviously a very intelligent individual, who didn't seem necessarily filled with the usual rock star ambitions. Rock was one of the many things he did to pass the time." Poneman went to a show at the Central Tavern in Seattle. He liked what he saw, and after several more gigs, the Sub Pop guru invited Nirvana to record a ten-song demo with Endino at Reciprocal Recording in Seattle on January 23, 1988. Because Foster was unavailable to attend the session, Kurt and Krist called on Dale Crover to play drums.

The "Dale" demo was completed and mixed in about five hours, at a cost of $152.44. Ten songs were recorded: "If You Must," "Floyd the Barber," "Paper Cuts," "Spank Thru," "Hairspray Queen," "Aero Zeppelin," "Beeswax," "Mexican Seafood," "Pen Cap Chew," and an up-tempo version of "Downer."

"Five of these songs went on *Incesticide* in their original rough mix form," said Endino of the Dale demo session. "Another, 'Spank Thru,' has never been officially released in [the original Dale demo] form. Two more, 'Floyd the Barber' and 'Paper Cuts,' were properly remixed and added to *Bleach*. Of the remaining two, 'If You Must' was never released because Kurt disliked it, and 'Pen Cap Chew' . . . was never finished . . . 'Spank Thru,' 'If You Must,' and 'Pen Cap Chew' have been widely bootlegged, all from cassettes that were given out to many people." When the session was completed, Endino exploded into Poneman's office with a tape fresh off the master.

"Jack was totally blown away by the demo," Poneman remembered. "He thought Kurt had this voice unlike anything Sub Pop had recorded up to that point."

Endino recalled the impact of the moment as well. "This guy's got a really amazing voice . . . I don't know what to make of [the tape] but his voice has a lot of power."

The first song on the tape was "If You Must." Poneman reflected on the moment when he first heard the song. "It had this bridge where he just did this . . . how do I put it? . . . opening up, and just letting it out. I just went, 'This guy is really incredible!' So I called [Kurt], and said I loved the tape and that we should be making a record."

At the end of April, Nirvana was asked by Sub Pop to play Sub Pop Sunday at the Vogue in Seattle. It was essentially an audition, but the band did not play up to their expectations. "We didn't really fuck up," Foster recalled, "like, we didn't have to stop in the middle of the song. But it was very intimidating, because we knew it was for getting a record deal." The small crowd did not provide the energy the band had hoped for, but their inability to shine stemmed from the decaying relationship between Foster and the group's two founding members. "I felt out of place, but I was into what they were doing,"

Foster added. "I loved to play their music." Also, his heavily mustachioed looks seemed sadly out of place in the band, and Foster got the boot after the poorly received gig. "I was so fuckin' pissed," he said about his departure. "It was just like if you caught your girlfriend in bed with someone else."

With no one else to turn to, Kurt and Krist brought Aaron Burckhard back into the band. But that wouldn't last long. Burckhard quickly exhausted Kurt's patience. He hated the long practice hours and the frequency of rehearsals. "They wanted to practice every night. *Every* night. I'm like, give me a break!" Burckhard said about his eventual departure from the band. "I didn't show up a couple of times and they got kind of pissed off. [My feeling was] we're not going to make no money off it or anything, you know?"

The band was now headed in a more serious and responsible direction. Burckhard was out of the group, and he left with no hard feelings.

"Seattle was, for a time, the world, and people were all keyed in to what was happening [here]," said Poneman. "The stuff that happened to Nirvana, the built-in mania around this band, I'd never witnessed before or since. There was some kind of supernatural quality to their performances. I don't mean to invoke the idea of Goth or anything, but they created an inexplicable frenzy. Great bands that create moving songs don't approach the craziness that Nirvana would create."

The simple act of playing in front of the home crowd really got things going for the band. "We started playing around Seattle, and people responded and that was great," Krist recalled. "That made us feel really good. We just locked ourselves in the cellar, a little tiny practice place, and just started jamming and having fun. It was not like, 'We're going to be the Sub Pop sound.' We [had been] doing this for years. We got on Sub Pop because they were close by." It didn't hurt that they had their own transportation as well. "And we were lucky 'cause we had a van," Krist commented years later. "We were the only band signed to Sub Pop at that time with a van."

Kurt and Krist began searching for a permanent replacement, briefly considering Tad Doyle, lead singer of TAD, to be their next drummer. After a few unsuccessful auditions, they checked out Tick-Dolly-Row drummer Chad Channing.

Channing, a native Californian, lived on nearby Bainbridge Island. Like Kurt and Krist, he was raised on a healthy dose of Aerosmith and, like Kurt, he was a high school dropout. When Kurt and Krist first met him he was a cook at a restaurant in Bainbridge Island, which meant Channing often had to load up his drums and take the ferry from the island to Seattle. But because it meant being able to play in the band, he didn't seem to mind.

"I remember Kurt telling me a long time ago when they were first checking us out, 'God, man, I wish we could get that guy!'" Channing remembered. "Look at those drums! Those are the weirdest things I've ever fuckin' seen!" Channing accepted an invitation to jam for a number of sessions at Krist's house. Properly inspired by his North drum kit as well as by the quality of his drumming, Kurt and Krist made the twenty-one-year-old the first official drummer of Nirvana.

Channing was an instant hit. His personality fell completely in line with the insurgent disposition already smoldering within Kurt and Krist. They all had in common a healthy resentment for authority. They were stubborn, and antiauthoritarian.

"I think we all have our own personal, political, and spiritual opinions," Channing commented. "But regarding our music, it's rock and roll, no message, no direction."

Kurt and Krist started to click with Channing and the band played several gigs throughout the Northwest. Krist remembered one gig happening "in this shitty old house. We'd play in front of five people. Everybody would be drunk and stoned." Undaunted, they played more shows in Tacoma and Olympia.

Kurt hated the travel, Krist didn't care either way, and Chad felt it was just another journey in his life. His father, Wayne Channing, was a radio disc jockey who was forever moving the family along with him to different jobs all over the country, from California to Minnesota to Hawaii to Alaska to Idaho and back. "Our [family] motto was, 'Move every six months.' So whatever friends I made, wherever I went, I knew they were just temporary," said Channing. "So that was kind of weird. You don't really hang out with many people because why make a friend if you're not going to be around?" The brief tour ended in Krist's adopted hometown at the Tacoma Community World Theater under one of their unfamiliar monikers, Ted Ed Fred.

The Seattle music scene was beginning to take shape, as bands like Skin Yard, the Fluid (transplants from Denver), TAD, Mudhoney, and Mother

Love Bone were now playing to sold-out audiences. Soundgarden had opened the door for them all and signed with A&M Records in the summer of 1988.

"Those were magical times," reminisced Kurt. "That was the Seattle scene. When Mudhoney was playing and we were playing, and TAD and the Fluid, that was a little time in history that you can compare to the Liverpool scene, the Cavern Club. It was innocent. It wasn't exploited . . . yet."

In June, with Nirvana finally enshrined as the band's permanent name, the trio went into the studio with Jack Endino to begin recording songs for a limited-edition Sub Pop release to be called *Sub Pop 200*; they also recorded a number of songs that would eventually constitute their first album, *Bleach*. (The *Sub Pop 200* compilation, a three-EP collection of Seattle sounds also featuring Soundgarden, TAD, Mudhoney, Beat Happening, and Screaming Trees, was limited to five thousand copies and became a collector's item.) In one session they finished several tunes, including "Spank Thru" (a remake done this time with Channing on drums), "Love Buzz, "Big Cheese," and an unissued version of "Blandest."

" 'Blandest' didn't come out very well and they opted to rerecord it at a later time because the song was just not ready yet," Endino said. "They instructed me to record over this version, which we did. I never even kept a cassette of it myself, so the bootleg copies of it that exist must have come from band members' rough mix cassettes, perhaps stolen ones."

The session was not without pressure and confusion, as Nirvana and Pavitt clashed when it came to recording the song "Love Buzz." Endino and Kurt arranged a collage of cartoonlike segments to start the song, but Pavitt felt it interfered with the song itself. "I collect children's records and obscure things like that," Kurt said. "Originally it was planned to have twice as much cartoon stuff included at the beginning of 'Love Buzz,' but [Pavitt] didn't like that idea, he said it went on too long."

Endino agreed. "The 'Love Buzz' single version had an intro, originally twenty seconds long, that was an audio collage of little snippets put together by Kurt at home through skillful use of the pause button on his cassette deck. We spliced it onto the beginning of the tape but the Sub Pop folks made us shorten it." The long version of the intro, bootlegged under the titles "Montage of Heck," "Buzz Cut," and "The Landlord," was eventually removed when "Love Buzz" was added to *Bleach*. But the edited segment remained on the single version when it was released later that fall.

"Another difference [between the single and *Bleach* versions] is that in the middle of the single mix, there's a 'noise break' which has extra noises from the same collage cassette added in," Endino continued. "Since all eight tracks were full on the master tape, we had to plug the studio cassette deck into the board like a virtual ninth track, and each time I ran through the mix, Kurt had to press 'play' on the cassette deck at the right instant so that the stuff would be blended into the mix I was doing. When we later went to remix 'Love Buzz' for the album, Kurt forgot to bring that cassette, so those noises are absent."

The uninspired sessions left Kurt and Krist unhappy with the recording of the final product, and they blamed Channing for the perceived "lightness" of "Love Buzz" 's sound. Used to the killer pounding kicks of Dale Crover's John Bonham style of drumming, Kurt felt they should "have recorded it a lot heavier . . . We weren't sure just what we wanted to do so it turned out kind of wimpy."

Even the amount of time put into the different mixes left all involved feeling less confident about the song itself. Kurt felt that they just could not get the song to sound the way they'd hoped it would. The absence of a powerful low-fi sound gave the recording a crisper, cleaner feel, and for years Kurt believed it was one of the weakest recordings they'd ever produced.

Bouncing back and forth between the live stage and Reciprocal Recording allowed the trio to play a few noneventful shows that summer under the name Nirvana, the first occuring at one of the July Sub Pop Sunday shows at the Vogue in Seattle. By the end of the month they remixed "Love Buzz" and "Big Cheese." They also remixed a new version of "Spank Thru" for the *Sub Pop 200* compilation.

On Halloween Eve, Nirvana played a dorm party at Evergreen State College in Olympia, followed by an official show at the college the following night. The Halloween Eve bash is said to be the first time anyone ever saw Kurt smash his guitar during a show.

The following month, the low-profit Sub Pop label released the debut single by Nirvana, "Love Buzz," with "Big Cheese" as its B side. It was the first single in a new Poneman and Pavitt moneymaking venture called the

Sub Pop Singles Club. For a fee, paid in advance of course, members of this mail-order club received a new Sub Pop single every month. Only one thousand copies of "Love Buzz" were released, much to the band's dismay. As Krist put it, the band felt burned putting out a single no one could buy. But the club single sold out quickly, and it remains the most sought-after Nirvana collectible.

Before heading back into the studio to finish recording the remaining songs for *Bleach*, Nirvana played a show at the Hoquiam Eagles Lodge on December 21. They tested "School," "Love Buzz," "Blew," "Spank Thru," and "Floyd the Barber." Kurt, mocking a particular group of people he despised, appeared on stage with his neck painted red. Krist, apparently making no statement at all, played in his underpants.

As 1988 came to a close, Nirvana played a record release party for the *Sub Pop 200* compilation at the Underground in Seattle on December 28. Seattle poet Jesse Bernstein introduced them as "the band with the freeze-dried vocals." Nirvana's booming drums, tuned-down guitars, and ferocious vocals blew away the sold-out crowd with an almost identical set list from the Hoquiam show, including earsplitting versions of "Paper Cuts," "Mr. Moustache," "Sifting," "Hairspray Queen," and "Mexican Seafood." By now it was very clear to all involved that Nirvana was dead serious about putting out a full-length album. They rehearsed endlessly with Channing with that goal in mind. Sub Pop, like many independent labels in the history of rock 'n' roll, was severely limited in funds, but they went ahead and booked recording time for Nirvana during the 1988 Christmas season.

Six

The problem with independent music
is you can't find it half the time.
—KURT COBAIN

The title of Nirvana's first full-length record came shortly after the sessions were recorded. One day during a short West Coast tour in February 1989, the band was riding around San Francisco in their van with Poneman and Pavitt. They noticed that there was a major anti-AIDS campaign going on in town, with signs posted everywhere urging drug users to "bleach your works"—that is, sterilize your needles with bleach. There was even a guy dressed up as a bleach bottle, walking around downtown handing out bottles of bleach to passersby. Nirvana became possessed by the notion that the epidemic might suddenly make bleach a precious commodity—and from there it wasn't hard to make the connection.

The recording of *Bleach* was completed on a budget of $600. Recuts of "Floyd the Barber," "Paper Cuts," and "Downer," all taken from the January 1988 demo tape, were attempted with Channing, but the band was unable to match the original intensity of the Dale Crover cuts. Since funds were tight, the original Crover versions from the demo were remixed for *Bleach*.

"We just recorded it . . . and made sure that [Endino] didn't put a lot of effects on it," Kurt said. "It was hard to find a studio that didn't sound high-tech 'eighties. So we just did it as fast as we could, and as cheap as we could. We attempted to record tuned [lower than] a D [chord]. I don't know if you know how fucking low that is! It's ridiculous . . . You couldn't hear anything. We thought, 'Well, we can't be that heavy!' " The low-end sound they were searching for was inspired by two bands not known for Nirvana-style songwriting, but revered by Kurt and Krist for their varied use of pounding, pulsating bass rhythms.

"About a week before we recorded *Bleach* we were listening to a tape that had the Smithereens on one side and Celtic Frost on the other," Krist explained. Asked if this had any effect on the recording of *Bleach,* Kurt joked, "How could we deny the influence?"

In all, there were six days of recording: December 24 (five hours), December 29 (five hours), December 30 (five hours), December 31 (four and a half hours), January 14 (five hours), and January 24 (five and a half hours).

"The only finished outtake from these sessions was 'Big Long Now,' which later appeared on *Incesticide,*" Endino said. "Kurt decided there were already enough slow heavy tunes on *Bleach,* so this song was left off. There was also an earlier, instrumental version of 'Sifting' with a wah solo, and similar early versions of 'Blew' with a different solo and gibberish words, and 'Mr. Moustache' with gibberish words. These seem to have been widely bootlegged. There are no other unfinished or partial songs from these sessions."

On the first day in the studio the band experimented with a different recording technique. Jack Endino recalled that "the band came in, and said, 'We're going to tune our instruments way down, really low and we are going to try and record all of the songs this way.' I think Kurt was having trouble singing and wanted to make it a little easier for himself. Well of course they were way out of tune, and didn't sound too good. So they ended up hating it, and then came back another day and rerecorded all of it!"

"On the first day of recording, we weren't satisfied. Only one song ['Blew'] came out of it," Krist said. "So we ended up recording everything else in the next two days."

Keeping it simple was the key to getting the sound Nirvana was trying to produce in the short time that was available. "A lot of people have said [*Bleach*] is very dry," Kurt would say later. "We wanted it to be as loud and as in-your-face as possible, as raw as we could. I think a lot of music today sounds far too polished, there's no energy. It's too programmed and fake; you hear too much. I want a little mud in my music. Lou Reed once spent about a year looking for a studio that was old enough to give him the sound he wanted, and [when] he finally found one, he just went in, turned up the power, and that was it. That's what we'd really like to do. I would think that the kind of people who'd prefer an 'eighties sound are the kind of people I wouldn't really want as our audience."

Kurt described the album's construction and dynamics: "*Bleach* just seemed to be really one-dimensional. It just has the same format [throughout]. We had a few hours every night for about six days. There were a few guitar overdubs, but that's about it. All the songs are slow and grungy and they're tuned down to really low notes. And I screamed a lot."

One of the unique elements that separated Nirvana from other grunge bands was Kurt's searing vocals. His wails were a separate, prominent instrument in Nirvana's overall sound. Kurt noted, "[It's] like what you get out of the Gyuto Monks from Tibet is not what they're saying. It's the power of their vocalizing . . . They reproduce three tonal chords in their voices, which is supposed to be impossible, but they do it and it takes over fifty years to develop this, it's chanting, it has a very eerie effect upon you.

"It's that energy we're trying to put out; we're not tight . . . it's the energy and the fun we try to project, not some heavy message in the lyrics."

It was that energy, along with Endino's engineering skills, that gave Cobain the comfort level to develop. As the band's act solidified, he was developing a writing style that only he could comprehend and interpret. "I write most of the lyrics," he said. "Half the time I can't finish a subject so I'll turn the rest of the song into something else. I don't know, it's really hard to explain . . . I don't consider lyrics a big deal at all . . . A good melody line, a hook, and live energy is far more important."

Clearly evident during the *Bleach* sessions was Kurt's knack for pop delivery. "At the same time that we were recording *Bleach*, we had a lot more songs like 'About a Girl,'" he said. "In fact, 'Polly' [a very sensitive and disturbing pop song that would appear on Nirvana's second album, *Nevermind*] was written at that same time, too. It's just that we chose to put the more abrasive songs on the *Bleach* album."

The decision to record more straight-ahead rock songs for *Bleach* was made jointly by Sub Pop and Nirvana, though Kurt regretted leaving other material off the album. "I wish we'd have put 'Hairspray Queen,' or something, but the idea of going into the studio again, instead of what we had on the demo already, was enough of a challenge.

"We purposely made [Bleach] one-dimensional, more 'rock' than it should have been," Kurt added. "There was this pressure from Sub Pop and the scene to play 'rock music,' strip it down and make it sound like Aerosmith. We knew that was the thing to do . . . We wanted to try and please people at first, to see what would happen."

For Chad Channing, Nirvana's simple formula for recording Bleach left little for him to contribute. "For me, recording always went weird," he said. "I was there, I did my job, and that was it . . . I'd bang on the drums, get the drum sound down and stuff like that, and then I'd just kick back and wait until they got the bass and guitar sounds and we'd do the song and that was kind of it. The rest of the time, I'd spend listening to see what they did with it . . . I really had nothing to say or do."

Nirvana chose to put one player's name in the album credits who didn't even play on the album. Jason Everman, a friend of Channing's and the guy who put up the $600 for the recording time, is credited with playing guitar on Bleach. The truth is, he only played with Nirvana live during their 1989 tours. (The band cut one session with Everman in June. They recorded a cover of the KISS song "Do You Love Me," which ended up the following year on the KISS tribute album Hard to Believe on Olympia's C/Z Records. At the same time they also recorded an early version of "Dive," which remains unheard and unreleased.)

However, you would have thought Everman was definitely in the band after reading his comments during a Nirvana interview about the making of Bleach that appeared in Flipside magazine in 1989:

Chad Channing: "We wrote down the lyrics on the way to the studio."
Krist Novoselic: "We were trying to be spontaneous."
Kurt Cobain: "We're really new in the studio, we never recorded before."
Jason Everman: "The studio is a pretty sterile environment, you can't get really psyched in the studio, but live it's different. It was really new material too, we just decided to go out on a limb and record five new songs."

"We basically were ready to take anybody [along on tour] if they could play good guitar," Kurt said in an effort to set the record straight about Jason Everman. "He seemed like a nice enough guy. And he had long Sub Pop hair." It was that head of Sub Pop hair, of course, that appeared with the others on the cover of *Bleach*.

Bleach also introduced Nirvana's official logo, set in Bodini extra bold condensed type. Because the typesetter was rushed to finish the logo, it contains typographic imperfections (such as the large letter spaces on either side of the V) that never got fixed.

Like each member of Nirvana, each song on *Bleach* represented a small piece of the entire personality of the project. "Blew," for instance, was written by Kurt in his traditional verse-chorus-verse-chorus-bad-solo-chorus-verse-chorus-chorus-chorus style of writing pop songs. Like his songwriting heroes the Beatles, Kurt would rely on this typical pop structure to write songs throughout his brief career. Kurt actually joked about his bad songwriting and rhyming in the chorus: *"Is there another reason for your stain? Could you believe who we knew stress or strain? Here is another word that rhymes with shame."* Freshly recorded with Channing on the drums, "Blew" was laid down on the first day, the low tuning lending it a very dark, dirgelike sound.

The most bizarre cut lyrically on the album is "Floyd the Barber," a song about an individual who has a nightmare about being shaved to death by Floyd, a character from the 1960s hit television comedy *The Andy Griffith Show*. Dropping the names Floyd, Opie, Aunt Bee, Barney, and Andy—they all watch the victim bleed from Floyd's deadly shave—the song is written as though it had been Kurt's own nightmare, though as he stated many times in explaining his songwriting, his use of the first person was usually merely a device.

Just before recording *Bleach*, Kurt's girlfriend, Tracy Marander, had complained that he hadn't written a song about her. Kurt responded to the challenge and effortlessly wrote "About a Girl," an instant pop classic, written in the same melody and manner as any of the Beatles' best material. Kurt spent hours listening to *Meet the Beatles!* the night he wrote the song, and the influence is abundantly apparent. Although far different from anything else Sub Pop had released, "About a Girl" is an example of the type of songwriting Kurt enjoyed most. It was also a sign of the songwriter that Kurt was becoming. It was always Kurt's idea to have heavy songs to mix with mellow songs. "I remember years ago asking [a childhood friend], 'How successful do you think a band could be if they mixed really heavy Black Sabbath with the Beatles?'" Kurt said. "'What could you do with that?' I wanted to be totally Led Zeppelin in a way and then be totally extreme punk rock and then do real wimpy songs.

"We wrote ['School'] about Sub Pop; if we could have thrown in Sound-garden's name, we would have. It was a joke at first, and then it turned out to be a really good song." Kurt later explained his idea of beauty, and the values behind "School": He claimed the song was about "antique craftsman-ship, something that is built well, to last, something solid. Values that my grandparents had—pretty much the opposite of the way things are going now. It's the same with music—sincerity, craftsmanship. If you do a job, you should do it well—that's just good business sense. Same thing my grandfather used to bitch at me about when I was a kid, and I never understood him. Our songs are about changing yourself, [about] frustration. There was this anthem the skate-rock kids were claiming for their own, 'Don't Resist,' to not resist against repression. 'No Recess' [aka 'School'], one of our new songs, was just some surreal idea I had about being in school and being in social cliques all the time, and then you grow up, having to deal with exactly the same things with your friends at parties and in clubs as you did in high school. It's exactly the same."

The lead single from *Bleach* is a scowling version of the Shocking Blue's "Love Buzz," the first of eight cover songs Nirvana recorded in their brief career. Songs like "Love Buzz" separated the band from the garage/metal groups of the Seattle scene, as they showcased the pop melody/thrashing guitar style that Kurt integrated into his own songs. The heavy, grinding groove served as a perfect complement to Krist's low-fi bass, and Kurt's trippy, dreamlike guitar leads and howling vocals easily make "Love Buzz" one of Nirvana's most memorable creations.

In contrast, the pounding sludge and horrifying lyrics of "Paper Cuts" were written with shocking intent. The song is believed to be based on a true story about an Aberdeen family who kept their children locked in a room with painted windows, entering the room only to feed them and remove newspa-pers the children used to relieve themselves. The version of this song that appears on *Bleach* is Nirvana's original 1988 demo, featuring the incessant thumping of Dale Crover on drums.

"Negative Creep" is more of a riff-based song whose sparse lyrics revolve around the chorus. The song features an ode to Mudhoney's "Sweet Young Thing," where they sing, "Sweet young thing ain't sweet no more"; in "Negative Creep" Kurt sings, "Daddy's little girl ain't a girl no more." However, the element that truly distinguishes "Negative Creep" from other Nirvana songs is that it fades out in the end with the band repeating the chorus. Usually their songs end cold; they play a final note to the end of the song. "Negative Creep" 's fadeout marks one of their few gestures toward a 'sixties commercial pop aesthetic.

Like "Negative Creep," "Scoff" sticks to the stripped-down approach of repeating verse and chorus over and over. The single verse of lyrics is repeated three times; Kurt throws in a bridge as well, giving the song a somewhat different flavor from some of the earlier material. However, Kurt still provides a powerful and emotional punch to "Scoff" 's apparent simplicity with a convincing, plainspoken chorus that screams an unveiled message of anger and pain.

"Swap Meet" is a wry, bittersweet love story about a man and a woman who sell their arts and crafts at the Sunday swap meet. Kurt's references to "sea shells, drift wood, and burlap" later cropped up as a prank in the *Nevermind* biography, where the band claimed they'd met in arts and crafts classes.

A fan favorite, "Mr. Moustache," is a play on the mustache, a Nirvana-inspired symbol of the kind of macho rednecks with whom Kurt obviously had problems. Drummer Dave Foster seemed to share some of these characteristics, but it is unclear whether the song was actually written about him.

The one song on *Bleach* that could be labeled as filler is "Sifting." The lyrics don't really make much sense, and the melody drifts along with no direction or purpose. It has a distinct faux Zeppelin vibe to it, as if it were a *Physical Graffiti* B side, and Kurt's Robert Plant-ish vocals do nothing to help dilute the comparisons.

"Big Cheese" is the tongue-in-cheek anthem for Sub Pop bigwig Jonathan Poneman. Kurt remembered writing the song as a reaction to Poneman's critical attitude toward the band. The song was the flip side of the "Love

Buzz" 7-inch single, but it did not make the original version of *Bleach*; it would only be added to the CD version after the success of *Nevermind*.

"Downer" is an original 1988 Nirvana demo version with Dale Crover on drums. "I was trying to be Mr. Political-Punk-Rock-Black Flag-Guy," said Kurt about the song. "I really didn't know what I was talking about. I was just throwing together words."

With the exception of "About a Girl," the songs on *Bleach* flow in a stereotypical stream of underground noise and on-the-spot punk creations. At one point in the mixing of the album, Nirvana wasn't quite sure exactly what they were working on, but they were enjoying the work nonetheless. "We were all sick by then," said Krist, "and we had this codeine syrup from the Pierce County Health Department. So we were drinking a lot of that for our sickness, but we were really on codeine and so we were mixing the record and getting really into it."

But the distinctiveness of Nirvana's embryonic sound had more to do with confusion than codeine. "There were a lot of real confused messages going on in our brains," said Kurt, remembering the roadblocks the band encountered when trying to refine their style for *Bleach*. "We just didn't know what we wanted to do at all. We just didn't have our own sound at all. Like everyone else, we were just coming to grips with admitting that we liked all different kinds of music. To be a punk rocker and if you were at a Black Flag show and you said you liked R.E.M. . . . You just couldn't do it."

It was hard enough for Kurt to choose an acceptable direction for his band. Now people were starting to approach him with stupid questions: "How come you don't mention the title of your songs in any of your songs?"

"I've never had any reason to name any of my songs," Kurt said, "That's the only difference between alternative bands and cock-rock bands. Alternative rock bands name their songs with titles that don't have anything to do with the song or the chorus." For *Bleach*, Kurt explained, "I decided to write songs that I would easily remember the lyrics to so I wouldn't fuck them up during the live show."

Few events in Kurt's life came close to matching the excitement the band experienced when they heard their songs on the radio for the first time. "It was amazing," Kurt remembered. "I never thought that I'd get to that point.

I just thought I'd be in a band and maybe make a demo, but for [disc jockeys] to play it on the radio was just too much . . . More than I ever wanted."

There were real-world reasons for their excitement. "[To] be able to pay my rent with this band," Kurt remembered thinking, "it would be really great. It made us step up mentally to another level where it was a reality that we could actually live off of this. I didn't think anywhere past ever being able to afford more than a hundred-dollar apartment."

On the surface, it appeared that everything was in place. Everyone in the Nirvana camp was psyched as Sub Pop geared up to release *Bleach* in February 1989. Yet beneath the facade, internal tensions were mounting. Sub Pop's micromanagement had fueled Nirvana's unhappiness with the finished product. "They were just constantly having control right away," said Kurt, "doing exactly what a major label would do, and claiming to be such an independent label." Sub Pop had its vision of what Nirvana's image and promotion should be, and, of course, the band had their own ideas. Kurt grew so fed up with the label that he finally resolved that "they can say whatever they want" about Nirvana in Sub Pop's press releases. "Our promotional sheet is really tongue-in-cheek stuff, like, 'When they're not impregnating their cousins, they're working on cars.' We don't have much of an image, so [Sub Pop] is trying to create one." Kurt didn't look kindly on Sub Pop's marketing efforts, which often seemed to blur the distinction between one band and the next on their roster. "A lot of people lump all the [Sub Pop] bands together," Kurt stated. "But they do it because of the marketing and packaging."

Krist attempted to explain the ball-and-chain effect the Sub Pop connection would have on the band. "People ask when the Sub Pop thing is going to die away, like they are waiting for the backlash to start. It's probably going to die away when the bands break up, or start putting out lousy songs."

The "Sub Pop thing" Krist talked about never went away. Their savvy marketing of blurry images, long hair, and flannel shirts created a culture that justified the coolness of the band, and it was their ticket into a lot of discriminating music circles. The often rocky Sub Pop–Nirvana relationship opened the doors and created previously unattainable opportunities for a number of Seattle's most promising bands in 1989. "For a few years in Seattle, it was the Summer of Love, and it was so great," said Kurt. "To be able to just jump out on top of the crowd with my guitar and be held up and pushed to the back of the room, and then brought back with no harm done to me—it was a celebration of something that no one could put their finger on. But once it got into the mainstream, it was over."

The Seattle scene was about to ignite. And Nirvana and Sub Pop Records were at Ground Zero.

Seven

Basically this is the real thing. No rock star contrivance, no intellectual
perspective, no master plan for world domination. You're talking about
four guys from rural Washington who wanna rock, who, if they weren't
doing this, would be working in a supermarket or lumber yard,
or fixing cars. Kurdt Kobain [sic] is a great tunesmith, although still a relatively
young songwriter. He wields a riff with passion.

—EVERETT TRUE,
Melody Maker, March 18, 1989

Bruce Pavitt's propaganda machine for the Sub Pop family of artists was
well oiled by the time *Bleach* hit the streets on June 9, 1989. That same
day, another Sub Pop creation, Lame Fest '89, a showcase of some of the label's newest acts, sold out Seattle's revered Moore Theater. Nirvana headlined
the gig that also featured TAD and Mudhoney. With their summer tour
scheduled to begin in just a few days, Kurt, Krist, and Chad used Lame Fest to
debut Jason Everman as the fourth, though unofficial, member of the band. It
was an uneventful performance, but it marked the first time that hundreds of
kids would have the chance to buy Nirvana's music right at the show.

For those who couldn't make it to Lame Fest, nearly one thousand white
vinyl copies were made available through chain and mom-and-pop record
stores across the Pacific Coast. Sub Pop's catalogue prophetically listed *Bleach*
as "hypnotic and righteous heaviness from these Olympia pop stars. They're
young, they own their own van, and they are going to make us rich!" Word
was spreading throughout Seattle's music community and college radio sta-

tions across the country; after hearing *Bleach,* alternative music circles everywhere raised their critical eyebrows. Nirvana's subsonic bass lines, scorching guitars, and heart-pounding drumbeats were taking everyone into uncharted waters.

For some, like Mark Lanegan, the effect was immediate. "In the spring of 'eighty-nine, Nirvana played a show at the community center in my hometown of Ellensburg, Washington," recalled Lanegan, the lead singer of Screaming Trees. "They completely blew me away; it was like seeing the Who in their prime. After two songs some jerk who worked there stopped the show—they'd gone over their time limit because the ten local bands who opened had gone over time. So they just stood there for a second and then Krist started throwing his bass in the air, up to the top of this twenty-foot ceiling, and catching it with one hand. Meanwhile Kurt was letting his amp go loud as hell, and their road manager got in a fist fight with the jerk guy. The whole thing was completely crazed. And this was in Ellensburg, of all places! I still believe to this day [Nirvana's] the best fucking band I've ever seen."

Seattle rock producer and musician Steve Fisk remembered his first Nirvana show without sentiment. "I hated them," said Fisk, who was at the same Ellensburg gig as Lanegan, but walked out after the first song. "The P.A. system was set up really bad[ly] by this jock guy from Yakima. Kurt had broken a string and was really upset and stood in the corner trying to change his guitar string. They were just clowning off and they were all nervous—except for Krist . . . Even when it was obvious that Kurt wasn't playing his guitar they kept playing."

For Steve Turner of Mudhoney, it was a stunt pulled off by Kurt during a gig with Nirvana that put him into orbit. "We played this tiny club in San Jose in early 'eighty-nine . . . Nirvana opened for us and during one of the songs they were hopping around, and Kurt somehow ended up balancing on his head—still playing guitar—and stayed there for a good long time. It was one of the coolest things I'd ever seen. I tried it after that. It didn't work as well."

Others, like Superchunk's Mac McCaughan, took a while to warm up to the band. "The first time I saw Nirvana, I thought they sucked," McCaughan said, referring to the Lame Fest show. "I thought the trashing of gear was contrived, and that *Bleach* was sort of low-rent Melvins. The next time I saw them was around the time the 'Sliver' single came out [in 1990]. It took the first thirty seconds of 'School' to make me realize I had severely misjudged the power of this band; the crowd was going completely nuts . . . The songs were amazing, the energy manic, and the trashing of gear seemed inevitable, not contrived."

As the summer tour to support *Bleach* approached, leaving home proved more difficult this time around. Krist and Shelli found it hard to say good-bye to each other after just getting back together after a long breakup, and even Kurt had a hard time facing the reality of being without Tracy for the longest time in their short relationship. It was a challenging test for the four friends—Tracy and Shelli were more than just Kurt and Krist's girlfriends. In many ways they acted as the band's managers: They sold the band's merchandise at shows, made sure the right press was around the band, got the guys to rehearsal, kept them fed, and always gave them a place to lay their heads. The two den mothers would undoubtedly be missed over the next few months.

With Krist's van filled to the top with gear and bodies, Nirvana departed on an almost thirty-date tour of the United States with fellow Seattle grungers TAD. The first stop was in San Francisco, where Nirvana played to a small audience at the Covered Wagon on June 22. Krist, who loves the Golden Gate City, was able to find room for sentimentality in the midst of a blossoming hate-everything punk lifestyle. "It's one of my favorite cities," he said. "The Roaring Twenties, art deco architecture, the climate, the vibe." Sentiment vanished immediately, though, when a pleasant punk memory kicked in. "We've just been hanging out on Haight-Ashbury . . . flipping off a lot of people, giving them our new attitude. Sometimes people will be walking down the sidewalk and they'll hear 'Kiss the Goat' and see us flipping them off! We're gonna get our asses kicked one day," he remarked at the time.

The opportunity for the locals to do just that didn't come up too often. A limited budget kept the band on the road, often leaving town after a show on the same night they had arrived. It was not unusual for the entire group to end up staying at the house of someone they'd just met on the tour. And, of course, there were the times when they just didn't have a place to stay at all. The benefits of superstardom were still a long way down the road.

"We stayed at this one place in Texas, out in the woods, next to a lake where there were signs all over the grass that said, 'Beware of Alligators,'"

Kurt recalled. "We slept with baseball bats at our sides." Krist remembered what happened to the bats: "We hacked up a baseball bat or something, put motor oil on it and tried to cook Cup-A-Soups. That's how we lived. It was fun, though; we were a hardy bunch. What's the word . . ." Krist paused. "Youthful enthusiasm! It was Kerou-wacky."

But as the tour motored on, the band's initial excitement began to wane. The audiences weren't always big, and the venues themselves were often depressing. Nirvana had to find other means to keep themselves entertained and upbeat. Krist recalled: "We played in San Jose, which was a shit-hole. We played in Sacramento, which was a shit-hole. There was this guy in Sacramento called the 'Master Blaster,' he's Sacramento's most hated DJ. And we loved him. He was such a wiseass. This guy said something to him and he just went, 'Look at him. See why brothers and sisters shouldn't marry?' "

With so many people crammed into such a small space for long periods of uneventful time, the mind tends to wander into some pretty strange areas. Kurt explained one such moment. "We've got this stupid record by a band called 'Witchcraft Coven,' who had that hit in the ['seventies], 'Ode to Billy Jack.' On its cover is a picture of the female singer lying naked on the altar, with the other members of the band holding daggers above her. On one side are sappy songs and on the other there's a Satanic sermon, which sounds like a TV announcer saying stuff like, 'Kiss the goat,' 'Satan, Leviathan.' So we'd turn that up really loud at intersections." Krist chimed in, "We asked this guy for directions and just when we're about to drive off, Kurt shouts out, 'Hail Satan!' "

At times, bands on the road forget the special privilege that they have when visiting town after town. The tediousness of traveling in the same vehicle, with the same people, to towns and cities that after a while start to look like the same place can distort the fact that a band is seeing a side of culture and society in a few months that most people never get to see in a lifetime. But the memories of this tour stayed with Kurt for a long time. "We were totally poor, but, God, we were seeing the United States for the first time. And we were in a band and we were making enough money to survive. It was awesome. It was just great. And if Jason wasn't such a prick, it would have been even better."

At some point during the tour it had become apparent that Jason Everman was not exactly conforming to the image Nirvana was attempting to send out to its audience. "He was like a peacock on amphetamines," said Kurt about Everman's constant, out-of-rhythm head-bobbing and hair-wagging. "He was so posey I couldn't believe it. It was embarrassing. It was so contrived and *sexual*. It was gross."

Even though they knew he wasn't an official member of the band, Krist and Kurt still depended on Everman to participate in the duties he was hired to perform. But Everman showed no interest in rehearsing new material. When he showed up for their first day of practice with a bevy of female admirers, Kurt realized something wasn't right about the decision to bring Everman on board.

Nevertheless, with nerves on edge and Everman's departure imminent, the first official Nirvana tour continued. "Traveling is fun," Novoselic added, "and so is keeping yourself busy. Every night is like a different party, for free. Every night is like Saturday night."

Nirvana was having so much fun on the tour that Kurt began to express his joy by smashing a new guitar at every show. On July 9, 1989, at Sonic Temple Hall in Wilkinsburg, Pennsylvania, Kurt destroyed an old Mustang in his own unique way in front of a very small crowd.

"Why do I do it?", Kurt asked in a confrontational manner. "Why not? It feels good. Somebody already cut down a nice old tree to make that fucking guitar. Smash it! We only ever do it if the feelings right; it doesn't matter where we are."

Said Krist, "It seemed like you couldn't end a show without doing something spectacular or sensational. No matter how good you played, it seemed like you didn't give it enough. So if you smashed all the gear and had this big gala ending, we could say, 'There, we did it.' We couldn't just walk off the stage . . . It was fun, and if you were doing a shitty show, it kind of made it spectacular. Then it became addictive."

"When we started smashing our equipment it was out of frustration because I felt that we weren't playing very good," Kurt explained "So I'd get mad and throw a rock-star temper tantrum, you know. And just break things to cool myself off. It's really not a very wise form of rehabilitation, but it worked." Kurt got scientific about the whole process. "Normally, only the neck will break. So I'm able to keep the body for a few more times. We just put necks on the bodies again. People expect it also. Give the kids what they want."

Following a consistent *Bleach* playlist while throwing out a few surprises like "Blandest" and "Polly," the tour wound through Pennsylvania and New Jersey and landed, tired and exhausted, at the *College Media Journal*'s New Music Seminar at the Pyramid Club in New York City on July 18, 1989. The best part of the gig, which was largely uninspired, occurred when Nirvana pummeled a drunk who kept jumping onstage and knocking the equipment over. It turned out to be a bad night for the band, perhaps because they all knew it was going to be Jason Everman's last one with Nirvana.

The three-day journey from New York City back to Seattle was driven in absolute silence. Kurt and Krist completely ignored the doomed guitarist. "No one said a word for the entire drive," recalled Everman. "We drove nonstop, only stopping for gas." Though Everman would go on to say he quit the band, he was asked to leave indirectly. "We were just too maladjusted to tell him to his face," said Krist. "We just didn't want to hurt anyone's feelings and that just compounded the problem."

Kurt explained that Jason's departure "was very mutual. I don't really want to elaborate on it. It was just musical differences, we're really glad it worked out the way it did . . . He really did help keep the band together. It gave me more freedom to jump around into the crowd in the middle of the solo, stuff like that. Get a little more wild. I'm becoming a lot more comfortable playing by myself, so we really don't need another guitarist. It's very rare to get people as really compatible as we are, the three of us." Jason Everman had been brought in to round out the sound live, but, as Kurt explained, Nirvana had always been, first and foremost, a three-piece band.

"I always felt kind of peripheral," Everman said, looking back. "I don't remember ever being asked for input on songs in that band, which is ultimately why I left . . . I probably wanted to do things that were not simple enough for them, ideas that were *mine* as opposed to Kurt's. There wasn't a tremendous musical difference—maybe it was just a control thing. Basically, anybody besides Kurt or Krist is kind of disposable. At the end of the day, Kurt could get in front of any bass player and any drummer and play his songs and it's not going to sound that much different."

On August 12, 1989, *Bleach* was released in the United Kingdom by Tupelo Records. Eight days later, the trio took a break in touring for the first recording session of The Jury, a side project that featured Kurt Cobain on guitar, Krist Novoselic on bass, and Mark Pickerel and Mark Lanegan of Screaming Trees on drums and vocals. The session lasted six hours, with the quartet cutting two Leadbelly songs: "Where Did You Sleep Last Night" (aka "In the Pines") and "Ain't It a Shame." Lanegan took lead vocals on "Where Did You Sleep Last Night," and Kurt sang on "Ain't It a Shame," with Krist and Pickerel providing backing vocals. The songs were supposed to come out on a Sub Pop single under the name *The Jury,* but the single was never released. Lanegan would eventually use the version of "Where Did You Sleep Last Night" on his solo album, *The Winding Sheet,* while "Ain't It a Shame" remains in the Sub Pop vaults. Pavitt and Poneman have both commented that it is Kurt's best vocal performance ever. Kurt had fallen in love with Leadbelly's music after reading an article by William S. Burroughs about him. "It's so raw and sincere," Kurt said of his music, "it's something that I hold really sacred to me. Leadbelly is one of the most important people in my life. I'm totally obsessed with him." Kurt was enamored with the simplicity of Leadbelly's melodies and the sincerity of his lyrics. Nirvana revived "Where Did You Sleep Last Night" many times live, most notably on 1993's *MTV Unplugged in New York* session.

In September, after the *Jury* sessions, Kurt, Krist, and Chad began recording the *Blew* EP with producer Steve Fisk at the Music Source in Seattle. The band laid down tracks for five songs, but only "Stain" and "Been a Son" were included on the EP.

This version of "Been a Son" is the definitive take, as it encompasses Nirvana's thrashing signature sound (the version on *Incesticide* was taken from the 1991 BBC performance). Krist's bass solo is much more pronounced in this mix, and Kurt wailing the sad story of a girl who should have been born a man is more powerful and emotional. On the other hand, "Stain" is upbeat and bouncy. In a unique twist, it features dual Kurt vocal tracks and dual Kurt guitar solo tracks.

The *Blew* EP version of "Even in His Youth" (along with "Token Eastern Song") has never been released, although a different version of "Even in His Youth" is available on *Incesticide*. The version of "Polly," described as falling somewhere between the *Nevermind* version and the "New Wave Polly" version on *Incesticide*, was never finished.

The artwork on the *Blew* EP compared favorably with what appeared on *Bleach*, strengthening the chosen image of the band. The *Blew* EP cover has a black border with "Nirvana" and "Blew" in the Bodini font. The black-and-white photo of Kurt lying on the stage was, like the cover of *Bleach*, taken by Tracy Marander. She is also responsible for the photo on the back of the EP, which was shot in her gynecologist's office after one of her appointments.

As soon as the fall recording session was complete, Nirvana was back on the road again, heading to Mexico and back up through the midwestern United States. On this leg, the band introduced "Immodium" (aka "Breed"), "Stain," "Been a Son," "Even in His Youth," and "Junkyard" into its *Bleach*-dominated playlist. When the tour landed in the United Kingdom in October, Nirvana quickly discovered (while record shopping in a store) that Tupelo Records had released the *Blew* 12-inch EP in conjunction with Nirvana's English concerts. "Ha! We didn't even know it was out!" Krist Novoselic said with honest surprise. This foreshadowed things to come, as Sub Pop's failure to keep Nirvana informed of many promotional decisions created serious tension in their relationship.

While in England, Kurt Cobain talked about his first impressions of the motherland, and noted the similarities between the English and Seattle music scenes. "England is very Americanized, actually. I was surprised to see Burger King and McDonald's dotted everywhere . . . I thought English society would be above that.

"But I love their television. It's so boring, you don't have to watch it. You can find an outlet to do something else. That's the way it should be!"

Kurt's cynicism about American culture was only being confirmed by what he saw of European society. "Most Americans are . . . drunk on their goodies. It's like some kind of tribal thing, marking out your territory, the guy with the prettiest beads or washing machine is respected in the tribe . . . And it's really easy to play that game too . . . it's easy to be ignorant and not accept anything aside from your own tribe and your own values. It's weird, but it seems Europe is much more open-minded, at least towards music and the arts."

Kurt seemed aware of his own perspective, and how Nirvana's background might have influenced their reactions. "It's because we are secluded, out on a limb up here. The local scene has always had an element of rock in it, but it's been a gloomy element. That's why I reckon you guys in the UK like it—because your rock is on the gloomy side too. Maybe it's the weather—we have the same sort of miserable climate!"

In another interview, he reflected on the differences between life in Seattle and life on the road. "I like the isolation, because it makes me appreciate being on tour more. I don't do very much at home at all; I stay in my apartment for weeks. It sure broadens your outlook, all the different attitudes you come across. We're getting fed up with this backwoods image kind of thing we're getting. It's like, you know there's an Aberdeen in every state in the United States, which is redneck, hillbilly. We're not unique."

The first of thirty-six European dates on the forty-two-day tour was held on October 23, 1989, in Newcastle, England. Touring with old pals TAD made the grueling tour initially pass more quickly; on opening night, the Scottish band the Cateran was added to the bill. After a show at the Duchess of York Public House in Leeds on October 25, Nirvana headed over to BBC's Maida Vale Studios in London. There they met the famous disc jockey John Peel, who took the producer's chair to record Nirvana's "Love Buzz," "About a Girl," "Polly," and "Spank Thru" for a session later released on the hard-to-find compact disc *The John Peel Sessions.*

In an interview with *Zip Code* magazine, Kurt explained how much fun he had playing at the School of Oriental and African Studies in London on October 27. "That was definitely my favorite show, excellent. Very good crowd, I was amazed at it. They were more energetic than a Seattle crowd."

Never one to shortchange fans, Nirvana continued with its fourteen- to seventeen-song set through four more shows in the United Kingdom. Meanwhile, back in the States, the first original Nirvana recording to be released on a label other than Sub Pop appeared in November. "Mexican Seafood," taken from the early Crover sessions, was included on the compilation EP *Teriyaki Asthma,* on C/Z Records. Daniel House, who ran the label, was in the band Skin Yard with old friend Jack Endino. It was Endino who had turned House on to the Dale Crover demo tape.

The audiences were enthusiastic, but the touring was hard. Nirvana and TAD were traveling in a small Fiat van. They didn't eat well and the conditions were rough. The pressure and anxiety caused Kurt to withdraw.

Landing in Holland on November 1, Nirvana headed to Hilversum for a VPRO radio broadcast, which featured uninspired versions of "Dive" and "About a Girl." The band continued to add new songs to their burned-out set list, and on November 5 at the Melkweg in Amsterdam, "Help Me, I'm Hungry" made its debut. Five nights later, at the Forum Enger in Germany, "Molly's Lips" joined the mix. At the Kapu in Linz, Austria, on the twentieth, "Verse Chorus Verse" was heard for the first time. The John Peel sessions from October debuted on the BBC two nights later.

On November 27, 1989, at the Piper Club in Rome, an exhausted Kurt "had a nervous breakdown onstage," Sup Pop's Pavitt recalled. "He was just going to jump off. The bouncers were freaking out and everybody was just begging him to come down. And he was [saying], 'No, no I'm just going to dive.' He had really reached his limit . . . People literally saw a guy wig out in front of them who could break his neck if he didn't get it together."

Poneman, who was also at this show, recalled trying to console an obviously distraught Cobain after the show. "I was walking around the club with him, and he was saying, 'I just want to go home, I don't want to play for these people, these people are fucking idiots, they're stupid, they expect me to go up there and perform like a trained animal. I don't respect them. I want to be with my girlfriend and I want to quit music. This is not what I'm about.'"

According to Kurt, the first words out of Poneman's mouth were, "Well, now that you're quitting Nirvana, we'd still be interested in you as a solo artist." It was comments like these that would stick with Kurt for quite some time, an unsettling reminder that his passion for performing was quickly becoming a financial catalyst for people he once trusted as friends.

There was every indication that the tour was beginning to fall apart, but the band rallied and put on a good face for the remaining shows in France and Belgium. Nirvana played "Negative Creep" for the first time on the tour December 2 in Ghent, Belgium. The next night at the Charing Cross Astoria in London was the last show of the tour, teaming Nirvana with TAD and special guests Mudhoney. It was billed as the Charing Cross Astoria's Lame Fest, and it proved to be a disaster for Nirvana. Kurt's equipment was screwed up and the band was sloppy from the start. Frustrated, tired, and emotionally drained from playing thirty-six shows in forty-two days, Kurt, Krist, and Chad destroyed their equipment beyond repair.

By the time the band returned to Seattle in mid-December, the final plans were being put in place for Krist and Shelli's wedding. On December 30, 1989, the Novoselics were married in their apartment in Tacoma, Washington. In attendance were Krist's mother; Shelli's mother and stepfather; Kurt and his girlfriend, Tracy Marander; Kurt Danielson, Tad Doyle, and other members of TAD. Matt Lukin was Krist's best man. But the honeymoon was short: Nirvana's torrid seven-week United States tour was scheduled to start the following week.

Eight

This was going to be our second record, right. It was
supposed to come out probably around September 1990 and,
well, once we got off tour, that's when we lost Chad, so there was
uncertainty with that. We didn't want to release it.

—KRIST NOVOSELIC

Nineteen ninety opened with both promise and sadness for Nirvana and the entire Seattle rock community. Kurt, Krist, and Chad were busy touring the West Coast and making plans to lay down tracks for a second album for Sub Pop. In spite of their delicate relationship, Nirvana was optimistic about their future on the now nationally hip label. Mudhoney's 1989 self-titled release, TAD's debut album, *God's Balls*, and Nirvana's *Bleach* were all receiving substantial airplay on college radio stations across the United States. There was every indication that Sub Pop would be able to grind out a few more releases from a number of Seattle bands-in-waiting before the summer. But while the future looked bright, the frightening truth was that Sub Pop was having financial problems of its own, the effects of which would be felt by Nirvana before the year was out.

The band went into Reciprocal Recording with Jack Endino on January 2 and 3 to record the song "Sappy." That version "pretty much sucked and is still in a Sub Pop vault somewhere," Jack Endino claimed. "Several other versions exist." "Sappy" was another name for "Verse Chorus Verse," which Nirvana had tested live on the European tour. The studio version of "Verse

Chorus Verse" appears as the hidden track on the *No Alternative* benefit compilation CD.

On January 7, with reworked versions of their European set list in tow, Nirvana began their guitar-smashing, drum-trashing U.S. tour in Seattle. They would carry on through Washington, California, Arizona, and Canada, but the tour was interrupted when the Emerald City lost one of its favorite sons to a battle with drug abuse.

On March 16, 1990, Andrew Wood, who had been through drug rehabilitation a couple of times for cocaine abuse, stuck a needle in his arm, filling his frail body with an overdose of heroin. He died a few days later. A longtime member of the Seattle music scene (he had founded the influential band Malfunkshun in 1984), Wood was the lead singer of Mother Love Bone. Unable to continue under the name Mother Love Bone but not willing to let the memory of Wood fade away, the remaining members, along with Eddie Vedder, Soundgarden's Chris Cornell (Andy Wood's roommate), and Matt Cameron, devoted an entire album to Wood's memory. The finished product was named *Temple of the Dog*. Later, two of the members of Mother Love Bone, Jeff Ament and Stone Gossard, started Pearl Jam.

Shortly after Wood's death, Nirvana took a brief break from touring and headed to Smart Studios in Madison, Wisconsin, to cut demos with Butch Vig for their second album. Vig, now one of alternative music's most respected and revered producers, was mostly known for his work with TAD, and he was the perfect choice for the raw and inexperienced studio ranting of Nirvana. "He's so easy to get along with, it's just a perfect relationship because we still do whatever we want to do," said Kurt, one of Vig's biggest admirers. "But Butch has a few suggestions, and a lot of times they're great suggestions. He's just a really good coworker."

Vig's experienced ear recognized something special in Kurt. "If you took all his songs and had someone else sing them, it wouldn't be the same," Vig noted. "There's something in Kurt's persona that takes them to another level. There's mystery and passion and intensity and something that's almost otherworldly in his voice."

At the time of the recording, Kurt talked about the newer, mellower side Nirvana was beginning to reveal. "We're definitely not completely changing our style. There'll just be maybe three songs about a girl on the next record, instead of just one. We'll always still play really heavy, raunchy."

Seven songs were recorded during the Vig session, including the basic structures for "Polly," "Lithium," and "In Bloom." With the exception of the never-released "Sappy" and "Dive" (later used as a B side for the Sub Pop single "Sliver"), all songs from these sessions were rerecorded for the final project, which became *Nevermind*. But as Nirvana fans had come to expect, these early recordings (some of which have been heavily bootlegged) had different lyrics from their finished products: "Stay Away" became "Pay to Play," while "Breed" was known as "Immodium" at this stage of recording.

A few weeks after the Vig sessions wrapped up, tapes of the demo were mixed and distributed to the band, Sub Pop, and many others; as a result, bootlegs were leaked into the underground. Meanwhile, Nirvana wasted no time getting back to what they did best, playing live and often, going back on the road to complete a fifteen-date U.S. and Canadian tour. They debuted "In Bloom" on April Fool's night at the Cabaret Metro in Chicago and continued through Illinois, Michigan, and Massachusetts, playing a set of tunes that now regularly included "Spank Thru," "Been a Son," "Immodium" ("Breed"), "Negative Creep," and "Stain."

On April 26, the tour landed in New York City at the renowned Pyramid Club. Former Stooges lead singer Iggy Pop was in the audience that night, and the show was a tremendous opportunity for Nirvana to leave their influential mark on the most respected minds of the punk scene. When Kurt saw Iggy before the show, he ran out to the van, got his Stooges T-shirt, and wore it during the show. But the realization of playing to a house of punk rock's elite overwhelmed Nirvana, and they choked miserably.

Iggy, ironically, remembered the show, marred by technical problems and sound issues, with fondness. "It was hard to hear the guitar, but the guy playing and singing had a vibe; he hopped around like a muppet or an elf or something, hunched over his guitar, hop hop hop, hippety hippety hop. I loved that. When he sang, he put his voice in this really grating place, and it was kind of devilish sounding. At the end of the set he attacked the drum kit and threw cymbals, other bits, and finally himself into the audience. Later I saw the same guy passing the bar. He was little, with stringy blond hair and a Stooges T-shirt. I felt proud."

Krist Novoselic saw the show in a different way. "We knew Iggy Pop was there, Sonic Youth was there, but we just bombed. It was no good. Something happened . . . I was so bummed out that night that I shaved my head after the show. I needed to absolve myself from that whole bad scene. It's a very hygienic thing to do; shave your head."

During Nirvana's stay in New York they met with Steve Brown, a video director who'd done some video work for Sub Pop. The band worked with Brown for a week, shooting scenes that would make up the first "In Bloom" video. During the video Krist has some shots with hair and some with his shaved head. The video ended up on the Sub Pop video compilation *Sub Pop Video Network Program 1.*

Changes were beginning to occur both within and outside of the band. It was during this period that Kurt began breaking up his long relationship with Tracy Marander, one of the earliest signs that his personality and life were headed in a new direction. He began the process by telling her over the phone, on her birthday, that he didn't want to live with her anymore, though he said he still wanted to be her boyfriend. Then, too, Kurt and Krist were beginning to think about changing the makeup of the band—starting with a new drummer.

"Seven weeks, fucking seven weeks," Kurt remembered. "And it's just the three of us in the van, nobody else. We've got to drive, load up our stuff, and everything. We didn't bring anybody, we just left [Seattle to tour]. We attempted to get a sound man two weeks before we left, but you've got to worry about the guy's personality. We did want the guy who worked for Mudhoney but we didn't know him; we may be too weird for him."

The love for what Kurt did best had not escaped him. "But nothing is better than playing live, even though we may say we hate it and have said we may not continue to play live if we have to keep doing these seven-week tours. Playing in front of a bunch of people who react well is the best thing in the world."

Nirvana added a Velvet Underground cover, "Here She Comes Now," and "Dive" to their set list as the two-month tour wound its way through New Jersey, Washington, D.C., Florida, Georgia, Nebraska, and Idaho. At the end of May, with Nirvana back in Seattle, Kurt and Krist sat down together to make one of the toughest decisions of their professional career. They agreed that it was time to let drummer Chad Channing go.

"Chad wanted to express himself in a way that really didn't gel with what we wanted to do," Novoselic explained. "We needed somebody to just straight ahead rock hard. Chad really compromised his style to suit the band. I don't think he was happy about doing that. But his leaving the band was a good departure; it worked well for everybody."

Removing Channing from the band was not an easy thing for Kurt to do; he later said he felt like he'd killed someone.

"I was really hoping to participate more and become part of what was going on," Channing said, "at least to have a say in how my own drums sounded. I wanted to get more involved in the band and feel like I was actually doing something. I was still happy dealing with the album, but I wanted to be more a part of it. It was then that I realized that it really is Kurt's show and that what he says goes and that's it, no questions asked.

"[But] it wasn't like we weren't getting along," Channing added. "We always got along as human beings. It was strictly along the musical line that it just wasn't working anymore. That's where it ended, right there."

Channing had come to feel like a hired hand; he complained that Kurt and Krist would have been better off with a drum machine. For their part, Kurt and Krist had been stymied by Channing's behavior for some time; his playing would sometimes seem to drop out all together, leaving the band stranded without a beat, and Kurt remembered that it was over Channing's eccentricities that more than one guitar got destroyed. Clearly, something had to give.

"I'd spent the last [couple of] years with these guys in really close quarters," Channing recalled. "We'd gone through hell together. We'd been in shit together, in little vans, playing for no money. There wasn't any big daddy with the big bucks bailing us out . . . I knew that when we said goodbye, I wouldn't see them for a long time."

Once the pangs of Channing's departure faded, Kurt remembered why they had become a band in the first place, and their angst over the breakup was quickly brought down to earth. "Overall, I have massive love for that guy," said Kurt. "I kind of admire him because he's really satisfied with the way that he is. He seems like a really happy person and he always has been."

The seat behind Nirvana's drum kit, which seemed like a revolving door, was vacant again. Taking full advantage of the opportunity to fill it was Mudhoney's twenty-three-year-old Dan Peters, who sent the word to Kurt and

Krist through mutual friends that he wanted to jam with them. "So I got a call from Kurt, and he was like, Wow, you wanna play with *us?*" Peters said. "I was like, 'Hell yeah, let's hook it up and have some fun.' " Honest enthusiasm got the Mudhoney drummer into rehearsal, but it wasn't enough to make Peters a permanent member of Nirvana. Kurt had his own clear and concise vision of how he wanted the band to grow, even asking Peters if he would use a drum kit similar to the huge North kit Channing pounded to get the heavier sound Kurt loved. Rehearsals did not develop the symmetry the threesome hoped for, but their hard work did produce the band's first true single, "Sliver," a Pixies-influenced formula of soft verses and exploding choruses.

Kurt's songwriting continued to develop at a time in his life when everything seemed to be falling apart. Tracy was no longer by his side to provide him with inspiration or support, and he filled the void of Tracy's absence by seeking the attention of a young girl named Tobi Vail. The Olympia native was such an influence on the shy guitarist that many of the songs he wrote evolved from their relationship. Vail and her best friend, Kathleen Hanna, founded Bikini Kill, the "riot girl" band that opened several times for Nirvana.

On July 11, 1990, Kurt and Krist headed back to Reciprocal Recording to lay down the basic tracks for their new and final Sub Pop single, "Sliver." The recording was done with a quick-and-dirty intensity that Kurt later looked back on with pride. Special arrangements were required to make "Sliver," which caused a little friction. The band TAD was recording in the studio when Krist and Kurt arrived with Mudhoney drummer Dan Peters. As Jack Endino recalled, "Jonathan [Poneman] called up and was begging. 'We want Nirvana to cut this one song really fast while they're in town. And is there any way they can use TAD's equipment?' And Tad [Doyle, the band's singer] was like, 'This is our time, we're trying to record something here.' " Doyle resented Poneman's intrusion, but a compromise was struck: TAD took an hour for dinner, and Nirvana used the hour to make their record.

"There were two takes of 'Sliver,' " Endino remembered. "Only one of them was finished. And they're almost identical. And then we spent an entire day [July 24] redoing the vocals and maybe some guitar and then mixing it." The single was the second Nirvana single released through the Sub Pop Singles Club, with the Vig session version of "Dive" as the B side.

At the end of the 7-inch version of "Sliver" there is a recording of a phone call between Sub Pop's Jonathan Poneman and a very hungover Krist:

Jonathan: What's up?
Krist: Oh.
Jonathan: This is Jonathan.
Krist: Oh.
Jonathan: Just waking up there? [long pause] Hey. Hello?
Krist: Hello.
Jonathan: Yeah. Just waking up there or something?
Krist: Yeah.
Jonathan: Tough night, eh?
Krist: [pause] Yeah.
Jonathan: Just calling to touch base to see what's going on.
Krist: Uh-huh.
Jonathan: Should I give you a couple minutes here?
Krist: Yeah.
Jonathan: Can I, uh, call you back at one point?
Krist: Yeah, call back at five or so.
Jonathan: Okay, take care man.
Krist: See ya. Bye.

Soon after that session, Kurt started mapping out more tracks for the next Nirvana album. But because the original plans to cut it for Sub Pop had been scrapped and they no longer had a permanent drummer, Kurt and Krist almost decided not to do anything at all. "If we wanted to do anything, we wanted to release a new album with a new drummer," Krist said. "There were so many variables to consider that Kurt and I felt it wasn't wise to put out a record at all."

In August, Nirvana got the opportunity to open a few West Coast gigs for their longtime idols, Sonic Youth. A quick phone call to old friend Dale Crover, and the three-piece band was back on the road, testing a couple of new tunes—"Endless Nameless" and "Lithium." But the tour lasted only a short while, until Crover headed back to his duties as the drummer for the Melvins. Nirvana's problems keeping a drummer were starting to remind people of *This Is Spinal Tap*.

With Nirvana's biggest concert looming just weeks away, Dan Peters started rehearsing for the upcoming show. But several problems stood in the way of Peters officially becoming Nirvana's next drummer. Even though things seemed fine in the Mudhoney camp, their future together as a band was very much up in the air.

"Yeah, it looked like he was gonna be in our band," Krist said. But he was concerned about "another case of compromising [his] style for our band, y'know he was gonna go out and buy a bigger drum set and y'know you can really hear his style; it's just Mudhoney. Y'know those snare rolls." But due to Mudhoney's cloudy future and Nirvana's empty seat behind the bass drum, Peters saw the opportunity to join a band that was seemingly on the rise, and he went for it.

On September 22, 1990, Peters played his first gig with Nirvana. They introduced "Sliver" in their set list that night, and shared the stage with the Melvins, the Dwarves, and the Derelicts, in front of fifteen hundred people at Motor Sport International in Seattle. It was Peters' first and last gig. "I was totally made a fool of," said Peters. "I'm on the cover [of *Sounds*], with Nirvana, blissfully ignorant. Matt from Mudhoney told me that Krist had come up to him at the actual show and told him I wasn't going to be in the band anymore. And Matt's like, 'Have you told Dan?' And he's like, 'No, we haven't told Dan.' Matt's like, 'You gotta fucking tell him, that's bullshit.' If they were honest with me and up-front with me I would have totally accepted it, but the way they went about it bummed me out, because they didn't have the balls to tell me. The last thing I wanted to do was look like a chump, and I looked like a chump."

The reason Kurt gave for Peters's departure seemed noble enough: Simply put, if Peters had left Mudhoney, that would have sealed that band's fate, and Kurt didn't want that on his conscience. Three days after the Motor Sport show, Kurt played three songs live on Calvin Johnson's KAOS radio show, "Opinion," "Lithium," and "Dumb," and, unbeknownst to Peters, announced that Nirvana had a new drummer. "He's a baby Dale Crover," Kurt said to all who had tuned in. "He plays almost as good as Dale. And within a few years' practice, he may even give him a run for his money."

The new drummer's name was Dave Grohl.

Nine

I dropped out of high school when I was seventeen.
I started touring right after I dropped out.
And that's all I've been doing since then.
—DAVE GROHL

David Eric Grohl, son of James and Virginia Grohl, was born on January 14, 1969, in the small town of Warren, Ohio. When he was three, the family, including older sister Lisa, moved to Springfield, Virginia, where, just three years later, Dave's parents, like Kurt's and Krist's, divorced. The responsibility of raising the two Grohl children fell to Virginia, who became a high school English teacher to help support herself, Lisa, and Dave. And somehow, without any direct source, music always found its way into the Grohl home. In fact, there was always a guitar lying around the house, but, as Dave tells it, that guitar would have had to jump up and bite him on the ass to get him to notice it. "I never got around to really learning how to play it until I was about ten years old," said Dave, whose appetite for playing quickly blossomed and eventually led him to taking guitar lessons, whether he liked it or not. "I was told to take lessons because everyone was sick of hearing 'Smoke on the Water.' Took lessons for about one year and stopped because it wasn't teaching me how to play music." Dave tried to continue his lessons on his own, teaching himself to play along with his favorite Beatles songs. "I was always really good at figuring out songs by ear," he said. "I always thought that it was in my blood, seeing as my mother was in singing groups as a teen and my father was an accomplished flautist. At eleven, I started recording songs on a Fairfax County public-issue cassette player with my best friend Larry Hinkle."

Dave got his first guitar, a 1960s Silvertone version with the amp built into the case, as a Christmas present when he was twelve. By spring, dropped and broken, the Silvertone was replaced by a black Gibson Les Paul, which helped introduce Dave to the world of distortion. Before the year was out, he joined a neighborhood cover band, playing classic rock to anyone who would listen, including a nursing home where people danced to Dave's rendition of the Rolling Stones' "Time Is on My Side."

As with Kurt and Krist, Dave's introduction to punk was a memorable event. When he was thirteen years old, his family left their home in Washington, D.C., to visit relatives in Evanston, Illinois. Dave explains how his cousin, Tracey Bradford, became his Buzz Osborne.

"Tracey was two or three years older than me. We arrived, and my aunt Sherry says, 'Tracey, they're here. Come downstairs.' I hear this 'chink, chink, chink,' coming down the stairs," Dave recalled. "I was greeted at the front door by Tracey. But this wasn't the Tracey I had grown to love, this was punk-rock Tracey. Complete with bondage pants, spiked hair, chains, the whole nine yards. It was the most fucking awesome thing I had ever seen! That few weeks in Evanston changed my life forever. I was totally amazed at the extensive underground of fanzines and labels and bands. Her record collection was incredible! Hundreds of singles from all over the world. I no longer thought that punk rockers existed only on *CHIPs* and *Quincy*." From that moment he was a convert.

Completely inspired, Dave quickly made the switch from classic rocker to punk rocker. He had been introduced to punk about a year earlier, diving into Devo's first album, *Q: Are We Not Men? A: We Are Devo!* That was an album that really changed the horizon of punk rock, helping Devo become one of the first New Wave/punk bands to cross over into mainstream rock. For Dave, this album helped to open up his appreciation for punk, and inspired new ideas about the kinds of punk rock he was quickly becoming attached to.

Dave's new punk lifestyle followed the typical course of juvenile delinquency and the pains that come with it. "After I had been doing the punk thing for a while, I was in a bunch of bands and um, started . . . smoking pot," Dave said. "I started smoking a lot of pot when I was about fourteen and just started playing more guitar . . . I just started listening to melody and song structure and stuff, and taking a bunch of acid and smoking a lot of pot and listening to Led Zeppelin. You know, just your typical type of high school stoner shit . . . I'd sit there with a bong in my hand and listen to 'Rain Song' or something. There was this little group of all my friends, we were all in bands and we were all going through our little drug-experimental-sort-of-freak-out phase and we rehearsed in my friend Barrett's house . . . and we would sit around every Friday night listening to CDs and selling pot to each other . . . I was the high school stoner. But see, I was the Vice President of my freshman class, but still like a stoner. So, I was this real weird, sort of mutant, intellectual, stoner type. My mom was a teacher at the school and my sister was a senior so I couldn't really flaunt my 'stonerness' around school. I definitely had to keep it behind closed doors. And you know, holding a responsibility, such as being the vice president of the freshman class, you can't just let some scandal like that slip out."

Having a teacher for a mom made Dave particularly conscious of the perils of the American educational system. And Dave's strong feelings on the injustice educators face is right on the button. "The way America's money is budgeted by our government . . . leaves nothing to the education system . . . Teachers are dealing with the future; teachers are dealing with kids growing up who are going to take care of me or you someday. They're gonna decide how much the teachers are gonna be paid in twenty-five to thirty years and that should be the most valuable of all decisions, when it comes down to the rights of a teacher. And most schools now are just so overcrowded, it's amazing. Classes with thirty to forty kids in them, seven classes a day. Kids can cheat their way through high school. You can cheat your way all the way to graduation, and not even know how to read.

"Having my mother as a teacher and hearing all the horror stories . . . the education system in general in a lot of places is really screwed. And it has more to do with the government than it does the teachers themselves. There are a lot of really great teachers. I went to Catholic school for two years and I got an incredible education, because the classes were smaller and the teachers had time to sit down and actually talk to their students."

By the time he was fifteen, Dave began reaching in other musical directions, and he quickly became a fan of live shows. In the summer of 1984, at a Void show in Washington, D.C., Dave met some guys from the band Freak Baby, who were looking for a new guitarist. One successful audition shortly thereafter, Dave's career as a punk rocker was under way.

A few high school shows led to the completion of a four-track demo with local studio producer Barrett Jones, and that convinced a neighborhood punk-rock store called Smash to sell Freak Baby cassettes. After they kicked out their bass player a few months later, Dave switched to drums and Freak Baby's drummer switched to bass. But that move didn't yield the success the band had hoped for, and a short time later Freak Baby called it quits after only a few months together. Dave wasted no time hooking up with another band, Mission Impossible, in 1985, playing revved-up hardcore and getting the freedom to put his drum chops to good use. Mission Impossible's subsequent touring and the bands they played with were Dave's hardcore dream come true.

"Over the course of that year, I'd had many great experiences," Dave recalled years later in the official Foo Fighters band biography. "Opening for the legendary Troublefunk at a high school prom, Ian MacKaye of Fugazi publicly declaring that he liked my band, finally being able to send demo tapes to all the pen pals I'd acquired over years of fanzine collecting, even releasing a split single with local heroes Lunchmeat." But Mission Impossible eventually bit the dust, and Dave quickly met up with Reuben Radding, another local rocker. Radding was an extraordinary bassist in a band called A.O.C., which had broken up at about the same time.

Radding wasn't into the same hardcore scene Grohl had become attached to; he leaned more toward the indie scene where groups like Mission of Burma and Television drew the raves. Nonetheless, their common fondness for the alternative arena led them to form the band Dain Bramage. It was in this band where Dave discovered a love for songwriting and varied arrangements and dynamics, as Dain Bramage broadened itself into an extremely experimental band. Demos were again recorded with Barrett Jones, which piqued the interest of the Los Angeles independent label Fartblossom. The label paid to record the album *I Scream Not Coming Down* in a twenty-four-track studio in Annapolis, Maryland.

Excitement died as quickly as it took to record the album, and interest in Dain Bramage soon faded. Needing an outlet to pound his drums, Dave joined the Washington, D.C., band Scream. "In 1987, I saw a flyer that read 'Scream looking for drummer, call Franz,'" said Dave. "Now, Scream was legendary in D.C. They had been a band since nineteen seventy-nine or 'eighty and I had seen them many a time. Their first two records were among my all-time favorites. Originally, I'd just wanted to call Franz, jam with them once or twice, then be able to tell my friends, 'I got to play with Scream!' So I called Franz a few times and finally got an answer. I explained that I was a huge fan, told him which bands I played in, and that I'd love to give it a shot. When he asked how old I was, I lied and said I was twenty. I think I was seventeen. He never called back."

A few months passed; Dave called Franz again, convincing him to give him an audition. Dave knew Scream's repertoire backward and forward; he had even gotten ahold of an advance copy of a new demo of theirs. So when he showed up ready to play their own material, instead of just a bunch of Zeppelin covers, the band was floored, and Dave jammed with them for hours.

After a few more practices, it became very clear to Dave that Scream wanted him in the band. The remote possibility of joining Scream had never even been a consideration for him, but soon he found himself faced with a difficult, heart-wrenching decision: Either leave his seven bandmates in Dain Bramage behind to travel the world with Scream, one of his favorite bands ever, or stay loyal to Dain Bramage and hope for the best.

Dave almost backed out. "I called Franz and told him no. I explained my situation and apologized. I think he understood and invited me to their next show a few weeks later. It was one of the greatest Scream shows I'd ever seen. I changed my mind."

Scream had been under contact to Dischord, but they had just moved to Ras Records, a reggae label looking to get into the rock market. Under the direction of a reggae producer, they cut *No More Censorship,* Scream's fourth LP.

Scream hit the road to tour in 1987 and hit it hard, traveling across America, Europe, and Canada again and again and again until 1988 came roaring into their headlights. The constant touring didn't present great profits for the band, but it solidified their affection for playing live and kept them from the redundant routine of just playing in the same clubs over and over at home. Besides, this was what life is supposed to be about, Dave thought. "I was eighteen years old, doing exactly what I wanted to do," he said. "With a seven-dollar-a-day per diem, I traveled to places I'd never dreamed of visiting. And all because of music. The feeling of driving across the country in a van with five other guys, stopping in every city to play, sleeping on people's floors, watching the sun come up over the desert as I drove, it was all too much. This was definitely where I belonged."

Scream traveled to Europe in February 1988, landing in Amsterdam, and they played in the Netherlands, France, Germany, Italy, Scandinavia, England, and Spain. They were one of the few American hardcore bands to visit Europe, and the group went over big almost everywhere, often performing in punk squats. They played relatively few shows in clubs or traditional concert venues.

After another short tour in the United States, Scream headed back to Europe for three months in the fall of 1988. They continued writing new material and recorded the album *Live at Van Hall in Amsterdam*.

When he was able to enjoy the few minutes in between Scream tours, Dave found himself hanging with Barrett Jones. Jones was working on a solo project of his own, and since he had an eight-track setup in his basement, he had Dave record some parts, playing bass or guitar on some of Jones's songs. The experience was one that would permanently affect Dave's approach to songwriting.

"I realized that if I were to write a song, record the drums first, then come back over it with a few guitars, bass, and vocals, I could make it sound like a band," he said. Working up a handful of new riffs, Dave cut three songs of his own with Jones in a quarter of an hour. It was a useful trial, one he would think back to when he finally got his own band.

Scream toured Europe one final time in the spring of 1990: twenty-three shows in twenty-four days. Somehow Dave found time to write songs, including some that made it to the last Scream release, *Fumble;* others were put away for later use. One of their shows was recorded and later released as *Live in Germany.*

But when they got home to the apartment they shared, Scream vocalist Pete Stahl and Scream bassist Skeeter Thompson found an eviction notice awaiting them. They would have to be out the next day, ready or not. So Scream did the only thing they could think of doing: They got back on the road.

It became very clear to the band that this was to be their last tour together, as cancellations and low attendance deeply depressed all involved. Skeeter split without even so much as a good-bye and headed back to D.C., and the remaining members decided to stay in Los Angeles and search for a new bassist.

Frustrated, tired, unmotivated, and stranded, Dave picked up the phone and called Buzz Osborne. The two had become friends over the past several months, thanks to the corresponding touring schedules of Scream and the Melvins that often had them playing the same room. Osborne suggested he look up these two guys who were in a band called Nirvana, who happened to be looking for a new drummer. Dave hesitated; he was really just calling to get help with his own situation, not necessarily to jump blindly into another. He'd never met Kurt and Krist, and only knew a little about them from the buzz that had been created after the release of *Bleach*. What Dave didn't know was that Kurt and Krist had wanted him in the band ever since they'd seen him play at a Scream show several months earlier. Dave remembered seeing Kurt and Krist after the Scream gig, but he never introduced himself. "The Melvins were playing in San Francisco, I was backstage talking to Buzz and Dale, and there's this real huge, tall guy going, 'Wuh-uh, wuh-uh,' he waves his arms like Shaggy imitating Robbie the Robot. And there was this other guy sitting in the corner like he was taking a shit," he recalled in a 1992 interview with Shaun Phillips. Dave remembered finding Kurt and Krist quite amusing.

At a party in Olympia, Washington, shortly after, Dave and his friends crossed paths with Kurt and Krist again. The amusement wasn't mutual. "They were real rocker dudes," Kurt recalled. "I hated them, I thought they were assholes. [Dave] brought up this Primus tape from their car and tried to play it and everyone got mad at him."

But Dave's taste in music didn't sway Kurt and Krist's appetite to have Dave audition for Nirvana if the opportunity presented itself. "I'd been a Scream fan for about seven, eight years and we were just blown away by the whole band, especially the drummer. Dave was really good," said Krist.

Buzz Osborne knew this was a chance of a lifetime for Grohl, and he did his best to talk Dave into taking the job. It took days, but Grohl finally mustered up the courage to call Krist, who told Grohl he remembered seeing him play with Scream. But Krist explained that Nirvana had already recruited Dan Peters for their upcoming UK tour. Convinced it wasn't going to work out, Dave wished them luck and hung up. But Krist called back later that night and asked if there was any way Dave could be in Seattle right away. He didn't have to ask twice.

Ten

Corporate music has been [stagnant] forever.
I can't think of hardly anything in the corporate world that I've
liked for years. Maybe R.E.M. and the Pixies, that's about it.
—KURT COBAIN

With only a couple of bags of clothes and a set of drums to his name, Dave Grohl scrounged up a few bucks and flew to Seattle to catch Nirvana's Motor Sport gig with the Melvins and audition for the band. He had never seen the band play live, and though he liked *Bleach*, he was more impressed with the Melvins than with Nirvana.

Perhaps that was because of the incredible amounts of hype surrounding the Seattle music scene in the latter half of 1990. It had Dave thinking that Seattle, and Nirvana for that matter, was nothing more than a black-and-white still photo of a flannel shirt as seen through the blurry lens of noted underground photographer Charles Peterson. But the truth was, Dave didn't know much about Seattle at all. The only thing on his mind on the plane ride up there was the torture he was putting himself through for leaving his friends in Scream behind. It was the toughest decision he would ever have to make, but once he left, Dave knew there was no turning back. And he still wasn't quite sure what he had gotten himself into when he landed in the Emerald City and met his two new friends. "I was greeted at the Seattle airport by the biggest guy I had ever seen and the scrawniest guy I had ever seen."

Still broke when he got to Seattle, Dave moved in with Kurt and lived on his couch in a less-than-attractive setup for eight months. When Dave first arrived, Kurt had just broken up with Tracy and was totally heartbroken. He would sit in his tiny shoebox apartment for eight hours at a time without saying a word. It was an odd beginning to their friendship, but eventually Kurt overcame his heartbreak.

The first time Dave visited the house where Kurt grew up, a strange connection had formed, for there, on a wall in Kurt's room, amidst a plethora of garbled graffiti, was a drawing of a brain with a question mark over it. Dave had drawn the exact same thing in junior high school.

Even their mothers noticed the similarities. When they eventually met a few years later and exchanged the usual proud-mother stories about their sons, Wendy Cobain and Virginia Grohl were taken aback by the similarities of their sons. "We were just amazed at how much these two kids are alike," said Wendy. "They're like twins that got separated somehow."

Dave settled quickly into the Nirvana routine: practice, practice, practice. His first gig of a short tour with the band was just a few weeks away, and Dave recognized his responsibilities immediately. And it only took a run-through of the songs on *Bleach* to become crystal clear that the band needed a straight-ahead, rock-hard drummer like Dave Grohl. "If he ever leaves the band, we're breaking up," said Krist.

Kurt discovered another gem in the Grohl package: his outstanding ability to harmonize with Cobain's scratchy leads. It was something Kurt had wanted to expand upon for a long time, feeling it would strengthen their overall live sound.

It was Kurt's songwriting that first caught Dave's ear. "He just writes really catchy pop songs that are simple and repetitive and just pound this melody into your head over and over again until the song's over . . . Simplicity is so much more important than showing off your technical side. Some of the best bands in the world, the Beatles or this great band called the Vaselines from Scotland, they write songs with two chords, the catchiest pop songs I've ever heard in my life."

In October 1990, Nirvana began preparing to hit the road for another UK tour. Dave Grohl debuted on October 11 at the North Shore Surf Club in nearby Olympia, Washington. Their set list that night echoed lists from the previous two tours, adding "Son of a Gun," "Stay Away," "In Bloom," and "Sliver."

eople, and social
̶arted listening

̶hen Kurt
̶ething
̶nsed
̶ck

Three

People think that you sold out 'cause you made money,
you know? I think if you make money and start voting
Republican, because you get tax breaks . . . and they're the party
of the rich, I mean, that's sold out.

—KRIST NOVOSELIC

Krist Anthony Novoselic was born in Compton, California, on May 16, 1965, the son of Croatian immigrants Maria and Krist Novoselic. Novoselic, which roughly translates as "newcomer," is a common Croatian name. Krist should know; he's gone back to Croatia many times, and has acquired a broad knowledge of his heritage. "Both of my parents were born and raised in Croatia. Our family comes from the small island of Iz, two hours by boat from the town of Zadar. The Novoselics' roots there trace back to the mid-1700s." Krist's newlywed parents lived up to their family name, transplanting to the United States in 1963 and setting up a new home for Krist, his brother, Robert, and his sister, Diana. By 1979, the Novoselics were newcomers again, this time living in gloomy Aberdeen.

Unlike most residents who move to Aberdeen, Krist's family did not come to work in the logging industry. Krist's dad, a machinist, relocated there simply because work was available. For the Novoselic children, life in their dreary new surroundings was a far cry from their sunshine-filled neighborhood in Compton, which gave Krist, a lanky, gentle teenager, an almost sympathetic vision of Aberdeen. "It's isolated. It's a wood-industry town, you know. They've been through a lot of hard times. When the economy goes down,

listen

Osb
by the ti
encounters
my younger b
to jam together.
see his first Black
the average redneck,
was 'Fuck with them a

̶hborhood

Gay] was the worst thing I

̶ Aberdeen were in abundance and in full bloom

his parents divorced. He moved with his father to the neighboring town of Montesano, just a few miles east of Aberdeen. The divorce devastated Kurt. "I just remember all of a sudden not being the same person, feeling like I wasn't worthy anymore. I didn't feel like I deserved to be hanging out with other kids, because they had parents [who lived together] and I didn't anymore." Kurt expressed his unhappiness in his own unique way, sketching rude caricatures of his parents on his bedroom walls, captioning them "Dad sucks, Mom sucks," and "I hate Mom, I hate Dad, Dad hates Mom, Mom hates Dad, it simply wants to make you sad."

Don Cobain remarried shortly after the divorce, and it was a difficult adjustment for the whole Cobain family. In an effort to get closer to his son, Don thought Kurt would enjoy the time-honored father-son tradition of hunting. But Kurt wanted nothing to do with it. "Now that I look back on it," Kurt said, "I know I had the sense that killing animals is wrong, especially for sport. I didn't understand that at the time. I just knew that I didn't want to be there."

Don agreed that his relationship with Kurt had taken an awful turn for the worse, that Kurt had come to the conclusion that only his mother had his best interests at heart. He has also admitted to having a bad temper, and remembered hitting his son. "I do probably blow up before I think. And I hurt people's feelings and, I get over it, I forget about it, and nobody else does," said Don. "My dad beat me with a belt, gave me a black eye. I spanked [Kurt] with a belt, yes."

Ignoring his son's protests, Don pushed Kurt into playing sports; the teenager even won a medal in wrestling in junior high. But Kurt hated every moment of it. He once blew a big wrestling match by allowing his opponent to pin him, just to piss off his father who, after witnessing Kurt's stunt, walked out of the gym in disgust.

Kurt's attitude toward his parents and its effects on his life carried over into his days at school. "I felt alienated. Right around the age of nine, I started feeling more confused. I couldn't understand at the time why I really didn't want to hang out with the kids at school. Years later I realized why: I obviously didn't relate to them, because they didn't appreciate anything artistic or cultural . . . It was their bread to become loggers. That's it. I think the fact that

by the time Kurt returned to try and finish high school. Withdrawing into his own realm seemed to be the only way to deal with the world around him. "I was chased around a lot by rednecks in

Nothing would have been more ef-

negative things about

wed to go to

jock

could hav

fective.

on their backs

an upscale restaurant in town, where the other patrons gave us all the "who the hell are these guys?" look as we entered wearing jeans with holes in them, T-shirts hanging out of our pants, and sneakers untied. It was a relaxed and casual time, and Krist and Kurt and I talked about how I'd first met them at a Nirvana show in Cambridge almost a year and a half before. After dinner, we bid our good-byes and good wishes and the group headed over a few blocks to see their friends the Melvins play the celebrated Boston underground club the Rat. It was a great night, and I was looking forward to transferring the vibe onto the airwaves for all of Boston to hear the following evening.

But somehow, none of this mattered by the time the trio from the tiny town of Aberdeen, Washington, got behind the mic with me the night of the concert to conduct one of their few American radio interviews. Kurt and Krist weren't exactly excited about doing the interview, and Dave was pissed off because I hadn't introduced him as a member of the band (he was late arriving for the start of it). The live discussion was absolutely terrible—because of the complexity of the huge concert, bands were constantly being shoved in and out of the interview area, creating a hectic scene that bordered on chaos. By the time they got behind the radio mic, Nirvana wasn't paying attention, and the proximity of the wasted crowd caused distractions at every turn. What a contrast compared to the serenity of the interview session I would conduct with the band just a few months later after their first appearance on *Saturday Night Live.*

MTV was in town to cover this multiband, multigenre concert, about which Krist commented, "Variety is a wonderful thing, There's something for everybody." MTV initially showed little interest in covering the event until they found out Nirvana was playing. For reasons still unknown, their marketing team had set up a game of Twister in a nightclub next door that included the use of Crisco shortening, and Krist did not hesitate to put his six-foot-seven-inch frame into the center of the action. In an attempt to get some of the Crisco off his pants, Krist grabbed a nearby American flag and wiped his ass with it, in clear view of a jarheadlike creature who undoubtedly took offense to this seemingly innocent gesture. It ignited a fight with several testosterone-filled individuals who were watching the game, and the sudden increase in the room's energy level ignited the band, who by now were undoubtedly primed for a sonic assault unlike any other that had graced the Axis stage.

played the song, our telephones rang off the wall. In the two decades of being a disc jockey, I have never seen, before or since, the phone lines light up they way they did when we first played "Smells Like Teen Spirit."

Most of the time when we played the song, our listeners weren't really listening at all. They were reacting. "Who does this song?" "What song is this?" "Who are these guys?" were the most common questions at first, and they were followed by "Can you play the mosquito song?" and "I wanna hear that mulatto song." It didn't matter that they didn't know the name of the song or the group. And it definitely wasn't just Kurt Cobain's hard-to-understand lyrics that were driving them to the phones. It was the energy of Dave Grohl's concussive drumming, of Krist Novoselic's throbbing bass, and of Kurt's gut-wrenching screams that made them absolutely stop what they were doing and clog up our request lines for hours. Playing "Teen Spirit" on the air wasn't the first time we'd ever played Nirvana—"Here She Comes Now" actually received some exposure earlier in 1991, and our nighttime disc jockey regularly defied the format orders of our program director by playing *Bleach*, sometimes in its entirety, during the overnight hours. But neither generated the response and reaction that "Teen Spirit" inspired that August.

It was the keen insight of people like Mark Kates, the head of alternative promotion at DGC Records, that stoked the fire of Nirvana's marketing machine for the support of *Nevermind*. His undying passion for antiestablishment was one of the reasons both Sonic Youth and Nirvana joined DGC's roster of artists, but his tenacity for recognizing talent in its incubation stage began much earlier when he was a regular fixture in the burgeoning Boston underground music scene. Working for the local independent record label Ace of Hearts allowed Kates to form a relationship with Mission of Burma, the seminal punk group whose impact on alternative music made it possible for bands like Nirvana to be heard in the mainstream. This well-earned credibility helped push "Smells Like Teen Spirit" to the level of American radio airplay it needed to reach the masses, and Kates, along with DGC's head of college promotion, John Rosenfelder, was very instrumental in bringing Nirvana to Boston to play our benefit concert.

By the time the show rolled around in September, I was thoroughly prepared for an in-depth and insightful conversation with Nirvana just prior to their noteworthy performance. The night before, I had dinner with them at

The first time they actually played out was at a house party in Raymond, Washington. The crowd wasn't expecting anything like the trio and their dates, so Krist and Kurt seized the opportunity to educate them all on the finer points of the punk aesthetic. Krist started the ball rolling, running past all of the startled guests, who were gathered in and around the house, screaming and jumping through an open window. The fake vampire blood he wore on his face and hands ended up on everything he touched. "We were out there and partied, tore the place [up], and scared the hell out of everybody," Burckhard recalled. "Krist was drunk, running, jumping through the window, coming [back in] through the back door. Krist's old lady, Shelli, and Kurt's girlfriend, Tracy [Marander], started making out. That really freaked everybody out. [The crowd] were yuppie-type people, all huddled in the kitchen. They didn't know what to think. Kurt w...

pouring beer down the couch."

By the time they got behind their ins...
to listen. "We had everyone so scared ...
hiding from us," said Kurt. "We had th...
the rest of the house." The band's set li...
like "Hairspray Queen," "Spank Thru,"...
Zeppelin," "Beeswax," and "Floyd the B...
Tramps and Thieves" that featured Kr...
scure song from the Dutch band Shock...
"White Lace and Strange" (first record...
der and Roses), and Flipper's raucou...
nature gut-wrenching style was begi...
spirit he and Krist picked up from O...

The trio's first big live test came ...
of Gescco Hall in Olympia. A ver...
preciated what they heard; reports...
sheeting on the walls and rolling ...
town. The still-unnamed trio's ne...
ater in Tacoma. The Circle Jerks...
the past, and the owner, Jim May...
to put a name on the marquee. ...
went up in lights that night.

demo with Endino at Reciprocal Recording in Seattle on January 23, 1988. Because Foster was unavailable to attend the session, Kurt and Krist called on Dale Crover to play drums.

The "Dale" demo was completed and mixed in about five hours, at a cost of $152.44. Ten songs were recorded: "If You Must," "Floyd the Barber," "Paper Cuts," "Spank Thru," "Hairspray Queen," "Aero Zeppelin," "Beeswax," "Mexican Seafood," "Pen Cap Chew," and an up-tempo version of "Downer."

"Five of these songs went on *Incesticide* in their original rough mix form," said Endino of the Dale demo session. "Another, 'Spank Thru,' has never been officially released in [the original Dale demo] form. Two more, 'Floyd the Barber' and 'Paper Cuts,' were properly remixed and added to *Bleach*. Of the remaining two, 'If You Must' was never released because Kurt disliked it, and 'Pen Cap Chew' . . . was never finished . . . 'Spank Thru,' 'If You Must,' and 'Pen Cap Chew' have been widely bootlegged, all from cassettes that were given out to many people." When the session was completed, Endino exploded into Poneman's office with a tape fresh off the master.

"Jack was totally blown away by the demo," Poneman remembered. "He thought Kurt had this voice unlike anything Sub Pop had recorded up to that point."

Endino recalled the impact of the moment as well. "This guy's got a really amazing voice . . . I don't know what to make of [the tape] but his voice has a lot of power."

The first song on the tape was "If You Must." Poneman reflected on the moment when he first heard the song. "It had this bridge where he just did this . . . how do I put it? . . . opening up, and just letting it out. I just went, 'This guy is really incredible!' So I called [Kurt], and said I loved the tape and that we should be making a record."

At the end of April, Nirvana was asked by Sub Pop to play Sub Pop Sunday at the Vogue in Seattle. It was essentially an audition, but the band did not play up to their expectations. "We didn't really fuck up," Foster recalled, "like, we didn't have to stop in the middle of the song. But it was very intimidating, because we knew it was for getting a record deal." The small crowd did not provide the energy the band had hoped for, but their inability to shine stemmed from the decaying relationship between Foster and the group's two founding members. "I felt out of place, but I was into what they were doing," times, but never reached a level of obnoxiousness that would cause a rift in their friendship.

Without a name or any immediate plans other than to rehearse, the band began a series of sessions in the apartment above the beauty shop. When Krist's parents eventually divorced, Maria moved into the space, forcing the band to move its rehearsals to Kurt's shack. "I had the apartment decorated in typical punk rock fashion with baby dolls hanging by their necks with blood all over them," said Kurt, describing the layout. "There was beer and puke and blood all over the carpet, garbage stacked up for months. I never did do the dishes. Jesse [Reed] and I cooked food for about a week and then put all our greasy hamburger dishes in the sink and filled it up full of water and it sat there for the entire five months I was there." In the living room, Kurt kept a bathtub full of turtles. He had a few pet rats, too, that had complete run-of-the-house privileges.

The trio tried to practice as much as possible, but Burckhard and Krist didn't share Kurt's zeal for rehearsal. Often Krist would miss practice for one reason or another, and it was almost impossible to keep Burckhard interested, especially on the first of every month. That was the day when his live-in girlfriend's welfare check came in. Burckhard would end up blowing most of it at the local tavern, like the rest of Aberdeen's residents, who viewed the first as if it were a holiday.

"There really wasn't much [to do]," Burckhard said without apology, "except sit around, drink beer, smoke pot, and practice. Kurt practiced. He was a diehard. Every night we'd do our set three or four times." In time Krist began to appreciate Kurt's enthusiasm, dedicating himself to practicing even harder. Some sessions were so intense that the slightest mistake would set them off. "I'd get all pissed off if we had a bad rehearsal: 'God, it's gotta be good, it's gotta be rock, it's gotta be fucking fun,' " said Krist. In time their hard work and determination paid off. They grew more confident in their abilities and their set list, and they landed a few gigs to test out their material on a live audience.

Their first gig really wasn't a performance at all. Scheduled to play a party in Olympia, Washington, they loaded up Krist's VW, arrived at the house to find the party had already been broken up, turned around, and drove home.

---

and Nirvana became the label's first offici
band relationships were often started this
Wanna make a record?" It was that simple
brought Nirvana into the Sub Pop family.

The Sub Pop founders were friends w
band Skin Yard, and the producer of Gr
dhoney. Along with Chris Hanszek (pro
Endino founded Reciprocal Recording.
the spotlight, Endino liked to list himse
and not as a producer.

Endino explained why people consid
Seattle grunge sound. "It was a combina
and Sub Pop's choice of what bands to
1989, the so-called 'Seattle sound' bec
but prior to that, Sub Pop was definite
out a certain kind of record, and gener
sound."

The approach to producing that
music harmonics. Endino was kn
amounts of distortion, and he wa
muddy the mix of a band's songs. W
method of recording big guitar s
mixing one guitar to the left speak
a quasi-stereo effect. It's an old bu
the roomy, warm guitar resonance Endino love

This effortless appreciation for raw feedback drew Endino to Kurt's music. When Kurt and Crover first met Endino in 1987 and played him the Aunt Mari demo, Endino couldn't wait to tell Poneman about the band's "embryonic ingenuity." Poneman then met Kurt at the Broadway Espresso in Seattle. "Kurt was pretty laid back," said Poneman. "Obviously a very intelligent individual, who didn't seem necessarily filled with the usual rock star ambitions. Rock was one of the many things he did to pass the time." Poneman went to a show at the Central Tavern in Seattle. He liked what he saw, and after several more gigs, the Sub Pop guru invited Nirvana to record a ten-song started playing more guitar . . . I just started listening to melody and song structure and stuff, and taking a bunch of acid and smoking a lot of pot and listening to Led Zeppelin. You know, just your typical type of high school stoner shit . . . I'd sit there with a bong in my hand and listen to 'Rain Song' or something. There was this little group of all my friends, we were all in bands and we were all going through our little drug-experimental-sort-of-freak-out phase and we rehearsed in my friend Barrett's house . . . and we would sit around every Friday night listening to CDs and selling pot to each other . . . I was the high school stoner. But see, I was the Vice President of my freshman class, but still like a stoner. So, I was this real weird, sort of mutant, intellectual, stoner type. My mom was a teacher at the school and my sister was a senior so I couldn't really flaunt my 'stonerness' around school. I definitely had to keep it behind closed doors. And you know, holding a responsibility, such as being the vice president of the freshman class, you can't just let some scandal like that slip out."

Having a teacher for a mom made Dave particularly conscious of the perils of the American educational system. And Dave's strong feelings on the injustice educators face is right on the button. "The way America's money is budgeted by our government . . . leaves nothing to the education system . . . Teachers are dealing with the future; teachers are dealing with kids growing up who are going to take care of me or you someday. They're gonna decide how much the teachers are gonna be paid in twenty-five to thirty years and that should be the most valuable of all decisions, when it comes down to the rights of a teacher. And most schools now are just so overcrowded, it's amazing. Classes with thirty to forty kids in them, seven classes a day. Kids can cheat their way through high school. You can cheat your way all the way to graduation, and not even know how to read.

"Having my mother as a teacher and hearing all the horror stories . . . the education system in general in a lot of places is really screwed. And it has more to do with the government than it does the teachers themselves. There are a lot of really great teachers. I went to Catholic school for two years and I got an incredible education, because the classes were smaller and the teachers had time to sit down and actually talk to their students."

By the time he was fifteen, Dave began reaching in other musical directions, and he quickly became a fan of live shows. In the summer of 1984, at

n at Lon
," "Molly's
er Cuts" to
Edinburgh,
was October
na's abbreviated

1989," said Euls about this band
a couple of our old
when I heard they
others, and we had
na. On that occasion,
de a couple of records
no had sold out a fairy filmed the show, and
verential to *us*. Very odd,

rvana would later return the
genius, two side projects of
e heard a tape of both bands
bers. "Eugene is a great songrica's gotta go on tour with us.'
very well, very clever."

of Nirvana, playing live sets with
coming heroes themselves to fans
g before their eyes and they all being good. What they did not undertent of the bad that would come with

been home for a short while from the
al bomb on Kurt and decided to break
t was a position Kurt had never been in
the one writing the Dear John letter. No
on, whom he respected and loved so dearly,

D.C., Dave met some guys from the band Freak
...ist. One successful audition shortly
...ay.

Kurt longed for a distraction from his feelings and sought out new friends to fill the void. He even went back to seeing his old girlfriend, Tracy Marander.

One evening, the two went to see Vail and her band, Bikini Kill, play a show in Olympia. Tracy, who knew Kurt pretty well, noticed him nodding off in the car on the way to the show. She had never seen him like this, and she was concerned that his condition was something he'd brought upon himself.

After the show, Kurt asked Tracy to stop at his house so he could use the bathroom before the two headed over to a friend's party. But Kurt took longer than Tracy had the patience for, and she went looking for him in the bathroom. What she found horrified her: Kurt was passed out on the toilet with a bottle of bleach on the floor and a spoon with residue on it in the sink. Kurt's sleeve was rolled up; when Tracy tried to pick him up, he laughed, then nodded off again. Marander left the room, horrified.

Dave called Krist the next day to ask for a loan. Instead, Krist dropped a bomb on Dave that blew the drummer out of the water: Kurt had been doing heroin. Dave called Kurt immediately, and in their conversation, Kurt convinced Dave he wouldn't do heroin ever again. Dave felt the whole event seemed innocent enough, like a little boy getting caught doing something he knows he shouldn't be doing, and he didn't think much of it again.

"I told [Kurt] he was playing with dynamite," said Krist, who viewed the situation much differently than Dave. "It bummed me out. It was shocking. I didn't like it at all. I just don't see anything in that shit. I just told him that's the way I feel."

Krist, Dave, and Kurt were more than just bandmates: They had become friends, loyal not only to the band's vision but to each other. It was clear that Nirvana was finally the solid three-piece unit it had set out to become. They convinced everyone of that at a gig at the Off Ramp Cafe in Seattle, where the trio enthralled a packed house with versions of "Aneurysm," "Oh the Guilt," "In His Room," and "Swap Meet." The three were ecstatic over the idea of settling down in the studio for the first time to record together. They booked some time in the familiar surroundings of the Music Source in Seattle, the same studio where Krist and Kurt had recorded *Blew*.

Only this time the band did not work with Jack Endino. Instead, they chose to rely on the talents of their sound engineer, Craig Montgomery, to

...ck demo with
...borhood punk-
...they kicked out
...and Freak Baby's
...success the band
...t quits after only a
...with another band,
...ore and getting the
...possible's subsequent
...hardcore dream come

...t experiences," Dave re-
...biography. "Opening for
...u, Ian MacKaye of Fugazi
...ing able to send demo tapes
...ne collecting, even releasing
...ut Mission Impossible even-
...ith Reuben Radding, another
...assist in a band called A.O.C.,
...e.

...cene Grohl had become attached
...here groups like Mission of Burma
...ss, their common fondness for the
...band Dain Bramage. It was in this
...songwriting and varied arrangements
...dened itself into an extremely experi-
...rded with Barrett Jones, which piqued
...endent label Fartblossom. The label paid
...*ming Down* in a twenty-four-track studio

...t took to record the album, and interest in
...ding an outlet to pound his drums, Dave

handle the sessions. Keeping it simple, Nirvana picked two songs to record, the freshly penned "Aneurysm," one of the first songs the trio wrote together, and another new song entitled "Even in His Youth." Both songs would end up as B sides to the yet-to-be-written monster, "Smells Like Teen Spirit." The songs, the sound, the whole package—Nirvana was falling into place.

Everyone involved appeared comfortable with the creativity spawned from those early sessions. There was no real formula to the production: The band jammed until they found a groove that they liked and stuck with it until it became a song.

"We like to delve into different areas and influences from song to song," said Krist. "Our influences range from Patsy Cline to Black Flag and we like to run the gamut when we write. It keeps things interesting."

Rehearsal was just as important, as the group gave equal time to perfecting old songs as well as the new ones. Discipline, one of the earliest hallmarks of Nirvana, was still very much alive by the time Dave became a full-time member of the group.

"We were practicing a lot," Dave recalled. "We were writing a lot of material. We'd come up with something, and we just started jamming. There were so many songs. We'd write them, they'd be great for, like, two weeks, 'Oh my God, this is the best song ever,' and we'd forget them."

With no great expectations for himself or the band, Dave used his free time simply to settle in and become part of another new family. He didn't feel like the new guy anymore, but he also didn't feel like a significant cog in the machine. It would take him a while to get over the jitters—after all, he was only the latest in a long line of drummers—but something about the groove they'd found together must have reassured him more thoroughly than Kurt or Krist ever would have directly.

Years later, Dave reflected back on those early days. "I really had no idea what to expect once I got up [to Seattle]," he said. "I knew that there was some [major] label interest, but I didn't know how insane it would be. Six months after I moved to Seattle, we had everyone in the world after us."

From the underground to the corporate towers, the word was out about Nirvana, and everyone sought the attention of alternative music's best-kept secret. Despite the temptations and enticements, Nirvana fought to stay loyal to Sub Pop, never making public any desire to leave the label that had helped to give them this newfound notoriety. But by the end of 1990, the relationship between Sub Pop and Nirvana began to deteriorate dramatically. The fallout wounded Kurt and Krist tremendously: They loved the hip reputation of Sub Pop, their great label bandmates, and their standout packaging. Sub Pop owners Jonathan Poneman and Bruce Pavitt had supplied the trio with almost everything a band could want or need . . . except good distribution. Nirvana was playing in more and more towns whose record stores were not carrying their records, and it was starting to concern them. They got tired of kids coming up and asking, "Where can I find your record?" Sub Pop told Nirvana of their plans for expansion, which was intended to benefit all bands on the label. But by now Kurt and Krist had lost patience. It was clear to them that the time had come for the band to move on to a major label.

Nirvana wanted out of their contract with Sub Pop, but they were having problems approaching the label to tell them about it. "We wouldn't return their phone calls for weeks and weeks at a time," said Kurt. "Every time I talked to Jonathan, I feel that I made it clear that there was definitely an uncertainty in our relationship. I just don't understand how you're expected to come right out and tell someone something like that. I suppose it's the more adult thing to do, to tell someone that you don't want to have anything to do with them anymore. It's a really hard thing to do."

Talking to other labels "was just something we had to do," Kurt explained. "There was no reason other than to get our music out, just distributed better, like in Kmart! It'd be nice for a fifteen-year-old in Aberdeen to have the choice, the opportunity to buy our record. That was an opportunity I never had. All I could get was Judas Priest."

But when Sub Pop eventually found out about Nirvana's plans from an outside source, it crushed the band. "I felt really bad," Kurt said. "I felt guilty because I wanted to be on their label still because I knew that these are people who share similar thoughts. I kind of felt like the enemy at the time. But still, there was nothing that [Pavitt] was going to do that would change my mind. They were just too risky."

"I think it's inevitable that Nirvana would go on to a larger label, but I don't think it was inevitable that the relationship between Sup Pop and Nirvana, which disintegrated to a large degree, necessarily needed to," said Poneman. "I accept my responsibility in that deterioration, but in my own defense I will say it was driven by the times, my age, unfamiliarity with the circumstances . . . When you're in your twenties and still feeling your way around and suddenly these media barons and tastemakers are telling you that you're God—it goes to your head. And it went to my head, it went to Bruce's head, it went to Kurt's head and Krist's head, and it would have been nice to have a little bit more trust."

Kurt's relationship with the two Sub Pop gurus had changed dramatically since the early, innocent days. "It was just obvious that [Pavitt] thought of himself as an educated white upper-middle-class punk rocker who knows everything and I'm just this idiot from Aberdeen," he said. "That was always something that we sensed and we totally resented him for it."

Kurt had actually begun laying the groundwork for their departure almost a year earlier. Krist had usually handled most of the complicated management issues, but when Sub Pop issued a long and confusing contract in May 1990, they sought the legal advice of Soundgarden's manager Susan Silver. She recommended that Nirvana meet heavyweight booking agent Don Muller and the powerful, influential entertainment lawyer Alan Mintz. Mintz was dedicated to representing new artists. He was awed by Nirvana's music, though somewhat confused by the band's desire to leave Sub Pop. But at Kurt's insistence, Mintz helped them get out of their deal and soon after began shopping them to major labels.

In a short amount of time A&R (artists and repertoire) people from an array of major labels began expressing interest, and before long a genuine bidding war was under way. "They were all asking [for us]," said Krist. "MCA, Capitol, Charisma, Columbia, Slash, Polydor, Polygram, all the Polys! A lot of schmoozing." The one label that made the greatest impression was David Geffen's DGC Records.

For a successful band that joins the recording roster of a major record label, financial success, at least for the moment, is assured. Whether you've been showing a profit or merely a promise, distribution and promotion inevitably improve under major-label guidance. When a band is looking to sign with a major label, they often scrutinize the careers of other bands on the label to see if their needs have been satisfied. But in some instances, a band will sign with a label simply because they are impressed by the presentation and reputation of the label's A&R person, and not unwisely, for in the end that is the person who will be responsible for the welfare of the band itself. The person who did just that for Nirvana was Gary Gersh, who at the time was one of Geffen/DGC's A&R people and had also worked in the business for Capitol and EMI Records.

What really spoke to Nirvana was that during his tenure Gersh had signed the New York punk band Sonic Youth to DGC. Like Nirvana, Sonic Youth was also born of a local underground music scene. After a number of successful releases on independent kingpins SST and Homestead Records, Sonic Youth had shifted quite naturally from the indie rock world to the corporate rock world. While other up-and-coming independent bands were signing with major labels and losing their credibility by becoming part of that label's moneymaking marketing machine, Sonic Youth, with the help of Gersh, were able to keep their creative control and freedom. That was most important to Nirvana, and it solidified their decision to sign with DGC. "Yeah, we knew Sonic Youth were happy," Krist said. "And we always loved and respected Sonic Youth."

"This whole business is full of shit," Dave contended. "Of all the labels we looked at, Geffen seemed the coolest. They knew where the band was coming from. They weren't old fogeys, big old fat men with cigars in their mouths sitting up in their presidents' offices looking at how much MC Hammer is making."

"There were a lot of other labels that we talked to that just had no clue," Kurt noted. "DGC just really knew the boundaries of our music, and, plus, our contract was really well written in terms of artistic freedom and all that stuff. We're in control of what we do, where we tour, exactly what our music sounds like. We have a lot of say-so. Still, I don't think a lot of that matters as long as the band still plays good music. Most of the bands who were on independent labels and then signed to majors ended up writing shitty songs mostly because they had been together for over ten years. You can't blame that on the label they were on. Then again, I've heard horror stories about bands that have been completely fucked over by major labels. You can lose your A&R guy and end up getting ignored for months, just put on the back burner. It happens all the time."

"[We] are proud to be label mates with Sonic Youth and Teenage Fan Club," said Krist. "We're totally aware that we're a commodity for [DGC].

They're there to help us, to put our records in the store. We're satisfied 'cause they work for us. Besides, the worst thing they could do is drop us."

As their new contracts were being drawn up, Nirvana hit the pavement in 1991 with Screaming Trees for a brief April tour of Canada and Washington, welcoming "Territorial Pissings" and "Stay Away" into their mushrooming live set list. The Charles Peterson photo of Kurt standing on his head playing his guitar was taken during this tour at one of the Commodore Ballroom shows in Vancouver. Kurt had attempted a flip on stage and Peterson caught it on film, giving the illusion that Kurt is standing upside-down, strumming away.

A few days later, on April 17, Nirvana played before a sold-out all-ages show at the OK Hotel in Seattle, with Fitz of Depression and Bikini Kill. That night, Nirvana debuted a song that Kurt had recently written. The trio had jammed hard on it in rehearsal and was anxious to play it live. The crowd had no idea that "Smells Like Teen Spirit" would become the anthem for a new generation. Their response, however, was instantaneous, and the moment was caught on videotape and appeared in the movie *Hype*.

On April 30, Nirvana formally signed a recording contract with DGC Records. The signing benefited all involved. The money Sub Pop would receive from the deal, including percentage points from future Nirvana releases, would help them to overcome their financial woes and to better service their own bands—a point Kurt cited as a mitigating factor in his painful decision to leave the label. Most important, Nirvana finally got the distribution deal they'd always wanted.

They got an advance of $290,000 to pay for future studio time and to put some cash in their pockets. Or so they thought. Like many bands who sign their first real record contract, Nirvana's dreams of instant financial success faded quickly. "Thirty-three percent of it immediately went to taxes," said Krist. "Fifteen percent went to our manager, Sub Pop got their chunk . . . We just set enough aside so we get some money every month. If you worked steady at Jack in the Box forty hours a week, you'd probably get the kind of money we get, but we don't have to work at Jack in the Box."

"It's nicer [being on DGC] because we have the freedom to spend a bit more money," Krist said at the time. "We can take our time now and we're guaranteed to get our album in any store . . . We're not getting any pressure . . . from DGC to change our style in any way. We're wearing exactly the same clothes that we were wearing two years ago."

The legal process Nirvana went through to sign with a major label gave them an appreciation for how the big music business works, but it also taught them how to look out for themselves professionally. One of the things that had always bothered the band was the perception people had of them because they were on Sub Pop, that they were simply hicks and nothing more.

And there were other public perceptions that bothered them. "There were all these rumors that we got, like, a million dollars," Krist said. "In *Spin* magazine, it was printed that we got seven hundred and fifty thousand dollars, and we didn't even get a quarter of that. What we did was, instead of going for the big dough, we went for the strong contract—more freedom and more percentage points on the record. There were a lot of little clauses that are in our favor. We're not in it for the money. We're in it for, you know, the 'Let's put out a record, and let's do this thing right' kind of attitude."

Nirvana's signing was the first opportunity for huge numbers of people, kids especially, to have access to the underground or "alternative" sound on such an enormous scale. Kurt understood that more than anyone. "The opportunity came and I just thought, 'Fuck it.' These are the songs we're writing right now . . . There are a lot of kids out there who couldn't quite swallow Black Flag by listening to it for the first time, so you've got to kind of ease them in . . . You pose as the enemy to infiltrate the mechanics of the empire."

Nirvana's signing with Geffen opened the door for other independent bands to begin gaining national exposure—and, in time, to begin reshaping the mainstream music industry. "Most mainstream music is so stale and bad," Krist said. "Then again, it might be a reflection of society's tastes. So who knows if what we want to do stands a chance. I believe that there's a lot of good music out there and people have to hear these bands. Somebody's got to spread the gospel and I hope we can do that. That is kind of how we justify what we did by moving to a major. We want to break the way for these bands."

Along with a new recording contract came a new manager named John Silva, who represented Danny Goldberg's Gold Mountain Management. Silva, who worked in the same capacity with Sonic Youth, created a comfort level that allowed Nirvana to concentrate solely on writing and recording the songs they had always dreamed of creating. No longer hindered by Pavitt's unwanted micromanaging style, Krist, Kurt, and Dave headed into the studios to commence recording what in time would prove to be the most influential rock album since the Beatles' *Sgt. Pepper's Lonely Hearts Club Band*. In May 1991, the trio began laying down the tracks for Nirvana's second full-length album, *Nevermind*.

Eleven

Someone at MTV says, "I knew *Nevermind* was gonna be a big hit."
Nobody did, man! Nobody did! And I don't care if someone at DGC says,
"Man, I saw this coming." Nobody knew! No-Body! I mean, it just happened.

—DAVE GROHL

Nirvana set up camp to begin work on *Nevermind* at Sound City Studios
in Van Nuys, California. In its heyday in the 1970s, rock dinosaurs like
Fleetwood Mac, Cheap Trick, Tom Petty, and Foreigner had recorded albums there, and the studio's simple, decades-old analog technology was exactly what Nirvana was looking for. "We were afraid to record in a big studio
with a professional sound mixer," Kurt noted. "If we wanted to make it really
raw, we could have. We didn't feel we had to compromise at all."

"We didn't want to get lost in technology," Krist said. "I've heard other
people talk about digital technology and all the new things it offers and the
drawbacks . . . We got a warm sound out of [Sound City]." Krist later added,
"It was like a time machine. It was like an old pair of corduroys that was
starting to wear out. Just like a studio Abba would have recorded in. We'd
just stagger in late, then get intense with it."

"It hadn't been touched since like nineteen seventy-four," remembered
Dave Grohl. "And all the equipment was really old and fucked-up and it had
corkboard all over the walls . . . It's a great studio. It's fucking excellent. All
the equipment we used was analog. None of it was digital, so we got this
beefy, warm, fat 'seventies sound to the basic tracks."

Despite their vaunted discipline, Nirvana had no particular focus when they entered the studio. "We really weren't thinking about anything," Dave said. "I mean, it was about time the band recorded something, finally. It had been two years since *Bleach*, so it was more of like, 'Wow, okay, we're in the studio, let's just get this done. Let's just do it.' There wasn't really any massive analyzing. It was just sort of 'Well, let's just put down the drums and bass and then put down the guitar, and eventually get to the vocals.' We didn't spend six months and five million dollars on it. We tried to hash it out as quickly as possible."

Even Kurt's songwriting was completed in this casual fashion. "I very rarely write about one theme or one subject," he explained. "I end up getting bored with that theme and write something else halfway through the rest of the song, and finish the song with a different idea."

Kurt's songwriting method benefited from a kind of inspired anarchy. "It's just thumbing through my poetry books and going, 'Oh, there's a line,' and writing it down. That's all I do. None of my poems are coherent at all. They have no themes whatever. They're not based on anything. It's just a bunch of gibberish. I mean, I try to have relations to some of the lines, and there's a lot of double meanings, and in certain senses, they do relate to something, but it's always changing. But when I say 'I' in a song, it's not me, ninety percent of the time."

"Kurt is the meister behind the songs," said Krist. "He'll sit on his couch and hack off a riff and a vocal melody and then he brings it to the band and we throw in some dynamics."

Logically, there was only one person to produce *Nevermind*, one person who fully understood the current mindset of the band, and that was Butch Vig. Nirvana had worked well with him when they recorded the basic *Nevermind* demo tracks at Vig's studios in Wisconsin. "He was just easy to work with," Kurt said. "Laid back and really attentive to what's going on. He works hard, but he doesn't work the band hard. That's the thing. That's a good balance there."

In another interview, Dave agreed. "It took about three weeks to do the record, which was a lot more time than *Bleach* took, but our producer, Butch Vig, was really great to work with. He didn't put any pressure in the wrong places. He was just easy to work with and the record came out just as we wanted it to."

Compared to *Bleach, Nevermind* demonstrated the band's growing attention to detail, accounting for the extra time it took to record. The three-week recording time was still rather quick compared to most major-label–released records, and the extra money and time saved allowed Nirvana to lay down a few more tracks and work on overdubs a little more than usual.

For example, Kurt's guitar sounds were drawn from a handful of guitars, including a late-model 1960s Fender Mustang and a Fender Jaguar. He also used newer-model Fender Stratocasters. Armed with several different distortion pedals, the speaker cabinet for Kurt's amp was mic'd with four different mics. Butch Vig used the best-sounding one for the overdubs of Kurt's guitar parts. The songs were recorded live, and additional vocal and guitar dubs were added later.

The increased attention to Kurt's guitar sound gave each of the songs on *Nevermind* a distinctive flavor. Yet they still seem to flow together like a finely braided cord. Kurt talked about how one of the songs set the tone for the entire album: "We'd been practicing for about three months. We were waiting to sign to DGC, and Dave and I were living in Olympia, and Krist was living in Tacoma. We were driving up to Tacoma every night for practice, trying to write songs. I was trying to write the ultimate pop song, I was basically trying to rip off the Pixies. I have to admit it. When I heard the Pixies for the first time, I connected with that band so heavily I should have been *in* that band— or at least in a Pixies cover band. We used their sense of dynamics, being soft and quiet and then loud and hard. 'Teen Spirit' was such a clichéd riff. It was so close to a Boston riff or 'Louie, Louie.' When I came up with the guitar part, Krist looked at me and said, 'That is so ridiculous.' I made the band play it for an hour and a half."

Both Krist and Kurt thought the same thing once the playing of the song fell into place. "The Pixies," Krist says. "We saw it right away. Both of us said, 'This really sounds like the Pixies. People are really going to nail us for it.' "

When they were listening to the mix-down, it was Dave who first spoke out and said he didn't think "Smells Like Teen Spirit" was that hot. "I don't know, everybody else was flipping out on it and thinking, 'Ooh, this will be the first single,' " Dave said. "We sort of wanted 'In Bloom' to be the first single. I mean, 'Teen Spirit' wasn't a favorite or anything. It was just sort of another song."

Many theories have been offered to explain the song's title, but Kurt's explanation seems to fit best. "Well, this friend of mine [Kathleen Hanna] and I were goofing around in my house one night. And we're kind of drunk and we were writing graffiti all over the walls in my house and she wrote, 'Kurt smells like teen spirit.' Earlier on we were kinda having this discussion on revolution and teen revolution and stuff like that, so I took that as a compliment. I thought that she was saying that I was a person who could inspire, in a way. I just thought that was a nice little title. And it turns out she just meant that I smelled like the deodorant Teen Spirit. I didn't even know that deodorant existed until after the song was written."

"['Smells like Teen Spirit'] is a typical teenage aggression song," Kurt said in the fall of 1991. "It has revolutionary themes, but I don't really mean it in a militant [light]. The generation's apathy is getting out of hand. [I'm] pleading to the kids, 'Wake up!' " This explanation was echoed in another interview: "It's about 'Hey, brother, especially sister, throw away the fruit and eat all the rind' . . . No longer is it taboo for the tattooed to take their generational solidarity and shove it up the ass of The Byrds and Herman's Hermits—loving disgraces we call parents, posing as the enemy to infiltrate the mechanics of the system, to slowly start its rot from the inside. It's an inside job, it starts with the custodians and the cheerleaders."

"No one, especially people our age, wants to address important issues," Kurt said. "They'd rather say, 'Never mind, forget it.' The song 'Smells Like Teen Spirit' addresses that subject, in a way." He recalled the origins of the line, "Here we are now, entertain us." "That came from something I used to say every time I used to walk into a party to break the ice. A lot of times, when you're standing around with people in a room, it's really boring and uncomfortable. So it was 'Well, here we are, entertain us. You invited us here.' "

Dave dismissed the song's deeper implications. "Just seeing Kurt write the lyrics to a song five minutes before he first sings them, you just kind of find it a little bit hard to believe that the song has a lot to say about something. You need syllables to fill up this space or you need something that rhymes."

However, those within the Nirvana management saw this song almost immediately as an anthem of sorts, a song that would speak to a troubled generation of people. "Every once in a while, a song *is* that powerful," said Danny Goldberg about "Smells Like Teen Spirit." "And in their instance, they not only had a song that was that powerful—it combined with an image that was very attractive to a certain subculture."

The version of "In Bloom" on *Nevermind* is a remake of the 1990 version that featured Chad Channing on drums. The audio track of that 1990 version is on the "In Bloom" video, but it has never been officially released by DGC. For this version, it is clear that Dave simply mimics Channing's original drum part, but he pounds the skins just a little bit harder, adding his own flavor. The production is crisper, and overall the song's new version kicks harder.

Kurt explained how his old peeve, high school jocks, inspired the lyrics. "Football players who become stage-divers. There were some very violent, macho guys there [in the pit], who we can't stand, and hopefully we can weed them out. The only thing we can do is make jokes about them." And don't forget the guys with bilevel haircuts, rednecks with guns. "Yeah. I suppose it leans toward that more than anything," said Kurt. "I really don't have any explanation for that song. I mean of course it does have those things in it. Obviously I don't like rednecks, I don't like macho men, you know, I don't like abusive people. I guess that's what that song is about. It's an attack on them."

In a DGC Records press release for *Nevermind*, Kurt, tongue in cheek, referred to "Come as You Are" as just "an old-fashioned love song coming down in three-part harmony." Kurt used a Small Clone Chorus Pedal on his guitar to give it that underwater feel to the opening guitar riff; the result sounds remarkably like the opening guitar riff to the classic Killing Joke song "Eighties."

"I really don't know what that song is about," Kurt said. "I guess it's about expectations of people. The lines in the song are really contradictory . . . you know . . . One after another they're kind of a rebuttal to each other. I really don't have much to say about it. It's just about people and what they're expected to act like."

Originally titled "Immodium" (culled from the bottle of the antidiarrhea medicine Tad Doyle was taking during TAD's European tour with Nirvana in 1989), "Breed" was first recorded with Chad Channing on drums and Butch Vig overseeing the production during the *Nevermind* demos. A leftover from the *Bleach* era, the new version of "Breed" (now with Dave on drums) has many of the characteristics of the songs from *Bleach*. Kurt's punk-rock rantings "I don't care, I don't care, I don't care," Krist's heavily distorted bass, and Dave's incessant pounding on the skins make "Breed" one of the heaviest songs on the album.

Another song first recorded with Channing in 1990 and recut with Dave for *Nevermind is* "Lithium." "It's another story that I made up, but I did infuse some of my personal experiences," said Kurt, "like breaking up with girlfriends and having bad relationships, feeling that death void that the person in the song is feeling, very lonely, sick." In the official DGC press release for *Nevermind,* Kurt expanded on the subject. "People who are secluded for too long go insane and as a last resort they often use religion to keep alive. In the song, a guy's lost his girl and his friends and he's brooding. He's decided to find God before he kills himself. It's hard for me to understand the need for a vice like that but I can appreciate it too. People need vices."

Kurt played guitar through a Fender Bassman amp, and used an Electro Harmonix Big Muff Fuzz to achieve a darker sound.

In late May, Nirvana took a break from recording *Nevermind* to play a special surprise concert at Jabberjaw in Los Angeles. Guitarist Eric Erlandson from the band Hole was at the show, which still featured a *Bleach*-heavy playlist but included rough, commanding versions of "On a Plain," "Come as You Are," "Lithium," and "Smells Like Teen Spirit." He remembered that "About four hundred lucky souls crammed into this dingy, dinky art space to sweat and stink as one. Every rock voyeur and band geek in town was there to hear, for the first time, the songs that would be *Nevermind*. The show was a mess, but, as always, Nirvana's wild, yet child-sweet spirit filled the room. I remember somehow deciphering parts of 'Smells Like Teen Spirit' and 'Lithium' out of the noise and confusion and feeling overwhelmed. Nirvana were beautiful like no other." Later that evening, the band attended the Butthole Surfers, Red Kross, L7 show at the Hollywood Palladium. It was at this show that Kurt Cobain met Courtney Love for the first time.

She was born Love Michelle Harrison on July 9, 1964, in San Francisco, California. She toyed with many versions of her name, including Courtney

Michelle Harrison, Courtney Michelle Rodriguez, and Courtney Manely, before finally settling on the well-known Courtney Love. Her father, Hank Harrison, went to college with Grateful Dead bassist Phil Lesh and thus became an early Grateful Dead associate. Harrison even managed the group when they were called the Warlocks, and he has written two books about the band.

Courtney's mother, Linda Carroll, is an Oregon therapist who made headlines of her own in the 1990s when she convinced one of her patients, 1960s radical Katherine Ann Power, to turn herself in after twenty-three years as a fugitive. Linda and Hank lived in Northern California in the late 1960s, but their marriage dissolved in 1969. Linda took Courtney and returned to Oregon shortly thereafter. It was a painful separation for Courtney, who would not have contact with Hank again until she was fifteen years old. According to an article that appeared in *Premiere* in February 1997, Courtney spent much of her early life living off a $400-a-month, $100,000 trust fund left by her grandmother. She left home at age thirteen, and exhausted the trust by the time she was twenty-two.

Growing up in Oregon was not easy for Love, and she eventually left for Japan, where she found a new way to earn a living without being under the watchful eye of those who knew her: She became a stripper.

The late 1980s found Love surfing the globe in search of her own identity. She dabbled in college in Ireland; was in a relationship with rock star Julian Cope; moved to Portland, Oregon, where she formed the band Sugar Baby Doll; found herself singing in an early version of the band Faith No More; developed another incarnation of Sugar Baby Doll with Babes in Toyland's Kat Bjelland and Jennifer Finch (a founding member of the punk band L7); auditioned for Alex Cox's film *Sid and Nancy* (where she got a small part as Nancy Spungen's best friend); played in an early incarnation of Babes in Toyland; went to Spain to appear in Alex Cox's spaghetti western *Straight to Hell* with Joe Strummer of the Clash; and finally, in 1989, ended up in Los Angeles, where, after placing an ad in Los Angeles's *Recycler* newspaper, she formed a new band, Hole, with Eric Erlandson. "After I called her, she didn't call me for two weeks," Erlandson said. "Then she called me back at three in the morning and talked my ear off."

Perhaps that was a sign of things to come for Courtney, whose never-ending search for people who would listen to her speak, to listen to how she felt, would become legendary. Even her marriage in 1989 to James Moreland, the leader of the punk band Leaving Trains, appeared to be a relationship built more on a public relations move than one of romance. The marriage didn't last long, and within two years it was over. "I think the main problem was that I was on SST Records," said Moreland of their brief rendezvous. "[Courtney] thought that was too small of a label for her husband to be on. That wasn't very punk rock of her, was it?"

Kurt and Courtney's first meeting after Love's departure from Moreland didn't exactly plant the seeds for a promising, blissful romance. But at least they weren't strangers to each other. "I saw him play in Portland in 1988," Courtney said. "I thought he was really passionate and cute, but I couldn't tell if he was smart or had any integrity."

Kurt thought she looked like Nancy Spungen. She had a classic punk-rock-chick look he was attracted to. But there seems to have been some question about Kurt's ability to reveal his feelings. "I wasn't ignoring her. I didn't mean to play hard to get. I just didn't have the time. I had so many things on my mind," said Kurt.

"I really pursued him, not too aggressive, but aggressive enough that some girls would have been embarrassed by it," added Courtney. "I'm direct. That can scare a lot of boys. Like, I got Kurt's number when they were on tour, and I would call him. And I would do interviews with people who I knew were going to interview Nirvana, and I would tell them I had a crush on Kurt. Kurt was scared of me. He said he didn't have time to deal with me. But I knew it was inevitable."

Getting serious with a new girlfriend in the middle of recording an album was an idea Kurt fought. "I couldn't decide if I actually wanted to consummate our relationship," he said. "She seemed like poison because I'd just gotten out of the last relationship that I didn't even want to be in. I was determined to be a bachelor for a few months. I just had to be. But I knew that I liked Courtney so much right away that it was a really hard struggle to stay away from her for so many months. It was harder than shit. During that time that I attempted to be a bachelor and sow my oats and live the bachelor rock-and-roll lifestyle. I didn't end up fucking anybody or having a good time at all."

Soon after that first encounter with Love in the summer of 1991, Nirvana returned to the studio to continue work on *Nevermind*. The production on the album was becoming slicker than Nirvana's earlier work, and with more tracks to work with, the band had more opportunity to do overdubs. But as Kurt explained it, the difference between *Bleach* and *Nevermind* went deeper than production values. "The production is obviously different; a lot of people think that it's a major change between the two albums, but it's really not. *Nevermind* just has a lot more pop songs on it."

Kurt told Everett True of *Melody Maker*, "It's fine, because we do play a lot of grunge, but we consider ourselves a bit more diverse than just full-out raunchy heavy music. We're aiming towards a poppier sound, and we've been into pop music for years; it's just that when we were recording *Bleach* we happened to be writing a lot of heavy songs at the time."

Nirvana's conscious attempts at simplicity in their songwriting may have had a lot to do with their awareness of what happened to electric jazz in the 1970s. Like Nirvana's heavy-rock timbre, fusion jazz was a fast-growing underground sound that was being embraced by pop culture. But it died out quickly because it was not simple in its melody structure and, therefore, made it hard for the average listener to remember a song. So as a collective group, the three members of Nirvana would make sure that their songs would be simply written, like kids' songs, so that the more simple the melody, the more likely fans would be able to recall their song. This, of course, is a key factor in a pop song's success.

And if there was any doubt about whether Nirvana was abandoning its punk roots for a simpler, pop-leaning sound, Kurt explained that there was more to the punk lifestyle than just guitar chords. "Punk is musical freedom. It's saying, doing, and playing what you want. In Webster's terms, *nirvana* means freedom from pain, suffering, and the external world, and that's pretty close to my definition of punk rock. By definition pop is extremely catchy, whether you like it or not. There are some pop songs I hate but I can't get them out of my head. Our songs have a standard pop format: verse, chorus, verse, chorus, solo, bad solo. All in all, I think we sound like the Knack and the Bay City Rollers being molested by Black Flag and Black Sabbath."

Major-label celebrity status did not affect the creative process behind *Nevermind*. The only difference between producing *Bleach* (which took six days to make) and *Nevermind* (three weeks) was the band had more time to play around in the studio. Nirvana knew the record would have turned out the same if they had made it themselves. However, what they hadn't anticipated was the pressure to stay underground in their sound. As Kurt noted, they experienced the indie-band-signing-with-a-major-label punk identity crisis when recording *Nevermind,* and weren't quite sure if it was even important to label themselves when the recording was completed.

Determining the band's image was always a struggle for Kurt. "On one hand, we're not a political band—we're just some guys playing music—but we're not just another mindless band asking people to forget, either. There's no rebellion in rock 'n' roll anymore. I hope underground music can influence the mainstream and shake up the kids."

Though he didn't know it at the time, Kurt's words were truly prophetic. When Kurt wrote "Polly," he intended only to write an unopinionated story about rape. "It's definitely an antirape song, but I threw a few twists in," he explained. "Actually, the story is about a rapist and a girl who is picked up by the rapist. The girl is a sadomasochist, so she played along with him while he was trying to rape her, and eventually escaped because of that."

"Polly" was apparently based on a true story that occurred in Tacoma, Washington, in June 1987. A man ironically named Gerald Friend kidnapped and tortured a fourteen-year-old girl who was on her way home from a punk-rock show at the Community World Theater. After raping the young woman, Friend hung her upside-down from a pulley attached to the ceiling of his mobile home and tortured her with a leather strap, a razor, hot wax, and a blowtorch. He dragged her to his car, where, after he stopped for gas, she was able to escape. Friend was later arrested and convicted for the crime.

Songs like "Polly" gave Kurt an opportunity to write and sing from the first-person perspective and to explore the possibility of writing through the voices of others. "Just because I say 'I' in a song doesn't necessarily mean it's me. A lot of people have a problem with that. It's just the way I write usually. Take on someone else's personality or character," said Kurt. "Hardly anything I've written is autobiographical, you know. Well, I mean, it's autobiographical in the sense that I have the same feelings and emotions that some of these songs are written about, but I'd rather just use someone else's example because my life is kinda boring. So, I just take stories from things that I've read, and off television, and stories I've heard."

About "Polly," Kurt said, "I think the reason 'Polly,' in particular, has such impact is because it could be considered a Top Forty song, a very simple, easy-listening song, with acoustic guitar and harmonies. But I decided to put some disturbing lyrics in, just to counteract that and make that the statement—that the song should not be that kind of song."

Written three years before the *Nevermind* sessions, "Polly" has since emerged in various solo acoustic versions that have been leaked out onto bootlegs. The version on the album is actually the same one recorded at Smart Studios in 1990, remixed and mastered for release with an uncredited Chad Channing on drums.

The delicate melodies in "Polly" played by Kurt come from an acoustic guitar tuned unmistakably flat. It only had five strings, and it was tuned a step and a half below E. "That's a twenty-dollar junk shop Stella guitar—I didn't bother changing the strings!" Kurt joked. "It barely stays in tune. In fact I had to use duct tape to hold the tuning keys in place." Vig recorded Kurt playing the raggedy guitar using one microphone.

"Territorial Pissings" opens with Krist venturing an unplanned and very strange interpretation of the Youngbloods' classic "Get Together." "They just said 'Sing something,' so I did it in just one take," Krist explained. "It just kind of happened. I wanted to put some kind of corny hippie idealism in it. But it wasn't really that thought into. I *like* that Youngbloods song."

According to Kurt, the song was loosely based on and somewhat inspired by a book he read by Valerie Solanas called *The Scum Manifesto*. Solanas, a radical feminist who died in 1988, had been an unpopular regular at Andy Warhol's Factory in the late 1960s, but she gained most of her fame by shooting the pop artist in 1968. *The Scum Manifesto* was a satire on the genetic inferiority of the male gender, the word *Scum* being an acronym for the Society for Cutting Up Men. It contains lines like "a man will swim a river of snot, wade nostril-deep through a mile of vomit, if he thinks there'll be a friendly pussy awaiting him," which entertained Kurt, who found the book strangely insightful: "It's an amusing little book; I laughed really hard when I read it. It's really cool. I was almost embarrassed to realize that I agree with a lot of it.

"Basically, it's just women taking over the world and men agreeing to go out with a bow of grace. They should all be assassinated, and those who agree with the ideals of this little manifesto should be in concentration camps and fed bread and water."

Kurt was intrigued by Solanas's writing. "[Solanas] was a militant feminist who, in my opinion, had some incredible ideas. Everybody called her insane because the ideas are pretty violent. [The book] pretty much says women should rule the earth, and I agree with it."

Kurt took the inspiration and wove it into a song. "I guess you could call it an ode to women, my love and respect for them—and how they're mis-treated."

Taking a different spin on love is "Drain You," the story of the friendship between two babies, or more to the point, two young lovers. Originally called "Formula," this song directly links Kurt to his old girlfriend Tobi Vail. Kurt said in *Nevermind*'s press release, "Come to think of it, almost all of the songs on *Nevermind* are about love or confusion, which is usually the result of love. Outcries of confusion about love and not understanding relationships, not just with your mate but with anybody, with yourself, with animals, et cetera."

Kurt's relationship with Vail was the inspiration for a number of songs on *Nevermind*, including "Lounge Act," which, obviously enough, is written in the style of a lounge song. And that's as far as the similarity goes, because "Lounge Act" was actually written as a result of his heart-wrenching breakup with Vail and being the dumpee instead of the dumper. "That song is mostly about . . . being smothered by a relationship," said Kurt, "and not being able to finish what you wanted to do artistically because the other person gets in your way."

Which might explain how and why "Stay Away" was written. "God Is Gay," a line from the song itself, and "Pay to Play" were some of the earlier working titles for this song. "There are also some ridiculous, even more em-barrassing titles than that," said Kurt. "Like, 'The Rocker,' 'The Eagle Has Landed,' 'Stay Awake,' but there's no story behind that at all. That's just typical cliché punk rock, like, 'Fuck off! Stay away—get away from me!' Just bitching about something, I guess."

A demo version of "Pay to Play" eventually appeared on the DGC Records–released compilation *DGC Rarities*. In a 1989 interview, Krist noted that in big cities like Los Angeles and New York, "there's so many bands and so much competition that bands have to pay to play. It's ridiculous."

"On a Plain" is a really simple song about Kurt recognizing how good his life is, despite all of his bitching and complaining about how bad things appear to be. In his typical flippant regard for some of his songwriting, Kurt dashed off the lyrics for "On a Plain" without much thought or direction, as the song opens, "I'll start this off without any words."

Perhaps the most artistic and impressive song on *Nevermind* is the down-tempo "Something in the Way." Kurt, Krist, and Dave play nearly all of the instruments on *Nevermind*, but for "Something in the Way" they brought in Kirk Channing (no relation to Chad) to play the beautiful and sad cello harmonies. Again, Kurt used the cheap Stella guitar to add depth to the dark and flowing imagery of the song. The lyrics in this song refer hauntingly to Kurt Cobain's personal refuge under a North Aberdeen bridge located just blocks away from his mother's house. This spot has now become a sort of graffiti museum for Nirvana fans, who visit it from all over the world. Kurt explained in 1992 how quickly the song came about: "That song really wasn't even written until a week before we went into the studio. And, uh, I knew I wanted cello on it, but after all the music was recorded for it, we'd forgotten about putting a cello on it, and we had one more day in the studio, and we decided, 'Oh geez, we should try to hire a cellist,' y'know, and put something in, and we were at a party, and we were asking some of our friends if they had any friends who play cello, and it just so happened that one of our friends in L.A. plays cello, so we took him into the studio on the last day and said 'Here, play something,' and he came up with something right away, it just fell like dominoes, it was really easy."

"My favorite song on the album is the song that's after the twelfth track . . . It doesn't have a name," Dave said about "Endless Nameless." Because the band intended it to be a hidden track on *Nevermind*, the song wasn't supposed to have a name; Dave thinks "Endless Nameless" might have come from something Butch Vig scribbled on the tape box of the master.

Creating a gold mine for collectors, the first pressings of *Nevermind* did not include "Endless Nameless." The oversight by DGC was corrected shortly thereafter when a new pressing was immediately sent out once the error was discovered. "It got screwed up and it didn't get on the first bunch of them," said Dave, "and when we got our first CD we listened to it and 'Endless Nameless' wasn't there. So we called Geffen immediately."

Burying the song thirteen minutes and fifty-one seconds after "Something in the Way" ends was an intentional strategy; the band hoped it would jump out at people when they least expected it. Said Dave, " 'Something in the Way' is sort of like your slow song, the last song on the record, and most likely to be listened to by yuppie folk or someone that would have, like, a carousel CD player. So, why not just screw up their little carousel deal?"

"We made the record we wanted to make," said Krist proudly about *Nevermind*. "We didn't want to make 'the number one' record. We didn't want to make some big hit record. It would've been the same record if it was on Sub Pop. It probably would have sounded as slick, but I hear our songs on the radio next to some other total mainstream music and it sounds a lot rawer. That's what we wanted to do. We thought, 'Well, it's like a major-label release, but let's make it raw enough to where we don't totally compromise.' "

"It's not like we had some scheme," Dave said defensively. "We're the last ones to analyze anything we're doing. Other people are a lot better at deciding what we're thinking than we are . . . let them spend their own time doing that—I've got better things to do."

In another interview, Dave added this sentiment: "I just thought *[Nevermind]* would be like another successful independent record vibe. I didn't think it would be that much different than *Bleach*—just a progression."

"What we've turned into over two years [shows that] our appreciation for pop music has just gotten greater," said Kurt. "During the time we were recording the *Bleach* album we were into more aggressive, meaner music and now I like all of it—I haven't denied any of that—I just think we've put together a good mixture of both elements."

Dave concurred. "It's just really heavy pop songs played by punk-rock children. I think that to give it a definition would be a contradiction. Punk rock is just freedom."

The freedom Nirvana experienced in working with DGC spilled over into other creative avenues as well. The band insisted on creative control of itself when it first signed with DGC, and they exercised that right immediately when it came time to design the artwork for *Nevermind*.

"Dave, Krist, and I were sitting around watching a documentary on babies being born underwater and we thought that was a really neat image," Kurt recalled. "So we thought, 'Let's put that on the album cover.' And then when we got back a picture of a [naked] baby underwater I thought it would look nice for a fish hook with a dollar bill [to be] on it, and so the image was born."

Controversy over the taste of the album cover was brought to light when someone suggested that the combined visual of a baby, which is actually a photo of a then-five-month-old Spencer Elden with his penis in clear view, being lured to a fishhook by money, might distort the image of Nirvana that DGC was trying to present to the public.

Even harder to understand was the back cover of the album, which features a photo taken by Kurt. It shows a monkey with a bomb on his back in front of a strange collage of images. "I was in a bohemian photography stage, taking a bunch of weird arty pictures, and that's one of them," said the singer. "Everyone thinks it's a real monkey, but it's just a rubber monkey that I've had for years. The collage I made many years ago. It's pictures of beef. I got these pictures of beef from a supermarket poster and cut them out and made a mountain of beef and then put Dante's people being thrown into hell and climbing all over it. If you look real close, there's a picture of the band KISS [taken from the *Love Gun* album] in the back, standing on a slab of beef."

Though it would become more disturbing years later, after Kurt's sudden and tragic death, there is a running theme in *Nevermind* that was a cause for concern for many involved in its making. "Yeah, I realized that after everything was written," Kurt said sadly about the many references to guns in the album. "I have no idea why it turned out that way. I really don't know why. Geez, I went shooting once with my friend Dylan . . . God, it was weird. Because I'd never shot a gun before and it reminded me of how totally violent those things are. They can rip right through you. I guess I'm opposed to guns because they're a violent tool . . . but . . . I'm not one of those anti-NRA people."

DGC's attempts to properly present and promote their new superstars were to be commended, but there isn't a single band on the planet who is ever entirely happy with a label's marketing perspectives. Nirvana, certainly, was not an exception to that rule. "The band bios that record companies send to press and radio people are so stupid," said Dave. "They all say the same thing. 'We're the best band in the world.' So we thought we'd write our own and put in all those 'rock band meets in art school' clichés. It's all lies! But it's sort of unfair because nobody knows. Radio stations are *still* going, 'This next track's from Nirvana, three guys who met in art school and walked around reading Rod McKuen poetry . . .' We should issue a public disclaimer."

Those close to Nirvana understood the band's inside jokes in the biography, but the different spellings of Kurt's name on *Nevermind*'s liner notes needed an explanation. "I think I wanted to be anonymous at first," said Kurt. "I was really thinking about changing my name for the *Nevermind* record. But then I just decided to spell it the right way. I just wanted it to be confusing. I wish I would have done the same thing that Black Francis did. He's changed his name so many times that nobody really knows who he is. I wish nobody ever knew what my real name was. So I could some day be a normal citizen again. I have no real reason. I just didn't bother with spelling it correctly. I didn't care. I wanted people to spell it differently all the time."

With the release of *Nevermind* just around the corner, Nirvana found themselves to be completely uncomfortable with the sudden notoriety. "And now we're snubbed by people who think we're big rock stars," said Dave. "They think that when you get signed to a major label you get all this cash to spend."

"We're guaranteed two albums [by DGC] and then after that they can drop us at any time," said Kurt. "I imagine we'll get dropped eventually, and after that it doesn't matter. We'll start another band."

The hyperbole surrounding the release of the album was starting to build. "It's becoming a bit exaggerated," Kurt said. "I'm looking forward to some backlash, at least in criticism, because there's so much anticipation, so much encouragement by our friends and label, that I'm afraid."

"If anything, we're trying to deny the fame," said Dave. "We don't want to be recognized on the street. We have lives outside the band. Fame isn't what we were looking forward to at all."

Twelve

Eugene [Kelly] was in a band called the Vaselines,
who's definitely our number-one favorite band. That's his new band,
Captain America, and they're really good.

—KURT COBAIN

In June 1991, Sub Pop released a compilation album, *The Grunge Years*, featuring Nirvana's "Dive." The tongue-in-cheek cover says "Limited edition 500,000," along with a photo of several corporate-looking record weasals. During the same month, Nirvana wrapped up the recording of *Nevermind*, leaving the mixing to Andy Wallace (who had worked with Slayer) and the mastering duties to Howie Weinberg. Preparations were also being made for another tour, this time opening up for underground kingpins Dinosaur Jr. But before the tour started, Dave headed back to Virginia to see his old friend Barrett Jones.

"On my [previous] trips back to Virginia, I started recording more and more at Barrett's studio," Dave recalled. "I had probably finished six or seven songs and was writing a lot of stuff in my spare time in Olympia. After recording *Nevermind*, I went home for a few days and recorded at a different local D.C. studio. This tape was heard by a friend named Jenny Toomey, who had a label called Simple Machines. She had heard [some of my] other recordings and asked if I was interested in doing a cassette release. I was a little hesitant, always having been very shy about people listening to me sing, but I eventually said yes." Dave listed himself under the pseudonym "Late" to draw attention away from his singing; the cassette that resulted included versions of "Winnebago" and "Marigold."

By the time Dave landed back in Seattle, Kurt and Krist were rehearsing the new songs from *Nevermind* for the upcoming tour. "We will tour until we go insane or die of exhaustion," Krist said, almost prophetically. Indeed, for the next two years, Nirvana would travel around the world in manic fashion, visiting Europe, Australia, South America, and Japan. This never-ending tour began on June 13, 1991, at the famous Warfield Theater in San Francisco. Opening for Dinosaur Jr., Nirvana introduced more *Nevermind* tunes into their playlist. "Drain You" was among the first songs added to the repertoire of Kurt-penned tunes.

After a sneak-over-the-border gig at Iguana's in Tijuana, Mexico, Nirvana wound its way back through California, Oregon, and Colorado, adding the soon-to-be-controversial "Rape Me" and "Endless Nameless" as steady entries in its trimmed-down set list of twelve to fourteen songs. Meanwhile, the buzz over Nirvana began to stir in hipper, alternative-friendly American cities, and soon shows were regularly selling out.

In August, Hole released their indie album, *Pretty on the Inside,* which received positive press from alternative critics in the United Kingdom. Contrary to published reports, the name of the band had no derogatory intent: Love explained that the name was drawn from Euripides' *Medea.* "Medea would speak of a hole piercing right through her soul," Courtney explained. "It's about the abyss that's inside." However, in the United States it was completely overshadowed by the release of Nirvana's "Smells Like Teen Spirit," which was shipped to both commercial alternative and rock radio stations. For many radio programmers, this was the first time they heard the music of Nirvana.

On August 16, the Los Angeles college radio station KXLU broadcast the announcement that Nirvana was looking for punk rockers to be in the band's video shoot for "Smells Like Teen Spirit," to be held the next day. The shoot took place at GMT Studio, a sound stage in Culver City, California, that was made up to look like a high school gymnasium, complete with bleachers and basketball hoops. Dave described it as "a pep rally from hell." The response was so overwhelming that hundreds of heartbroken kids were turned away.

It was Kurt who came up with the treatment for the "Smells Like Teen Spirit" video, drawing ideas from two 1970s punk rock movies: the Ramones cult classic *Rock 'n' Roll High School* and *Over the Edge,* a movie about a band of crazed juvenile delinquents who smoke pot, get liquored up, vandalize a Southern California suburb, and eventually lock their parents inside their high school and set the building on fire. Kurt pointed to the film as a defining factor in his psyche, but some of his wilder ideas were not as warmly welcomed by video producer Sam Bayer. Kurt wanted the shoot to expand outside, where the kids could go wild, demolishing things in their path. He wanted the extras in the gym scenes to come down to the floor and empty their wallets into a raging bonfire, complete with burning effigies. The cheerleaders, also Kurt's idea, were initially supposed to be unattractive, awkward-looking girls, in a gesture of disgust with the familiar cheerleader image. All of the ideas were done away with by Bayer, whose refusal to cooperate with the young anarchists earned him the moniker Jethro Napoleon. "He's got a little Napoleon complex," Kurt said of the diminutive Bayer. "He was just so hyper, such a rocker guy. I just couldn't believe it. I couldn't believe we actually submitted to that."

During the shoot, Bayer lost his cool, telling everyone—band included—to shut up. Undaunted, everyone in the audience laughed and heckled Bayer. "It was just like we were in school," said Kurt. "He was the mean teacher. But by the end of the day, we were having fun."

To close out the shoot, Kurt wanted everyone to come down from the bleachers and mosh. Bayer didn't like the idea, but Kurt eventually talked him into it. It is undoubtedly the defining moment of the message Kurt was trying to express. "It's sort of funny, because people look at the video like it's some monumental statement," said Dave. "So many people think it's the epitome of this rebellious high school teenage vibe."

Eventually a series of creative solutions was readied (the janitor was played by Rudy Larosa, who was actually the janitor in Bayer's apartment building), and the shoot was completed for a modest $33,000. All the same, Kurt was self-conscious about the expense: "That's a hell of an embarrassment," he said in a *Musician* magazine interview. "We definitely could have used some film student who would have done just as good a job."

Perhaps, but Bayer was hired to make a video that had to be accepted by the biggest critics in the video industry: MTV. DGC knew that in addition to radio exposure, success on the enormous cable outlet would be the ticket to huge album sales and mass audience appeal. "MTV is a really weird corporate machine," said Dave Grohl. "Labels throw them a bunch of videos. Like Capitol Records, they'll give them an MC Hammer video. Then there's some band like Fetchin' Bones, that no one's really heard of. The label will say, 'Play the Fetchin Bones video. If you don't, you can't have MC Hammer.' " This was a common practice in the music industry in the early 1990s, for video airplay on MTV gave major labels the power to influence radio station airplay. Music was no longer sellable on its own merits: To reach the masses, video had become an equal, and necessary, partner. The MTV generation created new guidelines for record promotion, and Nirvana's "Smells Like Teen Spirit" video was the benchmark for all to follow.

"Actually, MTV really does try and be as subversive as it can," Kurt said, "as subversive as it's allowed, especially the news. They're constantly exposing all the rights that are being taken away from Americans. But no one gives a fuck, they just wanna see that damn Warrant video!"

The public reaction to Nirvana's exposure on MTV caught the band by surprise; they had predicted nothing more than respectable record sales. "I expected our core audience to buy *Nevermind* within the first couple of weeks, and sales would decline after that," said Kurt. "But after I realized that we were on MTV, I suspected we would sell a lot more."

By the end of August, with preparations for the video release being made for MTV and the single "Smells Like Teen Spirit" being promoted on American radio, Nirvana launched itself on a nine-date tour of the United Kingdom and Europe with Sonic Youth, Dinosaur Jr., Mudhoney, and Smashing Pumpkins. Much of the tour would be filmed for the classic film *1991: The Year Punk Broke*.

"Lounge Act," a fan favorite from *Nevermind*, broke into the live rotation of songs as Nirvana landed in Ireland on August 20. The following day, the *Kill Rock Stars* compilation was released. Nirvana's song "Beeswax," from the Dale Crover sessions, was featured on the fourteen-track set. It quickly became a hard-to-find collector's item, as only one thousand original vinyl copies came with hand-screened covers. The compilation also features Bratmobile, Courtney Love, Unwound, Steve Fisk, Bikini Kill, Witchy Poo, the Melvins, Kicking Giant, Fitz of Depression, Jad Fair, 7 Year Bitch, and Kreviss.

Three days later, at the Reading Festival in Reading, England, the three members of Nirvana asked Eugene Kelly to come onstage and join them in a rendition of the Vaselines' "Molly's Lips." Kelly later described the moment as unforgettable.

Sonic Youth were headlining the festival, but Nirvana left the biggest impression. "Toward the end of an absolutely raging set, Kurt leapt over the monitors and into the photo pit where Dave Markey just happened to be shooting our tour film, *1991: The Year Punk Broke*," remembered Sonic Youth's Lee Renaldo. "Hundreds of arms reached out to grab him. Kurt, still playing, made his way over to Markey, stuck his mouth to the camera mike, and said, 'This is a blues scale in E,' poking fun at himself and every guitar hero ever."

Dave gave his spin on the show and large venues like the annual Reading Festival. "Personally, I don't really like playing to big crowds," he said. "I mean, playing the Reading Festival was cool and everything, but it's one of the most impersonal things you can ever do—play to a crowd of thirty-five thousand people with a distance of about twenty feet between you and the people in the front row. It's just sort of perverse and disgusting—like a circus show."

Dave also regretted not being back in the United States during this period, for going on at the same time was the K Records International Pop Underground Convention in Olympia, once the hippest independent music event in the business. Kurt had promised himself not to miss it: The members of Nirvana had always had a deep-rooted respect for independent labels like K Records who stuck to their punk-rock ethics, and the trio wanted to be at the convention to show their support. One of Kurt's white Stratocasters had a K Records sticker blazoned across it, but his real sign of admiration and devotion surfaced when he tattooed himself with the K Records logo on his left forearm. "You can do it with just a regular sewing needle, string, and some India ink," said Dave, who shared this experience with Kurt. "Wrap the thread around the needle, dip it in the ink, and jab it in."

Kurt messed up the process. "When I did it, the thread unraveled. So I ended up jabbing in the needle and pouring ink all over my arm," he said.

After Reading, Nirvana shot through Germany for one uneventful show;

then it was on to the Pukkelpop Festival in Hasselt, Belgium, on August 25 for a huge show with Sonic Youth, Dinosaur Jr., the Ramones, and the Pixies' Black Francis playing solo. At this point Nirvana was loose, the gigs rocked, and the camaraderie between the bands was so strong that practical jokes began cropping up everywhere. At the Pukkelpop Festival, Kurt, Dave, and Krist switched around the dinner table placement tags backstage, seating the Ramones and their party of twelve at a table for two meant for Black Francis and his girlfriend. John Silva got into a food fight. Kurt wore Black Francis's name tag all day; by the time Francis hit the stage for his performance, some of the Dutch press covering the festival had no idea whom they were interviewing. When Kurt hosed Francis down during his set with a fire extinguisher he found by the side of the stage, a large group of security men charged him, and Kurt dropped the extinguisher and ran into the darkness backstage.

On the return trip through Germany, Nirvana's playlist began to tighten and reflect more *Nevermind*-based material, with only "Floyd the Barber," "School," "Negative Creep," and "Blew" remaining from *Bleach*. Before they played their final show of the abbreviated tour at the Rotterdam De Doelen, "Pennyroyal Tea" and "Something in the Way" had become crowd favorites. Back in the States, "Smells Like Teen Spirit" was ripping apart car and home stereos in every major city. Radio stations couldn't keep up with their audiences' demands to hear the song, and DGC broke out a full-scale promotional campaign.

On September 5, Nirvana stopped in London before bringing the tour to the United States and Canada. There they cut another session with John Peel at the Maida Vale Studios, recording stripped-down versions of "Dumb" (a song they would record for their next album, *In Utero*), "Drain You," and "Endless Nameless."

The "Smells Like Teen Spirit" CD-5 was released in the United States on September 10. It featured "Smells Like Teen Spirit (edit)," "Even in His Youth," and "Aneurysm." A record release party for *Nevermind* was thrown three days later at the Re-Bar in Seattle. On September 16, Nirvana prepared for an in-store acoustic appearance at Beehive Records in Seattle, but the acoustic plan changed when the sound man showed up with a ton of equipment, rigging Nirvana to play full on. Members of the Posies and Soundgarden watched in amazement as Kurt, Krist, and Dave created a sonic concussion that rattled the store's windows. The band exploded through most of *Bleach* and *Nevermind*. Kids were moshing in the store. It was complete and total mayhem.

Four days later, the Melvins opened the sold-out Nirvana show at the Opera House in Toronto. "My favorite memory of Nirvana was watching an audience of dumbfounded Canadians getting their asses kicked while Nirvana played their best song, 'Endless Nameless,' for the first time," reflected the sentimental Dale Crover. The crowd also got to hear "Aneurysm" for the first time live. The next day, "Smells Like Teen Spirit" debuted on the *Billboard* Modern Rock Chart, where it would remain for twenty weeks. Before long, it would reach number one.

Nirvana arrived in Boston on September 22 on the eve of the start of the American tour. With a free night off, the band headed over to see their old friends the Melvins play a gig at the Rat. At the show, Kurt met a woman named Mary Lou Lord, a local rock artist who was known around town for playing acoustic gigs on platforms in Boston's subway system. It was an association Kurt often denied having any part of, but for a short while, the two were friends of sorts. Lord even followed Nirvana to London to surprise Kurt, only to be scared off by a threatening Courtney Love. He may have sincerely liked her, but Kurt wasn't prepared to develop the kind of relationship that Lord later spoke of as being more than it really was.

On September 24, as Nirvana's major-label debut was released to retail stores throughout the United States, *Nevermind* debuted at number thirty-six on the UK pop charts. Krist and Dave had seen firsthand the impact their new record was having on kids, as hundreds of them lined Boston's famed Newbury Street to get into one of the hip local record stores to buy their own copies of the album. That night Nirvana played a special, unscheduled all-ages show for many of those same kids who were standing in line. Kurt, Krist, and Dave were upset over the fact that the previous night's benefit concert had been a twenty-one-plus show. The band negotiated with the management of the club, called Axis, which was reluctant at first to give up the alcohol revenues of an adults-only show. But smarter heads prevailed, and Nirvana got their wish. "[We want] to play as many all-ages shows as possible," said

Krist, "because we hate control and we don't want to participate in it." By night's end, another eight-hundred-plus kids went home extremely grateful and happy.

The audience at Club Babyhead in Providence, Rhode Island, the following night may have seen one of the most interesting sets that Nirvana would ever play. With their best friends and spiritual advisers the Melvins opening up, Kurt blew up his amp, setting the edgy tone for the rest of the evening. The band was sloppy and loose that night, but the song selection was amazing. The group kicked off with the Vaselines' "Jesus Doesn't Want Me for a Sunbeam," played in a dramatically different way from their later *Unplugged* version. The second song of the set, a song they rarely played live, was the Velvet Underground's "Here She Comes Now." They had recorded the song for the Communion label's tribute album *Heaven & Hell, a Tribute to the Velvet Underground—Volume One*. That was followed by a cover of the Wipers' classic "D-7." Three songs, three covers. By the time they got to one of their own songs, even sneaking in a rare performance of "Help Me, I'm Hungry," the audience was transfixed.

After gigs in New Haven, Connecticut, and Trenton, New Jersey, Nirvana's tour landed in New York City on September 28, where the trio dished out an afternoon in-store performance at Tower Records. That night at the Marquee, the Melvins opened up for a rabid, packed house. *The College Media Journal's New Music Report* review of the show, published on October 18, noted that "if pot plus sweat plus more sweat equals the odor of the soul of today's youth, then okay, yes the Nirvana show at the Marquee did indeed smell like teen spirit."

Opening with a Vaselines cover, Kurt stayed in the corner of the stage most of the show, Krist laughed throughout the gig, and Dave pounded the hell out of his skins. At the end of the encore, "Help Me, I'm Hungry," Kurt dove into the crowd. Everyone who could reached to support him over their heads while Kurt sang the rest of the tune.

While *Nevermind* continued to gain momentum on the playlists of alternative and rock radio stations across the United States, Nirvana concerts sold out more and more often. And even though DGC and Gold Mountain were ecstatic over the speed of the groundswell, the members themselves were inclined to take all the notoriety with a healthy helping of self-deprecation.

"We're as exciting as when you see a rock band on a 'sixties sitcom," said Krist. "There's gonna be chaperones, a table with punch on it and records on a little console. Fred McMurray is gonna be a chaperone." At the JC Dobbs show in Philadelphia on October 1, their increasing popularity seemed momentarily to backfire: When the band left without an encore, there were no chaperones to control the pissed-off crowd that sent Nirvana back to the van with a chant of "Sellout!"

Nirvana's radio profile was growing, but the trio was still not a household name. On October 2, the night Nirvana played at the 9:30 Club in Washington, D.C., the local DGC promotion person had the responsibility of taking the band out to eat before the show. When the band arrived at a trendy restaurant, the maitre d' refused to seat the raggedy trio. It was 1991, and "grungewear" had not yet hit the mainstream. But payola was still very much in vogue. The maitre d' was slipped some cash, and the band was swiftly seated.

The snub left an impression on Kurt, Krist, and Dave, but not one of inadequacy. "We're not like some kinda archaeologists or historians, digging out a certain style and a certain look, and putting it altogether," said Krist. "People are so image-conscious . . . whereas we just wanna look like ourselves . . . You got other things to live for, which are more important."

Kurt presented a visual worth considering: "Can you imagine us in spandex pants? Why, we'd look like starving Ethiopians!" Then he got serious. "Like, we're purposely going to go for the greasy scum-hooligan look. I mean, people are just so conned by the consumer society."

They'd played the 9:30 Club before, but Nirvana wasn't prepared for what greeted them this time around: The room was packed. After the gig, Krist talked about the changes they were encountering in their recent concerts. "Last night we played the same type of club we always play, but it was like playing in a sauna."

The show was a quick forty-five-minute set, opening with "Smells Like Teen Spirit." During the set, Kurt left the stage for almost five minutes. Krist chatted to the crowd to keep them interested while Kurt was gone. When he returned, Kurt jumped into the audience, and was passed around like a beach ball.

The carnival-like atmosphere of Nirvana's concerts continued through

North Carolina and Georgia; in mainstream media, meanwhile, the critics were falling over themselves to be heard on the topic. Wrote the *Los Angeles Times*'s Jonathan Gold, "The hooky, awesomely catchy songs on *Nevermind* have the inevitability of folk songs—as if all the band had to do was dig them up and not write them—but in sheer pop craft, *Nevermind* may be the *Meet the Beatles* of grunge."

Some even sensed a dramatic change occurring in the rock mainstream. "*Nevermind* is more hump than punk rock," blared the October 4 edition of *CMJ*. "Nirvana is gunning to take over the world, with Kurt Kobain [sic] the consummate dropout savant."

Chicago's Urge Overkill jumped on the Nirvana tour on October 12 at the sold-out show at St. Andrew's Club in Detroit, Michigan. Nirvana were huge fans of Urge Overkill; their label at the time was the well-respected indie Touch and Go, and their producer, Steve Albini, was a favorite of Kurt's. As "Aneurysm," "On a Plain," and "Lithium" became regulars on the set list, fans on this leg of the tour were treated to a twenty- to twenty-two-song set list of *Bleach* and *Nevermind* favorites.

Nirvana and Urge Overkill found themselves at the Cabaret Metro in Chicago, Illinois, the next evening. Courtney Love flew in for this gig, and it is said that this was the night that Kurt and Courtney decided to get serious about their relationship. They had exchanged a few phone calls along the tour when Courtney told Kurt she wanted to see Nirvana in Chicago. "So he got on the phone and spent, like, one thousand dollars and bought me a ticket and I went," Courtney said. "And that is when we got together."

But the beginning of the relationship was far from storybook, though it did set the tone for what lay ahead. When they first started dating, Courtney has said, "We didn't have an emotion towards each other. It was, like, 'Are you coming over to my house?' 'Are you going to get it up?' 'Fuck you.' That sort of thing. [Kurt] thought I was too demanding, attentionwise. He thought I was obnoxious. I had to go out of my way to impress him . . . I just knew he should ask me [to marry him] if he had any brains at all." Kurt expressed his newfound romantic happiness that night in Chicago by smashing the crap out of Dave's drum kit with the splintered remains of his guitar neck.

Four nights later, the tour stopped at Mississippi Nights in St. Louis, Missouri. The show the night before at Mississippi Nights had been a Guns

N' Roses concert that eventually turned into a rampage between band members and the audience. Nirvana found the idea of a riot at a Guns N' Roses show pretty hilarious. "I mean, what does Axl Rose have to say to anyone?" Krist wondered. "What is his platform, what's his core, where does he come from? There's nothing! He just talks shit. He just . . . he throws bottles!"

As Blackie Onassis of Urge Overkill, who opened the Nirvana show, tells the story, Nirvana thought they would show folks how a real concert riot is conducted.

"The whole day there had been this running joke in the Nirvana camp about how Guns N' Roses had just had that big riot there. Kurt mentioned that he'd like to start a riot, too, but I don't think anyone took him seriously. Nirvana needed to use our gear that night because the previous evening they had just trashed *everything*. It was only twenty minutes into their set and Dave runs in and says that Kurt just invited the entire club onstage because there were so many kids stage-diving. We realized our gear was up there, so we all went running on stage to save our equipment. We found Krist and Kurt sitting on the edge of the stage, totally bewildered, with five hundred kids swarming all around them. The whole place was going crazy, the owners were calling the cops." Meanwhile, the security staff, fresh off the Guns N' Roses incident, were heating up. "The police showed up and Krist gave this long speech about how everyone needed to get along and he talked everyone back into their seats and the cops agreed not to arrest anybody. Nirvana started playing again and they kept the club open late so they could finish their set. Even the cops stayed and watched the show. What started out as total mayhem ended in peaceful resolution. That's how badly people wanted to hear Nirvana."

On October 17, a battle of the bands of sorts took place in Los Angeles federal court, but, unfortunately, stage performances had nothing to do with it. Lawyers for Kurt Cobain, Dave Grohl, and Krist Novoselic were in court to settle a dispute with an unknown quartet out of Los Angeles over which band had the legal right to the name Nirvana. The Los Angeles band had been issuing cease-and-desist orders to radio and video outlets playing "Smells Like Teen Spirit."

"I have to practically apologize for 'Teen Spirit's' success to people," said Kurt. "It's not our fault. I mean the label is totally supportive in letting us do what we want but that's pretty much all they did. They pushed the record in radio and they got it on, and I think the success has a lot to do with the programmers at the radio stations liking the music, they sincerely like it. So they played it."

Walter Wiggins, the lawyer who represented the L.A. band Nirvana—his brother and cousin were members—claimed the band had had the name since 1983, and had registered a trademark in 1990 with the State of California. When the case reached the U.S. District Court, both parties agreed to share the name, but the L.A. band would agree to sell its trademark to Cobain, Novoselic, and Grohl.

Nirvana's touring schedule continued through Kansas and into Texas, for a show on October 19 at the Trees Club in Dallas. A weak opening performance of the virtually unknown song "Formaldehyde" set the tone for an overall awful concert. But it was certainly one of the most exciting live shows Nirvana ever played, for reasons entirely unexpected.

Kurt had been suffering from an ongoing battle with bronchitis, and earlier in the day a doctor had prescribed a potent antibiotic to ease his illness. What he had failed to do was warn Kurt not to drink alcohol that night. Kurt explained: "I started drinking and I just felt insane, like I did a whole bunch of speed or something. I just wasn't very rational at all."

The overcrowded club had Nirvana fever, and by the time the trio hit the stage it had reached a surging pitch of frenzy and frustration. It was impossible for people to breathe or move, and equally impossible for Nirvana to hear what they were playing. "I started to get more and more frustrated with the monitors as the tour went on," said Kurt. "The ones we'd been given were ridiculous. They made it impossible for us to hear ourselves and I can't fake a good show." Finally, Kurt lost it in the middle of a song, smashing his favorite Mustang guitar across the monitor board, damaging it so badly that it created an uncomfortably long delay in the show. "So I get pretty mad and throw a rock star fit once in a while," he said, "and at that particular show I destroyed a five-thousand-dollar monitor board—that's how much it would have cost to bring our own PA system on the road!" Eventually, after repairs were made, the show continued.

However, the incident itself was far from over. The system Kurt destroyed belonged to the best friend of one of the club's burly bouncers, who took it upon himself to set matters straight. When Kurt jumped into the audience to surf during "Love Buzz," the bouncer in question—even as he appeared to be helping Kurt back onstage—started pulling Kurt's hair and landing a few chops on him as well. "I decided to get one good blow in before he beat me up after the show," Kurt said. "So I smacked him in the face with my guitar. He got a big gash on his forehead." The melee continued with Kurt and the bouncer exchanging kicks and punches. Dave jumped over his drum set and into the riot. Two roadies pulled the bouncer off Kurt, and Krist got in the middle of the warring parties. Order was eventually restored, and the show continued.

When the show finally ended and the crowd left, the bouncer and a few of his friends were waiting outside for Kurt. "They all happened to be wearing Carcass and S.O.D. T-shirts," Kurt said. "He was screaming, beet red with blood all over himself, 'I'm gonna kill you!' " Kurt, Dave, and Krist bolted for a waiting cab, only to head right into a traffic jam in front of the club. The bouncer and his pals jumped on the cab and kicked in one of the windows, trying to grab at anyone they could get their hands on. Eventually the cabbie caught a clear lane and gunned the engine, leaving the hoods rolling on the pavement behind him.

Lost in the hysteria of the evening was a favorite Fender Mustang guitar, the one Kurt had used to assault the bouncer. "I've smashed three Mustangs," Kurt said; "they're my favorite guitars to play. I love them. And they're kind of hard to find. Especially in the left-handed version. The last one I broke was in Dallas—I definitely regret breaking that guitar. I tried to baby it as long as I could."

At the Vatican in Houston on October 20, another frothing crowd stirred up a swirling pit, encompassing the entire floor. During "Polly," the mob sang so loudly they could be heard over the PA system. A fiercely drumming Dave broke his snare drum during "Breed." Krist played barefoot the whole show.

By now the hysteria over Nirvana had reached a fever pitch nationwide, and their shows were starting to sell out weeks in advance. At a record store appearance in San Diego, California, on October 23, the kids packed in so tightly that the set list was cut to just six songs. But those who could hear were treated to stripped-down versions of "Dumb," "Here She Comes Now," "About a Girl," "Polly," "On a Plain," and "Been a Son."

The following day, Nirvana made a trip to Mexico to play the Iguana Club in Tijuana, with opening bands Sister Double Happiness and Hole. The show, to no one's surprise by now, was sold out. The band agreed that this was one of the most uncontrollably violent shows they'd ever witnessed. Kids leaped from eighteen-foot balconies into the crowd below. Fans fell or, more likely, were shoved into teeming mosh pits, only to be trampled by fellow patrons. Security did little to prevent over a hundred people from diving from the stage. By the time they kicked into "Smells Like Teen Spirit," mayhem was already entrenched.

Perhaps the main reason the place got so out-of-hand was that the gig was packed with the kind of macho, fear-inducing jocks Kurt and Krist had tried to leave behind in Aberdeen. It was a pretty pungent irony: The very people who had inspired Kurt's outsider ethos were now filling the halls for Nirvana shows.

"There were these very buff, testosterone-type jock guys up front just reeking of Man," said Kurt, recalling the Tijuana show. "It was gross. They were fighting. You could tell that they were just out of the service, and they were there just to beat people up. It was really shameful. It's a shame, but the majority of people in the mainstream don't have the mental capacity to understand what we're talking about. It's not entirely their fault, either. I think it's totally organic. They're born without a brain, and the only thing they can relate to is being sexist and being misogynist and working with their arms and sweating and enjoying sports. I don't think that we're going to have a large enough impact to change this, but it'll be fun to at least try." As the band left the stage, Krist yelled to the crowd, "Thanks for having a good attitude and for having a little fun."

At this time, record sales of *Nevermind* were approaching 350,000 in the United States. Three weeks after its release, the album reached number sixty-five with a bullet on the *Billboard* 200 Albums Chart. They were labeled "alternative music's hottest band" by the music industry, a moniker that never mattered much to the band. "There are also a lot of poser alternative bands that are being marketed as alternative, but they're not," Krist said. "The word 'alternative' is just a crock of shit anyway. It's just a dodge. It just protects the old guard; it gives them a place. They're trying to say, 'Not only is there this old, musty, redundant stuff, but there's also this alternative to that.' Instead of the new stuff coming out and pushing that old stuff out of the way."

"The only way I can describe 'alternative' anymore is 'good music,'" Kurt added. "I don't care what it sounds like—I don't care if it's abrasive or clean or retarded. It doesn't matter anymore. I mean, there are so many bad bands and so many bad songwriters out there that the only alternative to bad music is good music. And that's very rare."

Back in Los Angeles on October 24, Krist and Kurt, who wore a bulky yellow promlike dress, taped an interview for MTV's big-haired rock video show *Headbangers Ball*. When asked by the host, Rikki Rachtman, why he wore a dress, Kurt replied, "It's *Headbangers Ball*, so I'd thought I'd wear a gown." After the show, the band questioned why they were booked on the popular metal show. "Is Nirvana a heavy-metal band? That's fine; let them be fooled!" said Kurt. "I don't have anything against *Headbangers Ball*, but it is strange to see our faces on MTV."

Later that night, Nirvana played a gig at the Palace in L.A., the first of two sold-out performances, with Sister Double Happiness, L7, and Hole opening up. Twelve hundred fans sold out the show at $15 a ticket, with proceeds benefiting an abortion rights group called the Feminist Majority. Kurt, who had always believed that women should rule the world, honored their presence at the show with a fresh coiffure of blue hair. Krist voiced his opinion about the fund-raising issue from the stage during the set: "If you think abortion is wrong, don't have one." Scalpers were getting $100 a ticket by the time Nirvana hit the stage.

"Drain You" opened the show, but when "Teen Spirit" boomed through the PA, the pit in front of the stage exploded into an enraged ocean of testosterone. Mötley Crüe's Tommy Lee was pissed off that he had to pay to get into the benefit show. It exemplified one of the things Kurt despised most about Nirvana's sudden rise to the top: the emergence of Johnny-come-lately fans who, for some reason, felt they understood what Nirvana was all about and sought to emulate them. "Most of the new fans are people who don't know very much about underground music at all," Kurt said. "They listen to Guns N' Roses, maybe they've heard of Anthrax. I can't expect them to understand the message we're trying to put across. But at least we've reeled them in—we've gotten their attention on the music."

During the band's stay in Los Angeles, they received a fax from heavy-metal superstars Metallica. It read: "We really dig Nirvana. *Nevermind* is the best album of the year. Let's get together soon, love, Metallica. P.S., Lars hates the band."

"We'll rub elbows with Metallica!" said Kurt. "That way they'll wear our T-shirts and we'll become an instant success . . . We've gotta get Kirk Hammett a Melvins T-shirt."

Sudden sadness dimmed the tour on October 25, 1991, with news that legendary concert promoter Bill Graham had died. Nirvana was booked into San Francisco's Warfield Theater the next evening; uncharacteristically, the boys stopped the applause from their introduction to dedicate the show to Graham from the stage. In what may have been an offhand tribute to Graham, Nirvana opened the show with the Vaselines' "Jesus Doesn't Want Me for a Sunbeam." During "Love Buzz," Kurt climbed on the drum riser and smashed his guitar into Dave's kit.

Kurt's only stage interactions with the crowd occurred when he interrupted "Smells Like Teen Spirit" with an enormous burst of feedback and then waved good-bye at the end of the set. Perhaps caught up in the frenzy of the whole show, Kurt spent the evening knocking over mic stands, falling over backward, and banging up his equipment. The crowd, like many before it, went crazy during "Teen Spirit," forming what is considered by regulars in attendance to be the largest mosh pit the Warfield had ever seen.

At the Palace in Los Angeles on October 27 and 28, Hole opened for the band along with one of the band's heroes, Greg Sage, lead singer/guitarist of the legendary Northwest underground band the Wipers. (Nirvana later paid homage to Sage by recording two of his songs, "Return of the Rat" and "D-7.") Kurt dove into the swirling stage-front mosh pit with his guitar, and later destroyed Dave's drum kit. The kids filled the Palace's gigantic floor, pogoing to every song during both sold-out shows.

The following night, Sub Pop's promotional kingpin and Nirvana friend Susie Tennant alerted the band that *Nevermind* had been certified gold. The only dark note on this leg of the tour was the death of Jesse Bernstein, a friend, a Sub Pop labelmate, a Seattle poet, and a respected musician who committed suicide the same day.

The tour continued through Oregon, Washington, and British Columbia.

Old pals Mudhoney and Bikini Kill opened the final show of the tour's first leg on Halloween night at Seattle's Paramount Theater. The show was recorded and mixed by Andy Wallace on the Dogfish Mobile Truck, and filmed for the BBC. Versions of "School" and "Drain You" recorded that night eventually ended up as B sides to the "Come as You Are" single. "Negative Creep" appeared on the live CD *From the Muddy Banks of the Wishkah*, where the venue was mistakenly identified as New York instead of the Paramount Theater.

Nirvanamania spilled over into the fanzines of the world as the punkers became international magazine cover stars, appearing on the front of London's *New Musical Express* on November 1, 1991. "You know what I think is great?" said Dave Grohl during an interview about being interviewed. "The interviews in English magazines, because they sort of tidy up the grammar. You're free to tidy up any of our grammar. Just make us sound smart."

The following day, Nirvana embarked on a new six-week UK and European tour at this, the height of their popularity in Europe. Before they left U.S. soil, "Smells Like Teen Spirit" had debuted on the *Billboard* Album Rock Chart. It would eventually chart as high as number seven, and make a home on the chart for six months. *Nevermind* became a platinum record, passing one million sales worldwide after just six weeks.

BBC radio got most of the band's attention during this leg of the tour, as they aired Nirvana's *John Peel Sessions,* cut two months earlier, for the first time on November 3. Meanwhile, Nirvana blasted the United Kingdom, playing a melange of tunes culled from *Bleach, Nevermind,* and some of the songs that eventually appeared on *In Utero.*

On November 8, the trio appeared on the BBC TV program *The Word,* performing, naturally, "Smells Like Teen Spirit." It is here that Kurt first officially revealed that he was involved with Courtney, romantically declaring: "Courtney Love, the lead singer of the sensational pop group Hole, is the best fuck in the world." The following evening, the boys headed into BBC's Maida Vale Studios to record for Mark Goodier's radio show. Nirvana played electrified versions of "Polly," "Been a Son," "Aneurysm," and "Something in the Way," and the show aired on November 18.

Much of November was spent jumping around Germany, Italy (the live version of "Spank Thru" from this show appears on *From the Muddy Banks of the Wishkah*), and Austria. The tour hit its low point at a gig at the Vooruit

Krist, Kurt, and Dave in Los Angeles, California, 1992. © Kevin Estrada/Retna Ltd.

Kurt, Krist, and Chad under the Tacoma Narrows Bridge in Tacoma, Washington, August 1988. © ALICE WHEELER/RETNA LTD.

Tracy Marander and Kurt, 1988. © ALICE WHEELER/RETNA LTD.

Kurt, Krist, and Chad. © CHARLES PETERSON/RETNA LTD.

Slim Moon, Kurt, Jonathan Poneman, and Amy Moon, 1989. © ALICE WHEELER/RETNA LTD.

Krist on tour, 1990, Cambridge, Massachusetts. © CHRISTIAN CAMPAGNA

Kurt on stage during the *In Utero* tour. © IAN TILTON/RETNA UK

Kurt at Maxwell's in Hoboken, New Jersey, July 13, 1989. © Ian Tilton/Retna UK

Kurt, Dave, and Krist, 1992. © Youri Lenquette/Retna Ltd.

Kurt and Eugene Kelley. © Mick Hutson/Redferns/Retna Ltd.

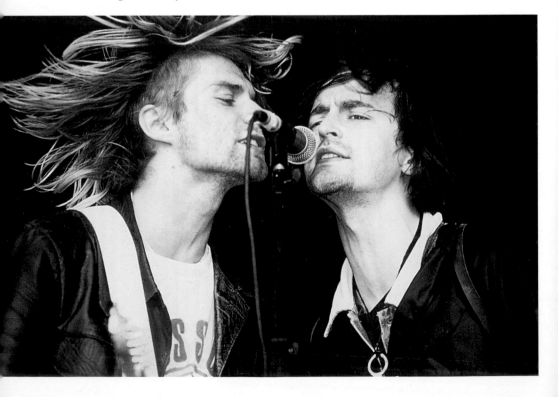

Kurt at the Oakland Coliseum in Oakland,
California, December 31, 1993.
© Jay Blakesburg/Retna Ltd.

Dave, Krist, Pat, and Kurt in Paris, France, March 1994. © YOURI LENQUETTE/RETNA LTD.

in Ghent, Belgium, on the twenty-third. Natural exhaustion caused infighting and anxiety that hampered the band's performance, and the quality of Nirvana's show suffered considerably. "It wasn't rock-star posing. A lot of what happened had to do with alcohol and with some really weird tension in the air," recalled Krist. "The whole course of events just couldn't be stopped. We were just on the train, and wherever it took us, we went. We're dealing with an extreme business here, so reactions are extreme."

Later that week, Nirvana played live on VPRO radio in Hilversum, Holland, just as "Smells Like Teen Spirit" was entering at number nine on the UK charts; it would peak at number seven one week later. That same night Nirvana played at the Paradiso Club in Amsterdam; the show was recorded by the Fudge Mobile for the BBC. Some of the footage from this gig appears in the video *Nirvana Live! Tonight! Sold Out!!*; the versions of "Lithium," "School," "Been a Son," and "Blew" all ended up on *From the Muddy Banks of the Wishkah.*

Before they embarked on a tough touring stretch—five shows in five nights—Nirvana made an appearance on the long-running UK TV show *Top of the Pops*. An English analog to *American Bandstand*, the program required Kurt to sing the now-ubiquitous "Smells Like Teen Spirit" over a prerecorded backing track. A true punk under any circumstance, he sang the song in a lounge lizard vocal and didn't even attempt to play his guitar. Dave mocked playing the drums, missing them most of the time entirely. Krist goofed off on the stage. This version is another highlight on *Nirvana Live! Tonight! Sold Out!!*

"All Apologies" entered the set list as Nirvana scooted around Scotland for several more sold-out shows. As *Nevermind* continued to sell in unbelievable weekly amounts worldwide, the underground community that Nirvana felt so close to began to turn its back on them. To many in the underground/indie scene, success was immediately suspect—it was an attitude Nirvana might once have shared, but now it was hard to swallow. "You know, if people want to slag us off and call us sellouts for doing what we're doing before even hearing it, fine," said Dave, "Fuck 'em. Those are the people we don't really care about. Whatever. It's open to anyone's interpretation. If they want to slag us for signing to a major, cool. That's fine. If they don't, great. No big deal. No skin off my back.

"People are under the impression that we're doing this for all the wrong reasons and they're just wrong. Kurt wrote a lot of really good songs and Kurt's got a real good pop sensibility—if you want to call it that. But people think Kurt's writing these pop songs to make a buck, which is stupid. It's completely ridiculous. It's the music we all love to play and has nothing to do with money."

"We wanted to do as good as Sonic Youth," Krist said. "We totally respect those people and what they've done. We thought we'd sell a couple hundred thousand records at the most, and that would be fine. Next thing you know, we go Top Ten. I wish we could have a time machine and go back to two months ago. I'd tell people to get lost."

"Everyone is always asking if I'm afraid of the band's success going too far," Dave added. "That doesn't really make any difference. I just don't want to be David Grohl of Nirvana for the rest of my life. It's like the kid who got caught masturbating in the bathroom of high school. That's the only way he's ever known."

But the band's fame had begun to grow so quickly that it was beyond even their own control. As Alexandra Saperstein wrote in the *Mills College Weekly* that year, "Nirvana possesses an intriguing mixture of the unabashed sensitivity of the Replacements, the scything bass and guitar riffs of Sonic Youth, and the enrapturing hypnotic aura of the Cult—not an easy thing to do, certainly, but then most bands don't have one-tenth of Nirvana's talent."

Even some of Nirvana's mentors were recognizing the growth of the trio's talent. "Between the first Edinburgh show in 1990 and when we supported them at London Kilburn National in London on December 5, they'd got a lot better songs," said Eugene Kelly. "Some of the stuff that they'd been doing before was maybe a bit too Black Sabbath, but it was fairly easy to see how big they were going to be, how important.

"At the Kilburn National I had a real admiration for how they'd filled this enormous place with all these people going wild. The whole atmosphere was incredible. Backstage there were no real rock clichés; maybe the odd trashed dressing room, but nothing more. By this stage, we were the ones being the more reverential."

The maturity Kelly noted may have inspired Kurt to take on the responsible role as fiancé to Courtney. That night, after the December 5 show, Kurt and

Courtney, lying in bed together, decided to get married. While the two hardly expected that their friends would be overjoyed at the decision, they certainly never anticipated the disappointment in some of the reactions. Courtney offered her own chilling assessment of the reception: "Kim Gordon [of Sonic Youth] and Julia Cafritz [who plays with Gordon in the band Free Kitten] told me when me and Kurt got serious, 'You know what's going to happen?' They spelled out everything. 'You'll become junkies. You'll get married. You'll OD. You'll be thirty-five, you'll try and make a comeback.' And I was going, 'Yeah, I know what's going to happen. I don't give a fuck. I love this guy. My prince on a goddamn white horse. And I'm going to do it. I'm going to do both: be with him and do my thing.'"

After a quick dip in France to play the Trans-Musicale Festival in Rennes, Nirvana was back in the BBC's Channel 4 Studios to appear on the popular *Jonathan Ross Show*. According to the show's producers, the band was supposed to perform "Lithium," but when they were introduced, Nirvana exploded into a searing version of "Territorial Pissings." After the song they completely trashed their equipment, and Ross signed off with some witty commentary: "Thank you very much indeed. Boy, I hope we didn't wake the neighbors up. Nirvana there doing the tune we didn't actually expect, but they wanted me to tell you they're available for children's birthday parties and bar mitzvahs."

After the Ross show, the rest of the tour was canceled. Dates in Ireland, on December 9 at Belfast's Connor Hall and December 10 at Dublin's McGonagle's, became casualties. Band exhaustion was cited as the reason; Kurt's voice was fried and beyond medicinal repair, and doctors ordered rest for the entire band.

It wasn't long, though, before public demand, promoter pressure, and the trio's love for the stage spurred Nirvana to resume touring. And they returned in grand fashion, too, joining the Red Hot Chili Peppers and Pearl Jam at the Motor Sports Arena in Los Angeles on December 27 for the first of three consecutive sold-out California shows.

Nirvana's portion of the next show, at the O'Brien Pavilion at the Del Mar Fairgrounds in Del Mar, was recorded and was released as a Westwood One broadcast. Several songs were also released as Nirvana B sides; the entire show has been bootlegged, but in near-studio quality, because it was recorded, engineered, and produced by Andy Wallace and the Dogfish Mobile Truck. The Del Mar show featured a long set of twenty songs, including covers of songs by the Wipers, the Vaselines, and Devo. The versions of "Sliver" and "Polly" both appear on the "In Bloom" CD single, and versions of "Smells Like Teen Spirit," "Aneurysm," and "Drain You" all ended up on *From the Muddy Banks of the Wishkah*.

Nirvana's incredible and unpredictable year of 1991 ended on an upbeat note. *New Musical Express*'s annual year-end poll voted *Nevermind* album of the year, and it ranked "Smells Like Teen Spirit" the number seven single. MTV cast "Smells Like Teen Spirit" at number seventy in the top one hundred videos of 1991, with Guns N' Roses' "You Could Be Mine" at number one. Sales of *Nevermind* were well over one million by this point, and there was no sign of decline.

"I'm seeing two-year-old kids singing along to 'Teen Spirit,'" said Dave. "I've seen stockbroker yuppies slam-dancing to it on a disco floor. It's spreading like the plague. Hopefully, the original following who bought *Bleach* are listening to *Nevermind* and realize it's the same trip. The same ideal. The same band."

"I wasn't hoping for [the notoriety] or looking forward to it," Kurt said about Nirvana's budding yet seemingly unwelcome popularity. "But it's not surprising 'cause I see so many shitty bands on the cover of magazines. It doesn't surprise me when a band can write a few good songs [and] are appreciated."

"Things are just getting bigger and bigger, and it's kind of overwhelming," said Krist, who was clearly uncomfortable with the thought of becoming jaded superstars. "I don't mind, as long as we stay who we are and make the kind of records we want to make. We're just along for the ride."

Kurt felt there was still a sense of innocence to the whole experience. "We still feel as if we're teenagers," he said, "because we don't follow the guidelines of what's expected of us as adults, we still screw around and have a good time."

"Do you think that we're still a pain in the ass for the music industry?" Krist asked. "Are we still uncooperative? Is there still that vibe in the air?" The band seemed increasingly desperate, in interviews conducted during this first flush of fame, that they not be perceived as conspirators in their own success.

Thirteen

I'm not doing any more interviews, 'cause it's really
getting on my nerves . . . I mean they're so boring because you
have to say the same thing, you know.

—KURT COBAIN

Excitement clogged the air in the DGC Records offices nationwide early in 1992 as promotion plans for one of the biggest albums and one of the most noteworthy bands in DGC's short history began to unfold. As *Nevermind* bulldozed its way toward the top of the Billboard charts, a tour of Japan, Australia, and Hawaii was being put together. Nirvana kicked off the new year with a show at the famous Cow Palace in San Francisco. It was here that, almost twenty years before, on March 3, 1972, Kurt's hero Evel Knievel had wiped out his motorcycle attempting a sonic jump to superstardom. It seemed appropriate that Nirvana should use the same venue to lift off the earth and soar to a still-unmatched ride to fame as well. "There's definitely going to be a lot more people finding out about Nirvana," Dave predicted. "You know, Nirvana's done a little bit of touring and now I think radio is going to be some tool. I think the label is probably going to use it to get bigger shows going and more press."

On January 10, the threesome arrived in New York City to play a special performance in front of an invitation-only audience of industry hangers-on and hard-core fans at the MTV studios. The entire show was taped, and portions of it were played back on the MTV Sunday night show *120 Minutes*, a two-hour weekly feature dedicated to breaking alternative artists. Among the songs played during the gig were "Smells Like Teen Spirit," "Territorial Pissings," "Drain You," "On a Plain," and "Polly."

Also that day, Kurt was hit with the first piece of press suggesting that he was using heroin. The article, written by Jerry McCulley for *BAM* magazine, was filled with speculation and implication. Drawn largely from observations made backstage at a Nirvana show, the article read, in part: "Kurt soldiers gamely on alone, nodding off occasionally in midsentence. He's had but an hour's sleep, he says blearily. But the pinned pupils; sunken cheeks; and scabbed, sallow skin suggest something more serious than mere fatigue. The haggard visage and frail frame make him appear more like forty than twenty-four." Even though the word *heroin* was never used, the author's intent was duly noted.

"I'm a narcoleptic and I'm skinny and they have nothing better to talk about," said Kurt. "It all started with one interview . . . I was really fucked up and tired and drunk, and the guy thought I was on heroin. And he started the whole thing. And now everyone thinks I'm a heroin addict . . . It really pisses me off, because there are *no* drugs backstage at a Nirvana gig. There never have been. We don't allow them. It really pisses me off because I'm kind of an example for people, and there are nine-year-old kids who are into our band, and if they think that I take drugs and I think it's cool, then they're going to do it too. You know, I do drugs every once in a while. But I don't like bands who promote drug use, because it influences people and it isn't cool."

The following day saw the milestone everyone had been waiting for: *Nevermind* officially became the number one record on the *Billboard* album chart, astonishing the industry by leaping over Michael Jackson, Garth Brooks, Hammer, Michael Bolton, and Boyz II Men. On the same day, the single "Smells Like Teen Spirit" rose from number thirteen to number six on the Top 100 singles list. "Nirvana is that rare band that has everything: critical acclaim, industry respect, pop radio appeal, and a rock solid college/alternative base," wrote Paul Grein in the January 11, 1992, *Billboard*. That very night, millions of people worldwide saw the band perform live for the first time ever, as Nirvana made its first national television appearance on *Saturday Night Live*.

The invitation from NBC executives to play on the network's internationally famous comedy show was confirmation of Nirvana's meteoric rise up the music charts, but to no one's surprise, they were late for the biggest gig of their brief career. It had been a busy day for Kurt, whose photo shoot with Michael Lavine (which appeared in the April 1992 edition of *Sassy* magazine and on the inner sleeve of Nirvana's third album, *In Utero*) had caused him to oversleep. By the time he and Courtney stumbled out of the elevator and into the lobby of the Omni Park Central Hotel in New York City, their small entourage, including Krist and Dave, had lost their patience and were more than eager to get on the road. But when the chauffeured transports arrived, Kurt, Krist, and Dave hesitated. The first vehicle, a large van, pulled up to the small group of DGC record executives and Gold Mountain Management, while the second car, a large limousine, opened its doors to escort the members of Nirvana and their families. The band absolutely refused to ride in the limo. Everyone present knew the trio was about to step into a new life of international celebrity as of roughly midnight that evening, but Nirvana had grown tired of the pageantry that had led up to it. Without argument and with much relief, the band and their families jumped into the van and left the limo waiting for the suits.

Anticipation for Nirvana's performance on this night was high for weeks for both the public and those in the corporate Nirvana camp, but for the trio, it seemed like just another gig. At least that's the impression they gave on the outside. Kurt, Krist, and Dave seemed very loose backstage, blowing through rehearsal without incident, and calmly interacting with various *SNL* actors and comedians. By the time *SNL* host Rob Morrow announced, "Ladies and gentlemen, Nirvana!" and the band launched into "Smells Like Teen Spirit," the studio audience were bouncing their heads in unison. Hair flew everywhere. Kurt, wearing a homemade Flipper T-shirt, and Krist, wearing a Melvins T-shirt, paid homage to their favorite bands. As Kurt wailed "a mulatto!" one final time, screaming cheers blasted over the band's feedback before the APPLAUSE sign came on in the studio. The *SNL* cast, who had watched stageside through the whole song, knew they'd witnessed something unique. The scene was surreal: Two years before, the trio had been tuning up for practice alone in a cold, dirty, damp shack in Olympia, Washington. Tonight they were playing live to the whole planet on the world's biggest stage, and they were being showered with unending adoration.

For the second *SNL* song, it seemed logical to expect Nirvana to play "Come as You Are," the next anticipated single from *Nevermind*. Instead, the band scared the hell out of the studio and national viewing audience with a searing version of "Territorial Pissings." The song concludes with an almost untranslatable emotional explosion, but Nirvana needed no interpreter on this evening. At the song's end, they went ballistic, smashing their equipment to pieces. Kurt knocked over his mic stand; Dave grabbed his tom and threw it sky-high; Kurt then sent the neck of his guitar crashing into his speaker cabinet, as if he were stabbing it to death.

"I punctured every speaker in the cabinets," Kurt said after the show. "And there were twelve speakers to puncture. I can't think of anything better to do than to puncture speakers; that's my favorite piece of equipment to destroy. It's a lot of fun."

Krist, now wearing an L7 T-shirt, hurled his bass up in the air; he couldn't catch it on the way down, and it narrowly missed the bass drum that Dave had sent flying off the stage. Dave picked up the toms and whipped them off the platform. Kurt punctured his cabinet over and over, Dave tossed cymbals everywhere, Krist threw whatever came his way. The producer, fearing the unknown, and perhaps for his future as a producer, screamed to get the *Saturday Night Live* logo up on the screen so they could cut away. In an interview almost a year later, Krist looked back on Nirvana's second song, which had included a big surprise: "For me, the point is to do anything spontaneously—open the car door and I'll hop in. That's what happened with that 'controversy' at the end of *Saturday Night Live,* when we were all kissing one another. It wasn't planned. When we finished playing, I just looked at Kurt and Dave and started chompin' them. It was funny." (The kissing episode has since been cut out of repeats of the show.) Parts of the audience cried out with applause, others ran for cover, and suddenly the show went to a commercial and wasn't live anymore. Kurt, Dave, and Krist, mission accomplished, calmly walked off the stage.

It's been said that the best way for a band to tell how good their New York City gig was is to count how many members of Sonic Youth were still in the audience by the time it was over. On this Saturday night, Kim, Thurston, Lee, and Steve were the first to stand and applaud as Nirvana jumped offstage and headed to their dressing rooms.

If their first *SNL* performance established nothing else, it certainly proved to Nirvana that their international popularity was something very tangible, and it wasn't going to go away anytime soon. Kurt even found it strange that so many people wanted to meet him after the show and get his autograph. "Oh geez. The autographs. They're really annoying. I've never understood why anyone would want an autograph. There are a lot of people who I admire, look up to, respect and all that, but I never wanted their autograph. If I ever wanted to say anything to them, I'd just walk up and say 'Hi.' If I didn't have anything interesting to say, I wouldn't say anything to them. [Asking for autographs] just gets really annoying. It's distracting. [I'll be] sitting around backstage and all these people are coming in—'Hey, I'm sorry to bother you,' . . . they're all really nice about it, and they feel guilty and I'm sure my attitude toward them doesn't help them, you know, feel any better. When I was a kid, Evel Knievel was a real big thing for me. But I never really wanted his autograph. I just don't understand it."

When asked about the band's performance that night in front of an international viewing audience, Kurt explained, "I kinda felt like we accomplished something. We played pretty abrasively tonight, you know, wrecked our equipment as usual." Destroying equipment had become a Nirvana trademark, and the band seemed to be weary of the routine. Did it feel good to smash a guitar in front of millions of people who'd never seen the act before? A smile broke his tired expression. "Actually, it did."

No sooner was the show over than Nirvana found themselves getting right back to business to help sell even more copies of *Nevermind*.

On January 18, two new singles, "Come as You Are" and "On a Plain," debuted on the *Billboard* Modern Rock Chart. "Come as You Are" charted for eighteen weeks, climbing as high as number three. "On a Plain" hung around for just two weeks, disappearing from view after reaching number twenty-five. One week later, "Come as You Are" debuted on the *Billboard* Album Rock Chart, where it spent twenty-five weeks and would chart as high as number three.

Nirvana now faced the daunting task of making a follow-up video to the hugely successful "Smells Like Teen Spirit." With the somewhat sour experience of working with Sam Bayer fresh in their minds, Kurt, Krist, and Dave agreed that working with Kevin Kerslake to make a video for "Come as You

Are" would better satisfy Nirvana's unique interpretation of the song. Kerslake had worked with Sonic Youth and Iggy Pop. After meeting with Kerslake, the karma was set. There would be no extras in the video, no fancy props or hyped-out messages, just the three members of Nirvana enjoying themselves and doing whatever the hell they wanted to do.

The video for "Come as You Are" was shot on a soundstage that included running water and a chandelier for Kurt to swing around on. Blurry scenes shot of the threesome a few days earlier (done intentionally to give the feeling of wetness) were projected behind Nirvana as they performed to the video cameras. There's never a clear view of the band in any part of the video. It is possible that this was done intentionally to prevent too much focus on Kurt's deteriorating health. However, the ongoing and controversial gun theme that permeated Kurt's lyrics was visually evident in the end of the video: a revolver softly floats in water and slowly drops to the bottom of the screen.

At the end of January, in the middle of their tour of Australia, New Zealand, and Japan, the band were asked to do a photo shoot for an upcoming cover for *Rolling Stone* with photographer Mark Seliger. In a message for anyone who had become convinced that Nirvana had sold their souls for the almighty dollar, Kurt showed up at the shoot with a homemade T-shirt reading CORPORATE MAGAZINES STILL SUCK. It was a classic punk T-shirt, handmade, just like the Flipper T-shirt Kurt had made and worn on *Saturday Night Live*. "We were on tour in Australia, and I had completely forgotten that I had promised to do the *Rolling Stone* piece," Kurt said. "And that day, they called and said, 'Are you ready to do the photo shoot?' And it was like, 'No, I really don't want to do this.' I had so much pressure from my management and the band members—they wanted to do it, and I just agreed."

Kurt's T-shirt message wasn't exactly a personal attack on *Rolling Stone*, in spite of the fact that he had never liked the magazine. He was simply growing tired of the endless demands that hounded Nirvana wherever they went. "On my way there I just decided, 'I'm going to write something on my shirt that's offensive enough to stop getting our picture on the cover'," Kurt admitted. "This way I could say that I actually played along with it and still didn't get picked to be on the cover. I wasn't necessarily challenging *Rolling Stone*, saying, 'You suck' and 'We don't want to have anything to do with you, but we'll still use you for our exposure.' *Rolling Stone* sucks, has always sucked, and still sucks just because they have a hip band on their cover. We're not as cool and hip as everyone thinks. Having us on the cover isn't going to make *Rolling Stone* any cooler." But having Nirvana on their cover did help make the magazine a little richer. When one of Seligar's Nirvana shots made the cover of the April 1992 edition of *Rolling Stone,* it became one of the best-selling issues in the history of the magazine.

On February 8, "Lithium" debuted on the Billboard Modern Rock Chart; it stayed there for three weeks, charting as high as number twenty-five.

By the time the tour landed in Japan in February (Nirvana's first-ever show in the land of the Rising Sun was at the the Kokusai Koryu Center in Osaka on Valentine's Day), "Where Did You Sleep Last Night" had been introduced into a revolving set list of songs from *Bleach* and *Nevermind,* along with a few songs that showed up on *In Utero* and *Unplugged in New York.* The Japanese experience was an enjoyable one for Krist, Dave, and Kurt, as the video version of "Something in the Way" on *Nirvana Live! Tonight! Sold Out!!* (culled from the February 16 performance at Club Citta in Kawasaki) demonstrates.

Before returning to the mainland United States for some much-needed rest, the threesome played a couple of sold-out shows at Pink's Garage in Honolulu; Hawaii, on February 21 and 22; performances of "Negative Creep" and "Noise" from one of the shows also appear on *Nirvana Live! Tonight! Sold Out!!* Two days later, in Waikiki, Kurt Cobain and Courtney Love, to the surprise and chagrin of many, were married. Courtney's wedding dress, a white diaphanous item with creeping dry rot, was supposedly a dress originally worn by actress Frances Farmer in one of her movies. Dylan Carlson, one of Kurt's first true friends, was the best man. He was also one of Kurt's few friends at the ceremony, since Courtney had decided on a small and exclusive guest list. Her reasons were not easily swallowed by those left off the list.

"They [Dave Grohl's few guests, including Barrett Jones] all came from Seattle and they were all going to go back and say, 'We were at Kurt and Courtney's wedding!' and lie about things," said a suspicious Courtney. She even purposely left off Krist's wife. "Shelli and Krist were being really shitty to us and they thought I was doing all these drugs," Courtney explained. Shelli and Krist had been friends with Kurt for a long time, much longer than Kurt had known Courtney, and Krist felt it was rather strange being invited without Shelli. "That was fucked up, but I don't want to dwell on it," Krist said, keeping the incident private. "It was resolved, more or less."

Although Courtney maintains that she was not on drugs, Kurt later admitted to shooting up before the ceremony. "I wasn't *very* high, though. I just did a little teeny bit just so I didn't get sick." Although they were presumably happy in their union, Courtney's exceeding caution spilled into her relationship with Kurt when she requested that they sign a prenuptial agreement. "I didn't want Kurt running away with all my money," Courtney joked.

Upon their return from Hawaii, the newlyweds moved into an apartment in Los Angeles. It was a far cry from the solace Kurt was used to in Washington. "I hate L.A.," Kurt said. "I love the weather, but I can't stand being there. I absolutely hate it . . . People are so rude there."

His disdain for his new surroundings kept Kurt in the house most of the time, often high on heroin, but not completely inactive. "I didn't find myself just sitting in the house and nodding off and sleeping," Kurt explained. "I was always doing something artistic. I got a lot of paintings done and wrote a lot of songs. I did all my best songwriting on heroin [that] year." Kurt began to justify his increased heroin use, even though he could almost see his future becoming destroyed by it. Hiding his heroin use from Courtney, he was trying to find a way to be a junkie and a husband, and the unknowing Courtney was just happy to be his wife. "Life is like a perennial honeymoon right now," Courtney said at the time. "I get to go to the bank machine every day!"

But Kurt's heroin use was not unknown to those who knew him well. Visitors and trips outside the apartment were limited. It upset Krist more than words could express. "Kurt's a fucking junkie asshole and I hate him!" he blurted out one day, shocked by what Kurt was becoming. In a more reflective mood, Krist expressed a sense of helplessness about Kurt's decline. "I felt like he left me. I was really concerned and worried about him and there was nothing I could do about it. I don't know how much heroin Kurt was doing because I never saw him. I never went to his house. I saw him high a few times, but never really a fucking mess. I never saw that. That's just what I heard or what I assumed."

While the turmoil between Kurt and Krist continue to boil, Dave kept busy writing his own songs. "The explosion of my real band [Nirvana] kept me pretty busy for a while," Dave recalled in the Foo Fighters press biography, "but I always managed to bring along a guitar so that I could write songs to record upon returning home [from touring]. By this time, Barrett [Jones] had moved to Seattle and become my roommate. The eight-track studio was in the basement, at our disposal anytime we came up with an idea." Dave's work during those weeks would later crop up on his Foo Fighters debut.

With Dave Grohl writing new material, Krist flustered over his relationship with Kurt, and the newlyweds beginning their life together, the future of Nirvana, unbeknownst to the public, was changing course dramatically. The band would begin to resent the one thing they had loved the most: touring and playing live. Now, it seemed, fans were dying to see them not because of what Nirvana's songs meant to them, but because the band was the newest pop sensation, the flavor of the week.

Any band in the world with an album as big as *Nevermind* would spend all the time they could in an attempt to exploit the groundswell as fully as possible. Income in the music business is usually made through touring, especially for the most popular acts. But with *Nevermind* continuing to outsell every rock record in the stores, Nirvana resisted touring—a decision that was mainly Kurt's.

"I needed time to collect my thoughts and readjust," he said. "[The success and promotion of *Nevermind*] just hit me so hard, and I was under the impression that I didn't really need to go on tour, because I was making a whole bunch of money. Millions of dollars. Eight million to ten million records sold—that sounded like a lot of money to me. So I thought I would sit back and enjoy it. I don't want to use this as an excuse, and it's come up so many times, but my stomach ailment has been one of the biggest barriers that stopped us from touring. I was dealing with it for a long time. But after a person experiences chronic pain for five years, by the time that fifth year ends, you're literally insane. I couldn't cope with anything. I was as schizophrenic as a wet cat that's been beaten."

Touring the United States compounded that feeling. "On average it's a ten-hour drive a day, said Kurt. We've always been in this very small compact van, very clammy, with seven people and all the equipment. For the tour in

Europe we had a stereo, a real luxury." Plans were made for a few select gigs in the States, but not until later in the year; for the moment Nirvana was out of circulation.

In March 1992, *Bleach* was rereleased in the United Kingdom, debuting on the charts at number thirty-three. At the same time, "Come as You Are" debuted on the UK charts at number nine.

The next month, Kurt and Courtney confirmed that they were expecting their first child, due in August. The announcement would ruin plans for Courtney's band, Hole, to play 1992's Reading Festival. The small setback to the band would change for the positive. After a small bidding war, Hole was signed to Geffen Records for a reported million-dollar deal. "I had one A&R guy tell me, 'Sleeping with Kurt Cobain is worth half a million dollars,'" said Courtney.

One thing Hole had on its side during negotiations was the experience Nirvana had gained in its own negotiations with DGC. "I got excellent, excellent contractual things," Courtney said at the time about Hole's record deal. "I made them pull out Nirvana's contract, and everything on there, I wanted more. I'm up to half a million for my publishing rights and I'm still walking."

Almost immediately, because of the obvious parallels, the press formed its own opinion about Hole's music, citing songwriting similarities between Hole's lead singer and Nirvana's lead singer. "If those sexist assholes want to think that me and Kurt write songs together, they can come forward with a little more [money]," said Courtney. "No matter what label I'm on, I'm going to be his wife. I'm enough of a person to transcend that."

Meanwhile, in the April 1992 edition of *Select* magazine, Kurt let out that the follow-up album to *Nevermind* was scheduled to be recorded in September, after Nirvana's summer tour and the expected birth of his child. "It's gonna be a tight squeeze," Kurt said. "Our touring schedule is getting in the way of being able to finish the songs we've been writing."

As spring began to bloom, the band recorded the song "Oh, the Guilt" with Barrett Jones at the Laundry Room Studios in Seattle; they released it as a split 7-inch with the Jesus Lizard's "Puss" on Touch and Go Records in January 1993. The artwork for the single, a striking painting by Malcolm Bucknail, features a dog with human hands and a portrait of a Native American. During this same session they also recorded a cover of the Wipers'

"Return of the Rat" for an upcoming Greg Sage tribute record, and "Curmudgeon," the B side to the "Lithium" CD single.

Meanwhile, the artwork for the cover of *Nevermind* was suddenly threatened by a proposed new law in Seattle that would have classified the picture of the infant underwater as adult material, calling it suitable only for those over eighteen years of age. The law was not passed, though at the Wild Planet record store in Ventura, California, store managers were advised by a city official to cover up the baby's penis on the cover of *Nevermind*. The store used blank pink Post-it notes to censor the album cover.

During the entire month of April, Kurt remained out of the public eye. "I think that after our last tour, when Courtney and I went into seclusion and she got pregnant and I started doing drugs, that seclusion was a time that was needed," Kurt explained. "I know that sounds almost like an endorsement for drug use, but I honestly don't regret at least taking that time off. I regret taking drugs, but I really needed the rest and time to sort things out." Fans of Nirvana and Hole got an opportunity to hear from newlyweds Kurt and Courtney for the first time in an interview with the teen magazine *Sassy*, in which the couple discussed what marriage was like.

"In the last couple of months, I've gotten engaged and my attitude has changed drastically," said a blissful Kurt. "I can't believe how much happier I am and how even less career-oriented I am. At times I even forget I'm in a band, I'm so blinded by love. I know that sounds embarrassing, but it's true. I could give the band up right now. It doesn't matter. But I'm under contract."

"We get attention for our relationship, but if we didn't have bands, no one would care," said Courtney, quite pointedly. "I mean, the reason we're doing this interview is girls have been trained to look up to rock star boys as these . . . objects. They grow up their whole lives with horses or rock stars on their walls. For me, I didn't want to marry a rock star, I wanted to be one. I had a feminist hippie mom, and she told me I could do whatever I wanted to do. But a lot of girls think that to go out with somebody who's cool or successful, they have to be pretty and submissive and quiet. They can't be loud and obnoxious like me, and they can't have their own thing."

Obviously, Courtney did have her own thing, and putting it together with Kurt's own thing enabled the two of them to purchase a new house. "It's really beautiful, it's Victorian," said Courtney with schoolgirl wonderment. "And my favorite thing to think about while we're doing major label meetings and stuff is basically what color we're going to paint the walls. I want to have a baby really bad, but I want to be able to afford it myself. I want my own money. I couldn't imagine marrying someone with money and then living off them."

When May 1992 rolled around, the second *Nevermind* single, "Come as You Are," peaked on the *Billboard* charts at number thirty-two. At the same time, the name Nirvana came under challenge again, this time by the 1960s Irish psychedelic band also known as Nirvana. This new battle brought out some unexpected friends: Guns N' Roses made a statement of support for Kurt, Krist, and Dave and their rights to the name, and Axl Rose even tried to get Nirvana to tour with them. Kurt, for his part, made it very clear that he was not interested in touring with Guns N' Roses.

In an interview that appeared that month in *Musician* magazine, Rose asserted that his intentions were good and his feelings of support genuine. "I just think that Nirvana are having a lot of problems with who they are and who they want to be and trying to hold on to it at the same time," Rose said. "At least Kurt is. I'd like to be as supportive as I can, but I don't know how much he will allow support. To write a song like 'Smells Like Teen Spirit' . . . and then have it used as an anthem has got to be a complete mindfuck.

"The man definitely has a mountain to rise above," Rose continued. "I think there is a part of him that has the strength and desire to do it. I just don't know if he's able to get in touch with it."

For Dave, the spring and summer of 1992 were a blast. "With little action on the Nirvana front, I could pay more attention to my music," he later said, without a hint of insincerity. "Recording became a full-time deal. Between sporadic Nirvana trips and visits to [Washington,] D.C., most of my time was spent writing and experimenting with harmonies and arrangements. [Future Foo Fighters] songs like 'Good Grief' and 'Exhausted' were written around this time . . . 'For All the Cows' [another Foo track] was done around the same time, and my growing love of recording cover songs led me to record 'Ozone' from Ace Frehley's solo record and the Angry Somoans' 'Gas Chamber' [two Foo B sides]."

By summer, the personal life of Kurt Cobain was becoming front-page news everywhere. One of the first prominent mentions of his growing reputation as a heroin junkie came in the form of an article printed in the weekly radio and record industry trade magazine *HITS*. Known for its biting humor aimed at various record executives and radio programmers, the editors of *HITS*, in the magazine's June 1 edition, insinuated that Kurt Cobain was "dancing with Mr. Brownstone," a reference to the Guns N' Roses song about shooting heroin. But rumors of Kurt's heroin use were still unconfirmed at this time, and Kurt would publicly deny that he was suffering from any debilitating illness or heroin abuse.

Before the month of June ended, Nirvana began a ten-date tour of Europe, a tour that would mark the beginning of the dark and tragic side of the final years of Kurt Cobain's life.

Fourteen

My father said this to me: "I know why you guys have sold
so many records—cause the video's got a bunch of kids trashing
a gymnasium." And, I mean, that sort of works.

—DAVE GROHL

Good news wasn't hard to come by for Nirvana as the band prepared to depart for its ten-date 1992 European tour in June. Their live set list hadn't changed much since the beginning of the year, though now and then a curveball like "Scoff," "Son of a Gun," or "Swap Meet" would be added to the mix. They even played the very obscure "The Money Will Roll Right In" when the band landed in Sweden and Spain. *Nevermind* had officially sold over one million copies in the United States, there were 300,000 copies sold in the United Kingdom, and the new single, "Lithium," had debuted on the *Billboard* Album Rock Chart on June 20 (it peaked at number eleven on the UK chart and at number sixteen on *Billboard*).

However, suspicions of Kurt Cobain's drug addiction had begun to fester, causing subtle rifts in the Nirvana camp. In an interview with *New Musical Express* magazine, Kurt denied suggestions that he had a heroin addiction. With plans for a follow-up to *Nevermind* now being made, Kurt predicted the band would lose half of their audience, because the new album (which Nirvana did not record until 1993) would not be as accessible, or radio-friendly, as *Nevermind*.

June 23, 1992, a rainy and gloomy day, began with a terrifying episode: Kurt collapsed in convulsions over breakfast. After an uninspired gig at the

Point Depot in Dublin, Ireland, the night before, Kurt had forgotten to take the methadone pills he had been taking to battle his increasing heroin dependence. The press was all over the story, some attributing the incident to a drug overdose. Nirvana's management doused the story with unwavering denials, and the tour continued uninterrupted later that evening at King's Hall in Belfast.

The Breeders and Teenage Fan Club opened the show in front of more than ten thousand screaming fans, but before Nirvana hit the stage, Kurt clashed with overenthusiastic security guards. A reporter for *Select* magazine saw the frightful-looking lead singer nibbling on food that night, his hair dyed deathly white. Wearing glasses to disguise himself, Kurt looked like a ghost. The reporter asked him about drugs, but Kurt again denied his heroin use.

Nevertheless, after the gig, Kurt was rushed to a local hospital with abdominal pains. He was suffering from what doctors called stomach ulcers, due partly to the strain put on his abdomen from his ferocious vocal technique and partly to his unwavering diet of junk food.

While he couldn't confirm Kurt's heroin problem, the *Select* reporter did get one of the first looks at the pregnant Courtney, whom he found hanging around backstage smoking a cigarette.

Before the band finished the tour, articles in newspapers and tabloids the world over called Courtney an unfit mother. But while in Europe, Kurt and Courtney got to see a sonogram of their child in Courtney's womb. "Oh god, it was incredible, it was one of the most amazing things," Kurt recalled. "It wasn't just a picture—it was a video, so you could see her moving around. It was the first time we realized she was a living thing. You could see her heart beating."

Nirvana's touring machine closed out June with stops in France, Denmark, Finland, Norway, and Sweden, and landed in Spain in July. But the tour was cut short as Courtney struggled with her pregnancy. She was admitted to a Spanish hospital out of fear that the baby was in danger. Following the instructions of the baby's doctor, the Cobains immediately flew home.

On July 21, DGC released the "Lithium" single to retail, along with, in a welcome gesture, a transcript of the lyrics from *Nevermind*. For the first time, people could actually figure out what Kurt was saying in "Smells Like Teen

Spirit." The single also included the song "Curmudgeon," and a live version of "Been a Son" recorded during the October 31, 1991, Halloween show.

Scenes shot at that Halloween gig and clips from *1991: The Year Punk Broke,* make up the video for "Lithium," which was released shortly after the release of the "Lithium" single. Kevin Kerslake handled the directing duties. The original idea for the video involved some very detailed animation, but when told that process could take up to four months to create, both Kerslake and the band agreed it would be easier to make a video montage of past performances quickly and efficiently.

On August 4, with the birth of his child just a few weeks away, Kurt checked into Cedars-Sinai to detox, spending a total of twenty-five days there. In that month's issue of *Vanity Fair* magazine, an article written by Lynn Hirschberg profiling Kurt and Courtney included a comparison to Sid Vicious and Nancy Spungen, the punk rock Romeo and Juliet who died tragically in the early 1980s. Hirschberg was not the first to depict the Cobains this way, and the recurring reference was starting to wear thin on Kurt. "It's just amazing that at this point in rock-and-roll history, people are still expecting their rock icons to live out these classic rock archetypes, like Sid and Nancy," he said. "To assume that we're just the same because we come from the underground and we did heroin for a while—it's pretty offensive to be expected to be like that."

The article was the most damaging portrait of Cobain and Love that had yet appeared. Courtney spoke openly about her and Kurt's drug and alcohol abuse; the revelation's shock waves would be felt throughout the rock community.

"We went on a binge. We did a lot of drugs," Courtney said candidly to Hirschberg, referring to a trip to New York City earlier in the year. "We got pills and then we went down to Alphabet City and Kurt wore a hat, I wore a hat, and we copped some dope. Then we got high and went to *Saturday Night Live* [Nirvana's first appearance]. After that, I did heroin for a couple of months . . . [Kurt] tried to be an alcoholic for a long time, but it didn't sit right with him."

Hirschberg's article quoted sources who claimed that Courtney had been using drugs during her months of pregnancy, though Courtney said she had begun detoxing immediately after she found out she was pregnant. "I didn't have a baby to stop doing drugs," Courtney said later. "But I knew that if I would continue to do drugs my career would go to hell and I wouldn't give a shit and I'd be one of those junkies that I've seen at N.A. [Narcotics Anonymous] meetings with track marks on their hands and neck."

"Courtney was honest about the heroin excursion we went on for a few months," said Kurt. "Then Courtney found herself pregnant, realized she was pregnant and had a drug problem, and got off of drugs. It's as simple as that. But [the *Vanity Fair* story] made it look like . . . Courtney was nine months pregnant and still doing drugs." Still, the article was a devastating blow to Kurt and Courtney's relationship. "I wouldn't have thought that I could be dwarfed or squashed or raped or incredibly hurt by a story in that magazine, but the power of it was so intense," Courtney recalled. "It was unbelievable. I read a fax of it and my bones shook. I knew that my world was over. [Kurt cried] for weeks. It was nothing but crying. All we did was cry. It was horrible."

Hirschberg's story cited the prevalent belief that Courtney had turned Kurt on to heroin. Shelli Novoselic knew that Courtney had nothing to do with Kurt's heroin addiction. "Everybody was blaming Courtney," she said in an interview cited in Michael Azerrad's *Come as You Are*. "She was the big scapegoat. If Kurt wouldn't have hooked up with her, he would have hooked up with somebody else and done heroin. That's just the fact of the matter. It was easy to blame her . . . because she's loud and outspoken and has her own point of view."

A few weeks after the article was published, Kurt was detoxing in the same hospital where Frances Bean Cobain was born at 7:48 A.M. on August 18, 1992. Had she been a boy, Frances would have been named for Eugene, after Eugene Kelly of the Vaselines; instead, Kurt and Courtney agreed on Frances, after Kelly's partner in the Vaselines, Frances McKee. They added Bean as a middle name because they both felt Frances looked like a kidney bean in her early sonograms. Or was she named Bean from Carolyn Chute's novel, *The Beans of Egypt, Maine*? "Let's start saying, 'Yes,' because it'll be the intellectually correct answer," Courtney said. In an interview in the December 1992 issue of *Spin* magazine, Kurt and Courtney failed to verify either story:

Spin: Well, there is a white-trash mythology that surrounds both your bands to a certain degree. *Beans of Egypt, Maine,* is, like, the ultimate white-trash novel.

Kurt: Well, that's the reason we named her.

Spin: It's a great book.

Kurt: We're waiting for it to come out on video.

Courtney: We don't like them books.

Kurt: Them books is hard to read.

Contrary to previously published reports, Courtney's smoking habit did not affect Frances Bean's birth weight; she was born a healthy seven pounds, one ounce. Courtney recalled the day of Frances Bean's birth: "I'm having the baby, it's coming out, [Kurt's] puking, he's passing out, and I'm holding his hand and rubbing his stomach while the baby's coming out of me. It was pretty weird." Kurt, in spite of his ailment, was overcome by the father-in-waiting emotion. "I was so fucking scared—it was probably a classic case of what the typical father goes through. I was just so weak and sick and afraid that something was going to happen to Courtney or the baby."

The horror of Kurt being high on heroin while she was giving birth is still fresh in Courtney's mind. "The day Frances was born this dealer came to the hospital [to see Kurt]. There were eight thousand nurses and doctors outside the door, and Kurt was in the hospital, on a morphine drip for his stomach. He's already on a fucking morphine drip, and then he arranges for this dealer to come and stick a needle into the IV!"

"Although I was doing drugs right up to before she was born, I did try to stop a couple of times during that period," said Kurt sadly. "I didn't get it out of my system, but I knew I had to keep on trying. Otherwise there might have been a chance that I would dabble in it when she was around. And I didn't wanna do that at all, that's a totally dangerous thing. Again, I don't regret anything—it's something I had to do, it was part of my rehabilitation. But the whole thing seriously almost ruined us, it was a really hard thing to go through."

His burgeoning addiction to heroin, the pressure and publicity of the *Vanity Fair* article, the birth of Frances Bean, and the unwanted burden of being an international icon: All of these were beginning to overwhelm Kurt, and pulled him into depths of depression he had never before experienced. In response to the *Vanity Fair* article, the Los Angeles County Department of Children's Services took action, threatening to relieve Kurt and Courtney of custody of Frances Bean. Two weeks after her birth, a judge ordered that Frances Bean be turned over to the custody of Courtney's sister until Kurt completed a thirty-day detoxing. Courtney pleaded with those who would listen that she had been clean from the moment she found out that she was pregnant, and that she was perfectly fit to care for the child.

"It was all a total scam," Kurt told Michael Azerrad about the incident. "It was an attempt to use us as an example because we stand for everything that goes against the grain of conformist American entertainment. It was a witch hunt. Social Services literally took the *Vanity Fair* article and Xeroxed it and then took that pee test that Courtney took in the first trimester of her pregnancy and used that as an excuse to take our baby away.

"It was just so humiliating and it just felt like so many powerful people were out to get us that it just seemed hopeless. It didn't seem like we'd ever win. It was amazing. We were totally suicidal. It's not the right time for a woman trying to get rid of the hormonal problems of just having a baby and me just getting off of drugs and just being bombarded with this. It was just too much."

As the *Musician* magazine interview continued, Kurt's anger grew. "I just decided, 'Fuck this, I don't want to be in a band anymore. It just isn't worth it. I want to kill [Hirschberg]. As soon as I get out of this fucking hospital, I'm going to kill this woman with my bare hands: I'm going to stab her to death. First I'm going to take her dog and slit its guts out in front of her and then shit all over her and stab her to death.' She'd better hope to God that someday I don't find myself destitute without a wife and a baby. Because I'll fucking get revenge on her. Before I leave this earth, she's going out with me."

The anger and devastation had welled up so much inside the two of them that Kurt and Courtney, in one very sad chapter of their brief story together, considered suicide. Then Courtney thought of Frances Bean. "I was like 'I'll go first. I can't have you do it first. I go first.' I held this thing in my hand. And I felt that thing that they said in *Schindler's List*: I'm never going to know what happens to me. And what about Frances? Sort of rude, '*Oh, your parents died the day after you were born.*' I just started talking [Kurt] out of it. And he said, 'Fuck you, you can't chicken out. I'm gonna do it.' But I made him give me the gun, and I had Eric [Erlandson from Hole] take it away."

Miraculously, only those very close to the band knew any of this was occurring. Erlandson visited Courtney and Kurt frequently throughout this period, and the Cobains thanked him by putting him in their will. "[Eric] totally saved our lives during that whole time," said Kurt. "He was the only piece of reality, the only calm person who was there as any example of what life could be like afterward, once this crazy shit was over with." As far as the public was concerned, Nirvana's exclusion from the public eye merely suggested that the band was preparing for their upcoming live appearance on the 1992 *MTV Video Music Awards* in September. But before that would happen, Nirvana committed themselves to playing a special "No on 9" benefit concert at the County Fairgrounds in Portland, Oregon, on August 22. The "No on 9" campaign was a hot voting issue in the Pacific Northwest. It was a measure that if passed could prohibit any positive or neutral mention of gay people or issues involving the gay community in Portland's classrooms. The tension from protesters and supporters at the event fueled the already strained relationship between Kurt and Axl Rose. Nirvana had turned down the invitation to tour with Guns N' Roses, but until this show they had kept quiet about their true feelings about their label mates. Then, in a bizarre onstage incident, a fan demanded that Kurt lay down his sword and he responded.

"When we played that 'No on 9' benefit in Portland, I said something about Guns N' Roses," Kurt explained. "Nothing real nasty—I think I said, 'And now for our next song, "Sweet Child O' Mine." ' But some kid jumped onstage and said, 'Hey man, Guns N' Roses plays awesome music, and Nirvana plays awesome music. Let's just get along and work this out, man!' And I just couldn't help but say, 'No, kid, you're really wrong. Those people are total sexist jerks, and the reason we're playing this show is to fight homophobia in a real small way. [Axl Rose] is a fucking sexist and a racist and a homophobe, and you can't be on his side and be on our side. I'm sorry that I have to divide this up like this but it's something you can't ignore. And besides, they can't write good music.'"

After a gig at the Seattle Center Coliseum on August 23, Nirvana landed in England on the thirtieth to play the Reading Festival, a show in which

Kurt was inexplicably brought onstage in a wheelchair. Kurt was making a joke about the noise that he was a junkie. He proceeded to sing "The Rose" and then fall down on the stage. The trio launched into "Breed," a performance that was captured in the Sonic Youth video chronicle *1991: The Year Punk Broke*. At that year's festival, Nirvana stormed through a twenty-five-song set of *Bleach, Nevermind,* and *In Utero* tunes, including a version of "tourettes" that can be found on *From the Muddy Banks of the Wishkah*. Also appearing at the festival were Screaming Trees, the Melvins, L7, Mudhoney, Eugenius, Pavement, Nick Cave, and Björn Again, an Abba tribute band.

On September 8, at the Pauley Pavilion on the campus of UCLA in Los Angeles, California, the 1992 *MTV Video Music Awards* took center stage on television sets across the United States and throughout the world. In less than a year, MTV had not only introduced mainstream America to some of the newest alternative genres in pop music, they had also institutionalized a new buzzword that even parents seemed to understand: grunge. It didn't necessarily define the culture of America's youth, but it certainly labeled it. And that night's show featured live performances by what the American music industry considered to be its top two grunge acts, Nirvana and Pearl Jam, along with performances by the Red Hot Chili Peppers, the Black Crowes, Guns N' Roses, the Cure, Brian Adams, Eric Clapton, En Vogue, Elton John, and Michael Jackson. Nirvana, riding the crest of the successful "Smells Like Teen Spirit" video, had been nominated in three categories by MTV viewers: Best New Artist, Best Alternative Video, and Best Video of the Year. In an example of how far Nirvana had crept into the American mainstream, Weird Al Yankovic was nominated for an award for his parody video, "Smells Like Nirvana." Though he did not win, the video rejuvenated Yankovic's career. "We were the foundation of Weird Al Yankovic's comeback," Kurt noted a few months later.

Marring what should have been a celebratory event for the band, the staff at the MTV Awards gave Nirvana problems from the moment they arrived in Los Angeles. The day before the show, the band had been rehearsing two songs, "Rape Me" and a new song called "New Poopy," but MTV predictably demanded that the band perform "Smells Like Teen Spirit" or its current national single, "Lithium." The band gave in to playing "Lithium," though they still wanted to play "Rape Me." But Danny Goldberg tried to convince the boys to do as they wished. "[Danny] was the only person Kurt trusted," Courtney said. "At that time, you didn't say 'fuck you' to MTV; you just didn't do it. A lot of people were saying, 'You've got to do it [play what MTV asked for]. Do you understand the consequences for your career if you don't? They will kill you.' Then Danny called up and said, 'Neil Young wouldn't do it, and neither would Bob Dylan. Don't do it.' That sold Kurt on Danny for the rest of his life."

They had decided to play "Lithium," but just as they were introduced, Kurt started playing the chords of "Rape Me." A few seconds later, they kicked into "Lithium." Toward the end of the song, the band ripped into the usual equipment destruction, this time with dangerous consequences: When Krist threw his bass way up in the air, it came flying back down on his head. He stumbled away, but as they were leaving the stage, Kurt kicked Krist in the ass, unaware that Krist was hurt. (He later apologized.) Krist explained how it felt to have his bass fall on his head: "It was tremendously liberating. It was like an epiphany. Everyone needs a good knock on the head once in awhile, be it actual or metaphorical. Some religious people actually go so far as to crucify themselves, so either it had a lot of meaning or it doesn't mean shit. Did it hurt? Yeah, I was a bloody mess."

For the first award that Nirvana won, Best Alternative Video, they sent a Michael Jackson impersonator onstage to accept the award. As Kurt explained it, his intention was to show the viewers of America that he was being treated with the same public scrutiny and invasion of privacy as was Michael Jackson, so it didn't matter who accepted the award. "I wanted it to be used as a reminder that I'm dealing with the same thing," Kurt said afterward. "All rock stars have to deal with it. It's the fault of the fans and the media." But the bit went down like a lead zeppelin: the joke was lost on nearly everyone in the audience.

When it was announced that they had won the award for Best New Artist, MTV personnel urged them to accept the award themselves. They agreed, but they regretted it almost immediately. The stage was unlike any they had been on before. "I was just kind of nervous up there," Kurt recalled. "When we played, I didn't look out in the audience to realize how big it was. And once I got up there, I realized millions of people are watching and it's a really big place and these lights are really bright and I don't want to be here, this is really stupid. I just wanted to leave right away." When Kurt finally looked into the camera, he said, "You know, it's really hard to believe everything you read," no doubt alluding to the *Vanity Fair* article and the subsequent bad press.

By now, Kurt's comments about Guns N' Roses made several days earlier had made their way back to Axl Rose, who was anxious to greet Nirvana when they returned backstage. "They actually tried to beat us up!" Kurt said. "Courtney and I were with the baby in the eating area backstage, and Axl walked by. So Courtney yelled, 'Axl! Axl, come over here!' We just wanted to say hi to him—we think he's a joke, but we just wanted to say something to him. So I said, 'Will you be the godfather of our child?' I don't know what had happened before that to piss him off, but he took his aggressions out on us and began screaming bloody murder. These were his words: 'You shut your bitch up, or I'm taking you down to the pavement.' Everyone around us just burst out into tears of laughter. She wasn't even saying anything mean, you know? So I turned to Courtney and said, 'Shut up, bitch!' And everyone laughed, and he left. So I guess I did what he wanted me to do—be a man. Later [when] we were walking back to our trailer, the Guns N' Roses entourage came walking toward us. They have at least fifty bodyguards apiece— huge, gigantic, brain-dead oafs ready to kill for Axl at all times. They didn't see me, but they surrounded Krist, and [Guns N' Roses bassist] Duff [McKagan] wanted to beat Krist up, and the bodyguards started pushing Krist around. He finally escaped, but throughout the rest of the evening, there was a big threat of either Guns N' Roses themselves or their goons beating us up."

It was this kind of small-minded, violent gesture that confirmed for Kurt how entirely different the two bands were. Kurt even attempted to deflate talk of competition for fans between the two bands. "I don't feel like I'm competing at all. I've said in public enough times that I don't give a fuck about his audience. We do come from the same kind of background. We come from small towns and we've been surrounded by a lot of sexism and racism most of our lives. But our internal struggles are pretty different. I feel like I've allowed myself to open my mind to a lot more things than he has. His role has been played for years. Ever since the beginning of rock 'n' roll, there's been an Axl Rose. And it's just boring, it's totally boring to me. Why it's such a fresh and new thing in [Axl Rose's] eyes is obviously because it's happening to him personally and he's such an egotistical person that he thinks that the whole world owes him something."

The evening was winding down, and the Nirvana entourage headed back into Pauley Pavilion to watch the rest of the show. The band was particularly keen to see another one of their rivals, Pearl Jam, play in front of a huge national audience. When his band was done with their performance, Eddie Vedder stood at the side of the stage watching Eric Clapton play his big hit, "Tears in Heaven." Courtney walked up to Vedder and started to slow-dance with him. Kurt eventually made his way over to him. "I stared into his eyes and told him that I thought he was a respectable human," Kurt said plainly. "And I did tell him straight out that I still think his band sucks. I said, 'After watching you perform, I realized that you are a person that does have some passion.' It's not a fully contrived thing. There are plenty of other more evil people out in the world than him and he doesn't deserve to be scapegoated like that."

It was becoming increasingly difficult for Kurt to avoid talking about his heroin problem as 1992 began to wane. For the press, the story was familiar enough. Throughout the history of rock 'n' roll, drug use had led plenty of musicians to their deaths. But there was always that insatiable desire to get to the bottom of truth or rumor. And until that truth or rumor was fully exposed, it could continue to harm to all involved. Kurt knew this, and it tore at him every day. In September, a profile on Cobain by pop critic Robert Hilburn appeared in the *Los Angeles Times*, revealing that Kurt had done heroin for three weeks earlier in 1992. In a detailed interview with Amy Raphael the following year in *The Face* (September 1993) Kurt spoke about that troubled period.

"It's a part of my life that I'm not too proud of. It's been going on for years. Then I slowly decided not to self-destruct. I wasn't familiar with what heroin does to people. I did it first in 'eighty-five/'eighty-six in Aberdeen. I'd wanted to try it forever. I wanted to be a junkie for a few months after *Nevermind* and the tour. It was a really stupid idea. I didn't understand how evil it is, how hard it is to get off it. It's the most addictive thing I've ever tried. It's an ongoing dilemma. I still have problems with it. This year I've fucked up a few times. But I'm not addicted anymore. I haven't had any drug dealings for a long time. I couldn't fool myself or anyone else that I won't do it again; I'll always be a junkie. I've had to excommunicate my drug-taking friends and focus on my family and my music.

"I'm afraid of dying now, I don't want to leave behind my wife and child, so I don't do things that would jeopardize my life. I try and do as little things as I can to jeopardize it. I don't want to die. I've been suicidal most of my life, I didn't really care if I lived or died, and there were plenty of times when I wanted to die, but I never had the nerve to actually try it."

Kurt claimed that the changes in his family circumstances would be what saved him. "Fatherhood has completely changed my whole outlook on everything. I don't know . . . It's nice to know that we can have the luxury of a nanny. It's great that [Frances Bean is] never ignored. And she's learning to have relationships with people. When we were young, Courtney and I were both very trusting and naive. But . . . Just finding a marriage partner, a soulmate, I never expected it to happen. I wasn't nearly as self-destructive as has been sometimes reported."

For friends close to the Nirvana camp, Kurt's heroin use would not fade away as quickly or as simply as they or he would have hoped. But there was still good news around the corner to lift their spirits and take the spotlight off all of Kurt and Courtney's private troubles. There were more shows to play in the places where Nirvana always felt at home.

Two unannounced shows with Mudhoney put a familiar spark back into Kurt, Krist, and Dave. The first gig was at Western Washington University in Bellingham on October 3. The following night, Nirvana opened for Mudhoney at the Crocodile Cafe in Seattle (the last Nirvana show legendary photographer Charles Peterson would shoot). Happiness seemed to overcome Kurt on this evening. He was back in his element, with his people, away from public curiosity and scrutiny. He took a flying stage dive during Mudhoney's set, got back on the stage, was handed a guitar by Krist, and jammed on some punk covers with the band. Kurt's interaction with the audience was priceless. Many watched Nirvana in amazement, others with sheer joy.

The demos for the upcoming album, *In Utero*, were also cut in October, with Jack Endino at the control board. Naturally, a bootleg CD called *In Utero Demos* hit the streets, featuring alternate versions of the entire album, plus the outtakes from the sessions—"I Hate Myself and I Want to Die," "Marigold," and "MV."

After all that had happened to them over the past few months, Nirvana seemed to be back to their old anarchic selves again. They packed up their gear and headed to Buenos Aires, Argentina, for a show on the night before Halloween. "When we played Buenos Aires, we brought this all-girl band over from Portland called Calamity Jane," Kurt recalled. "During their entire set, the whole audience—it was a huge show with like sixty thousand people—was throwing money and everything out of their pockets, mud and rocks, just pelting them. Eventually the girls stormed off crying. It was terrible, one of the worst things I've ever seen, such a mass of sexism all at once. Krist, knowing my attitude about things like that, tried to talk me out of at least setting myself on fire or refusing to play. We ended up just having fun, laughing at them [the audience]. Before every song, I'd play the intro to 'Smells Like Teen Spirit' and then stop. They didn't realize that we were protesting against what they'd done. We played for about forty minutes, and most of the songs were off *Incesticide*, so they didn't recognize anything. We wound up playing the secret noise song ["Endless Nameless"] that's at the end of *Nevermind*, and because we were so in a rage and were just so pissed off about this whole situation, that song and the whole set were one of the greatest experiences I've ever had."

The fourth video from *Nevermind* came out in November. "In Bloom" is one of Nirvana's best videos, and to produce it the band again called on the talents of video vet Kevin Kerslake, who had directed "Come as You Are." The concept for "In Bloom" was simple: filmed in black and white, the video would give the impression that Nirvana was on a 1960s Ed Sullivan–like television show debuting their new hit single. Hiring the right characters, having the right look, and displaying the right attitude was the key to the concept's success. First, Nirvana hired Doug Llewelyn from the TV show *The People's Court* to be the Ed Sullivan–like emcee character at the beginning and end of the video. His introduction, like the video, was intentionally directed at those in the media who lambasted Nirvana as out-of-control grungers and a menace to society: "Next, ladies and gentleman, we have three fine young men from Seattle [crowd cheers]. They're coming, hold on, they're coming. They're thoroughly all right and decent fellows with their hit single, 'In Bloom.'" The trio even got a dig in at all the phonies who professed to be hip to the underground scene but clearly were not, as Llewelyn mispronounced the band's name: "Here they are, Nirvannah!!"

The brilliance of this video shines through as Nirvana kicks into "In Bloom," with Kerslake using camera angles and set designs that accurately mimic television music shows of this time period. Kurt, smiling stupidly as he sings and staring straight at the camera, wears thick black-rimmed glasses, and his hair is slicked back behind the ears. Dave wears a short blond wig, and Krist cut his hair really short to complement the high-water pantsuits the trio are wearing. Vintage footage of kids screaming in the audience coupled with sharp camera cuts to the band acknowledging those screams with smiling head nods make the video hilarious.

But midway through the "In Bloom" video, footage of Nirvana wearing dresses and playing on the same stage are inserted. Now the images are flashed back and forth, with an applause track added to broaden the cheesy TV feel. Typically, Nirvana-in-drag trashes their set, while Nirvana-in-suits continue to play as though they were the Chesterfield Trio. Finally, Doug Llewleyn walks back onstage and says, "All right, everybody, let's hear it for these three nice decent clean-cut young men. I can't really say enough nice things about them. They're gonna be really big stars."

In December, Nirvana was named *Spin* magazine Artist of the Year, and four Nirvana songs were ranked in MTV's *Top 100 Video Countdown* ("Smells Like Teen Spirit" at number eight, "Come as You Are" at number twenty-one, "In Bloom" at number forty, and "Lithium" at number fifty-nine). On the day after Christmas, the latest single, "In Bloom," debuted on the *Billboard* Album Rock Chart. For seventeen weeks it remained there, charting as high as number five. Dave seemed a little overwhelmed by it all. "See, this thing is like a first for me, it's like this new experience and it's something that I never really expected to happen," he said, looking back on the year. "But now that it's happening I'm sort of thinking, 'Well, maybe it's not that I didn't expect it, it's that I really didn't want it to happen.' I just want to go out and play music to people who are gonna dig it."

"I get recognized every day, *every* day," Krist said with amazement. "I just kind of get used to it."

Added Kurt, "I'll never get used to it."

Even Krist, who usually enjoys the spotlight, appeared uncomfortable with the idea of being beamed into so many homes on a regular basis. "*Nevermind* goes platinum and we're all over MTV and it's like weird, like, now what?" he asked no one in particular. "Where do we go from here? Are we going to be Led Zeppelin and the big band of the 'nineties or are we just going to fall apart?"

Numbers, sales figures, and chart action were annoying subplots to Nirvana's artistic vision of themselves. "That's what I'm not excited about, 'Hey! We're number four! with Garth Brooks' and all that other shit," said Krist. "I don't give a shit about that."

Understandably, Kurt's vision of what he would do with his fifteen minutes of fame reflected back to his original dreams as a teenager for what he thought would lead to a happy life. "We'd like to buy a house. And live in it. To actually have a place to live. Yeah. I'd like to put money into the bands that I like and help promote them. I'd like to toss a few bills to some independent bands."

True to the punk-rock ethic, Kurt was always looking for a way to help other underground bands. "I guess the best part would be being in the position to take other bands, whom you like a lot, on tour with you. It's definitely a nice thing to be able to do. We took Shonen Knife, a three-piece all-girl Japanese band, on tour with us in England. They've been a favorite of ours for years. And no one really knows who they are in England or anywhere in Europe."

That sort of precious anonymity was no longer within Kurt's reach. "I wanted to at least sell enough records to be able to eat macaroni and cheese, so I didn't have to have a job," said the now-wealthy Kurt. "I can't stand it when people come up to me and say, 'Congratulations on your *success!*' I want to ask them, 'Do you like the songs? Do you like the album?' Selling two million records isn't successful to me unless it's good."

Fame and success often go hand in hand, and Kurt was finding them both to be increasingly annoying elements of his life. He was constantly under the public's microscope, and it was steadily pushing him further and further away from living his life on his own terms. "I don't want to have a long career if I have to put up with the same stuff that I'm putting up with. I'm trying it one last time, and if it's more of a pleasant year for us, then fine, we'll have a career. But I'm not going to subject myself to being stuck in an apartment building for the next ten years and being afraid to go outside of my house. It's not worth it. I would gladly give up music for my life. It's more important."

Fifteen

I really don't have much sympathy for people who buy *[Nevermind]*,
or who buy anyone's record, who just buy it because it's popular
and they think they should be hip and cool.
Those kind of people I can do without.

—KURT COBAIN

To celebrate their remarkable leap from beer parties in Aberdeen to live performances on national and worldwide television in the winter of 1992, Nirvana released *Incesticide*, a collection of B sides and hard-to-find recordings. Jack Endino recalled that "when they were planning *Incesticide*, Krist called me up and wanted to know if I remembered 'Blandest' [an unreleased song from the *Bleach* sessions] and if there was a tape of it anywhere. I told him, 'No, you guys told me to erase it.' Imagine how spooked I was when I later heard it on a bootleg . . . tenth-generation cassette tape hiss, horrible fried three A.M rough mix and all."

Though most of the material on *Incesticide* was familiar to serious fans ("Sliver" and "Aneurysm" had been performed live by Nirvana extensively over the previous two years), three of the songs—"Aero Zeppelin," "Hairspray Queen," and "Big Long Now"—had never been made available.

The songs and performances on *Incesticide* offered a welcome, if random, glimpse at the band's development since the late 1980s. "Dive" originally appeared as the B side of the 1990 7-inch "Sliver;" it was recorded in April 1990 and produced by Butch Vig. Chad Channing played drums on this song, another rewrite of the heavy string-band grunge formula.

"Stain" had first been released on the 1989 Sub Pop EP *Blew*. It was produced by Steve Fisk at a studio that mostly recorded TV and radio commercials. The *Incesticide* version of "Been a Son" is taken from the 1991 BBC Mark Goodier recording session; it is an upbeat version of the same song that appears on *Blew*.

The two *Blew* songs were followed by three covers. "Turnaround" is a remake of the B side of Devo's breakout single "Whip It." Nirvana's version was recorded in England at the 1990 BBC John Peel recording session, and can also be found on the Japanese/Australian EP *Hormoaning*.

"Molly's Lips" was Nirvana's favorite Vaselines song, with "Son of a Gun" a close runner-up. Those, too, derived from the 1990 John Peel session, and were also released on *Hormoaning*. The lyrics Kurt sings on "Molly's Lips" are incomplete; apparently Kurt forgot to write them down. The power-pop version of "(New Wave) Polly" is taken from the 1991 BBC Mark Goodier session. This is a more amped-up version than the softer acoustic rendering that appears on *Nevermind*.

"Hmm . . . 1 think I may have grown a bit as a lyricist" since writing "Downer," Kurt said in DGC's official press release for *Incesticide*. "Downer" was first released as a bonus track on import CD versions of *Bleach*. It was recorded in 1988 at Reciprocal Studios with Jack Endino; Dale Crover played drums. Also taken from this session for *Incesticide* was "Mexican Seafood," which first appeared on the compilation *Teriyaki Asthma* on C/Z Records, and "Beeswax," released the previous year on the various-artist collection *Kill Rock Stars*. "Hairspray Queen" and "Aero Zeppelin," both early demo versions, also featured Dale Crover. The band didn't think much of these tunes originally; in the press release, Kurt made short work of "Aero Zeppelin." "Christ! Let's just throw together some heavy metal riffs in no particular order," he gibed, "and give it a quirky name in homage to a couple of our favorite masturbatory 'seventies rock acts."

"Big Long Now," with Chad Channing on drums, was recorded in 1989 for *Bleach*, but failed to make the final cut. "Aneurysm" was taken from the Goodier BBC session. It had originally appeared as a bonus track on the "Smells Like Teen Spirit" CD maxisingle, and was also included on the *Hormoaning* EP.

Ironically, though tongue-in-cheek, the original title for *Incesticide* was

"Cash Cow." It had first been intended as a Sub Pop release, but after some consideration, the band decided the joke wasn't that funny after all. And while it would have been very punk to put it out on Sub Pop, distribution was still an important issue for Nirvana, and Sub Pop couldn't deliver the way Geffen could.

The album features some Kurt Cobain artwork and, for the first time, liner notes written by Kurt. When the record was first released, critics viewed the notes as a gesture by Kurt toward people who had recently made his life a living hell, but it was really directed at people Kurt looked at from the stage, people who simply wanted a piece of him and the band just because they were popular, riding their fifteen minutes of fame. "That's been the biggest problem that I've had being in this band," Kurt said. "I know there are those people out in the audience, and there's not much I can do about it. I can talk about those issues in interviews . . . I think it's pretty obvious that we're against the homophobes and the sexists and the racists, but when '[Smells Like] Teen Spirit' first came out, mainstream audiences were under the assumption that we were just like Guns N' Roses. Then our opinions started showing up in interviews. And then things like Krist and I kissing on *Saturday Night Live*. We weren't trying to be subversive or punk rock; we were just doing something insane and stupid at the last minute. I think now that our opinions are out in the open, a lot of kids who bought our record regret knowing anything about us."

He continued, "There is this war going on in the high schools now between Nirvana kids and Guns N' Roses kids. It's really cool. I'm really proud to be a part of that, because when I was in high school, I dressed like a punk rocker and people would scream 'Devo!' at me, because Devo infiltrated the mainstream. Out of all the bands who came from the underground and actually made it in the mainstream, Devo is the most subversive and challenging of all. They're just awesome. I love them."

The liner notes for *Incesticide* provide the Nirvana fan with a deep look into the mind of the group's embattled lead singer. But, fearing the flak of unnecessary negative press, Geffen edited one portion of Kurt's rantings. "I just went into the *Vanity Fair* and media scam," said Kurt, about his never-seen attack. "It was really negative, although it was very truthful. It came straight from my heart and I really felt that and I still do. Anyone looking back on it would see complaining. No one has enough empathy for me or Courtney to look beyond that and realize that it should be a legitimate complaint."

The last paragraph of Kurt Cobain's liner notes from *Incesticide* sum up the year 1992 for Nirvana, the most exciting year in the too-short history of the band.

I don't feel the least bit guilty for commercially exploiting a completely ex-hausted Rock youth Culture because, at this point in rock history, Punk Rock (while still sacred to some) is, to me, dead and gone. We just wanted to pay tribute to something that helped us to feel as though we had crawled out of the dung heap of conformity. To pay tribute like an Elvis or Jimi Hendrix impersonator in the tradition of a bar band. I'll be the first to admit we're the 90's version of Cheap Trick or The Knack but the last to admit that it hasn't been rewarding. At this point I have a request for our fans. If any of you in any way hate homosexuals, people of different color, or women, please do this favor for us—leave us the fuck alone! Don't come to our shows and don't buy our records. Last year, a girl was raped by two wastes of sperm and eggs while they sang the lyrics to our song, "Polly." I have a hard time carrying on knowing there are plankton like that in our audience. Sorry to be so anally P.C. but that's the way I feel.

Love,
Kurdt (the blonde one)

Sixteen

Start a band . . . Especially girls. They should start bands.
There aren't enough girl musicians.

—KURT COBAIN

To say that 1993 was tumultuous for Kurt Cobain would be an under-statement. Nevertheless, the events of that year helped to free him from the bondage of bitterness that had become rooted within his mind-set. "My attitudes and opinions have only got more optimistic in the last couple of years and that's because of having a child and being in love," he said that year. "It's the only thing I feel I've been blessed with. For years, that's the life I was searching for. I wanted a partner. I wanted security. I wanted a family. Every-thing else is totally irrelevant."

"Two years ago I never thought about the future, not at all," he told an interviewer for *Melody Maker*. "But now I have this huge responsibility to my family and it's probably more pressure than I've ever had dealing with this band. Now I'm thinking about not leaving the child in the car, not even for a second, in case someone snatches her, all kinds of things like that.

"In the last year and a half, even before we found out Courtney was preg-nant, I've started to evolve a little bit from being a completely negative bastard, pretending to be punk rock and hating the world and saying clichéd things like, 'Anyone who brings a child into the world at this point is completely selfish.' "

Courtney and Kurt met and married faster than expected, and Courtney's subsequent pregnancy surprised everyone; Kurt himself expressed some regrets about its timing. "We wanted to have a baby," said Kurt. "We definitely wanted to have a baby. But not at [the] time [that we did]. It happened too soon. I really wish [Frances's birth] could have waited. But . . . I'm totally happy about my family situation."

"Kurt's the right person to have a baby with," Courtney told Lynn Hirshberg in the *Vanity Fair* article. "We have money. I can have a nanny. The whole feminine experience of pregnancy and birth—I'm not into it on that level." And yet there was a perverse streak to her attitude. "But it was a bad time to get pregnant," she said, "and that appealed to me."

Though he had few positive memories of his father, fatherhood came naturally for Kurt Cobain. "Oh yeah, embarrassingly so," he said. "I'm always making noises and acting the fool. It's really fun though, it gives me an excuse to do that again. And it's great to have Frances around. We took her to the photo shoot and [Frances] took my mind off the monotony of having to stand in front of the camera. Every few seconds, I would look over to [her] and make fart noises to make her smile."

Asked if being a father was having any effect on his songwriting, Cobain reflected that it was still too early to judge, that he was enjoying the role of daddy too much to be to concerned about writing new material. "The biggest impact of having a child is personally," he said. "I've always been chronically depressed, or at least pessimistic, for part of each day. Now I only have to see Frances for ten minutes and my spirits are lifted so high I feel like a completely different person."

It would seem almost impossible to think that two volatile personalities could get along so well and make each other happy, but somehow Kurt and Courtney seemed to be making it work. "It's a whirling dervish of emotion," said Kurt, "all these extremes of fighting and loving each other at once. If I'm mad at her, I'll yell at her, and that's healthy. If we weren't married, just living together, there would have been three or four times when one of us would have walked out on the other. But because we're so committed to each other, we've never had a fight last longer than an hour. We make up every time."

Even the question of family leadership had never become an issue in the Cobain household. "God! I don't want to say something like, 'Well, if anything, I wear the pants in the house,'" Kurt told Kevin Allman from *The*

Advocate. "It's completely divided. We have influence on each other. It's totally fifty-fifty. Courtney insists on this: She has a tab when she borrows money from me that she has to pay back. She's only up to six thousand dollars. We're millionaires, and she goes to Jet Rag [a Los Angeles vintage-clothing shop] and buys clothes—five-dollar dresses. Big deal! I'll gladly buy her some five-dollar dresses. We don't require much at all."

In hindsight, the glue that kept this husband and wife stuck together seems to have been Kurt's undying devotion to Courtney. While the media looked for any opening to slam her, while friends and family grew ever more suspicious over his wife's motives, Kurt, like the faithful dog who would knowingly die to save the family child from harm, supported and defended Courtney's honor against all critics.

"When I first met Courtney," Kurt said, "I thought of her as this totally independent self-serving person and I really respected her for that—that's why I fell in love with her. Since we've been married, I've found that she's a bit more insecure. I'm glad—it's nice to know she isn't going to take off one day. I didn't think I'd ever have a best friend, let alone a mate."

"Courtney's had misconceptions about herself all her life," said Kurt in *The Advocate.* "I talk to people who knew Courtney five years ago, and she was way more of a volatile, fucked-up person than she is now. She was insane at times. People would see her at parties just begging for attention. I never could have predicted a successful marriage with this person a few years ago. It just couldn't have happened."

By now, Kurt and Courtney had detoxed and were semiresponsible, with Frances Bean comfortably in tow. The Cobains could finally concentrate on beginning a happy family life together. Unfair comparisons of Courtney to Yoko Ono—as a band destroyer—soon seemed to disappear as an issue, at least with Kurt. "Krist and Dave liked Courtney before I even liked Courtney," Kurt said, recalling the trio's early friendships with her. "I knew that I liked her a lot, but I wouldn't admit it. She and Dave were really good friends—I shouldn't say this, but they almost wanted to get together for a time. When we were on tour in Europe, some of our shows collided with Hole shows, and Courtney would hang out on the bus with us, and Krist and Courtney were really good friends. And it hasn't changed at all. There hasn't been any bad blood except after the *Vanity Fair* piece." (According to Kurt, when the *Vanity*

Fair article hit, Courtney had asked Kurt, "Why don't you kick Krist out of the band?" The suggestion was made in jest, but Krist had taken it seriously.) "Dave and Krist are dealing with this fine, and they're defending us as much as they can, but we can't expect them to go on a defense crusade, because it doesn't affect them like it affects us."

As it happened, Krist was involved in a crusade of his own in 1993—one that began with a trip back to his ancestral homeland, Bosnia and Herzegovina. From his Croatian family, Krist learned firsthand of the horror of tens of thousands of women, Bosnians, Croats, and Muslims alike, who were raped and beaten by Serbian soldiers. He met with volunteers of the Trenjevka Women's Group, a dedicated organization that offers care to all female refugees and their children, to learn more about the devastation the worldwide press seemed determined to ignore. The experience moved Krist to organize a benefit concert featuring Nirvana, the Breeders, and Disposable Heroes of Hiphoprisy in April 1993 in San Francisco to provide assistance and raise awareness for the Trenjevka Women's Group.

Krist also wrote an article for *Spin* magazine to bring his concerns under a bigger public spotlight. *Spin* editor Bob Guccione Jr. offered Krist the opportunity to write a firsthand perspective of what he'd seen, and Krist jumped at the chance to share his views and observations. Though admittedly not an experienced journalist of any sort, Krist still hoped his article would be taken seriously enough to expose previously unreported accounts of civilian deaths and atrocities, and light a bureaucratic fire that would investigate further the brutalities of his homeland that had been so expertly silenced by both Bosnian and international authorities.

When the trio reassembled in mid-January, they hit the road for a short tour of Brazil with good friends L7. The gigs provided some of the footage for the Nirvana video *Nirvana Live! Tonight! Sold Out!!*, as "Dive" and portions of "Aneurysm" were taken from the band's first show of 1993, on January 16 at Murumbi Stadium in São Paulo. A week later, at Praca Da Apotoese in Rio de Janeiro, Kurt and Courtney did some of their first songwriting and recording together, a development that signaled their growing intimacy. (A few years later, Hole performed a song called "Drunk in Rio," written by Kurt and Courtney). During this period, "he knew he was the shit, but he had no rock star ego," Courtney remembered in a 1994 interview with MTV's Kurt

Loder. "And he needed a little. The funnest time he had as a rock star was when we went to Brazil, and we had a bodyguard, and we had to have a limo cause that's all they had. And we got these insane great meals, and he got two hundred fifty thousand dollars for one show! He had the best time that I saw him have."

The lavish accommodations provided for Nirvana whenever they traveled was something the band could never get used to; ironically, for the somewhat less famous Courtney—who had spent plenty of time on tour—they had become second nature. She seemed almost surprised by Kurt's appreciation for the simple things in life. "Kurt would carry his bag up cobbled Parisian streets," she said, "and he was scrawny, [but he] carried [his own] huge suitcase because everything had to be punk."

That night in São Paulo, Nirvana performed a twenty-three-song moshfest of tunes snared from *Bleach, Nevermind,* and *In Utero.* Even Flea of the Red Hot Chili Peppers joined the boys onstage, picking up a trumpet to play along with "Smells Like Teen Spirit." As they wailed away in Brazil, "Sliver," the first single from *Incesticide,* began a one-month stay on the *Billboard* Modern Rock Chart in the United States; it would peak at number nineteen.

In one year, Nirvana became one of the biggest rock bands in the world, with sales figures from their three albums reaching multiplatinum by the spring of 1993. Much to their chagrin, however, they had also released the concept of grunge into the world of mainstream marketing; by the middle of 1993 it seemed as though the word was interchangeable with "Nirvana."

More than a year earlier, Dave had complained publicly about the label. "I don't know who invented this 'grunge' term, I don't know who came up with the 'g-word,'" he said disgustedly. "I mean, people will ask [adopting an irritating nasal-whine], 'Oh, what's this band sound like?' 'Oh, you know, sort of grungy' . . . Someone said that we'll be a Sub Pop band for the rest of our life just because of that [grunge] thing. You know, who cares, it's all fucking rock 'n' roll anyway."

For Dave, there was a distinction to be made between his band's music and that of other grunge acts, which he linked with heavy metal. "It's the attitude that sets [Nirvana] apart from the [grunge and heavy metal label]. When you think of heavy metal, you think of sexist innuendoes and pseudo-Satanism."

Krist echoed the idea. "A lot of heavy-metal kids are just plain dumb. I'm sorry. We're heavy, but we're not heavy metal," he said in 1992. "Metal's searching for an identity because it's exhausted itself, so they're going to latch onto us. We're not metal fans."

Perhaps the constant labeling of their music and their way of life was what inspired Nirvana to move toward a more aggressive, confrontational style for the new record. All three members of the band had stated in several interviews before the record was made that they were eager to record an album more like *Bleach*. "We've been wanting to record a really raw album for almost a year and it looks like we are finally ready to do it," Kurt said. For Kurt, the idea of opening up the aggressive side of Nirvana's music seemed to go hand in hand with his attempts to alleviate his own inner turmoil, both physical and emotional. "I have been prescribed some stomach medicine that has helped ease the pain and I've been going to a pain management clinic. I also meditate. We'd like to put the album out before we go on tour again early next year . . . We might not go on any more long tours. The only way we could tour is if I could find some way to keep my stomach from acting up. We could record and play shows once in a while, but to put myself in the physical strain of seven months of touring is too much for me. I would rather be healthy and alive. I don't want to sacrifice myself or my family."

In February, a month after "Sliver" debuted on the *Billboard* chart, their song "Oh, the Guilt" was released as a 7-inch single on Touch and Go Records, with the Jesus Lizard's "Puss" as its B side. The Jesus Lizard's lead singer, David Yow, had previously sung for Scratch Acid, an early influence on Nirvana.

This single marked the first Nirvana release on Touch and Go, a label that had won Cobain's respect with its support of acts like the Jesus Lizard and Urge Overkill. It was through Touch and Go that Nirvana connected with producer-engineer Steve Albini, and before long they hired him to produce the band's third studio album, *In Utero*. Now, with those recording sessions just weeks away, Kurt was still scrambling to write songs.

"I haven't written any new lyrics, that's for sure," he said with some embarrassment. "We have about twelve songs for [*In Utero*] we're scheduled to record in February, and I don't have any lyrics at all. Within the past year, notebooks and poetry books I've had lying around have either been destroyed or stolen. So I don't have anything to go back on at all. It sucks. This past year I haven't been very prolific at all. A few months ago we went on tour to Europe, and before we went I took two of my favorite guitars and all my poetry books and writings and two tapes that had guitar parts I was going to use for the next record, and I put all this really important stuff in our shower, because we've never really used our shower before. And the roommates upstairs had a plumbing problem, so when we came back, everything was destroyed. I don't have anything to go back on at all. It's pretty scary."

During the weeks before the new sessions, Kurt did find the time to design a guitar for Fender, whose instruments he had always favored. His design was a combination of a Jaguar and a Mustang called a *Jag-Stang,* originally intended exclusively for Kurt's use onstage. In an interview with *Guitar World* magazine, Kurt was asked why he preferred the low-end Mustangs and Jaguars to the more popular Fender models. "I don't favor them—I can afford them. [Laughs] I'm left-handed, and it's not very easy to find reasonably priced, high-quality left-handed guitars. But out of all the guitars in the whole world, the Fender Mustang is my favorite. I've only owned two of them. They're cheap and totally inefficient, and they sound like crap and are very small. They also don't stay in tune . . . Whoever invented that guitar was a dork. I guess I'm calling Leo Fender, the dead guy, a dork. Now I'll never get an endorsement!

"I own a 'sixty-six Jaguar. That's the guitar I polish and baby—I refuse to let anyone touch it when I jump into the crowd!" A few months after his design was approved, consumers were able to buy the *Jag-Stang,* but only in very limited quantities.

In the third week of February 1993, Kurt, Krist, and Dave checked into Pachyderm Studios outside Minneapolis, Minnesota, to begin recording the songs that would make up *In Utero.* Registered under the alias "Simon Ritchie Group" (a nod to Sex Pistol Sid Vicious's given name), the trio spent the following two weeks recording with Steve Albini. Like Jack Endino, Albini, who once headed up the legendary band Big Black, credits himself only as an engineer, not a producer. But his well-respected reputation for his studio work with PJ Harvey, the Pixies, the Breeders, Urge Overkill, and other bands confirmed his producing skills. Kurt had always had a fondness for the Pixies and for the production methods and styles Albini used on the first two Breeders albums. Working with Albini seemed inevitable as early as 1989, when Kurt was asked in an interview with *Zip Code* about getting him to produce the next record. "That's a thought," Kurt said. "I like his drum sound, he gets a really good drum sound." In another interview, Krist said he knew Albini was the key for producing *In Utero* "from hearing the way the songs sounded at the end of rehearsals. They're pretty straightforward songs, and Steve has a really straightforward approach, so he sounded like the best man for the job."

"When we went into the studio, only half of the compositions were ready," Kurt said. "The rest originated from messing around in the studio. This way we applied a pressure that was far more defining than the one that was applied from outside. We restricted ourselves to a deadline—two weeks—and a recording budget. I like to work that way. I also waited with the lyrics to the last moment. I know me; if I make something long before, I keep working on it and start to doubt [it]. Or else I'll decide it's not good anymore and throw it away. For the new album I fixed everything in my mind on the very day."

"That makes sense," said Dave. "We did almost no postediting on the songs. We recorded everything in one take, and did as little overdubbing as possible. *Nevermind* was polished; every mistake was taken out of it. With *In Utero* we meant to produce an honest group album again. Musically there is much more to be taken out of it. Take the track, 'Milk It,' for example: it has a very remarkable dynamic. There [are] some cracks and creaks in it, the bass screws up regularly . . . Those sorts of little things give the album character."

In the past, Kurt had always seemed dissatisfied with the way the band sounded on tape—Nirvana's sessions had usually been treated as an opportunity to try out new things. "Every recording we've done has been total experimentation," said Kurt to *Impact* magazine. "I wanted this band to sound like *[In Utero]* forever, since we started."

Kurt's instincts about getting a live sound in the studio dovetailed faithfully with Albini's methods, as he revealed in the same interview. "If you put a microphone in front of a snare drum, go into the control room and listen to somebody hit on it, it sounds really fake and weird. So instead of doing that, I thought [on *In Utero*] we should use more microphones. I suggested to Jack Endino and to Butch Vig that we should use a whole bunch of microphones to get an ambiance out of the room, but they wouldn't do it. It turns out that's exactly how Albini does it, and it was an assumption that I had. He came so close with the Pixies and the Breeders, who sound the way I've always wanted to sound. [On *In Utero*] you can hear the chair creaking because we had so many microphones around us. We had thirty for the drums alone."

Pachyderm Studios was a favorite place to work for Albini, and the house the studios were built into left a positive impression on Nirvana. "We were in this house built in the early 'sixties; it was like Mike Brady meets Frank Lloyd Wright," Krist recalled. "There were these architectural innovations, but there was also this 'sixties kitsch. It was a good working environment; you could really concentrate on having a good time."

And for Kurt, Krist, and Dave, their personal enjoyment in making *In Utero* was just as important as meeting the expectations of everyone involved. Somehow, the trio managed to shrug off the pressure to make another *Nevermind* that must have been coming at them from all directions. "Ugh. I'll never do that again," Kurt said. "It already paid off, so why try to duplicate that? And just trying to sell that many records again, there's no point in it."

"The pressure is on the record company, not us," said Dave at the time. "*They* have to sell the album. We just went into the studio and recorded what we liked to see recorded. No one meddled with that. Then we mixed everything, gave the master tape to Geffen and said 'this is it.' "

"Lou Reed once made an album called *Metal Machine Music* and lost all his credibility with it," added Kurt. "We could have done something like that, but our musical aims are somewhat bigger. We like to have a good feeling about an album."

"It's up to [Geffen] to make the link to the mainstream," said Dave. "I just think this time it will be harder to do that."

Seventeen

The only reason I would've deliberately put out
a really aggressive, raw album would have been to piss
people off, to get rid of half our audience and more.

—KURT COBAIN,
CIRCUS MAGAZINE

Initially, *In Utero* was to be titled *I Hate Myself and I Want to Die*, Kurt's token response whenever strangers would ask, "Kurt Cobain, how are you?" The name was eventually scrapped (along with the song of the same name) for *Verse Chorus Verse*, named after the simple formula for writing a pop song. Soon after, that title too was sent to the trash heap.

It wasn't until Kurt was reading some of Courtney's poetry that he noticed the phrase "in utero." It fit well with the artwork Kurt had planned for the album cover. "I just like the way it sounded," Kurt explained after the record was finished.

The final artwork for *In Utero* comprises two separate but related themes. On the cover is a classroom model of the human body that is known as Brunnhilde: The Transparent Woman and is used by schoolchildren to learn about different parts of the female anatomy. If you want to see where the heart is, for example, you push a button and it lights up on the body. It is the female counterpart on the "Sliver" single cover of The Transparent Man. For *In Utero*, Kurt added the wings to the body.

"The album's back cover," he said, "is a collage of rubber fetus dolls, orchids, and models of bodily organs, suggests the aftermath of a massacre." Whereas

Nevermind seemed to have guns as its repeated motif, *In Utero* had a different image—sickness. The theme was inadvertent enough: "I'm always the last to realize things like that, like the way I used guns in the last record," said Kurt. "I didn't mean to turn *[In Utero]* into a concept album." Inevitably, Kurt's experiences with Courtney and Frances seem to have reawakened a longtime interest in physicality for Kurt. He had always been fascinated by reproduction and birth and had been painting fetuses for years and making fetus dolls out of clay. However, it was his respect for motherhood that deepened his appreciation for pregnancy.

Kurt treated the work of creating the songs for *In Utero* with a sense of impatience. "But I'm getting so tired of that [verse-chorus-verse] formula," he said. "And it *is* formula. And there's not much you can do with it. We've mastered that, for our band. We're all growing pretty tired of it . . . Krist, Dave, and I have been working on his formula—this thing of going from quiet to loud—for so long that it's literally becoming boring for us. It's like 'OK, I have this riff. I'll play it quiet, without a distortion box, while I'm singing the verse. And now let's turn on the distortion box and hit the drums harder.' I want to learn to go in between those things, go back and forth, almost become psychedelic in a way but with a lot more structure. It's a really hard thing to do, and I don't know if we're capable of it—as musicians."

One thing was clear: There would be no willfully contrived megahit to follow up "Smells Like Teen Spirit." "If it wasn't for 'Teen Spirit,' I don't know how *Nevermind* would have done," Krist said after the recordings for *In Utero*. "There are no 'Teen Spirit's on *In Utero*. There are six or seven great songs, but no phenomenal big hit."

The band's casual attitude toward hit making alarmed some at DGC. "The label's all freaked out about it," Krist reported of the less commercial *In Utero*. "It's like, 'Shit, it's *art*—what are you going to do about it?' "

Remarks like this helped fuel the rumors that Nirvana was intentionally cooking a bad record. Kurt contemplated releasing a mediocre record as a response to the hype, but decided against it. "I would've done it for sure a year ago, but now I've learned to ignore everything, all that celebrity thing."

Kurt's comments at the time of *In Utero*'s launch revealed a kind of animated defensiveness about the final product. He was convinced that *In Utero* would not sell as many albums as *Nevermind,* but Kurt and his bandmates were comfortable with and aware of this possibility. From an artistic perspective, they were very happy with the results yielded on *In Utero,* and they were more satisfied with this effort than they were with *Nevermind.* Critics considered this new record to be more aggressive than *Nevermind,* and Nirvana would say later that this was intentional. They wanted to introduce a different recording style and thus introduce a raw side of the band to the mainstream. Recognizing their red-hot popularity throughout the world, the band clearly understood that no matter what they released, their new songs would be played on the radio without hesitation. For the members of Nirvana, this was nothing short of a satisfying accomplishment. They could finally put together a product they could be proud of and, perhaps, break through to newer, sometimes riskier, musical frontiers.

Thus *In Utero* became a bold songwriting challenge, to explore areas and expressions that, because of Kurt's previous songwriting stylings, the anticipating public certainly was not prepared to hear. "Scentless Apprentice" is a perfect example of this. The lyrics are based on the novel *Perfume* by Patrick Süskind. It is the story of Jean-Baptiste Grenouille, who at birth is discovered to have no scent. Ironically, though, Grenouille does possess an incredible sense of smell, and he eventually becomes an apprentice in a tannery. "He was born scentless and senseless, he was born a scentless apprentice," Kurt sings, following the story line in *Perfume.* But after Grenouille leaves the tannery, he murders an innocent girl because her smell overwhelms him. He is so enamored by her aroma that he yearns to make it a cologne. It becomes a lifestyle of the scentless apprentice, who continues killing virgin girls to obtain the smell he will use to create his master perfume. Though not a particularly popular Nirvana song, "Scentless Apprentice" represents some of Kurt's finest songwriting.

"Almost all my lyrics have been cut-ups, pieces of poetry and stuff," said Kurt. "And the pieces of poetry are taken from poems that don't usually have meaning in the first place. They were cut-ups themselves. And often I'll have to obscure the pieces I take to make them fit in the song, so they're not even true pieces of poem. But *[In Utero]* is the first record where I've written at least a couple of songs thematically. 'Scentless Apprentice' is one."

"I've always painted abstracts. I love dreams that don't make sense. I'd much rather watch a film that doesn't have a plot. Most of my lyrics don't connect because I've taken lines from lots of different poems of mine and put them together. I'll make up a theme well after the fact, oftentimes while I'm being interviewed. But there are a few more obvious subjects on this album than on the last."

Controversial expressions of art are featured throughout *In Utero*. "Heart-Shaped Box," originally titled "Heart-Shaped Coffin," is filled with disturbing imagery of cancer, disease, and death. Although some felt this song was about the well-publicized Kurt persona of being the complaining, bitchy, whiny guy ("Hey, wait, I've got a new complaint," he sings in the chorus), Kurt said "Heart-Shaped Box" was inspired by documentaries he'd seen about kids with cancer. Pulling out nonsensical lines and phrases from poetry that he'd written on other occasions to create new songs, Kurt utilized this methodology when writing "Heart-Shaped Box." He resurrected the unusual expression "umbilical noose," something he first penned in an early draft of "Smells Like Teen Spirit." During the recording of the song, Kurt laid down a long, distorted guitar solo. But the impromptu creation took away from the rhythm of the song itself, and it was later taken out in the mixing.

With its pop-influenced edge and addictive, singalong chorus, "Heart-Shaped Box," the perfect representation of the overall Courtney Love–inspired theme of *In Utero*, was the logical choice to be the album's first single.

Another song inspired a new Nirvana controversy. As if willfully ignoring the actual lyrics of the song after the album's release, the press exploded with criticism of "Rape Me." "I was trying to write an antirape song in a very bold way," Kurt explained delicately. "What I've realized is that in order to get your point across, you have to be obvious. That's how most people want songs to be. They need it thrown right in their face.

"I've gone back and forth between regretting it and trying to defend myself. Basically, I was trying to write a song that supported women and dealt with the issue of rape. Over the last few years, people have had such a hard time understanding what our message is, what we're trying to convey, that I just decided to be as bold as possible. How hard should I stamp this point? How big should I make the letters? It's not a pretty image. But a woman who is being raped, who is infuriated with the situation . . . it's like 'Go ahead, rape me, just go for it, because you're gonna get it.' I'm a firm believer in karma, and that motherfucker is going to get what he deserves, eventually. That man will be caught, he'll go to jail, and *he'll* be raped. 'So rape me, do it, get it over with. Because you're gonna get it worse.'"

Few lines in Nirvana's songs are as poignant or say so much about Cobain's sensitive side as "I miss the comfort in being sad" from "Frances Farmer Will Have Her Revenge on Seattle." Despite the ironic similarities between the life of actress Frances Farmer and his own, which he never denied, Kurt felt simply that this song was about Farmer herself, the way her life was exploited by those considered close to her. It captures the sadness of people being publicly humiliated without cause or sympathy, and the shame of a bureaucratic system that can't, or won't, do anything to protect them. Kurt wrote the lyrics because he was so moved by a Farmer biography. "The song is so feminine," he said. "Men don't often write poetry equating women with nature."

While "Frances Farmer" dives into an intriguing side of society, Kurt said "Dumb" was a song that required no deep interpretation whatsoever. "['Dumb'] is just about people who're easily amused, people who not only aren't capable of progressing their intelligence but are totally happy watching ten hours of television and really enjoy it. I've met a lot of dumb people. They have a shitty job, they may be totally lonely, they don't have a girlfriend, they don't have much of a social life, and yet, for some reason they're happy.

"At times, I wish I could take a pill that would allow me to be amused by television and just enjoy the simple things in life, instead of being so judgmental and expecting real good quality instead of shit. ['Dumb' is] not about me, but it has been. And just using the word 'happy' I thought was a nice twist on the negative stuff we've done before.

"I wish we could have written a few more songs like ['Dumb' and 'All Apologies'] on all the other albums. Even to put 'About a Girl' on *Bleach* was a risk. I was heavily into pop, I really liked R.E.M., and I was into all kinds of old 'sixties stuff. But there was a lot of pressure within that social scene, the underground—like the kind of thing you get in high school. And to put a jangly R.E.M.–type of pop song on a grunge record, in that scene, was risky . . . The big guitar sound is what the kids want to hear. We like playing that stuff, but I don't know how much longer I can scream at the top of my lungs every night, for an entire year on tour. Sometimes I wish I had taken the Bob Dylan route and sang songs where my voice would not go out on me every night, so I could have a career if I wanted."

"Very Ape" brought out the sarcastic side of Nirvana. Originally known as "Perky or Punky New Wave Number," "Very Ape" (like "Mr. Moustache" before it) gave Kurt a chance to mock the stereotypical "macho" man in two minutes. "I take pride as the king of illiterature," he sings. "I'm too busy acting like I'm not naïve." The unusually up-tempo focus—similar to that of "Mexican Seafood"—features a rare peek at Kurt's jerky, Devo-influenced guitar playing. The brief chorus of "Very Ape"—"Out of the sky, into the dirt"—reflects the hook of Neil Young's "My My Hey Hey," a song Kurt quoted from in his suicide note.

"Milk It" offered an unsavory look at codependency. It may even have been a subtle hint of things to come, as Kurt crooned, "Look on the bright side of suicide." Raw yet full of life, "Milk It" is surprisingly one of Nirvana's most well-written songs in spite of the formulaic use of the verse-chorus-verse style. It is a unique perspective on Kurt's chronic stomach pain and the copious ways of finding relief from the ailment itself.

The dark undertone of "Pennyroyal Tea" exposes the eccentricities of Kurt's songwriting, and perhaps his lifestyle. In it, Kurt envisions using "Pennyroyal Tea" (an herbal abortive used to end pregnancies) in a figurative sense to cleanse his soul, to rid himself of his own evil spirits. However, Kurt also intended the song to be about a person who had traveled way beyond severe depression and now lived on the edge of his or her own self-imposed death. "Pennyroyal Tea" was one of Kurt's favorite songs.

"Radio Friendly Unit Shifter," originally titled "Nine Month Media Blackout," is a lighthearted take on the damage negative press can do to one's life. "I just thought it had a nice ring to it," Kurt said plainly about the song's title. "I just wish things weren't taken so literally. Really, after all the shit I've had to read about me—and especially my wife—in the last year and a half, I should've put out a really hateful record. I should've used every chance I had to attack people. I wanted to, I feel that strongly about it, but there's just no point. I'm already known as a crybaby whiner."

Kurt felt "tourettes" was one of the poorer songs on the album. "Yeah, that kind of song didn't need to be written," he admitted. "If anything, it hurt the album. I could scream my guts out at any time, fool myself and everybody else. I can work up enough energy to scream my guts out for any fast punk-rock song, but ['tourettes'] wasn't as good as 'Territorial Pissings.'

"At the time, I felt the majority of the album was a little too middle-of-the-road, straight 4/4 rock songs, and I wanted to have some faster songs. I guess I didn't have time to write anything better. But I don't mean to complain about 'tourettes' so much, because the rest of the album devours it."

Perhaps the deepest, most emotional song on the album is "All Apologies," which would take on new meaning after Kurt's death. Some would point to the rhyme "I'm married/buried" as a slam on Courtney, but Kurt explained: "That was another line that was written before Courtney and I started going out." The band revisited this song on their *Unplugged in New York* album, and it is that version that still gets the most radio airplay to date.

"I Hate Myself and I Want to Die," once slated as the album's title cut, was even mastered and sequenced into an early DGC Records in-house promotional version of the album. Yet it was deleted from the album roster, and ultimately only saw the light of day on Geffen's *The Beavis and Butt-Head Experience* album (the title of the song is never referred to in its lyrics). Kurt explained the title as a joke. "As literal as a joke can be. Nothing more than a joke. And that had a bit to do with why we decided to take it off. We knew people wouldn't get it; they'd take it too seriously. It was totally satirical, making fun of ourselves. I'm thought of as this pissy, complaining, freaked-out schizophrenic who wants to kill himself all the time. 'He ain't satisfied with anything,' and I thought it was a funny title. I wanted it to be the title of the album for a long time. But I knew the majority of the people wouldn't understand it."

"Marigold" is the only Nirvana song neither written nor sung by Kurt. Instead, Dave Grohl garners songwriting and vocal credits while Kurt takes the backup vocals. Dave had recorded this song with his friend Barrett Jones during one of their many sessions. A very simple song with just a few lines, it ended up as the B side to "Heart-Shaped Box."

"MV" was credited with its complete name, "Moist Vagina," only on the German release of *In Utero*. Kurt uses the word "vagina" in a clever rhyme with "marijuana"; otherwise, this is another simplistically written and structured song. Like "Endless Nameless" on *Nevermind*, the German import version of *In Utero* contained a hidden bonus track—"Gallons of Rubbing Alcohol Flow Through the Strip." It is a punk rant with a long jam, with the lyrics in the liner notes listed simply as "whatever."

Before *In Utero* was released, Nirvana shot the video for the first single, "Heart-Shaped Box." Moving in a new direction with a new artistic vision, Nirvana hired Anton Corbijn to direct. The result contains startling vibrant-colored interpretations of Kurt's lyrics to "Heart-Shaped Box," including the crucified old man wearing a Santa Claus cap and a little girl dressed in what appears to be a Ku Klux Klan outfit. In all of its darkness a comedic light shines through as a black crow appears to sing the chorus. Two versions of this video were made; one shows Kurt lying in a field of poppies as if he is dead. Strangely enough, this scene was edited in after Kurt's death in 1994.

In Utero was recorded quickly and efficiently. "It was made really fast," Kurt concurred. "All the basic tracks were done within a week. And I did eighty percent of the vocals in one day, in about seven hours. I just happened to be on a roll. It was a good day for me, and I just kept going."

After the recording of *In Utero* was completed, the band returned to Washington with the tapes to listen to, and then the trouble began. With the luggage barely unpacked, Kurt already had problems with the mix of the songs. "The first time I played it at home, I knew there was something wrong," he later reflected. "The whole first week I wasn't really interested in listening to it all, and that usually doesn't happen. I got no emotion from it; I was just numb. So, for three weeks, Krist, Dave, and I listened to the record every night, trying to figure out what was wrong.

"My A&R man . . . said, 'I don't like the record, it sounds like crap, there's way too much effect on the drums, you can't hear the vocals.' He didn't think the songwriting was up to par. A few other people—our management, our lawyers—didn't like the record either."

The trio called Albini to talk about the problems but hadn't yet absorbed enough to identify them. They just knew something wasn't right. "I couldn't really say much to anyone because at the time I wasn't sure what I wanted to change on the album," said Kurt, though he was convinced that the problems did not lie in the songwriting.

"We finally came to the conclusion that the vocals weren't loud enough, and the bass was totally inaudible," Kurt explained. "We couldn't hear any notes that Krist was playing at all. I think there are a few songs on *In Utero* that could have been cleaned up a little bit more. Definitely 'Pennyroyal Tea.' That was not recorded right. That should have been recorded like *Nevermind,* because I know that's a strong song, a hit single . . . You hit and miss. It's a really weird thing about this record. I've never been more confused in my life, but at the same time I've never been more satisfied with what we've done."

Under time and money pressures, the band decided simply to remaster the album with mastering engineer Bob Ludwig in lieu of calling for a complete remix. As Kurt explained, it was a gamble—not least of all because they themselves weren't familiar with the mastering process. "We thought it was the last stage in the process where you just take the tapes in and run them through a machine that allows you to cut it onto a record. So we went to the mastering plant and learned that you can actually take the vocals right out if you want to. It's amazing, it's practically like remixing. So that's what we did, we just gave the bass more high-end so you could hear the notes, turned the vocals up, maybe compressed it a little, and that did it, cured everything. As soon as we'd done it, we knew we'd made the right decision, [and] it was over. And now I wouldn't change anything on it, I'm a hundred percent satisfied."

At first, the trio had been thrilled with Steve Albini's quick-and-dirty approach; in the end, though, his approach may have compromised the sonic success of the album. "The mixing we'd done with Steve Albini was so fast it was ridiculous, about one hour per track," said Kurt. "We decided to remix two songs, 'Heart-Shaped Box' and ['All Apologies'] with Scott Litt [R.E.M.'s producer]. The rest we were able to improve on during the mastering. That took care of it."

Using Litt wasn't intended to be a slap at Albini, just an opportunity to use an experienced and objective ear to see if Nirvana's anxieties over the original mix were justified. "He just remixed a couple of the songs," said Krist. "I just didn't think that the bass was loud enough [on 'All Apologies']. And Kurt said he wanted to add some background vocals to 'Heart-Shaped Box.' " Kurt agreed. "To remix any more would've destroyed the ambiance of the whole thing." Litt also removed a long stream of guitar feedback from "Heart-Shaped Box" that ran through the majority of the song.

Steve Albini was destined to take some flak for the production problems on *In Utero*, but from the start he treated his contribution as that of a hired worker, not a member of the creative team. "I get paid a flat fee," he explained, "which ensures: one, I have no stake in the commercial success of the record, so I have no reason to ameliorate what might be an 'uncommercial' creative impulse on the part of the band; two, If the band is getting fucked financially I am not responsible; three, I need not maintain any sort of 'relationship' with the record label beyond doing a good job on the record; and four, I get the satisfaction of knowing that the record sounds better and cost less than it would have otherwise."

This would have been an easy set of rules to break for Albini when Nirvana first approached him to work on *In Utero;* he could have insisted on taking a cut of the album's profits, an industry custom that could have made him a rich man. Then again, DGC wasn't exactly thrilled with the band's choice of Albini as producer. "Our A&R man at the time, Gary Gersh, was freaking out," said Dave. "I said, 'Gary, man, don't be so afraid, the record will turn out great!' He said, 'Oh, I'm not afraid, go ahead, bring me back the best you can do.' It was like, go and have your fun, then we'll get another producer." Still, Albini couldn't help but reserve a certain amount of professional pride in his work, and when the complaints started coming in about *In Utero*, he took them personally. And when Nirvana, DGC, and Gold Mountain Management expressed aloud their dissatisfaction with his mixing, Albini took steps to protect his reputation.

"You could put that band in the studio for a year and I don't think they could come up with a better record," Albini said, defending his work. "I think that's as good as they're going to be. If that doesn't suit their record company then their record company clearly has problems that go beyond this record. The record company has a problem with the band. The sooner everybody involved recognizes that, the easier it will be on everybody."

It was becoming obvious to all involved that *In Utero* was not going to be *Nevermind* in its sound or its sales. The people who had made lots of money off *Nevermind* were growing more and more concerned over whether or not *In Utero* could come close to the same success. Rumors began to spread that DGC would reject the record completely. "If they do, they know we'll break up," said Kurt. "Fuck, we made them fifty million dollars last year!"

Finger-pointing became the order of the day, and Nirvana felt that Albini's concern over his image was at least partially to blame. "The whole thing was Steve's fault," said Kurt. "He initiated the whole problem by convincing himself that people were out to get him, to discredit him. He's a paranoid person in general. He's told me a lot of terrible stories about how he's been fucked around by major labels, how they've insisted on remixing the stuff he's done, so it's understandable. But he really had no reason whatsoever to be as paranoid as he was. Basically, he heard from me—about a week after we got back from recording—that my A&R man had said he didn't like the record. But the thing to understand is that it never went beyond that, just these people were expressing their opinion . . . I just think he was trying to protect himself before he had any evidence that he was being fucked with. Like I say, it's understandable because he's told me some really nasty stories about what's been done to him. But still, I can't help but resent him for jumping the gun.

"I found him to be surprisingly pleasant when we showed up in Minneapolis, [and I] didn't find anything wrong with his personality. I just think he worked too fast for our tastes . . . He wanted to mix a song in an hour. He has this theory, that if something you transfer onto tape isn't immediately satisfying to you there's no point in remixing, you might as well throw it away and start again. I don't know why he's so against mixing but he is, and we're not used to working like that anymore . . . I don't have any desire to talk to him again."

Dave was more direct. "I happen to love Steve Albini. He really prides himself on being the biggest dick you ever met in your life and he does a good job of it. He's also an incredibly intelligent producer."

"I really liked the record after it got mastered," Krist said. "I think Albini did an amazing job—he's an amazing producer. Albini actually worked out great for us; he's really good at getting things in the first take, just getting a really great live sound. He's just an opinionated guy. If someone's gonna ask him about something, he's gonna speak his mind."

Even Kurt's disappointment with Albini couldn't dampen his enthusiasm for the record, though. "It introduced a whole new sound to the mainstream audience. That Steve Albini underground sound is pretty tired for people who are familiar with that stuff, but we had to do it. We *wanted* to record an album and have that sound, so it was pretty much the fulfillment of a childhood fantasy."

A few months before the release of *In Utero* in the fall of 1993, negative rumors had caught fire: The band was breaking up, the album sounded horrible, the label was unhappy. Soon the story spread from the music trade magazines to more mainstream venues. *Newsweek* even printed an article saying how disappointing the record sounded. "That was hilarious!" said Krist. "Some establishment news magazine! . . . It's just this stupid little controversy, because some people change their minds along the way, and some people didn't know what the fuck they were talking about . . . But I thought it was kind of cool to have a full-page ad in *Newsweek*. How much does Marlboro or Reebok pay for that? We got a full-page ad for nothing!

"I *really* want people to hear this record," Krist continued. "I get really idealistic about it. There's a lot of 'alternative bands' out there, and their music would basically fit in the repertoire of Rick Springsteen or some serious mainstream stuff. They're marketed as alternative, and they're confusing people. It's all part of that weird, MTV-televised music revolution bullshit!"

"We think *In Utero* will get three types of reactions," said Dave, in what may have been the most cogent analysis of the situation. "For the listener-by-accident spoiled by *Nevermind*, this album sounds like our commercial suicide; probably he/she will ignore it, and consider us one-hit wonders. The skeptics will rate it a pretentious album, 'Nirvana makes some noise and they think they are good at it.' Big deal. The fans, finally, will instinctively like it. They will rate the album at its true value; a spontaneously realized, no-nonsense album, without the postproduction polish."

"We are going to go out and promote *In Utero*," Krist said with determination. "We're doing interviews, we're doing videos, we're going to go out on the road—I want to do all that rock 'n' roll industry stuff. We were pretty much unanimous in that. The feeling [is] very much, 'Let's throw this record at the wall and see if it sticks.' Geffen Records lets us do whatever we want. But you have to think about the consequences of your actions. So if the record doesn't sell very well then we can't really bitch. We really want people to hear it, so we want to play ball with the label. We get along with everyone there. We have meetings with them, and it's like, 'Yeah, that's cool, we'll do this, we'll do that', or 'We won't do this.' They understand where we're coming from."

Lost in all the hype and production of *In Utero* was *Incesticide*, released just a few months earlier. Nirvana needed to make a video for "Sliver." The band got together in Kurt's garage and decorated it with a hodgepodge of knick-knacks that Kurt had collected and put in storage. Once again, they tapped Kevin Kerslake to direct the video, shot in March 1993 with a Super 8 camera, which gave the video the warm, grainy feel of home movies. Everyone in front of the camera appears to be having a great time, even Frances Bean, who is making her first appearance in a music video.

Meanwhile, Krist's highly anticipated Balkan relief concert, held in San Francisco in April, was a rousing success. All seemed well again, until Kurt and Courtney's married life turned an awful corner. Kurt's drug use was increasing, and life at home was growing far darker for the family.

One night that spring, Kurt injected himself with a large dose of heroin and then attempted to drive himself home. Once there, he began to shake uncontrollably. He was flushed, dazed, turned "beet red," and grew delirious, the police report noted. Courtney called 911. As Kurt's mother, Wendy, and his sister, Kim, stood by, Courtney injected her husband with buprenorphine, an illegal drug that can be used to awaken victims after a heroin overdose. She also gave him a Valium, three Benadryls, and four Tylenol tablets with codeine, which caused him to vomit. When police arrived, "Cobain was conscious and able to answer questions, but was obviously impaired to some degree," the report stated. Courtney told the police this kind of thing had happened before. Kurt recovered in a few days. The entire episode was recounted in the *New York Post*.

Two months later, on June 6, Seattle police were called to Kurt and Courtney's house after a neighbor reported a domestic dispute was taking place there. But the real trouble started only after the police arrived. The Cobains were in their garage jamming together, perhaps even yelling at each other, when the concerned neighbor phoned the police. Six uniformed officers arrived at the house and explained that the domestic dispute law required that they arrest someone before they could leave the premises. "Once the cops explained to me that they had to take one of us to jail because there was a domestic violence call from one of the neighbors, I understood that because they were so nice about it," Kurt said. "They explained it in full detail and made me realize that most domestic violence calls are real, and if one or the other people aren't arrested, then the cops will just be called back an hour or two later, and this time one of them may be dead."

Almost as if on cue, Kurt and Courtney begin to argue over who should be the one who gets arrested. "I have to admit I was rather drunk, I get drunk easily, and I don't remember the whole chain of events," Kurt said. "We got into a scuffle, Courtney was wearing a choker and I ripped it off because she threw juice in my face. She did that 'cause we were yelling at each other. It turned into a domestic fight in front of the cops! They asked out of the blue if there were any guns in the house. I said no, but Courtney thought she'd cooperate and said, 'Yeah, they're upstairs in the closet put away safely, with no bullets in them.' So they confiscated my three fucking guns! The police report came out as us fighting over guns, me assaulting her with a gun and trying to choke her. The last thing I want to be thought of as is a wife choker." The police confiscated the guns, and chose Kurt to ride with them to the nearby jail, where they held him in a cell for three hours. After he had cooled down, Kurt was released on $950 bail.

With Krist trying to help the women of Eastern Europe and Kurt concerned with violence and trauma closer to home, Dave was saving for his future. "Around the summer of nineteen ninety-three, I had been talking to a fellow in Detroit about possibly releasing some of my stuff [the recordings he made with Barrett Jones in 1992–93] on his small label," Dave said. Originally he wanted the music to remain out of the spotlight, but ultimately to have something to send to friends. With Nirvana's upcoming tour put on the back burner, Dave had a change of heart and looked forward to releasing his material.

As a prelude to their impending fall tour, Nirvana decided to play a surprise show with Jesus Lizard during the New Music Seminar in New York City, an underground convention of college and alternative radio programmers and independent record label scenesters. The purpose of the July 23 gig was to showcase songs from the as-yet-unreleased *In Utero*, and while there was great anticipation for playing that evening, the day itself started out in a harrowing fashion.

Courtney heard a loud thud in the bathroom of the New York hotel where the couple was staying. She opened the door and found Kurt unconscious. "Kurt totally died. His eyes were wide fucking open, like a cadaver. Dead. It was awful. I made Wendy come up, and I'm like, 'This is your fucking son!' and just threw Kurt at her. He just looked at her and said [affecting a junk rasp], 'I'm not on drugs, Mom. I'm not on drugs. Uhhh.' " Kurt had overdosed again.

Nevertheless, that night Nirvana somehow played an extraordinary show at the Roseland Ballroom in front of a few thousand very fortunate fans. The audience was filled with independent and underground music critics, and Nirvana lived up to their highest expectations. Before the show, while giving an interview with *The Face* magazine, Dave grabbed the microphone playfully and intoned: "Well, here we are at the New Music Seminar 'ninety-three and the hot ticket for tonight: Nirvana and Jesus Lizard. An alternative spectacle, something not to be missed. The phenomenon of [stumbling] . . . Nirvana is revealed on stage. Yes, a band that has become *the* godfather of grunge as we know it. Grunge: 'ninety-two's coined term. G-R-U-N-G-E. That Sound from Seattle, that crazy mix of Stooges meets Black Flag. Yes, that's grunge and that's tonight at Roseland with the Jesus Lizard, one of the most un-precedented freak-out bands . . ."

For the first time since the days of Jason Everman, Nirvana had a fourth player join them onstage during the NMS gig. Nirvana roadie and former Exploited guitarist Big John Duncan was hired to handle Kurt's second guitar parts for a few songs from *In Utero*. The move was an experiment. Kurt wanted to take some songs and thicken them up to see how it would work. "John played on four songs, just to see what it was like," Krist explained. "It worked out pretty good, but it was strange for me because I simply wasn't used to it. But I've had nothing but positive responses from [the crowd], which is what we wanted. I had to be open-minded." It would also be the first time Nirvana played a midshow acoustic set, which featured the debut of Lori Goldston as Nirvana's new touring cellist.

There was a star-studded cast in the audience, including Mike D from the Beastie Boys; Thurston Moore (who was heard outside after the after show saying, "It was all right!"), Lee Renaldo, and Kim Gordon from Sonic Youth; Nash Kato, Blackie O, and "Eddie" King Roeser from Urge Overkill; designer

Anna Sui; MTV veejay Kennedy; and Howard Stern producer Gary "Baba Booey" Dell'Abate.

"I'm glad to have that show behind us," said Krist backstage after the gig. "I'd been kinda anxious about it, but we really flowed. And we pulled off the acoustic set, even though I was a little disturbed at the way [the audience] writhed around while we did it, like, guys, gym class is Monday morning."

It annoyed Kurt as well. "The acoustic set was a very last-minute idea. I'd never done anything like it. It was strange because I could hear people talking louder than I could hear the band. Very rude. I mean, even if I don't like a band that much I'd still have enough respect not to do that. But I guess that's New York for you. I don't want to react in such an extreme way as maybe U2 have by turning their show into a kitsch vaudeville act and be so sarcastic about the whole idea of being a rock 'n' roll star that it becomes a sick joke."

A few days after the gig, Kurt returned to Seattle. As one friend reflected, "He just kept to himself. Every time he came back after a tour, he would get more and more reclusive. The only people that saw him a lot were Courtney, Cali [aka Michael DeWitt, the Cobains' nanny], and Jackie [Farry, a former nanny and assistant manager]."

"Ever since *Nevermind* came out, I've been kind of . . . lazy," Kurt admitted. "I don't have quite as much fire in me. It still comes, but in stages. I used to write all the time—every day, I picked up my guitar. And now I find myself not even playing for an entire month. At the same time, I'm always writing songs in my head. It used to really affect me. I would drain myself emotionally. I wouldn't be able to go outside or go to a party or anything because I was almost schizophrenic sometimes; I was like a mad scientist. And once you get into that frame of mind, your focus can't be distracted at all, by a stupid party or something."

But the Roseland gig did suggest a new direction for Nirvana. The addition of a second guitarist gave them a fuller sound, and the audience seemed to approve of the choice. It became clear that it was time to consider the idea of having a permanent fourth member for live appearances. Kurt was working hard to find a second guitarist for Nirvana's upcoming tour. "I was racking my brains for months, trying to track down all these old guitar players from punk-rock bands that I liked," he recalled, "[but] most of them were junkies. I met [Germs guitarist] Pat Smear when I was living in Los Angeles and instantly fell in love with him. Very rarely do I meet someone that I like so much right away, and we only spoke a few words to each other. That's one of the most important things to look for when you're starting a band, someone you can get along with. If they can't play guitar then, who cares? Personalities are more important. And he's so damn happy, I envy him sometimes! He plays rhythm guitar, has his big smile, and the rest of the band can soak into the vibe of what's going on."

As much as Kurt liked Pat, the thought of a fourth member in Nirvana was still an uncomfortable notion for the trio. In the fall of 1993, though no one was raising explicit objections, it was still unclear whether Pat Smear would become a permanent member of Nirvana. "I don't know," Kurt said; "we haven't tried writing yet, haven't had a chance to do that. I'd like to." The whole band respected Pat Smear and the L.A. punk sounds of the Germs, and his upbeat personality seemed to have a positive effect on all three members. "He's got this great sense of humor," Dave said, "and he's a good player. I can't wait till we start writing stuff with him." But Dave confirmed Kurt's vagueness about Smear's status: "It's unsaid within the band as to whether he is a member or just coming on to play guitar."

One thing was clear: Having a second guitarist in the band for live shows would relieve a lot of the pressure on Kurt to be perfect every night. "[Having another guitarist] gives me a lot of room," he explained. "If I screw up it won't matter. I might actually be able to have a little eye contact with the audience. I'm tired of having to concentrate on so many things at once—like remembering the lyrics, playing the notes perfectly."

The uncertainty over the inclusion of Pat Smear proved to be a good distraction for Nirvana, who were still being hounded by Kurt's drug habit. It was the number-one topic in conversations about the band, on talk shows, in music magazines, and in the supermarket tabloids. To avoid further public humiliation and speculation, it was time for Kurt to come clean with an admission, and he did so in a limited way in the October 1993 issue of *Musician* magazine. "I'm caught. So I may as well 'fess up to it and try to put it in a little bit more perspective. Everyone thinks I've been a junkie for years. I was a junkie for a really small amount of time. It was my idea, I was the one that instigated it. But I didn't really know how to get [heroin], so Courtney would take me to the place where we might have a chance of being able to find it. We only did it twice on the whole [1992] tour. I was so angry with my body [over his chronic stomach pains] that I couldn't deal with anyone socially. I was just totally neurotic because I was in pain all the time. People had no idea I was in pain and I couldn't complain about it twenty-four hours a day. If I'm going to kill myself, I'm going to kill myself for a reason instead of some stupid stomach problem. So I decided to take everything in excess all at once. I was determined to get a habit. I wanted to. It was my choice. I said, 'This is the only thing that's saving me from *blowing my head off* right now.' I've been to ten doctors and [there's] nothing they can do about it."

As if Kurt's established personal problems weren't enough to send him over the edge, there was yet another problem facing the band, an issue Kurt essentially created himself: the awkward dispute over the band's royalty-sharing arrangements.

Originally, Nirvana's contract with Geffen Records had given all three band members equal credit and royalties on every song. But now, after reassessing the amount of work he had put into writing the songs on the last two albums, Kurt had begun to feel he deserved a bigger slice of the pie. Almost all at once Kurt had found himself with a new wife, a newborn baby, and a new home; it was a position of responsibility to which he was hardly accustomed, and for a while he seemed to believe—hardly realistically—that he might soon find himself in financial jeopardy. By the fall of 1993, his concerns had abated, but it was a surprising moment of panic from the usually generous Cobain.

"At the time, when we were signing contracts and stuff like that, it was always divided equally and that was fine. But I never realized I would become a millionaire and then, all of a sudden, need money. It's a ridiculous situation really. Well, we didn't agree on [restructuring the royalties] right away. It took a bit of convincing on my part. I still believe in all-for-one, one-for-all, you know. We're a group, we're a three-piece. Krist and Dave are equally as important as I am as far as the persona of the band goes, in the way we're perceived. We're perceived as a band. But I had written ninety-nine percent of the songs and many were the times when I've taken Krist's bass away from him and shown him what to play, and sat behind Dave's drum kit and shown him what to play, stuff like that. I don't enjoy being in that sort of dictatorship position, but I came up with the songs at home and introduced the songs to the band and I could be asking for a lot more.

"I've been blown away by stories of how other bands split their percentages. Like, Perry Farrell in Jane's Addiction got ninety percent of everything just because he's the lead singer. But he didn't write all the songs. I know the bass player and guitar player wrote a lot of the music, fifty percent or more. In The Pixies, Frank Black had those people on commission, you know. So when I found out about things like that and found myself needing money, I didn't feel that guilty about asking for a higher percentage. And, anyway, it's only in one area of payment, just the songwriting credits. We still split the touring money, and royalties off the record, and stuff like that. It's only an extra few thousand dollars a year or something. But it was a touchy subject at the time. I felt really guilty about asking for it. I just feel I'm entitled to it."

Dave and Krist were seeing a side of their friend they definitely could have done without. "Krist and I [thought], 'If this is any indication of how much of a dick Kurt is going to be, then I don't want to be in a band with someone like that,'" said Dave. "Everybody was saying, 'Let him have this one because the band will break up. You guys could make fifteen million dollars next year. Just let him have this one.'"

One phone conversation among the three ended with Kurt hanging up on Dave. "At the time, I was ready to fucking quit the band over it," recalled Kurt. "I couldn't believe that [they were] giving me so much shit about this."

The controversy over royalties was now a moot point, at least where Kurt was concerned. "I have to deal with the pressure of writing the songs," he said. "I don't care if someone else gets the credit for it but I should at least be financially compensated for it."

Nirvana played a benefit gig on August 6 at the King Theater in Seattle; the show was intended to raise money for the Mia Zapata Fund. Monies went to help solve the murder of Zapata, a local singer from the band The Gits who was killed earlier in the year. The case remains unsolved as of this printing. "We're always doing benefits," Krist said after the show. "We just played one for Mia Zapata. None of us knew her, but we thought, 'This is where we live, and this is a terrible thing that happened.' And it's the least we can do, to play for an hour, give something back to the community." A live version of "Radio Friendly Unit Shifter," recorded at this show, appears on the compilation *Home Alive: The Art of Self Defense.*

In September, the Melvins released their long-awaited album *Houdini.* Kurt was the producer on some of the tracks, and he played guitar on the song "Sky Pup." Then it was time for Nirvana to pay their annual visit to the MTV Video Music Awards, being held at the Universal Amphitheater in Los Angeles on September 8. Hosted by Christian Slater, the show included musical guests Aerosmith, R.E.M., Pearl Jam, Soul Asylum, and Lenny Kravitz. Nirvana's "In Bloom" video, produced by Line Postmyr and directed by Kevin Kerslake, won the award for Best Alternative Video.

On September 14, 1993, the highly anticipated effort *In Utero* was finally released. It appeared first on clear vinyl only, in a limited number of twenty-five thousand copies. Four days later, the album's first single, "Heart-Shaped Box," debuted on the *Billboard* Modern Rock Chart, where it found a home for fourteen weeks and eventually hit number one. The same day, the song debuted on the *Billboard* Album Rock Chart, peaking at number four and charting for seventeen weeks. The *In Utero* CD came out on September 21, entering the *Billboard* charts at number one with first-week sales of 180,000; in the United Kingdom it peaked at number eight.

Later that week, the band once again played on *Saturday Night Live,* and it marked the band's first national TV appearance with a fourth member. The show was hosted by basketball great Charles Barkley. Nirvana played "Heart-Shaped Box," their new single, as their opening song, and "Rape Me" to close. Kurt's performance was unusually subdued during "Rape Me"; he seemed merely to be going through the motions, and his quiet exit made quite a contrast with the raucous behavior of their first *SNL* appearance. The man who generated the most enthusisum onstage that night was Pat Smear; this appearance solidified his role as a permanent member of Nirvana.

Behind the public eye, preparations were being made for Nirvana's upcoming North American tour. This time the band was planning to bring along an underage guest. "I'll be taking [Frances Bean] with me for some part of the tour," said Kurt. He hoped Nirvana's tour would coinside with Hole's, so they could bounce the baby between buses, but the recording of Courtney's album was behind schedule and Hole's tour was delayed.

The impending tour also gave Kurt an opportunity to catch up on a lot of reading. "I used to read [fan] mail a lot, and I used to be really involved with it. But I've been so busy with this record, the video, the tour, that I haven't even bothered to look at a single letter, and I feel really bad about it. I haven't even been able to come up with enough energy to put out our fanzine, which was one of the things we were going to do to combat all the bad press, just to be able to show a more realistic side of the band. But it's really hard. I have to admit I've found myself doing the same things that a lot of other rock stars do or are forced to do. Which is not being able to respond to mail, not being able to keep on current music, and I'm pretty much locked away a lot. The outside world is pretty foreign to me."

The forty-five-date fall tour commenced on October 18, 1993, at the Arizona State Fair in Phoenix. By now Nirvana was working with a twenty-five-plus rotating song list drawing on all three of their studio albums.

Sharing in the excitement were the band's longtime fellow scenesters the Meat Puppets and the Boredoms, who both opened the first leg of the journey, while the Breeders, Shonen Knife, Come, and Half Japanese closed out the rest of the tour.

In addition to having Pat Smear as part of the permanent live arrangement, cellist Lori Goldston rejoined the live act to add her instrument's beautiful texture to "Something in the Way," "Jesus Doesn't Want Me for a Sunbeam," and "All Apologies," among others. For Goldston, who was used to playing small venues with carefully tended acoustics for her cello, playing huge rock venues took some adjustment.

"I got used to it, but it was freaky," she said, still obviously awed by the experience. "[The first few shows on the tour] broke me from stage fright pretty permanently." Besides adjusting to playing with an unpredictable punk-rock band, the classically trained Goldston also had to get used to audiences who were liable to throw things onstage as a twisted show of approval.

"I got a ducking reflex going, I'm sitting and I've got this expensive instrument; I can't afford another cello, you know? So I'd just duck!"

Then again, some of the kids may have been reacting to what was missing from the live sets. For the first few gigs on tour, Nirvana chose not to play "Smells Like Teen Spirit," sending many in the audience home angry. The band had lost their appetite for the song, and their lack of interest only increased as they came to realize that it was the one song many wanted to hear them play. It is the burden of any band to have to plow through endless renditions of their biggest hits, and for Nirvana, "Smells Like Teen Spirit" had become a reminder of just how routine their shows had become.

Having to play the song live "would have been the icing on the cake," said Kurt. "That would have made everything twice as worse. I don't even remember the guitar solo on 'Teen Spirit.' It would take me five minutes to sit in the catering room and learn the solo. But I'm not interested in that kind of stuff. I don't know if that's so lazy that I don't care anymore or what . . . There are so many other songs that I've written that are as good, if not better, than that song, like 'Drain You.' That's definitely as good as 'Teen Spirit.' I love the lyrics, and I never get tired of playing it. Maybe if it was as big as 'Teen Spirit,' I wouldn't like it as much."

In the midst of the tour, arrangements were made for Kurt to meet one of his longtime influential figures, William S. Burroughs, when Nirvana landed in Kansas. Prior to the beginning of the tour, Thor Lindsay, an employee of Tim Kerr Records, helped orchestrate the production of "The Priest They Called Him," an almost-ten-minute-long recording of Kurt making feedback with his guitar and Burroughs reading a poem about a priest who, on Christmas Eve, finds a suitcase containing a dead body.

The collaboration was recorded on separate occasions—Kurt's feedback on tape, Burroughs's reading on another—then mixed together by the people at Tim Kerr. The artwork for this very rare vinyl release included Krist dressed as a priest on the cover, with Kurt's and Burroughs's signatures engraved on the back.

So enamored was Kurt with Burroughs and his work that earlier in the year he had asked the legend via fax if he wanted to play the role of the old man being crucified in the "Heart-Shaped Box" video, but Burroughs said no. So it was with great relief that Kurt had another shot to meet his literary hero in the living room of his Lawrence home.

"I heard he really liked my lyrics . . . it's a real compliment, fuck yeah. [Meeting him] is a total blessing," Kurt said in an interview just prior to his encounter with Burroughs. "I [didn't] want him in our video just because of who he is . . . he's also this really interesting-looking old man, I want to meet him too . . . I'd be nervous, but I've met other idols . . ."

Their brief experience together probably meant more to Kurt than to Burroughs. But the grizzled icon nonetheless came away with a telling memory of the troubled rock star. "There was something boyish about him," Burroughs said of his experience with Kurt. "Fragile and engagingly lost . . . there's something wrong with that boy. He frowns for no good reason."

After an exchange of pleasantries and gifts, Kurt and Burroughs parted ways and Nirvana's massive touring schedule forged ahead.

Meanwhile, Courtney and Hole went to Atlanta on October 28 to record their major-label debut for DGC Records. Loading into the Triclops Sound Studio, they worked with Paul Kolderie and Sean Slade to produce an album appropriately titled *Live Through This*.

The following evening, the Nirvana tour bus pulled into the Michigan State Fair Coliseum in Detroit. The show was not one of their better efforts—the sound system was ill-matched with the coliseum's hard walls, which echoed the grunge all evening. Still, the band found playing airy arena gigs far better than playing claustrophobic bars.

"We've been touring since the beginning of time, playing clubs over and over again, which gets a bit monotonous," said Kurt. "You can't breathe, it's smoke-filled, beer-ridden, and even though those are some of the best memories I have, it gets old after a while. When *Nevermind* blew up, we knew we had the chance to go on this huge arena rock stadium tour, but I just emotionally and physically couldn't have dealt with it at that time. But I've had a lot of time to sit at home and work it over in my mind. Now that we're playing on larger stages there's better circulation; we have an amazing PA system which allows me to hear everything. That's usually how I judge a good show: by the monitors. It's simply a matter of getting used to something."

"Before, we were just vagabonds in a van, doing our thing," Krist added. "Now [you've] got a tour manager and a crew and it's a production. You've got schedules and shit. It used to be an adventure. And now it's a circus."

That also pretty much describes the events surrounding the release of the November 1993 issue of *Details* magazine, which hit the newsstands as Nirvana rolled into Dayton, Ohio, on October 30. The magazine contained yet another revealing article about Kurt; in an interview for the article, he spoke openly about the recurring stomach distress that he said was responsible for his heroin habit.

"I know this sounds like a cop-out or a lame excuse, but I've been suffering from chronic stomach pain every day of my life for six years now. I've been to about eight different gastrointestinal doctors and it's always been diagnosed as irritable bowel syndrome. I've had ten or eleven endoscopes, where they stick the fiber optic tube with a camera down your throat, and they always find a red, inflamed piece of tissue in my stomach. Imagine the worst stomach flu you've ever had, every single day. And it was worse when I ate, because once the meal would touch that red area I would hyperventilate, my arms would turn numb, and I would vomit.

"I was suicidal on our last tour—I really wanted to blow my head off," Kurt said plainly. "And so when we got home I decided to do heroin every day because obviously a heavy narcotic is going to stop the pain. The whole time I was doing drugs I didn't have stomach problems . . . It's not my fucking fault that anyone knows that I did heroin. I've never talked about it. When I'm high, it's really obvious. That's why I've never gone out in public on it. I tried as hard as I could to keep it from everyone. I just hope to God nobody is influenced to do drugs because of me. I definitely have a responsibility to talk negatively about heroin. It's a really really evil drug—I think opiates are directly linked to Satan. I was a successful junkie for about a year—the only reason I was able to stay healthy and didn't have to rob houses was because I had a lot of money. I was up to five hundred dollars a day and it didn't do anything but keep me alive. When I finally quit, I had thirty days of excruciating pain."

The article reopened public speculation about Kurt's state of mind, and he did nothing to quell public interest at Nirvana's 1993 Halloween show at the James A. Rhodes Arena on the campus of the University of Akron in Ohio. That night, in a spontaneous gesture that recalled the days of Jim Morrison, Kurt whipped out his penis onstage. Derrick Bostrom of the Meat Puppets, who opened that show, witnessed the event: "About halfway through our Halloween show, an overexcited fan bopped Kurt on the noggin with a tennis shoe. Kurt grabbed the offending article and looked into the audience for the culprit. Unable to find him, Kurt dropped the shoe onto the stage, unzipped his fly, and midsong, filled the shoe with piss."

The stunt didn't appear to faze Kurt in the least. "I'm looking forward to a few more years of playing with this band," he said. "Then a few years later

I might say a few years more. I don't try to predict the future, but I know I'm not going to be rich for the rest of my life. I have money now, but within ten years we'll blow it. I'll have to get a job or have a solo career or something equally embarrassing."

Until then, however, Nirvana continued to enjoy the riotous juggernaut of their full tour. They blew into New York City on November 14 for a four-day stay in the New York metropolitan area. In just a few days, Nirvana was scheduled to perform an acoustic show for *MTV's Unplugged* series—but before they could tackle a performance like that, they needed serious practice time.

The group convened at the SST rehearsal facility in New Jersey on November 16 and 17, with the Meat Puppets and other assorted guests in tow. Lori Goldston recalled that a number of songs were rehearsed, but eventually cut from the *Unplugged* set list. "I was sorry to see 'Molly's Lips' go; it's a really fun song to play. I think 'Been a Son' was also talked about at some point."

Three of the songs Nirvana wanted to perform were Meat Puppets songs: "Plateau," "Lake of Fire," and "Oh Me," which appeared on the album *Meat Puppets II*. At some point during rehearsal Kurt decided to invite the Puppets themselves to come and perform onstage. "Why not? We weren't learning the songs right anyway," Krist said. Guitarist and vocalist Curt Kirkwood, with his brother Cris, joined the project, and performed a few nights later with Nirvana at the MTV taping.

As the band was rehearsing, *In Utero* continued its struggle on the *Billboard* charts; as predicted, the album had obviously failed to generate the momentum *Nevermind* had enjoyed early in its release. In a *New York Times* article by Jon Pareles, Kurt said with little concern, "I don't have high hopes of staying up in the charts. Meat Loaf [whose comeback album was outperforming *In Utero*] is so obviously more talented than I am."

November 18, 1993, saw the *MTV Unplugged* taping at Sony Studios in New York City. Tickets for this once-in-a-lifetime show were printed in two different colors: red tickets for fans, who were let into the show first, and blue tickets for music industry personnel. Most of the front rows were taken up by New York–area Nirvana fan club members; the rest of the seating, toward the back, was left for the press. Supermodel Kate Moss and comedian Bobcat Goldthwait were among the big celebrities in the audience, which also included a host of musicians the band had invited themselves.

"Doing *MTV Unplugged* was a lot of fun," recalled Krist. "We had a blast . . . It was a Nirvana triumph, but it's also Nirvana lite. But it was cool that we managed to pull it off. At least I got to play my accordion."

Even though they had performed acoustically before, the members of Nirvana were still concerned about risking exposure on the high-profile *Unplugged* series. They were also worried about not having enough material to cover the hour-long show. In between songs, Kurt played emcee, talking and cracking jokes with members of the band.

Dave used a small drum set and jazzy brushes instead of sticks. Despite such confident gestures, playing this way was a venture into uncharted waters for them.

"It was a step forward we weren't sure we could do," Dave remembered. "It wasn't supposed to work. Then, when it was over and we saw it, someone in charge of the program asked if we wanted to do anything over. We said 'No, leave it.' But it's hard for me to watch or listen to now. It's so stark and haunting, almost spooky.

"I didn't expect it to go as well as it did, but it did and that makes it special. [And] these are the only all-acoustic recordings of those songs we ever did."

The atmosphere was loose and comfortable. Nirvana and their guest performers played fourteen songs straight through—each in one take, a departure for the MTV producers. Songs taped for other *Unplugged* performances generally get several run-throughs so that MTV editors can pick the best versions to air for later broadcast. But this was an *Unplugged* session unlike any other, which is exactly what Nirvana intended. The session would eventually be released as a live album reproducing the entire fifty-three-minute show as it was performed. The album does have its imperfections, but they only make it more riveting. The final product, just like the band itself, was raw and honest.

Producer Scott Litt was in the control booth engineering the mix of Nirvana's performance. For the show, Cobain played a rare Martin D-18E he'd bought from Voltage Guitar in Los Angeles earlier that fall; it was Kurt's main acoustic guitar. The D-18E had been introduced by Martin in 1958, but production stopped a year later, and only 302 of the guitars were ever produced.

"We didn't want to do *Unplugged* the conventional way, where bands show up with acoustic guitars and the drummers drum as hard as they usually do," said Dave. "[Then] it's not different at all except it's not electric. We wanted it . . . more loungier." One of the things that made the *Unplugged* concert unique was its set list. The band felt sure that a number of its songs wouldn't translate acoustically, and they gave themselves the challenge of creating a new set list of intriguing material. "We knew we didn't want to do an acoustic version of 'Teen Spirit': that would have been horrendously stupid," Dave said. "We felt it would be better if we found other songs."

Nirvana performed six cover tunes that evening, including the three Meat Puppets songs with the Kirkwood brothers. They also performed the Vaselines' "Jesus Doesn't Want Me for a Sunbeam," which they had often performed live, as well as David Bowie's "The Man Who Sold the World," another frequent entry on their electric shows. Bowie was deeply touched by the gesture when he saw the show later on MTV. "I was simply blown away when I found that Kurt Cobain liked my work, and I always wanted to talk to him about his reasons for covering 'The Man Who Sold the World,'" Bowie commented. "It was a good straightforward rendition and sounded somehow very honest. It would have been nice to have worked with him, but just talking would have been real cool."

The final cover song performed was an acoustic version of Leadbelly's "Where Did You Sleep Last Night." The song had been on Kurt's mind for years; not only had Nirvana featured it on tour, but Kurt and Krist had performed it on Mark Lanegan's solo album *The Winding Sheet* back in 1990. "Where Did You Sleep Last Night" is the most memorable performance on the entire *Unplugged In New York* album, and it is a hallmark moment in any and all of Nirvana's live performances. It wasn't enough that Kurt found a way to brilliantly express Leadbelly's convincing emotional pleas that were written over fifty years earlier, but he did so in a gut-wrenching manner that pierced right through the heart of the absolutely silent studio audience. The performance was the perfect ending for a perfect night that many thought Nirvana could never pull off. But they did so undeniably. The impact of the session, however, would not be measured for another several months, when the session would air on MTV worldwide.

Nirvana's mega-arena tour continued without fanfare through the southern states, landing in Atlanta, Georgia, on November 29 at the Omni. The press covering the tour had often painted a picture of a band bent on leaving destruction in its path, but often it was the type of fan Kurt hated the most that instigated the destruction.

"I was always comfortable with [disruptive fans]," he said in an interview that night at the Omni. "I'm not nearly as judgmental as I've probably acted or come off as in print. A lot of times when I do say stuff like that it's in a sarcastic tone, and that doesn't come across in print. The main concern I've had is what we had to deal with tonight"—Kurt had stopped the show to yell at a "breast-groper" in the audience. "I don't want jerks to come to the rock show, cause problems and ruin it for people. One of the biggest reliefs I've had is that it doesn't happen very much at all.

"It's really hard to describe just why this tour's been going so well," he reflected. "Every night we go out on-stage and I realize that ninety-eight percent of those kids honestly like our band. They're not up there to see a circus act, and even if they did go to a show to see that, they realize that I'm not fucked up after the second song and I'm having a good time. To be able to sell out an arena and know that ninety-eight percent of those kids are honestly good kids, nice people who are sincere, conscious of things, aware of things, it's a great feeling to know that."

As December came into view, a new single, "All Apologies," debuted on the *Billboard* Modern Rock Chart. It boosted the relatively poor sales of *In Utero* nationwide, and it would go all the way to number one. The powerful and sad ballad, which tells so much about its troubled songwriter, remained on the charts for twenty-one weeks.

MTV entered the Nirvana picture again with an invitation for the trio to play a special gig with Pearl Jam, Cypress Hill, and the Breeders for their *Loud and Live* show. The taped performance took place on December 13 at Pier 47 in Seattle, Washington, but Pearl Jam canceled due to illness, giving Nirvana the time to play a longer set. They blew the crowd away with "Radio Friendly Unit Shifter," "Heart-Shaped Box," "Drain You," "Pennyroyal Tea," "Breed," "Serve the Servants," "Lithium," "Rape Me," and "Destruction." The live version of "Scentless Apprentice" from this show appears on the CD *From the Muddy Banks of the Wishkah*.

Three days later, Nirvana's *Unplugged in New York* performance premiered on MTV; it was simulcast on radio nationwide. Two songs from the session were cut from the hourlong presentation—the cover of the Meat Puppets song "Oh Me" and "Something in the Way." The audio of both songs ended up on the *MTV Unplugged* album. A portion of the video of "Something in the Way" was shown in 1999 on *MTV's Bare Witness,* a behind-the-scenes look at the making of Nirvana's *Unplugged* performance. The entire "Oh Me" still remains unseen by the public.

Thus, 1993 ended well. The Butthole Surfers and the Hawaiian band Chokebone opened for Nirvana on a few West Coast dates. The last two of the year were at the Great Western Forum in Inglewood, California, on December 30, and then the next night at the Oakland Coliseum Arena, in Oakland, California. Kurt led the audience in the year-end countdown as the band played a twenty-five-song set. "Okay, you trained monkeys, everybody jump up and down!" Kurt screamed from the stage. "We'd talk between songs but our TelePrompTer isn't working tonight," added Krist.

The new year kicked off with a New Year's night show at Jackson County Expo Hall in Medford, Oregon, with the Butthole Surfers and Chokebone opening. The next day, Kurt and Courtney took the domestic bull by the horns and bought a new car—and not just any car, but a luxurious Lexus. A few days later, Kurt, completely uncomfortable with the new status symbol in his driveway, returned the car to the dealer.

The tour continued throughout the Northwest, stopping at the Seattle Center Arena on January 7. That night Nirvana played "Smells Like Teen Spirit" in Seattle for the first time in two years. This was the first of two consecutive sold-out shows at the Center, and the band celebrated its homecoming with the announcement that Pat Smear and Lori Goldston (whose services were on loan from Seattle's Black Cat Orchestra) were now official members of the band.

While they were in town, Kurt and Courtney purchased a $1.1 million shake-covered house on Lake Washington Boulevard East in Seattle. Located in an affluent part of town, the 1902 house is only a block away from Puget Sound, with stunning water views and a small park, bench and all. The young urban professionals in the neighborhood could hardly have been happy at the sight of their new neighbors and their friends.

While the Cobains signed the deed on their new abode, Soundgarden played a gig six blocks away from the Center Arena at the 1,500-seat Moore Theater. A crowd of seventy-five close friends and family were invited to this private show, which began at 4:30 that afternoon so as not to conflict with Nirvana's performance.

With plans to begin another European tour firmly in place, Nirvana popped into the Robert Lang Studios in Seattle for three days, from January 28 to 30, to record a new song entitled "You Know You're Right." Ironically, this song would come to have a remarkable impact on rejuvenating Nirvana's popularity almost ten years after Kurt's suicide, but obviously, no one knew it at the time. In fact, the whole session almost didn't happen at all.

"You Know You're Right" was a song the band had been toying around with during sound checks on their North American tour. They had actually played the song at a Chicago gig the previous October, calling it "On the Mountain." They had never seriously considered adding it to their repertoire, let alone recording and mixing it. When it came time to enter the Robert Lang Studios to put it together, Pat Smear returned home to rest in Los Angeles and never became a part of the recording. Despite repeated phone calls, Kurt never showed up during the first two days of the session, leaving Krist and Dave with no plan to follow. The duo instead jammed on songs Dave had been writing.

"Kurt came in on the third day, and we did ["You Know You're Right"] in one take," said Dave. "He sang three vocal tracks [and] that was it." Engineered by Adam Kasper, this raw but melodic performance contains some of the most feedback ever heard on a Nirvana track. With quiet verses and exploding choruses, even Dave had a difficult time trying to explain the song's direction.

"With *Nevermind*, we wanted to capture the raw energy of the band with optimum performance. *In Utero* was all about capturing the vibe on tape. ['You Know You're Right'] is somewhere between the two—but stranger." Unmixed and left in the vaults for nearly a decade, the lyrics to "You Know You're Right" have changed several times. Courtney even sang her own version of the song, calling it "You Got No Right" and incorporating her own lyrical interpretation, during the *MTV Unplugged* taping of her band, Hole.

On February 4, Nirvana touched down in Paris, France, to appear on Nulle Part Ailleurs-TV. They performed three songs, "Rape Me," "Pennyroyal

Tea," and "Drain You," before heading to the Pavilhao Carlos Lopes in Lisbon, Portugal, two days later to play their kickoff gig for the *In Utero* European tour, with "Very Ape," "Where Did You Sleep Last Night," "Noise," "Demolition," and a cover of the Knack's "My Sharona" sprinkled in.

On the day before Valentine's Day, in Paris, France, photographer Youri Lenquette witnessed a chilling glimpse into Nirvana's future. Kurt showed up for a photo shoot (high on drugs, claimed Courtney) for the French magazine *Globe* with a sports pistol he had recently purchased. In one pose, Kurt pressed the gun against his temple, pretending to squeeze the trigger and miming the impact of a gunshot to his head.

Kurt had befriended Lenquette after a fight with Courtney. "Kurt didn't have any real friends," Courtney would say later in the year. "I have a larger group of friends, people I've known for a long time . . . Kurt would hear me on the phone, laughing, getting hysterical, talking about designers. So he made this great officious ritual about his friends, and he made a friend in Paris named Youri. He dared me to say that Youri was a piece of shit, which was very obvious to me . . . [but] I never said a word . . . So he makes friends with this Youri, and he does this photo session with a gun in his mouth."

Traveling by bus throughout the French countryside certainly had its advantages for Nirvana, who found themselves with two luxury buses at their disposal. As they were headed back through France, Kurt began to lose his voice; throat spray was purchased in Paris and then administered before the upcoming shows to help ease his discomfort.

The tour chugged through France and Switzerland (where Kurt celebrated his twenty-seventh birthday) and down into Italy, where they performed "Serve the Servants" and "Dumb" on Tunnel TV in Rome on February 23.

Kurt's voice was fading fast, and doctors along the route told him to stop singing or risk losing it permanently. "You shouldn't be singing the way you're singing," said Alex MacLeod, road manager for the tour, mimicking the advice Kurt was receiving from doctors. " 'You have to take at least two months off and learn to sing properly.' And [Kurt] was like, 'Fuck that.' "

After the Terminal Einz show in Germany on March 1, Kurt's health worsened dramatically. The drugs and his throat and stomach problems all contributed to the depths of depression into which Kurt was plunging. He finally lost his voice halfway through the performance, and according to

MacLeod he went to see an ear, nose, and throat specialist the next day. "[Kurt] was told to take two to four weeks' rest," MacLeod said. "He was given spray and [medicine] for his lungs because he was diagnosed as having severe laryngitis and bronchitis." With their lead singer out of commission, the band was obliged to cancel scheduled dates in Munich and Offenbach.

While they were stopped in Germany, Kurt picked up the phone in the middle of the night and called his fifty-two-year-old uncle Art Cobain back in Aberdeen. Kurt hadn't seen his uncle since he was a child, but he now confided in Art that he was distressed at the way things were turning out for him. "He said he was getting really fed up with his way of life," the older Cobain recalled. "He really seemed to be reaching out. I invited him to our family reunion, but he never showed up." Art's suggestion—that Kurt look for solace in a family that had played a major part in Kurt's emotional distress since childhood—could not have been very enticing.

The tour that had seemed to be going so well was suddenly spiraling out of control. In an attempt to escape the press and get some much-needed rest, Kurt, with Francis Bean in tow, checked into the majestic Excelsior Hotel on Rome's Via Veneto. There is every reason to believe that he had returned to heroin as he retracted into his depression. But the only explanation given to the press was that Kurt Cobain was suffering from a "sore throat."

Eighteen

Let's keep the music with us.
We'll always have it, forever.
—KRIST NOVOSELIC

Courtney finally rejoined Kurt and Frances Bean at the Excelsior in Rome on Thursday, March 3. Her responsibilities with Hole had taken her away for almost a month—"the longest we'd gone without seeing each other since we'd been together," Courtney said. Kurt missed Courtney terribly, and he welcomed her back into his world with the zeal of a committed romantic. "He knew how obsessed I [was] with Roman history, and he got this beautiful hotel room, and covered it with flowers," Courtney recalled. "And he bought me these beautiful jewels, some three-carat diamond earrings, and some roses, which I thought was beautiful. He even bought me lingerie!" Courtney would later make it clear that Kurt was seldom the romantic type; this reception must have made quite an impression.

As the clock struck midnight and Thursday disappeared into Friday, Kurt put Frances Bean down for the night and asked a member of the hotel staff to run to an all-night chemist in the city for a quantity of the prescription tranquilizer Rohypnol, usually used to treat severe insomnia, but also used to ease the symptoms of heroin withdrawal. A short time later, with Pat Smear joining the party, Kurt ordered a bottle of champagne from room service. After Pat left, Kurt and Courtney retired to the bedroom, but Courtney fell asleep before Kurt could consummate his romantic longings, leaving him alone to ponder his troubles. "The rejection he must have felt after all that anticipation—I mean, for Kurt to be that Mr. Romance was pretty intense," Courtney later said. Kurt's reaction to rejection that evening must have stemmed from more than sexual frustration, however. For the past several months, more and more of Courtney's time was being eaten up by her work with Hole, and Kurt, who supported her independence and her band, had begun to feel she was neglecting her family. "Even if I wasn't in the mood, I should have just laid there for him," Courtney said in retrospect. "All he needed was to get laid. He would have been fine. But with Kurt, you had to give yourself to him. He was psychic. He could tell if you were not all the way there. Sex, to him, was incredibly sacred. He found commitment to be an aphrodisiac."

By the early morning, Kurt was no longer in the bed. "I woke up to reach for him, basically to [make love to] him, 'cause I hadn't seen him in so long," said Courtney. "And he wasn't there. And I always get alarmed when Kurt's not there, 'cause I figure he's in the corner somewhere, doing something bad." Courtney's worst fears were realized sometime between 4:00 and 6:00 A.M., when she found Kurt out cold at the foot of their bed. He was fully clothed and clutching a large sum of money in one hand, a two-page note in the other. Terrified, Courtney called for the hotel staff, who immediately phoned for medical help.

"There's blood coming out his nostrils . . . [and] he's got one thousand American dollars clutched in one hand, which was gray, and a note in the other," Courtney remembered. "[The note] was on hotel stationery, and he's talking about how I'm not in love with him anymore, and he can't go through another divorce [like his parents']. And then the next page is like how we're destined to be together, and how he knows how much I love him, and please don't take this personally, and how Dr. Baker [a senior psychotherapist at Canyon Ranch, a health and wellness resort the couple attended] said that like Hamlet, he had to choose life or death, and that he's choosing death."

Around 6:30 A.M., an ambulance finally appeared, rushing Courtney and a still-unconscious Kurt to the Umberto 1 Polyclinic Hospital in the center of the city, where he was admitted and immediately placed on a life-support machine. Doctors pumped out the contents of his stomach, but Kurt slipped further into unconsciousness as five hours of emergency treatment failed to have any positive effect. By 11:30 A.M., Radio 1 in London carried the first news reports of the overdose, claiming that his life was in danger after slipping into a coma. Around noon, doctors transferred Kurt, still in critical condition, from Umberto 1 to the American Hospital, a private clinic on the outskirts of Rome. No reason for the move was given, but the staff at Umberto 1 described Kurt as being in "grave condition." It has since been revealed by Courtney that some fifty pills were found in Kurt's stomach, including Rohypnol. Rumors flew that a suicide note was found at the scene, but Nirvana's management company, Gold Mountain, denied that Kurt's overdose was a suicide attempt. "A note was found," said a company spokesperson, "but Kurt insisted that it wasn't a suicide note. He just took all of his and Courtney's money and was going to run away and disappear." An official statement regarding Kurt's condition was promised by American Hospital officials at 5:30 P.M.

As early evening arrived, with radio stations reporting that Kurt had gone into "an irreversible coma," Kurt regained consciousness for the first time. A spokesperson for Gold Mountain reported, "I don't know if he's talking lucidly but he's opened his eyes and is moving his hands. His wife and daughter are with him." At 5:30 P.M., the American Hospital declined to release any statement to the media after Kurt's family demanded that all information be kept secret—a request undoubtedly fostered by the press infiltration of Los Angeles's Cedars-Sinai Hospital in 1992, when Kurt was treated for illnesses connected with narcotics abuse.

Earlier in the day, Courtney had given a defiant finger to the media gathered in front of the American Hospital as she made her way inside. "I was hysterical throughout [the whole ordeal]. I mean, they had two tubes in his nose and two in his mouth, things coming out of every available artery . . . They had to put the glucose in through his neck. All of his life functions, including pissing, were being done by a machine. I mean, I have seen him get *really* fucked up before but I have never seen him nearly eat it. When Kurt came round and started responding, we gave him a clipboard and a pencil— and you know what the first thing he wrote was? FUCK YOU. I tell you, I'd take ten days of *Vanity Fair* after this."

Around 6:00 P.M. a statement was finally released by DGC. It said the twenty-seven-year-old singer "had suffered a complete collapse due to fatigue and severe influenza . . . Complications arose after he combined prescription painkillers and alcohol. Doctors report that he has made responsive signs." Nirvana fans began to gather outside the American Hospital, patiently waiting for news of Kurt's health. Many were crying, while others played Nirvana recordings on their car stereos.

The next day, according to the *New Musical Express* magazine, Nirvana's co-manager Janet Billig warned the media that the talk of Kurt's recovery might be premature. Medical reports confirmed that he was conscious, responding to treatment, and able to communicate with doctors. But they repeated that he was still in a very serious condition. One newspaper article cited a warning from a medical expert that Cobain might have suffered permanent damage. At 2:00 P.M. a press conference was held by Dr. Osvaldo Galletta, head of intensive treatment at the American Hospital in Rome. He confirmed that Kurt had emerged from his coma and could be released from the hospital as early as the next day. Later that night, at around 7:00 P.M., British DJ John Peel dedicated the Raincoats' "No One's Little Girl" to Kurt and Courtney during his Radio 1 show.

The next evening, at roughly 10:30, Billig told *NME* that Kurt was steadily improving, and had spent most of the day writing letters to fans and well-wishers, thanking them for their messages and prayers. The hospital announced that he was likely to be taken off the critical list within the next forty-eight hours if his condition continued to improve. As the scandal-hungry media shifted their attention elsewhere, Kurt checked out of the American Hospital on Wednesday, March 9. A hospital spokesman assured reporters that Kurt would suffer no permanent effects from the coma, but Kurt and his bandmates agreed to put Nirvana's European tour on hold. Together, Kurt, Courtney, and Frances flew back to Seattle, retreating to the house on Lake Washington Boulevard.

Sadly, Kurt had scarcely landed in Seattle before he let his addiction run away with him again. "I didn't find this out till later, but Kurt had called from the ICU in Rome and had arranged for a gram of heroin to be delivered in the bushes of our house," said Courtney. "It was fucking five or six days after Rome, and he was high as a kite."

Kurt's relationship with Courtney, like so much else in his life, was crumbling. On Friday, March 18, Seattle police were called to the Cobains' Lake Washington Boulevard East home by Courtney for another domestic-dispute call. She had attempted to kick in a locked door from the outside when she saw Kurt inside surrounded by his guns. Finally, Kurt rose from his chair and casually unlocked the door. "And there were the guns, out," Courtney said. "I grabbed the revolver, and I put it to my head, and I said, 'I'm going to pull this right now. I cannot see you die. I can't see you die again.' He grabbed my hand. He was screaming. 'There's no safety. You don't understand, there's no safety on that. It's going to go off. It's going to go off.' So he got it from me. And I was seriously going to blow my head off right in front of him, because I could not deal with it."

There are many conflicting reports on what actually happened that night. However, one thing is certain: It was a massive fight. When the police arrived and asked whether there were any guns in the house, Kurt said no and Courtney said yes at the same moment. Eventually, the police found and confiscated four guns: a .38-caliber Taurus revolver, a Beretta .380 semiautomatic handgun, a second Taurus .380 handgun, and a Colt AR-15 semiautomatic rifle. They also found twenty-five boxes of ammunition and quantities of an unknown medication. Because the dispute was limited to verbal exchanges, the police made no arrests. Kurt claimed he wasn't suicidal, that he was just trying to get away from Courtney. Kurt then left the house, the police report said. "Due to the volatile situation with the threat of suicide and the recovery of unknown medication, the weapons and the bottle of pills were placed into custody," the police reported.

The following day, Courtney and Krist begin an intervention with Kurt, confronting him about his drug use in the hope of persuading him that he urgently needed professional help. "The reason I flipped out on the eighteenth of March was because . . . couldn't take [Kurt's heroin use] anymore," Courtney said. "When he came home from Rome high, I flipped out. If there's one thing in my whole life I could take back, it would be that. Getting mad at him for coming home high. I wish to God I hadn't. I wish I'd just been the way I always was, just tolerant of it. It made him feel so worthless when I got mad at him. The only thing I can call it was a downward spiral from there. I got angry, and it was the first time I ever had."

Steven Chatoff, executive director of Anacapa by the Sea, a behavioral health center for the treatment of addictions and psychological disorders in Port Hueneme, California, was hired to help. "They called me to see what could be done," he said later. "[Kurt] was using, up in Seattle. He was in full denial. It was very chaotic. And [his friends] were in fear for his life. It was a crisis." Chatoff began interviewing friends, family members, and business associates in preparation for enacting a full-scale intervention. According to Chatoff, someone then tipped off Kurt, and the procedure had to be canceled. Gold Mountain claims that it found another intervention counselor and turned down Chatoff's services politely. When Chatoff learned Kurt would be headed to the Exodus Recovery Center in the Daniel Freeman Marina Hospital in Marina Del Rey, California, he was not encouraged. "I was not supportive of that at all," Chatoff said, "because that was just another detox 'buff and shine.'"

The first intervention had failed altogether. Krist and his wife, Shelli, then made a second attempt of their own, telling him how much they loved him and wished he'd get help. It didn't work. Finally, on Friday, March 25, a full-scale intervention took place at his house. Roughly ten friends, including Krist, Pat Smear, John Silva, Dylan Carlson, Danny Goldberg, Janet Billig, and Courtney attended. As part of the intervention, Pat and Krist threatened to break up the band, and Courtney threatened to leave Kurt. The session last five hours. At first Kurt was unwilling to admit he had a drug problem; he claimed not even to believe that his recent behavior had been self-destructive. By the end of the tense five-hour therapy, however, Cobain's resolve had weakened, and he agreed to enter a detox program in Los Angeles. He then retired to the basement with Smear, where they rehearsed some new material.

During the intervention, Frances Bean had been staying with Danny Goldberg's wife and children, playing with Danny's three-and-a-half-year-old daughter, Katie. When it was over, Goldberg called the Cobain house. "These things are so adversarial, and I just wanted to call him and tell him I loved him, just to change the tone," Goldberg said. "Frances had pinched Katie, so she wanted to talk to Kurt about that. Then I got back on and told him I loved him, and he went into rehab a day or two later." Later that day Courtney and Kurt were supposed to leave for Los Angeles. Once at the Seattle airport, though, Kurt changed his mind and refused to board the flight. Instead, on Sunday, March 27, Courtney wound up on a plane to Los Angeles with Janet Billig. That day was the last time Courtney saw Kurt alive.

In Los Angeles, Courtney checked into a five-hundred-dollar-a-night suite in the Peninsula Hotel in Beverly Hills, and began an outpatient program to detox from drugs. (Gold Mountain would maintain that it was for tranquilizers.) During her stay, Courtney had her final conversation with Kurt on the phone. "He said, 'Courtney, no matter what happens, I want you to know that you made a really good record.' I said, 'Well, what do you mean?' And he said, 'Just remember, no matter what, I love you.' " It was the last time she heard his voice.

On Monday, March 28, Kurt finally seemed to be reconciling himself to the detox program. Before boarding the plane, though, Kurt stopped by Dylan Carlson's condominium in the Lake City area of Seattle and asked Carlson to help him get a gun so he could ward off trespassers who had been frequenting his property on Lake Washington Boulevard East. As far as Carlson was concerned, the visit wasn't out of the ordinary. "[Kurt] seemed normal— we'd been talking," Carlson said. "Plus, I'd loaned him guns before." There was nothing criminal about what Carlson did: In Seattle, as of this writing, there is no registration or waiting period required to obtain shotguns. But Carlson believed Kurt came to him because he was afraid the police would confiscate any purchase, since they had taken his other firearms after the domestic dispute that had occurred ten days earlier.

The two purchased a six-pound Remington Model 11 20-gauge shotgun and a box of ammunition for roughly $300, which Kurt gave Carlson in cash. Dylan bought the gun and then, knowing Kurt was supposed to head off to Los Angles for detox treatment, offered to hold on to it until Kurt returned home. Kurt, however, insisted on keeping the shotgun himself. Police would later assert that he brought the weapon home and stashed it in a closet.

Finally, Kurt packed his bags and set off for rehab. Krist drove Kurt to the airport, where he got on a plane and flew to Los Angeles. There, Pat Smear and a Gold Mountain employee met Kurt and drove him to the Exodus Recovery Center. (This wasn't the first time Kurt had been there; he had spent four days detoxing at Exodus in 1992, but left the center before his treatment was completed.) Kurt talked to several psychologists there, none of whom considered him suicidal. By all reports, Kurt seemed to be in good spirits and looked healthy while at the clinic. He was visited by Frances and her nanny and by Gibby Haynes, but not once by Courtney.

On Tuesday, March 29, *In Utero* was rereleased specifically for Wal-Mart and Kmart. The song title "Rape Me" was changed to "Waif Me" on the album sleeve, and the nonoffensive section of bones and flowers in the cover art was blown up to cover up the fetuses. Kurt had apparently approved the gesture out of personal loyalty to Kmart, where he'd bought all his records when he was a kid growing up in Aberdeen.

On Thursday, March 31, one of the last people to see Kurt at Exodus was an artist known as "Joe Mama," an old friend from Olympia. "I was ready to see him look like shit and depressed," he said, since Kurt had only been at the clinic a few days. "[But Kurt] looked so fucking great." The treatment appeared to be working, and the relaxed atmosphere of the clinic may have sped up Kurt's temporary recovery and subsequent escape. Though Exodus is a low-security clinic, Kurt could have walked out the door if he had wanted to, but he had something else in mind. One of Kurt's visitors recalled, "When I went to visit him, Gibby Haynes was in there with him. I don't know Gibby, but he's a nut. He was jabbering a mile a minute about people who had jumped over the wall there, stuff like '[One guy] went over the wall five times.' Kurt probably thought it would be funny."

Sometime around 7:25 that evening, Kurt told the clinic staff he was stepping out onto the patio for a smoke. He looked around the compound, and then scaled the wall. "We watch our patients really well," said a spokesperson for Exodus, "but some do get out." A couple of hours after he scaled the wall, Kurt boarded a Delta flight back to Seattle, arriving around 1:00 A.M. Since most of his friends and business associates in Los Angeles were preoccupied with a Gold Mountain Management function, no one noticed he was missing.

Nirvana's European tour, scheduled to resume on April 12 in Birmingham, England, was officially postponed on April 1 after a previously released doctor's report found that Kurt needed more rest. Yet Kurt himself was nowhere to be found—not at the rehab center, not at home in Seattle. Courtney feared Kurt might have taken off on a heroin binge.

Courtney hired a private investigator, Tom Grant, to help her find Kurt; she also reportedly hired a second private investigator to watch the home of Kurt's drug dealer, a woman who lived in the town's Capitol Hill district. Kurt visited there on the evening of April 1, and the woman later told a Seattle newspaper that Kurt said to her that night, "Where are my friends when I need them? Why are my friends against me?" As April Fools' Day came to an end with no sign of Kurt, the friends Kurt felt were abandoning him were frantic in their search for him.

With the sun beaming off Puget Sound on April 2, Kurt, according to Courtney, called the Beverly Hills Peninsula Hotel looking for her. Trying to get through a block on the hotel phone, he stayed on the line for a reported uncharacteristically patient six minutes. When Kurt finally returned to his home soon thereafter, he found Cali staying there. "I talked to Cali, who said he had seen [Kurt] on Saturday [April 2]," said Carlson, adding that Cali described Kurt as looking ill and acting weird, but "I couldn't get a hold of him myself." The police believe Kurt wandered around town with no clear agenda. A taxi supervisor reported that Kurt was driven to a gun shop to buy shotgun shells; a receipt for the ammo was later found at Kurt's house. "After Kurt left [Exodus], I was on the phone with Courtney all the time," said Joe Mama. "She was really freaked out, so we drove around looking for him at all the places he might have gone." Neighbors told Courtney they spotted Kurt in a park near his house during the time of the search, looking ill and wearing an incongruously heavy coat. According to an article in the *Seattle Times* on April 9, 1994, the missing persons report filed by Kurt's mother suggests Kurt may have gone to a particular three-story brick apartment building in the Capitol Hill district, described as a location to buy narcotics. It is finally reported that Kurt may have spent time with some junkie friends, shooting up so much that they kicked him out because they were worried that he would OD on them.

Sunday and Monday passed. Still no one could find Kurt. On Sunday, Seattle police continued to follow the few leads they had, but most were dead ends.

During the night of Tuesday, April 5, there were reports of Kurt sightings at a dealer's place in Seattle's Capitol Hill district later that evening, where it is believed Kurt made his final drug purchase. But sometime during the late afternoon or early evening of that day, Kurt Cobain, under the influence of heroin, propped a stool against the French doors of the room above his garage at 171 Lake Washington Boulevard East, and shot himself once in the head, dying instantly.

Evidence at the scene suggests that Kurt removed his hunter's cap, which he wore when he didn't want people to recognize him, and dug into the cigar box that contained his drug stash. He completed a one-page note in red ink, addressing it to "Boddah," the name he had given his childhood imaginary friend. Kurt spoke of the great empty hole he felt had opened inside him, turning him into a "miserable, self-destructive death rocker." He also expressed his fear that Frances Bean's life would turn out like his own. Calling Courtney Love "a goddess of a wife who sweats ambition and empathy," he implored her to "please keep going for the child's sake." The trauma inflicted on Kurt's upper body was so devastating that Seattle police at first were unable to identify the shattered corpse that lay on the floor. It wasn't until they noticed Kurt's wallet, suspiciously lying wide open on the floor next to his body, that their worst fears were confirmed.

The position of the wallet and the manner in which it was found led many to believe that someone was with Kurt Cobain when he died. It was later discovered that Kurt and an unidentified person had spent at least one night during his disappearance at Kurt's other home, an eleven-acre estate east of Seattle that he and Courtney had purchased in March of 1993. There, a sleeping bag was found, as well as an ashtray filled with two brands of cigarette butts. One was a brand known to be used by Kurt; the other was not. Next to the sleeping bag was a picture of the sun, and drawn in black ink above it were the words, "Cheer up."

It was three more days before Kurt's death became known to anyone, but many of Kurt's friends had already assumed the worst. "That last week was unbelievably horrible," commented Jessica Hopper, a longtime friend of Courtney's who was the editor of the Riot Grrrl fanzine *Hit It or Quit It*. "Everyone was completely freaked out because you knew [Kurt's death] was going to happen soon. It was just a matter of *how* soon."

The search continued for Kurt the following day, as police looked into a report by two people who claim Kurt's Capitol Hill heroin dealer told them Kurt had come by her apartment the night before. But the dealer denied the incident to police.

On Thursday, April 7, the management of the Peninsula Hotel phoned Los Angles police to report a suspected drug overdose of one of its guests. When police arrived, Courtney was interrogated and brought to Century City Hospital for a suspected heroin overdose. When she was released into police custody later that day, Courtney was booked, under the name Courtney Michele Cobain, for felony heroin possession and receiving stolen property. Court-ney was released on $10,000 bail, and at her May 5 arraignment was cleared of charges that she had illegal drugs and syringes. Courtney's suspected over-dose was explained as an allergic reaction to a muscle relaxant.

The rumors surrounding Nirvana and its future as a band had by now gone completely out of control. Word of Kurt's suspected suicide attempt in Rome had saturated all corners of the music industry, and media outlets like the *Los Angeles Times* had read the band's latest tour postponement as a sign of its impending demise. Krist and Dave were unavailable for comment; Courtney had been arrested for a suspected drug overdose, and Kurt was nowhere to be found. The switchboards at DGC Records and Gold Mountain Management were flooded with calls from fans and press in search of an explanation. Add-ing fuel to the fire was Ted Gardner, the organizer of the Lollapalooza Fes-tival, who, on Friday, April 8, released a statement to the press that read: "Although we had been negotiating with Nirvana to headline Lollapalooza 1994, due to the ill health of Kurt Cobain, we cannot confirm them on the bill. We wish Kurt a full and speedy recovery, and look forward to the pos-sibility of working with Nirvana in the future."

There is a macabre aspect to the events of the following few days: An article ran in *Entertainment Weekly* about the newly sanitized version of *In Utero,* followed by a statement from DGC explaining the move—all while the real issue, the whereabouts of Kurt Cobain, went dismayingly ignored by all parties.

But not for long. For Veca electronics alarm technician Gary Smith, the morning of Friday, April 8, 1994, was nothing more than the last day of a very busy workweek. He headed to the house at 171 Lake Washington Boul-evard East to perform routine work on the alarm system there. Smith arrived sometime after 8:00 A.M. About thirty minutes later, while climbing an out-side staircase above the detached garage, he peered into the adjoining apart-ment and saw Kurt's body. "At first I thought it was a mannequin," Smith recalled. "Then I noticed [the body] had blood in the right ear. Then I saw a shotgun lying across [Kurt's] chest, pointing up at his chin." Oddly, instead of calling the police immediately, Smith called Veca Electronics. A Veca employee then called radio station KXRX-FM with what he claimed was "the scoop of the century," adding, "You're going to owe me a lot of concert tickets for this one." Marty Reimer, the on-air personality who took the call, said, "Broadcasting this information was kind of an eerie decision to make . . . We're not a news station." Gary Smith, or someone at Veca, then telephoned the Seattle police.

When they arrived, the police had to break into the cottage, perched above the detached garage, to get to Kurt's body. According to the King County medical examiner's report, a high concentration of heroin and traces of Valium were found in Kurt's bloodstream, but Chief Investigator Bill Haglund said that his death was the result of a gunshot wound to the head. The blast into his temple had done so much physical damage that he was identifiable only by his fingerprints. The following day, the *Seattle Times* ran a photo of Kurt's body; all that was showing was one dirty-jeaned leg, a badly tied Converse one-star sneaker with a white sock, and a light blue thrift store shirt.

News of Kurt's suicide came out in public that morning through various unconfirmed sources. Then, at 10:07 A.M. Pacific Standard Time, word that a body had been found at the Cobain residence hit the press wire services: *"Seattle—Seattle Police are investigating a report that a body has been found at the home of Nirvana singer Kurt Cobain. Spokeswoman Vinette Tichi (Tee'-Shee) says the body was discovered by an electrician who went to the home this morning to do some work."* Kurt's sister Kim and his mother, Wendy O'Connor, are said to have heard the first reports on the radio. The next Associated Press update came at 11:49 A.M., but there was still no confirmation that the body was that of Kurt Cobain. The Seattle Police would only say that the body of a young white man in his twenties had been found with a shotgun wound in the head. A police spokeswoman said the body had been there about a day; when pressed for a positive identification of the body, she was forced to demur to the medical examiner's office. Medical investigators said they presumed the body found at Kurt's home was that of the embattled singer. Then came the confirmation no one could bear to hear: At 2:25 P.M. Pacific Standard Time, the Associated Press released a statement by the president of Geffen and DGC Records, Ed Rosenblatt, confirming that twenty-seven-year-old Kurt Cobain had been found in his home with a self-inflicted gunshot wound to the head. "The world has lost a great artist and we've lost a great friend," the statement read. Wendy O'Connor revealed to the press that Kurt had been missing for seven days, and said that she had been fearing her son would be found dead, telling the Associated Press, "Now he's gone and joined that stupid club" of the drug-related rock casualties like Jimi Hendrix, Janis Joplin, Brian Jones, and Jim Morrison.

Gold Mountain Management echoed the DGC statement in a similar special release. "We are deeply saddened by the loss of such a talented artist, close friend, loving husband, and father. The intensity and creativity of Kurt's music and his thoughts will always be treasured. Kurt's art has transcended the popular to speak to millions around the world. Painfully, Kurt's passions and feelings about his fame overwhelmed him. We will miss him, his music, and his friendship deeply." Television stations broadcast the news as soon as it became official. And yet, in spite of the huge success of Nirvana over the past two years and Kurt's regular appearances in the press, it was clear that many news anchors reporting the event had little idea who it was they were reporting about. Some referred to him as "rock and roller Kurt Cobain" and "the leader of the grunge movement." Those who knew him accurately called him "the voice of a generation."

Two thousand miles away from Seattle, in a hotel in Fairfax, Virginia, Eddie Vedder reduced his room to a pile of rubble in reaction to the news. He later said that Kurt's suicide influenced him to work through his own problems to avoid getting swallowed up, too. Even though there had been friction between the Pearl Jam and Nirvana, Vedder undoubtedly had a deep respect for the troubled superstar. It was Kurt, after all, who provided for him a front-row seat to a world Vedder was trying so desperately not to fall into himself.

That night, from the stage, Eddie Vedder said to his audience, "Sometimes, whether you like it or not, people elevate you. It's real easy to fall . . . I don't think any of us in this room would be here tonight if not for Kurt Cobain." The suicide had such a profound impact on the members of Pearl Jam that they postponed a well-planned tour for at least two months to give themselves a chance to regroup emotionally.

Word of Kurt's death fell like a hammer into the heart of the music in-dustry. Sinead O'Connor recorded an emotional version of "All Apologies" in Kurt's honor; Patti Smith offered a song, "About a Boy." In his suicide note, Kurt quoted a line from a Neal Young song: "It's better to burn out than to fade away." Young was so moved by Kurt's gesture that he wrote a song for Kurt called "Sleeps with Angels." Young had made several attempts to reach Kurt shortly after Kurt's suicide attempt in Rome, but by the time the message reached Nirvana's management, Kurt had already disappeared from sight.

The Seattle music scene has lost many of its favorite musician sons and daughters in the previous few years, and the repercussions had echoed throughout the United States. Mother Love Bone singer Andrew Wood died from a heroin overdose in 1990. A year later, Sub Pop poet and Seattle scenester Jesse Bernstein shot himself to death. In 1992, Stephanie Sargent from the band 7 Year Bitch overdosed, and the Gits' lead singer, Mia Zapata, was strangled to death in July 1993. When Kurt died in the spring of 1994, no one knew which way to turn. Who would be next, many of us wondered. Millions of parents nationwide were suddenly urged to bridge the generation gap that Nirvana's music had highlighted, and to talk to the children about suicide. The message was clear for baby boomers everywhere: Kurt Cobain was not merely some rock 'n' roll icon who couldn't handle drugs. In ways that were important to recognize, he was every parent's child.

Within twenty-four hours of Kurt's reported death, the media blitz hit Seattle in a full piranha force. On Saturday, April 9, the television show *A Current Affair* offered Veca electrician Gary Smith $1,500 for the exclusive rights to his story. Smith politely turned them down. That night, at a previously scheduled and very subdued Sub Pop Records anniversary party at Seattle's Crocodile Club Cafe, staff members of another program, *Hard Copy*, actually offered guests of the party $100 for their invitations. They found no takers.

Meanwhile, collectors and fans swamped stores nationwide with a rush on Nirvana products of all kinds. *In Utero*, until now nothing more than a moderate success, jumped from number seventy-two to number twenty-seven in one week on the *Billboard* Album Chart in the short time since Kurt's death was reported.

Unannounced to the press or the public, a private funeral service for Kurt was held at Seattle's Unity Church of Truth on Sunday, April 10, 1994. Soft chamber music played over the sound system as mourners, including R.E.M.'s Peter Buck, who lived nearby, took their places in pews lined with childhood photos of Kurt. Minister Stephen Towles, who had spoken earlier at the public vigil, oversaw the private service. Courtney Love, Krist Novoselic, Bruce Pavitt, and Danny Goldberg also spoke to the small number of close and personal friends. Courtney, clad in black, read passages from the Book of Job and some of Kurt's favorite poems from Arthur Rimbaud's *Illuminations*. She told anecdotes about Kurt's childhood and read portions of his suicide note. He said that he had been faking his passion for too long, and could not do it anymore. "I have a daughter who reminds me too much of what I used to be," Kurt wrote, sadly.

Kurt's friend and best man, Dylan Carlson, read verses from a Buddhist poet. Krist Novoselic, speaking on behalf of Dave Grohl and Pat Smear, said Kurt's heart was his greatest asset. "His heart was his receiver . . . and his transmitter," said the gentle giant, with tender affection and grace.

Danny Goldberg gave the last eulogy of the service. "I believe [Kurt] lived several more years because of Courtney Love," he said. "When I met him, he was very depressed—[and] his love for her was one of the things that kept him going." Goldberg had been something of a mentor to Cobain, and he was one of the few people in the music business Kurt looked up to. "I certainly don't feel I did a very good job with Kurt if that was my role," Goldberg reflected remorsefully. "I wish I could have come up with something more spiritually inspiring about keeping him here."

When the funeral was over, mourners listened to a tape of some of Kurt's favorite music, including John Lennon's "In My Life." His body was cremated and Courtney, Wendy, and Krist decided together where the ashes would be privately spread.

Blocks away from the Unity Church, a memorial service for fans was held in Seattle's Flag Pavilion. In a rare Emerald City occurrence, three radio stations, KISW, KXEX, and KNND, joined forces to air the service. Krist Novoselic read a statement to those in attendance: "On behalf of Dave, Pat and I, I would like to thank you all for your concern at this time. We remember Kurt for what he was; caring, generous and sweet. Let's keep the music with us; we'll always have it, forever. Kurt had an ethic toward his fans that was rooted in the punk-rock way of thinking: no band is special, no player royalty. If you've got a guitar and a lot of soul, just bang something out and mean it. You're the superstar, plugged into tones and rhythms that are uniquely and universally human; music. Heck, use your guitar as a drum; just catch a groove and let it flow out of your heart. That's the level that Kurt spoke to us on, in our hearts. And that's where he and the music will always be, forever."

Courtney did not come to this service, but she prepared a taped message that was recorded earlier at 171 Lake Washington Boulevard East. The message was played in its entirety for all to hear who attended the public vigil at Flag Pavilion. She began her message by empathizing with the people at the vigil because she was as confused as they were. She said that Kurt had left a suicide note, and she characterized it as more like "a letter to the editor." She also declared that she wouldn't read all of it because "it's none of your fucking business." Clearly distraught, she called Kurt an asshole multiple times. The suicide note read, in part:

This note should be pretty easy to understand. All the warnings from the Punk Rock 101 courses over the years since my first introduction to the, shall we say, ethics involved with independence and the embracement of your community has proven to be very true. I haven't felt the excitement of listening to as well as creating music . . . and writing for too many years now. I feel guilty beyond words about these things. For example, when we're backstage and the lights go out and the manic roar of the crowd begins, it doesn't affect me the way in which it did for Freddie Mercury, who seemed to love and relish in the love and adoration from the crowd, which is something I totally admire and envy. The fact is, I can't fool you, any one of you . . . but I still can't get over the frustration, the guilt, and the empathy I have for everyone. There's good in all of us and I simply love people too much. So much that it makes me feel too fucking sad. The sad, little, sensitive, unappreciated Pisces. . . . I have it good, very good, and I'm grateful, but since the age of seven, I've become hateful towards all humans in general, only because it seems so easy for people to get along and have empathy . . . Only because I love and feel for people too much, I guess. Thank you all from the pit of my burning nauseous stomach for your letters and concerns during the past years. I'm too much of an erratic moody baby, and I don't have the passion any-more. . . . Peace, Love, Empathy, Kurt Cobain.

Before returning home from the private service at the Unity Church, Courtney and her friend Kat Bjelland, who would stay with Courtney for several weeks, stopped by the fans' candlelight vigil at the Seattle Center with a few friends. By now, though, the area was largely deserted. Courtney handed out a few pieces of Kurt's old clothes to the few who were still mourning. Bjelland was wearing Kurt's watch, given to her by Courtney.

In an interview with *Rolling Stone* later that year, Courtney explained that there was more to the suicide note than she read on tape to the fans. "He wrote me a letter other than his suicide note. It's kind of long. I put it in a safe-deposit box. I might show it to Frances—maybe. It's very fucked-up writing. 'You know I love you, I love Frances, I'm sorry. Please don't follow me.' It's long because he repeats himself. 'I'm sorry, I'm sorry, I'm sorry. I'll be there, I'll protect you. I don't know where I'm going. I just can't be here anymore.' There's definitely a narcissism in what he did, too. It was very snotty of him. When we decided we were in love at the Beverly Garland Hotel [a few years earlier], we found this dead bird. Took out three feathers. And he said, 'This is for you, this is for me, and this is for our baby we're gonna have.' And [now] he took one of the feathers away."

It did not take long for the news of Kurt's death to take effect on the youth who appeared to relate to his pain. Australian newspapers reported the suicide of a teen who killed himself in an apparent tribute to Kurt. Another depressed teenager in Turkey locked the door to her room and shot herself in the head while Nirvana's music played loudly in the background. Closer to home in Seattle, just a few hours after attending Kurt's candlelight vigil, a twenty-eight-year-old man shot himself to death.

On Monday, April 11, 1994, Seattle police officially confirmed that Kurt's death was a suicide. The news would make the covers of *People, Entertainment Weekly, Rolling Stone,* and *Newsweek* magazines. And in a bizarre reminder of the breadth of the generation gap, *60 Minutes* commentator Andy Rooney horrified viewers with an insensitive rant in which he wondered how a wealthy man could ever reach the point of suicide.

A few days later, on a sun-drenched Seattle morning, Screaming Trees singer Mark Lanegan remarked that Kurt might have thought differently about committing suicide had the weather been this nice on the day he died.

Nineteen

For a long time, I wouldn't listen to Nirvana.
It was too hard. But now I listen and
I'm rediscovering it and it's great.

—KRIST NOVOSELIC

T he U.S. legal system did not stop to mourn the loss of Kurt Cobain.
Immediately after the funeral service for her husband, Courtney Love
was obliged to turn her attention back to a series of legal battles stemming
from her arrest on April 7. Courtney's arraignment on May 5 found her
cleared of drug and possession charges; the syringes found in her Beverly Hills
hotel room were explained as necessary for injecting prescription painkillers.
On May 6 the Associated Press reported that according to Courtney's lawyer,
Barry Tarlow, police had been suspicious about a powdery substance found
in a locket in Courtney's possession, until an analysis proved the contents to
be a quantity of ceremonial ashes. "It's not a crime to possess Hindu ashes,"
Tarlow said. In a prepared statement, Courtney expressed relief: "I am de-
lighted that this nightmare is all over and I have been cleared of all drug
charges. I can now concentrate on putting my life back together and mourning
the loss of my husband."

Courtney mourned privately for a time after Kurt's death. Eventually and
inevitably, she returned to the public arena. In an interview with Kurt Loder
on MTV, she told the world that talking about Kurt's suicide helped her
mourn. She felt the need to express how Kurt was in private, and how she
felt about him. Her image was soon gracing magazine covers around the

world. While Hole's critically acclaimed album *Live Through This* (which had been given its title before Kurt's death) continued to climb alternative music charts in the United States, Courtney was gaining international fame—as a widow.

"Imagine this," Courtney explained to one interviewer. "You're peaking. You're in your youth. At the prime of your life. The last thing you want to be is a symbol for heroin use. You've finally met somebody of the opposite gender who you can write with. That's never happened before in your life. The only other person you could ever write with wasn't as good a writer as you, and this [new] person's a better writer than you. And you're in love with him, you have a best friend, you have a soul-fucking-mate, and you can't even believe it's happening in your lifetime. *And* as a bonus he's beautiful. *And* he's rich. *And* he's a hot rock star to boot. *And* he's the best fuck that ever walked. *And* he wants to have babies, and what you want is babies. You've wanted to have babies forever. *And* he understands everything you say. *And* he completes your sentences. *And* he's lazy, but he is spiritual, and he's not embarrassed about praying, and he's not embarrassed about chanting, he's not embarrassed about God, Jesus, none of it. He fucking thinks it's all really cool. He wants to fucking learn the path. He wants to be enlightened. Everything. And there's even room for you to fix him, which you like, 'cause you're a fixer-upper. He's perfect in almost every fucking way. The only fucking happiness that I ever had. And then it all gets taken away."

Mourning her husband proved difficult for Courtney, and she later admitted that her judgment about the sincerity of some well-wishers was clouded in the weeks following his death. "Michael [Stipe was] so persistent that it annoyed me, 'cause I just thought he felt sorry for me. But he called me two, three times a day, every day. And people that have gone through the same thing . . . it's really good to hear their stories."

People around the world continued to mourn Kurt's loss. One fan, Randi Hubbard of Aberdeen, Washington, erected a statue in Kurt's honor. "I think we all have a little Kurt Cobain in us," said Hubbard, who wanted to display the statue in Aberdeen. "We've all been on the edge." The statue, which weighed six hundred pounds and matched Kurt's height of five feet six inches, was initially embraced by the Aberdeen city council, which granted Hubbard's request to have the sculpture showcased for ninety days in a park at the eastern entrance to town. But it backpedaled after angry phone calls and letters from area residents hit city hall. Krist agreed, saying that Kurt himself would have hated the statue.

Dealing with his own emotions, Krist felt the need to speak to his fans via the Internet. Overwhelmed by their expressions of support, Krist wrote a lengthy e-mail to all from his heart. It read, in part:

> Thank you all for the messages. I cannot answer any of them. I am sorry. I don't have the time or the energy and frankly, I can't dwell on Nirvana. I can't spill my guts. It's too personal and again, I can't dwell on it.
>
> Remember that the music biz and the rock press have a symbiotic relationship.
>
> Remember that Nirvana was about music, first and foremost.
>
> Remember Leon Trotsky. The Fugs, "Dirty Old Man."
>
> Remember not to e-mail me. I will not answer.
>
> You are all good. Good-bye and God bless!

By now the national and international press were well bunkered in Aberdeen and Seattle, hounding anyone and everyone close to Nirvana for sound bites about Kurt. Krist's mother, Maria, said simply, "It's tragic, that we lost our nice boy."

Kurt's mother, Wendy, told the press many times that she and Kurt were like twins; that whenever she would think of him, he would call her, out of the blue. Wendy, like many in Kurt's life, tried to help the troubled rock star avoid his grievous path to death.

Kurt had dropped many clues of his manic depression and suicidal temptations throughout the years, and few listened. "For five years during the time I had my stomach problem, yeah, I wanted to kill myself every day," he once said. "I came very close many times. I'm sorry to be so blunt about it. It was to the point where I was on tour, lying on the floor, vomiting air because I couldn't hold down water. And then I had to play a show in twenty minutes. I would sing and cough up blood. This is no way to live a life."

Kurt even described Nirvana's sound and style as suicidal. "That pretty much defines our band. It's both those contradictions. It's satirical, and it's serious at the same time."

Courtney grew used to Kurt's not-so-subtle hints during their everyday life together. "Look, I lived with someone who said every day that he was going to kill himself," she said flatly, "and it wasn't like I was bored with it by any means. I did what I could to make sure that didn't happen. And that resulted in a lot of hysteria on my part. There was a lot of screaming, a lot of yelling. A lot of kicking the walls, a lot of broken fax machines and telephones. I started to feel like my purpose in life was noble—to take care of these two human beings, my husband and child, and make sure that they lived. And it was a fine purpose. I didn't have a problem with that.

"I remember going to a group-therapy thing we had at one of the rehabs. And these couples are all in there, talking and waiting to hear what we're going to say. And we thought, 'Fuck it, these couples all seem so dry.' What's the fucking point if you don't have soaring heights of passion, moments of intensity and beauty?"

In what is thought to be the last interview with Kurt Cobain, reported by the Associated Press on May 6, a writer for the magazine *RIP* had found the singer in a surprisingly "happy frame of mind." The interview appeared in two separate issues of *RIP* magazine, both released in May. Kurt said he was having the best time of his life, though he did remark, "I've always been a chronically depressed, or at least pessimistic, person for part of the day." The birth of Frances Bean, he said, had helped him "feel like a completely different person." Becoming a father made him feel "pig-headed enough to unnecessarily blame my parents for a lot of things they didn't deserve to be blamed for."

"Kurt and I used to be goofy together, we'd have these little laughs," said his mom, Wendy. "But then he stopped laughing. And that's what really flew the red flag up for me, that it was really getting serious. Kurt's problems were ongoing, and we struggled with them for years. I talked him through so many nights. He was probably a mis- or undiagnosed depressive, which runs in my family. My grandfather, I would say, died from that, 'cause he tried to commit suicide and eventually died from the injuries. Also, manic-depression is a progressive disease. Once you get past a certain stage it's almost unmanageable, even with antidepressants. I now know in hindsight that the sleeping he was doing in his teenage years was the very beginning of it. He was sleeping so much, but that was also masked by just being a teenager. But now I look back and go, 'Ah-ha, that was the very beginning of it.' And, of course, once they leave home, they're out of your control. He would call me crying and suicidal. He would always call when he got desperate. And then the last week he didn't call. That was horrible, because I knew."

To the surprise of many, it was announced in May that Kurt had not left a will behind. According to court papers filed in Seattle, there was no will on file, which would make Courtney and Frances the sole heirs to his estate. According to court papers Kurt had accumulated assets of at least $1.2 million.

And Courtney's pain would only get worse before it got better. On June 16, 1994, Hole's bass player, Kristen Pfaff, was found dead in her bathroom from a heroin overdose. On the advice of close friends, Courtney picked up her guitar and channeled her pain through song. On August 26, Courtney and Hole played for tens of thousands of fans at England's Reading Festival.

Three days earlier, DGC had issued a press release saying that a new album from Nirvana, to be called *Verse Chorus Verse,* was set for release in November 1994. The collection was described as a double album including live performances from 1989 to 1994 and the band's set from their *MTV Unplugged* appearance. But on September 1, DGC released another statement saying that the New Nirvana album would now consist of merely the *Unplugged* set. Dave and Krist were left with the heart-wrenching task of mixing the album. "It's hard to watch the show without thinking of Kurt," Dave said, "and it was very hard to get in the studio and mix the album with Kurt's voice coming through the speakers all day long. But I think you can especially hear the songs Kurt wrote in a different light on this album than anywhere else. It was great music."

In an unprecedented move, MTV, aware of the impending release of the album, repeated the *Unplugged* show several times, and it quickly became one of the highest-rated specials in the network's history. Despite its imperfections, Nirvana's *MTV Unplugged in New York* would win Nirvana a Grammy for Best Alternative Album.

Four months after Kurt's suicide, Krist and Dave performed for the first time since Nirvana's last show on March 1, 1994. Their unannounced appearance occurred at the Yo-Yo a Go Go Festival in Olympia, Washington, on July 12, with Dave and Krist playing in the backing band for

Simon Fair Timony, a ten-year-old singer who was fronting a band called the Stinky Puffs. The band also featured Simon's mother, Sheenah Fair, his stepfather, Jad Fair, and guitarist Don Fleming. The group performed Timony's tribute to Kurt, called "I'll Love You Anyway." Kurt, a friend of Jad Fair's, had nurtured Simon's interest in music since the boy was six years old; he had even agreed to collaborate with Timony on an upcoming Stinky Puffs record. In the *Incesticide* liner notes, Kurt had written that getting the Stinky Puff's 7-inch was one of the "greatest things" that had happened to him. Krist and Dave's appearance was a tribute Kurt would have appreciated.

Meanwhile, Krist was starting to take grieving in another direction. As his Internet statement suggested, Krist's political awareness had intensified in recent years, and now he began devoting his time to educating rock fans about politics by founding the Joint Artists and Music Promotions Action Committee (JAMPAC): "I looked at the Christian Coalition and saw how effective they were," said Krist, who has always been sympathetic toward causes that speak to the common man. "And I thought, 'Well, we can have a rock and roll coalition.'" Krist, who serves as JAMPAC's president, said the organization planned to lobby legislators and court them financially. "If you want to influence today, the reality is the bucks," he said. "You have to develop relationships with representatives and make campaign contributions. That's just American politics."

Dave, on the other hand, used his songwriting talents to help him get over the agonizing pain of Kurt's loss. "After Kurt's death, I was as confused as I've ever been," Dave recalled. "To continue [playing music] almost seemed in vain. I was always going to be 'that guy from Kurt Cobain's band' and I knew that. I wasn't even sure if I had the desire to make music anymore. [Then one day] I received a postcard from a fellow Seattle band, 7 Year Bitch, who had also lost a member [lead singer Stephanie Sargent]. It said, 'We know what you're going through. The desire to play music is gone for now, but it will return. Don't worry.' That fucking letter saved my life, because as much as I missed Kurt, and as much as I felt so lost, I knew there was only one thing that I was truly cut out to do and that was music. I know that sounds so incredibly corny, but I honestly felt that."

Dave had been writing and recording his own songs for several years, and his catalogue had grown considerably. "I decided to do what I had always wanted to do since the first time I'd recorded a song all by myself. I was going to book a week in a twenty-four-track studio, choose the best stuff I'd ever written out of the thirty-forty songs that had piled up, and really concentrate on them in a real studio." So in the fall of 1994, Dave organized his music, booked time at Robert Lang Studio in Seattle in October, and turned to his old friend Barrett Jones to handle the overall production work. Dave played all the instruments, and Jones ran the board and the tape deck. "The first four hours were spent getting sounds," Dave said. "This was a cinch for Barrett, whom I'd asked to produce since he was the one person in the world I felt comfortable singing in front of . . . Over the past six years, Barrett and I had perfected our own method of recording. Start with the drums, listen to playback while humming tune in head to make sure arrangement is correct, put down two or three guitar tracks—mind you, all amplifiers and everything are ready to go before recording begins—do bass track and move on to next songs, saving vocals for last."

For these songs, which would form the foundation of the Foo Fighters debut album, Dave and Jones made recording a game. "I wanted to see how little time it could take me to track fifteen songs, complete with overdubs and everything," Dave said. "I did the basic tracks in two and a half days, meaning I was literally running from instrument to instrument, using mostly first takes on everything. All vocals and rough mixes were finished on schedule: one week." After the songs were recorded and quickly mixed down, Dave's next move was deciding what he should do with the package. It didn't take long for him to make the wrong decision: He made one hundred copies to hand out to friends. "My next mistake was my blind generosity," Dave said regretfully. "That fucking tape spread like the Ebola virus, leaving me with an answering machine full of record company jive."

The excitement and anticipation over Dave's work were genuine, if unwelcome. It was clear that the songs were well written, that they'd be certain to appeal to Nirvana's audience. But Dave had played all of the instruments by himself, and was suddenly in need of a team of musicians if he was ever to duplicate the songs live. "I jammed around with a few people before meeting Nate Mendel," Dave said of the bassist from the Seattle band Sunny Day Real Estate. "His girlfriend was a good friend of my wife [Jennifer Youngblood, whom Dave married in 1993], and they joined us for a Thanksgiving party at my house. It was the night we discovered my house was haunted, but that's a different story altogether."

Dave then reluctantly gave the tape to his ex-Nirvana bandmate. "Not long after meeting Nate, I gave a tape to Pat Smear," said Dave. "I knew that the band would need two guitars, but [I] didn't think that Pat would want to commit to anything (or that he would even like the music). To my surprise, not only did he like the tape, he expressed interest in joining up. [Then] I just wanted to find the perfect drummer."

Not many drummers could fill Dave's shoes, but one who provided the drum sound he wanted for his new band was William Goldsmith of Sunny Day Real Estate. He didn't know much about the band, but Dave did know they had an album out on Sub Pop Records and had a solid nationwide following. "I saw them play their last few shows in Seattle and was blown away by Nate and Will. So you can imagine my first reaction when I heard the band was calling it quits. I gave the two of them tapes through my wife's friend and prayed they'd enjoy them."

Evidence suggests they enjoyed them indeed, as Mendel and Goldsmith gladly accepted the opportunity to play in Dave's band. With three first-rate musicians on board, Dave had the new band he had always longed to create.

"I didn't want this to become some ridiculous solo project," he said. "I sure as fuck didn't consider Pat, Nate, and William my backing band. I realized this was a bizarre foundation for a band, but that's exactly what my goal was: to have another band. We got together and it was soon apparent that this was to be the next band. I wanted everyone to have the freedom to do whatever they wanted to do within the songs, each member as important as the next."

The quartet named themselves the Foo Fighters.

For all practical purposes, the birth of the Foo Fighters officially ended Dave's association and career with Nirvana. It was time for Dave to move on, time to get over Kurt's death and focus on his own future. That was part of the reason Dave chose not to remain on DGC. He simply wanted a new, fresh start, a career built on his own merits. "You have to let [death] bounce off you and figure that it's just some guy you'll never talk to again," said Dave, but not without sensitivity. "Not that many people understand what I'm going through, and I don't expect them to. I don't expect people to be nice or understanding or compassionate, because it happens so rarely. I think about Kurt every day and I miss him, and I realize that I miss him. But at the same time things keep going, and I've got to make sure things keep moving for me. I don't know if [the Foo Fighters] makes anyone else feel better—I just know I have to do it for myself. I have to feel like I'm moving forward."

On September 8, 1994, the MTV Video Music Awards were held at a new home, Radio City Music Hall in New York City. Hosted by Roseanne Arnold, it included musical guests the Alexandrov Red Army Ensemble and Leningrad Cowboys, Aerosmith, the Beastie Boys, Boyz II Men, Green Day, the Rolling Stones, Salt-n-Pepa, the Smashing Pumpkins, Snoop Doggy Dogg, Bruce Springsteen, the Stone Temple Pilots, and Tom Petty and the Heartbreakers.

Nirvana's "Heart-Shaped Box," the only video made for the *In Utero* release, was nominated in four categories: Best Alternative Video, Best Video of the Year, Best Art Direction, and Best Cinematography. Produced by Richard Bell and directed by Anton Corbijn, the video won two awards, for Best Alternative Video and Best Art Direction. Without fanfare or sentimental speeches, Krist Novoselic, Dave Grohl, Pat Smear, and "Heart-Shaped Box" video art director Bernadette Disanto accepted their MTV statues.

The following month in *Rolling Stone*, R.E.M. lead singer Michael Stipe spoke publicly for the first time about his friend Kurt Cobain. To the surprise of many, Stipe let it be known that for nearly two years there had been talk between R.E.M. and Nirvana about touring together as co-headliners. The friendship between Stipe and Cobain was just beginning to take root when the latter passed away. They even spoke of writing and recording a few songs together. "We FedExed a few things back and forth, but nothing was ever recorded," Stipe said. "It was in the planning stages. I saw it as a window of being able to get him out of the head that he was in. That was what I threw out to him, like a rope, to try to pull him in—'Let's work on this project together.'

"I knew that [Kurt] had a great deal of respect for me and for [R.E.M.]. We had spent time together—he came to Athens [Georgia], he and Courtney and Frances, and stayed at the house. We talked a lot. The truth of the matter is, we really didn't know each other that well. It was more of a mutual respect.

He was very publicly an R.E.M. fan, which I think is incredibly daring for someone in his position."

After the Rome debacle, Michael Stipe felt that returning to the West Coast was not a good idea for Kurt. "I wanted to get him out of Seattle. [In Kurt's final days] I knew that he was there, and he was by himself. Everybody had tried everything they could, and [the proposed project] was my attempt to get him enough out of the head that he was in that he wouldn't kill himself or hurt himself. I thought it was going to be an overdose." He hesitated, reaching for his thoughts. "I wish he had . . . I don't know . . . you can't . . . what if?" He was silent momentarily. "[Our project together] was going to be very acoustic—and some organs. That's the kind of music [Kurt] wanted to do. He wanted to do something that was really not loud."

The one thing Stipe could relate to was the pressure artists like Kurt and Eddie Vedder had to endure in their newfound status as pop icons. "I feel so much like a contemporary of those guys, and yet I also feel like I've been there a little bit," the singer said. "I have great sympathy for anybody who's been thrown into . . . this as quickly as Kurt and Eddie have been. They got, in a way, the same tag that I did, where I was being positioned as the voice of a generation. It was something that I really, really did not want. It was like 'Wait a minute—I'm a fucking singer in a rock and roll band. I did not ask for this.' It's a lot of pressure. If *Murmur* or *Reckoning* [R.E.M.'s first albums] had sold five million copies, I wouldn't be alive to tell the tale."

On October 15, 1994, Nirvana's unplugged version of "About a Girl" debuted on the *Billboard* Modern Rock Chart. It would peak at number one, and remain on the chart for nineteen weeks. "About a Girl" also hit the *Billboard* Album Rock Chart; it peaked as high as number three. Two weeks later, on November 1, *MTV Unplugged in New York* hit the streets; it entered the charts at number one. It sold 310,500 copies in its first week.

"Punk rock should mean freedom . . . playing whatever you want, as sloppy as you want, as long as it's good and has passion," said Kurt Cobain in Nirvana's eighty-three-minute video, *Live! Tonight! Sold Out!!*, which hit the stores on November 15, 1994. Originally conceived and put together by Kurt in 1992, this powerful documentary featured previously unreleased footage of fifteen songs performed live around the world, as well as interviews, behind-the scenes exploits, and excerpts from the band's own home video archives.

"This is a celebration of how many rules Nirvana broke," said Robin Sloane, Geffen's head of creative services, about the video. "That's why it's so compelling and why Kurt wanted to make this and why we wanted to release it. It's about the power individuals can have because of their love for the music. When you first watch it, it's sad because you realize how much [Kurt] will be missed, but it's also testimony to the profound impact Nirvana had on music and culture."

Critics accused Geffen Records of trying to cash in on the Nirvana frenzy after Kurt's death, but in truth, this video project had begun a few years prior to its release. A rough 120-minute version had been completed by Kurt years before his death, but the project had languished when Nirvana went back on the road to tour. In addition, the task of obtaining the film footage that the band desired (and the necessary legal clearances) was massive. Footage from shows in England, Japan, Belgium, Brazil, Holland, and Denmark was gathered for the video, as well as from performances in Texas, Washington, Oregon, and Hawaii. Dozens of filmed interviews provided a special insight into the different perspectives of the trio. Kurt's death had put a temporary halt to the effort, but eventually the surviving members picked up the project as a part of their own healing process.

"Great care was taken to maintain the integrity and intent of the original edit," Krist and Dave said. They completed the project with editor Steve MacCorkle and supervising producer Greg Lapidus of Geffen, who added, "It was Krist and Dave's decision to put this [video] out, to complete what Kurt had started. It took a while before they were able to watch what we had. Everyone needed time to find some peace about what had happened. Then it became a labor of love. Everyone that worked on this had a real emotional involvement."

Highlights from the video range from Nirvana's appearance at a huge arena show in Brazil with Kurt and Dave appearing in drag to a stage dive by Kurt in Dallas that ended up in a bloody melee; from a performance at the Reading Festival to an instrument-shattering bash on *The Jonathan Ross Show* in London; from a truly bizarre semilive rendition of "Smells Like Teen Spirit" on *Top of the Pops* to a climactic orgy of guitar-smashing footage drawn from Seattle, Reading, Honolulu, London, Portland, Brussels, Belgium, Tacoma, and *Saturday Night Live* in New York.

By the end of the year, two videos from Nirvana's *Unplugged* album appeared on MTV's *Top 100 Video Countdown of 1994*. "All Apologies" came in at number seven, while "About a Girl" climbed to number thirty-three. Green Day's "Basketcase" video topped the chart.

As 1994 steamrolled to a close, Courtney showed up on the cover of the December issue of *Rolling Stone*. Public opinion of Courtney had often been buoyed by her public actions; now, eight months after her husband's death, she didn't seem bent on eliciting sympathy from Nirvana's fans. For the interview with David Fricke, Courtney donned the heavy brown jacket Kurt was wearing when he killed himself. "I washed the blood off it," she said unapologetically in the interview. "It's not even sentimental." The interview revealed a new Courtney Love, one who was clearly trying to move on with her own life. "I used to be able to talk to Kurt more, wherever he is," she said to Fricke. "But now he's really gone. I used to feel like mourning him was really selfish because it would make him feel guilty. And the best thing to do was to pray for him and show him joy, so he could feel the vibration of the joy. But now I know he's dissipated, and he's gone. There's not anything left. Not even to talk to."

As Courtney continued talk openly about her feelings, Krist and Dave shared their mourning with only family members and very close friends. Everyone in the Nirvana camp wondered if the two would ever play together again. As rumors spread in the music media about the idea of finding a new lead singer, Krist and Dave announced that they had made their first new recording together. In one of the most anticipated alternative releases of 1995, the duo joined Pearl Jam's Eddie Vedder and former Firehose and Minuteman bassist Mike Watt on the song "Against the 70's," which appeared on Watt's *Ball-Hog or Tugboat?* The album, an alternative-rock all-star collection released in the spring of 1995 on Columbia Records, also featured Jane's Addiction/Porno for Pyros' Perry Farrell and Stephen Perkins, Sonic Youth's Thurston Moore, Lee Ranaldo and Steve Shelley, Adam Horovitz of the Beastie Boys, Soul Asylum's Dave Pirner, Lemonhead Evan Dando, and Henry Rollins.

Krist and Dave's lengthy collaboration with Vedder left a lot of people suspicious that the songs on Pearl Jam's yet-to-be-released album, *Vitalogy*, were written about Kurt and his suicide. "No, [*Vitalogy*] was written when we were on tour in Atlanta," said Vedder in his defense. "It's not about Kurt. Nothing on the album was written directly about Kurt and I don't feel like talking about him because it [might be seen] as exploitation. But I think there might be some things in the lyrics that you could read into and maybe we'll answer some questions or help you understand the pressures on someone who is on a parallel train."

It wasn't long before Krist started his own band as well. After meeting singer Yva las Vegas in Seattle, the two collaborated and wrote songs for their new band, Sweet 75. Like Dave, Krist abandoned the instrument he played in Nirvana and returned to the first instrument he fell in love with, the guitar. Sweet 75's self-titled debut was released by Nirvana's label, DGC.

In July 1995, Krist and Dave (taking a break from touring with the Foo Fighters) spent hundreds of hours listening to tapes of Nirvana's 1989–1994 tours in an effort to nail down a track list for the live Nirvana album, *From the Muddy Banks of the Wishkah*.

The record was mixed quickly in Canada by Andy Wallace, the same mixer who had blended the sounds of Nirvana's *Nevermind*. Advance cassettes and compact discs were rushed to American radio, with emphasis on "Aneurysm" as the first single. When *Wishkah* was finally released on October 1, 1996, the CD became the third Nirvana album to enter the Billboard charts at number one, reaching 158,000 copies in the first week of sales.

In a first, Krist wrote the liner notes for the album:

In presenting this record, we hope that the ultimate allure of Nirvana and especially Kurt as well as the passion that we had—and have—for the music we made is once again brought to the forefront. Let all the analysis fall away like yellow, aged newsprint. Crank this record up and realize the bliss, power, and passion . . . TOTAL NIRVANA!

The release of *From The Muddy Banks of Wishkah* (an essential Nirvana collection) not only satisfied the pallets of die-hard fans of the band, it inspired a new generation of fans just being introduced to Nirvana to explore the group's brief history even further. The sixteen-song lineup covers a wide range of the trio's career, and though the performances appear unpolished and harried, they are true-to-life representations of what it was like to be at a live Nirvana show. Sloppy and loud in all its frantic beauty, the platinum-selling *From The Muddy Banks of Wishkah* is the exact opposite of the more popular and musically fluid compilation, *Unplugged*. Nevertheless, enthusiasts of the group came to appreciate the live album's unique contribution to the entire Nirvana catalogue of music, often referring to it as the most honest and real reflection of all of Nirvana's efforts.

Remarkably, despite minimal airplay on radio and no promotional vehicles in place to raise awareness of Nirvana, record sales of the trio's music continued to top the best-seller lists of retail stores throughout the world well after Kurt's death. But as happens with all rock 'n' roll tragedies, the controversy surrounding his demise was still being fueled by injurious gossip and spiteful journalism long after the official end of Nirvana the band.

"The culture of the dead is disgusting," said Billy Corgan, who shared the stage on a number of occasions with Nirvana as lead singer of Smashing Pumpkins. "I think everybody who is out there printing illegal Kurt Cobain T-shirts and trying to feed off the carcass is disgusting. Kurt Cobain was a great artist, and his music will endure for a long time and that's the best part about it. But the fascination and the glorification of his death just sends the wrong messages. It says that this is ultimately cooler than actually living and even failing."

In the years following Cobain's death, many believed his life and his actions were representative of the generation he inspired through his music, and numerous watch groups panicked unnecessarily, creating forums and help guides to steer their children away. It was that kind of knee-jerk reaction and senseless politicking that enraged many in the music community.

And then there are others who have rejected all attempts to link Kurt Cobain's demise with the supposed irresponsibility of his audience. "There's millions and millions of people in their forties who think they're so fucking special," said a clearly disgruntled and angry Kim Thayil, an original member of Soundgarden and a respected voice in the Pacific Northwest music scene. "They're this ultimate white-bread, suburban, upper-middle-class group that were spoiled little fuckers as kids 'cause they were all children of Dr. Spock, and then they were stupid, stinky hippies, and then they were spoiled little yuppie materialists. Now they're all at the age where they produce films and news reports . . . and we get *their* understanding of history. They're denying other age groups their own memories.

"All I've heard from them, ever since Kurt killed himself, is this nonstop criticism of Generation X. 'What's so great about Kurt Cobain?' *Fuck* you. They don't even understand their *own* heroes . . . Why are they so freaked out about Kurt Cobain? Because they don't understand his music, and they don't know who Kurt spoke to. It's just something they missed. It just went right by 'em."

Still, the macabre fascination of those not in-the-know surfaced again some eight years later, as Kurt's personal diaries were published in the fall of 2002 and sold nearly a quarter of a million copies before the new year. Putting to rest any theories that Kurt Cobain's popularity had waned since his death, *Journals,* a collection of disjointed diary entries, letters, and drawings taken from his personal notebooks, let fans into a world previously thought inaccessible. The publication revealed Kurt's deepest personal thoughts, and both Dave Grohl and Krist Novoselic initially refused comment on it. In fact, Krist felt it was wrong to talk about something this private, and he wanted no involvement with *Journals* on any level.

Though removed from the limelight because of her own professional troubles, Courtney Love continued to be a thorn in the side of the thousands of Nirvana fans waiting to hear the band's much-spoken-of, yet never released, studio tracks. In January 2000, Courtney's relationship with Geffen Records, her band Hole, and the Universal Music Group escalated into a lawsuit that threatened to prevent the release of any Nirvana music. By now, it was clear that a Nirvana box-set release was inevitable, but Courtney exercised her legal copyright to some of this music, which prohibited Dave and Krist from releasing any material without her consent. Finally, after a long and bitter dispute, Courtney and the two remaining members of Nirvana settled their differences and made good on their promise to release new, unheard Nirvana music to the world.

"Everything's great," said a very pleased Krist. "I'm happy it's all behind us. Now the music's out and I don't have any hard feelings against anybody. It's about liberation and going forward. If I have any regrets, it's that it went as far as the lawsuit. [But] I know it's not going to impact on [Kurt's] musical legacy."

Litigation prohibited any new and unauthorized Nirvana songs from being played on commercial radio or sold in retail outlets, but it didn't stop millions of fans of the band from downloading a previously unreleased song from various Internet sites throughout the world. By the time it was officially released on October 12, 2002, the ghost track "You Know You're Right" debuted at number twenty-two on the *Billboard* Modern Rock chart. Three days later, MTV2 debuted the world premiere video to the song, which featured a varied catalogue collection of Nirvana video and film clips culled from promotional releases and live concert footage.

Shortly thereafter came the release of *Nirvana*, the band's self-titled greatest hits collection, which featured the turbulent and previously unreleased single "You Know You're Right." "We bombed it together fast," Krist Novoselic said about laying down the initial tracks in that session. "Kurt had the riff and brought it in, and we put it down. We Nirvana-sized it."

Highly influential liner notes were written by the legendary rock critic David Fricke, who nailed the passion and subtleties of Nirvana's songwriting talents with his trademark exquisite and articulate fluency. Though hardcore Nirvana fans criticized the release for being so commodified, *Nirvana* is still a smart and legitimate accumulation of the best tracks taken from *Nevermind*, *Bleach*, early EPs, *MTV Unplugged*, and *In Utero*, and includes the long-sought-after 1994 Scott Litt remix of "Pennyroyal Tea."

With their financial futures secure, both Dave and Krist continued to play important roles in pop culture long after Nirvana had ended with Kurt's sudden and unexpected death. After his divorce from Jennifer in 1997, Dave turned his focus completely on the success of the Foo Fighters, becoming more involved in producing the band's videos and overseeing its promotion and marketing. The benefits were immediate. Riding the crest of Dave's strong songwriting, the Foo Fighters became one of the top alternative groups in the 1990s, selling millions of albums, playing in front of adoring teens and twenty-somethings in sold-out arenas, and crossing into mainstream success by the time the world crossed into Y2K. Krist, however, took a considerably different, though not unfulfilled, journey back to notoriety.

Shortly after an abbreviated tour in 1995, Sweet 75 broke up, and Krist quietly returned his focus to the Seattle political scene for the next few years. The experience enriched Krist dynamically and opened new creative doors for him. Along with former Dead Kennedys singer Jello Biafra and Soundgarden guitarist Kim Thayil, Krist formed the No WTO Combo, a short-lived project the three created just to protest the 1999 World Trade Organization conference in Seattle. Plans to get back together that same year with the Yva Las Vegas of Sweet 75 did not come to fruition, and Krist's long marriage to Shelli finally ended in divorce soon thereafter. Novoselic made one last attempt to return to the stage when he helped develop the band Eyes Adrift, a hip, alternative-country trio that also featured Meat Puppets guitarist Curt Kirkwood and Sublime drummer Bud Gaugh. It was an innovative venture that never received the recognition the trio was sure it would earn, and, with little interest from major labels, they released their self-titled debut on SpinArt Records. The challenges placed before them in working with the relatively unknown independent label left them with little money to promote the effort. As a result, they sold very few records, and, after playing live before several small, uninspired crowds, Novoselic suddenly decided to put his musical career back on the shelf.

"I quit," he wrote in a post on the band's official Web site, www. eyesadrift.com, in July 2003. "I can't deal. I can't read the magazines, listen to the radio or watch music television without feeling like I've just come in from outer space. I just don't get it and I probably never did.

"I'm relatively young and I want to follow my compulsions . . . If you've been following my politics, you know that I will continue to work for inclusion, fairness, and freedom."

Despite the dramatically different directions their careers had taken them, Krist and Dave remained solid friends. When Dave married former MTV producer Jordyn Blum on August 2, 2003, he made sure Krist was in attendance. Soon after, Dave returned to the stage as the lead singer of the Foo Fighters, while Krist sought new challenges to life in the political arena. But no matter what they chose to do with their lives, the craze and wonderment of Nirvana was never far from its two surviving members. And neither ever tried to turn away from it.

"People walk up to me and tell me how much (Nirvana's) music changed their lives," said Krist, shortly after the lawsuit between Nirvana and Courtney was settled. "I tell them how much they changed my life just by being fans and caring."

"You know, people find this hard to believe, but my memories of Nirvana are really good," said Dave. "I think of the people, the road trips. I think of that white Chevy van that we used to tour in that stunk of gasoline. I remember us having a really good time. Obviously, it did not end well, but my memories of Nirvana are just so much more powerful than any myth, and I won't let anything destroy that."

Selected Discography

ALBUMS

Bleach   Sub Pop SP 34
1989
First 1,000 copies on white vinyl; second 2,000 contain special poster on black vinyl; CD remaster of 1992 contains bonus track, "Downer"; A side has "T" shape on its label. Back cover illustration of tree with rings, with special slogans written in the rings, which also matches the band's T-shirt design. UK version switches "Love Buzz" for "Big Cheese"; Geffen CD release has "Big Cheese" and "Downer." There are approximately twenty different colors of vinyl among U.S. (Geffen/Sub Pop), UK (Tupelo/Sub Pop), and Australian (Waterfront/Sub Pop).

Bleach   Tupelo TUP34
1989
European issue. Only has 11 cuts. Everything except "Downer" and "Big Cheese."

Bleach   Sub Pop SP34b
1992
U.S., 13 cuts including "Downer" and "Big Cheese."

Bleach   Sub Pop SP34B
1992
U.S. There are 7 tracks on this version. It is a misprinted CD containing another group's music. The first 6 songs are the same song in different versions, and the last song is a different song, "Street of Dreams."

Bleach   Geffen/Sub Pop GEDGEFD24433
1992
European. Distributed by BMG. This has 13 tracks.

Nevermind   Geffen/DGC 24425
1991
First 50,000 CD copies do not include unlisted bonus track "Endless Nameless." On this CD the water is painted all the way to the center of the CD; on the second version the color stops and the center is clear. The LP was issued on black vinyl.

Nevermind   Geffen/DGC MFSL 1-258
1992
Mobile Fidelity Sound Master Recordings. This is the vinyl version.

Nevermind   Geffen /DGC UDGD666
1992
Mobile Fidelity Sound Master Recordings. This is the CD Version.

Incesticide   Geffen/DGC DGC 24504
1992
Rarities, oddities, and B side compilation plus 4 new tracks never heard, issued w/GEF 24504 label for UK release. The LP was released on blue/white swirl splatter vinyl.

Incesticide   Geffen/DGC/Sub Pop GED 24504
1992 German release
Comes in a medium green box numbered (of 500), has three postcards, green/blue/red.

In Utero   Geffen/DGC 24607
1993 (U.S.)
U.S. version is standard, versions outside North America contains contain "Gallons of Rubbing Alcohol," LP was issued on clear vinyl. The promo version is gold-stamped.

In Utero   Geffen/DGC 24705
1993
Cassette version
This features the artwork version of "Waif Me" instead of "Rape Me." This was made for Wal-Mart and KMart. The inside still lists "Rape Me" on the cassette shell.

In Utero   Geffen/DGC GEF 24536
1993
UK, includes "Gallons of Rubbing Alcohol Flow Through the Strip," not found on U.S. version.

In Utero   Geffen/DGC UDCD690
1993
Mobile Fidelity Sound Master Recordings, CD version.

MTV Unplugged in New York   Geffen/DGC DGC-24727
1994

Recorded live in New York City, Nov. 18, 1993, at the Sony Music Studios. Two songs were cut from the MTV broadcast, "Oh Me" and "Something in the Way." A 14-track LP. There is black and white vinyl in U.S., and the same colors in the UK.

From the Muddy Banks of the Wishkah   Geffen/DGC DGCC-ZS105
1996

All songs were recorded live. Originally supposed to be a double album with the *Unplugged* album attached.

Nirvana   DGC/Sub Pop 0694935072
2002

A compilation featuring the last song Kurt, Krist, and Dave recorded, "You Know You're Right."

EPs

Blew   Tupelo TUP CD 8
1989

Includes "Blew," "Love Buzz," "Been a Son," and "Stain"; issued on CD (TUPCD 8) and vinyl (TUPEP 8).

Blew   Sub Pop/Tupelo TUPEP 8 UK
1989

12-inch on black vinyl. Includes "Blew," "Love Buzz," "Been a Son," and "Stain."

Sliver / Dive / About a Girl (live)   Tupelo TUPEP 25 UK
1990

12-inch vinyl. The 12-inch comes on black vinyl and also a clear-type dark blue (German release).

Sliver / Dive / About a Girl (live) / Spank Thru (live)   Tupelo TUPCD 25
1990

Same tracks as vinyl version but adds a live version of "Spank Thru."

Hormoaning   DGC MVCG 17002
1992

Japanese release. Tracks include "Turnaround," "Aneurysm," "D-7," "Son of a Gun," "Even in His Youth," and "Molly's Lips".

Hormoaning   DGC

German version CD issue, and also Australia on purple-and-red swirl vinyl. The Australian version has the Australian tour dates listed. There is also a Japanese issue on black vinyl.

SINGLES (7-INCH)

Love Buzz / Big Cheese   **Sub Pop SP 23**
1988

Only 1,000 of the originals were made. It was the first single of the Sub Pop Singles Club. These were hand-numbered with a red pen. There are also promo copies. Kurt's name is spelled Kurdt Kobain. The A side has the following etched into the vinyl: SP-23A U-38426M-A WHY DON'T YOU TRADE THOSE GUITARS FOR SHOVELS? The B side has the following etched into the vinyl: SP-23B U-38426M-B. There is a stamp on both sides of the disc that says [kdisc].

Sliver / Dive   **Sub Pop SP 73**
A side SP73A L36293, B side SP73B L36293X.
1990

The first 3,000 copies were a blue-and-red-swirled vinyl. The second releases came in several colors, including clear blue, clear, raspberry, yellow, pink, and orange. The UK 7-inch is a gatefold and is pea green. The U.S. 7-inch is black. There is a phone call from Jonathan Poneman at the end. The UK versions were printed on the Erika label.

Molly's Lips / Candy   **Sub Pop SP97**
1991

Sub Pop Singles Club, January 1991. A side is a Vaselines cover done by Nirvana, recorded live in Portland in the spring of 1990 by Drew Canulette and the Dogfish Mobile Unit, mixed by Gary Held. The B side is written and performed by the Fluid; 7,500-copy limited edition, of which the first 4,000 copies were a black-and-green swirl. The second edition was on black vinyl. The A side has etched into the vinyl SP97A L37037 LAtER. The B side has SP97B L37037X LAtER.

Here She Comes Now / Venus in Furs   **Communion Comm 23**
1991

Split single; both songs are Velvet Underground covers. The A side is by Nirvana; the B side is by the Melvins. 1,000-copy limited edition on yellow vinyl. The second pressings were in various colors, including maroon splatter, blue, purple, orange, gray, blue splatter, and red.

Smells Like Teen Spirit / Drain You   **Geffen D6CS5**
1991

Released in the U.S. and UK on black vinyl. The UK release has European tour dates listed: November 26 Bradford University•27 Birmingham Hummingbird•28 Sheffield University•29 Edinburgh Carlton Studios•30 Glasgow QMU•December 2 Newcastle Mayfair•3 Nottingham Rock City•4 Manchester Academy•5 London Kilburn National Ballroom•9 Belfast Conor Hall•10 Dublin McGonagles. The A side has DGCS5A-1J-1-02 etched into the vinyl, the B side has DGCS5B-1J-1-02. (Promo copy has sample copy sticker on UPC code.)

Come as You Are (LP version) / Endless Nameless   **DGC/Sub Pop DGCS 7**
1991.

The UK version. There is no picture sleeve.

Come as You Are (LP version) / Drain You (live)   DGC/Sub Pop DGCS 7-19120
1991
The U.S. version. There is no picture sleeve. It is die-cut like the old-school 7-inch.

Lithium   DGC/Sub Pop DGC59
1992
UK version.

In Bloom   DGC/Sub Pop GFS34
1992
UK version.

Oh, the Guilt / Puss   Touch and Go TG83
1993
Split single; A side is Nirvana, B side is the Jesus Lizard; issued on blue vinyl for the UK edition, black vinyl for Canadian version. Cobain was a big fan of Jesus Lizard and the Touch and Go label. The Australian 7-inch was released as a limited-edition picture disc.

SINGLES (12-INCH)
Smells Like Teen Spirit   DGC/Sub Pop PRO-A-4365
1991
Promotional only. 12-inch (LP version), white label.

Smells Like Teen Spirit / Even in His Youth   DGC/Sub Pop DGCS7-19050
LP version. A side: "Even in His Youth," B side. Promo copy is gold/yellow vinyl. The regular 12-inch and UK 12-inch are on black vinyl.

Come as You Are   DGC/Sub Pop PRO-A-4416
1991
Promotional only. 12-inch (LP version), black label.

Come as You Are / Drain You   DGC/Sub Pop DGCS7-19120
1992
LP version. A side: "Drain You" (live). B side. Promo copy has sample copy sticker on UPC code.
A side, "Come as You Are." B side, "Drain You" (live).

SINGLES (CASSETTE/U.S.)
Smells Like Teen Spirit / Even in His Youth   Geffen/DGC CS 19050
1991
The B side is a non-LP cut.

Come as You Are / Drain You   Geffen/DGC CS 19120
1992
"Drain You" recorded October 31, 1991, at the Paramount Theater, Seattle, Washington.

Oh, the Guilt / Puss   Touch and Go TG83
1993
Nirvana and Jesus Lizard cassingle: Nirvana's "Oh, the Guilt" and the Jesus Lizard's "Puss."

CD SINGLES

Sliver / Dive / About a Girl (live) / Spank Through (live)   Tupelo/TUPCD 25
1990

"About a Girl" and "Spank Through" are taken from the Pine Street Theater show in Portland, Oregon, February 9, 1990. "Spank Through" is spelled "Spank Thru" on the earlier Nirvana releases.

Smells Like Teen Spirit (edit) / Even In His Youth /   Geffen/DGC/
Aneurysm   Sub Pop GED 21673
1991

A German release, with a slightly different cover from the UK version. The top says "Compact Disc Maxi-Single." "Even In His Youth" and "Anuerysm" were previously unreleased.

Smells Like Teen Spirit (edit) / Even in His Youth / Aneurysm   Geffen/
DGCDS-21673
1991

Comes as a digipak. "Even in His Youth" and "Aneurysm" were previously unreleased non-album tracks.

Smells Like Teen Spirit / Drain You / Even in His Youth /   Geffen/DGC/
Aneurysm   Sub Pop DGCTD 5
1991

UK release. Comes in a digipak. "Even in His Youth" and "Aneurysm" were previously unreleased. The back cover also includes tour dates: November 26 Bradford University •27 Birmingham Hummingbird• 28 Sheffield University •29 Edinburgh Carlton Studios• 30 Glasgow QMU• December 2 Newcastle Mayfair• 3 Nottingham Rock City• 4 Manchester Academy• 5 London Kilburn National Ballroom• 9 Belfast Conor Hall• 10 Dublin McGonagles.

Come as You Are / School (live) / Drain You (live)   Geffen/DGCDS-21707
1992

Comes as a digipak. "School" and "Drain You" are taken from the October 31, 1991, show at the Paramount Theatre, Seattle, Washington.

Come as You Are / Endless Nameless / School (live) /   Geffen/DGC/
Drain You (live)   Sub Pop DGCTD 7
1992

UK release. "School" and "Drain You" are taken from the October 31, 1991, show at the Paramount Theatre, Seattle.

Come as You Are / Endless Nameless / School (live) /   Geffen/DGC/
Drain You (live)   Sub Pop GED 21715
1992

German release. "School" and "Drain You" are taken from the October 31, 1991, show at the Paramount Theatre, Seattle, Washington.

Lithium / Been A Son (live) / Curmudgeon   Geffen/DGCDM-21815
1992

"Been a Son" is taken from the October 31, 1991, show at the Paramount Theatre, Seattle, Washington. "Curmudgeon" is non-LP. This also has the complete lyrics to the *Nevermind* album. The U.S. 7-inch and the U.S. 12-inch are both black vinyl.

Lithium / Been a Son (live) / Curmudgeon / D-7 Geffen/DGC/Sub Pop DGCTD 9
1992

UK release. Comes in a digipak. "Been a Son" is taken from the October 31, 1991, show at the Paramount Theatre, Seattle, Washington. "Curmudgeon" is non-LP. "D-7" is taken from the John Peel session recorded at Maida Vale Studios, London, England, on October 21, 1990. The UK 7-inch is red vinyl.

Lithium / Been a Son (live) / Curmudgeon   Geffen/DGC/Sub Pop GED21815
(previously unreleased)
1992

German release. "Been a Son" is taken from the October 31, 1991, show at the Paramount Theatre, Seattle, Washington. "Curmudegeon" is non-LP.

In Bloom / Sliver (live) / Polly (live)   Geffen/Sub Pop GFSTD 34
1992

UK release. Comes in a digipak. "Sliver" and "Polly" are from the performance at the O'Brien Pavilion, Del Mar, California, on December 28, 1991.

In Bloom / Sliver (live) / Polly (live)   Geffen/Sub Pop GED21760
1992

German release. "Sliver" and "Polly" are from the performance at the O'Brien Pavilion, Del Mar, California, on December 28, 1991.

In Bloom / Sliver (live) / Polly (live)   Geffen/Sub Pop GFSTD 34
1992

UK release. Comes in a digipak. "Sliver" and "Polly" are from the performance at the O'Brien Pavilion, Del Mar, California, on December 28, 1991.

Heart-Shaped Box / Milk It / Marigold   Geffen GFSTD 54
1993

UK release. "Marigold" previously unreleased.

Heart-Shaped Box / Milk It / Marigold   Geffen GED21849
1993

German release. "Marigold" previously unreleased.

All Apologies / Rape Me / MV   Geffen/Sub Pop GFSTD 66
1993

UK release. "MV" was previously unreleased.

All Apologies / Rape Me / Moist Vagina   Geffen/Sub Pop GED21880
1993
German release. "Moist Vagina" was previously unreleased. The same song is credited on the
English version as "MV." The CD label says "Made in Germany," but the CD shrinkwrap
has a sticker that claims it was made in England.

All Apologies   Geffen/Sub Pop GFST 66 UK
1993
12-inch; contains two seahorse art prints and is on black vinyl. Runs at 45 rpm.
A side: "All Apologies" (LP version), and "Rape Me" (LP version). B side: "Moist Vagina"
(previously unreleased).

Pennyroyal Tea (remix) / I Hate Myself and I Want to Die /
Where Did You Sleep Last Night? (In the Pines)
(*MTV Unplugged* version)   Geffen/Sub Pop GED21907
1995
This is a very rare Australian CD single.

BOX SETS

The Nevermind & In Utero Singles   Geffen NIR 9505
This is a blue package that features 6 singles:

GED21673	Smells Like Teen Spirit/Even in His Youth/Aneurysm
GED21715	Come as You Are/Endless Nameless/School (live)/Drain You (live)
GED21760	In Bloom/Sliver (live)/Polly (live)
GED21815	Lithium/Been a Son (live)/Curmudgeon
GED21849	Heart-Shaped Box/Milk It/Marigold
GED21880	All Apologies/Rape Me/Moist Vagina

The Nevermind & In Utero Singles   Geffen GED24901
This is a European version that is the same package as above, but it is wrapped in aluminum
foil.

GED21673	Smells Like Teen Spirit/Even in His Youth/Aneurysm
GED21715	Come as You Are/Endless Nameless/School (live)/Drain You (live)
GED21760	In Bloom/Sliver (live)/Polly (live)
GED21815	Lithium/Been a Son (live)/Curmudgeon
GED21849	Heart-Shaped Box/Milk It/Marigold
GED21880	All Apologies/Rape Me/Moist Vagina

PROMOTIONAL CDs (U.S.)

Smells Like Teen Spirit   Geffen/DGC/Sub Pop PRO-CD-4308
1991
Edit 4:30; LP version 5:05.

On a Plain   Geffen/DGC/Sub Pop PRO-CD-4354
1991
LP version.

Lithium   Geffen/DGC/Sub Pop PRO-CD-4429
1991

LP version. There was also another promo version. It looks like the same version, with the same numbers, but has "Promotional" stamped on the disc.

Come as You Are   Geffen/DGC/Sub Pop PRO-CD-4375
1992

LP version.

Nevermind It's an Interview   Geffen/DGC/Sub Pop PRO-CD-4382
1992

Interview with cued music and five listed tracks from the Paramount show: "About a Girl," "Aneurysm," "Drain You," "On a Plain," and "School"; hosted by the author.

Lithium / Been a Son (live) / Curmudgeon   Geffen/DGC DGCDM-21815
1992

"Been a Son" (live) is from the performance at the Paramount Theatre, Seattle, Washington, on October 31, 1991. The inside sheet contains all the lyrics to *Nevermind*.

In Bloom   Geffen/DGC/Sub Pop PRO-CD-4463
1992

LP version.

Aneurysm   Geffen/DGC PRO-CD 1033
1994

CD single from the album *From the Muddy Banks of the Wishkah*. The label says "(no version)." The "no" is in reference to the word "shit" being flipped backward for radio airplay.

Drain You   Geffen/DGC PRO-CD-1070
1996

CD single from the album *From the Muddy Banks of the Wishkah*. This is the same version as on the album.

Heart-Shaped Box   Geffen/DGC PRO-CD-4545
1993

LP version. This is an eco-pack.

All Apologies   Geffen/DGC/Sub Pop PRO-CD-4581
1993

LP version. Same cover as below, but without "Rape Me" on it.

All Apologies   Geffen/DGC/Sub Pop PRO-CD-4582
1993

"All Apologies" (LP version) and "Rape Me" (LP version). Includes the lyrics to "All Apologies."

All Apologies   Geffen/DGC/Sub Pop PRO-CD-4618
1993
"All Apologies" (acoustic version from MTV's *Unplugged*) and "All Apologies' (LP version).

About a Girl   Geffen/DGC GEFDS-21958
1994
Made in the U.S. This was released in the U.S. and Australia.

About a Girl   Geffen/MCA GED 21958
1994
Made in France.

About a Girl   Geffen/DGC/Sub Pop PRO-CD-4688-A
1994
"About a Girl" (acoustic version from MTV's *Unplugged*).

The Man Who Sold the World   Geffen/DGC PRO-CD 4704
1994
LP version from MTV's *Unplugged*.

You Know You're Right   DGC INTR-10853-2
2002
The last song Nirvana recorded as a band.

COMPILATION APPEARANCES

Sub Pop 200   Sub Pop SP 25-F
1988
Boxed set of 3 EPs that includes "Spank Thru." The UK version was issued only on white vinyl, but later rereleased for CD in 1992.

Sub Pop 200   SP 25b
1992
A compilation that has "Spank Thru."

Sub Pop Rock City   Sub Pop / Glitterhouse EFA-LP 04486-08
1988
Sub Pop compilation featuring TAD, The Fluid, Nirvana's "Spank Thru," Mudhoney, Soundgarden, Green River, Cat Butt, The Knights-2nd Days, Blood Circus, Swallow, and Thrown Up's.

Hard to Believe   C/Z 024
1990

A KISS tribute record, this is the only recorded appearance by Jason Everman with the band. Includes "Do You Love Me"; also released on CD.

The Grunge Years   Sub Pop SP 112B
1991

A compilation that features the track "Dive" (1991). Limited edition of 500,000.

Kill Rock Stars   Kill Rock Stars KRS 201
1991

Includes "Beeswax." The LP has 14 tracks and was also released on CD. The original 1,000 (first release) copies had a hand-screened cover.

Teriyaki Asthma Vol. 1–5   C/Z 037
1991

Includes "Mexican Seafood"; also released on CD. The release also includes L7, Babes in Toyland, Helios Creed, and Coffin Break.

Teriyaki Asthma Vol. 1–5   C/Z 009
1989

The same songs as the above CD, but split up over a set of five 45s that completes the *Teriyaki Asthma* series. The 7-inch with Nirvana also features Yeast, "Solid Alligators"; Coffin Break, "Hole in the Ground"; and Helios Creed, "America is in Good Hands." Kurt's name is spelled Kurdt Kobain, and Dale Crover plays drums. The 7-inch runs at 33 1/3 rpm.

Heaven and Hell, Vol. 1   Communion 20
1991

Includes "Here She Comes Now."

Eight Songs for Greg Sage   Tim/Kerr T/K 917010
1992

Includes "Return of the Rat"; originally issued in a boxed set of 45s, plus it also was on a 12-inch, also in a box, with picture sleeves; the compilation also includes Hole.

No Alternative   Arista 07822-18737-2
1993

Includes "Verse Chorus Verse"; the song is not listed on the CD; it is the last cut.

Burning Leaves Compilation   Geffen / DGC PROCD 4344
1992

Contains Nirvana's "In Bloom" and "Come as You Are." Also features Nymph, "Sad and Damned"; Teenage Fanclub, "Star Sign"; Galactic Cowboys, "Kaptain Krude"; The Candyskins, "For What It's Worth"; Circle C, "?"; The Freewheelers, "No More Booze (On Tuesdays)"; Terri Nunn, "89 Lines"; Warrior Soul, "Children of the Winter"; Teenage Fanclub, "The Concept"; Nymphs, "Imitating Angels"; Warrior Soul, "My Time"; Galactic Cowboys, "My School."

Burning Leaves 3 The Third Fall of DGC   Geffen PRO-CD-4474
1993

Promo-only compilation featuring Sonic Youth, "Youth Against Fascism"; The Sundays, "Love"; Sloan, "Underwhelmed"; Warrior Soul, "Shine Like It"; Cell, "Wild"; The Candy-skins, "Wembley"; Nirvana, "Curmudgeon"; The Sundays, "I Feel"; Sonic Youth, "Stalker"; Cell, "Auf Wiedersehen"; The Candyskins, "Land of Love"; Sloan, "Raspberry"; Half Way Home, "Push On!"; and Warrior Soul, "Punk and Belligerent."

The Beavis and Butt-Head Experience   Geffen H GEFD-24613
1993

Includes "I Hate Myself and I Want to Die"; eerily, this was the last song released before Kurt took his life.

DGC Rarities Vol.1   Geffen DGCD-24704
1994

Features "Pay to Play," an earlier version of "Stay Away." This was also released on vinyl in Holland.

Charles Peterson   Sub Pop PROCD#39
1995

CD comes with the book *Screaming Life*, photography by Charles Peterson, essay by Michael Azerad. Contains the Nirvana song "Negative Creep." Also features Green River's "Ain't Nothing to Do," Mudhoney's "No One Has," Tad's "Ritual Device," Soundgarden's "Entering," Screaming Tree's "Flashes," Beat Happening's "Midnight-a-go-go," Seaweed's "Selfish," and The Fastback's "What's It Like." The only way to get the CD is to buy the book, which contains the quintessential photos of Cobain and Nirvana, plus the other players of the Seattle scene. The book is dedicated to Kurt. A must for the Nirvana collection.

Hype! The Motion Picture Soundtrack   Sub Pop SPCD371
1996

The soundtrack from the movie features Nirvana's "Negative Creep."

Hype! The Motion Picture Soundtrack   Sub Pop SP378
1996

Box of four 7-inch singles. Nirvana's "Negative Creep" appears on green vinyl with the Wipers' "Return of The Rat" and Mudhoney's "Touch Me, I'm Sick."

Home Alive: The Art of Self-Defense   Epic E2K67486
1996

Includes a live version of "Radio Friendly Unit Shifter."

Sludge Sampler Cassette   Geffen/DGC PRO-C-4389
1992

Promo cassette sampler featuring the following groups and songs: Teenage Fanclub, "What

You Do to Me," Nymphs, "Imitating Angels," Tesla, "Song and Emotion," Roxy Blue, "The Cradle," White Zombie, "Thunder Kiss '65," Nirvana, "Drain You (Live)."

Caution Explosive Hits in Store CD   Geffen PRO-CD-4602
1993

Contains 3 Nirvana songs, "Pennyroyal Tea," "All Apologies," and "Heart-Shaped Box." Also features Guns N' Roses, "Hair of the Dog," Megadeath, "99 Ways to Die," Aerosmith, "Livin' on the Edge," Guns N' Roses, "Since I Don't Have You," Aerosmith, "Cryin,' " Cher with Beavis and Butthead, "I Got You Babe," Run-D.M.C., "Bounce," Guns N' Roses, "Raw Power," Aerosmith, "Amazing," Guns N' Roses, "Ain't It Fun," Primus, "Poetry and Prose," and Guns N' Roses, "Black Leather."

Celebrate the Seasons   Uni 3P2887
1993

Promo only containing the Nirvana songs "All Apologies" and "Dumb." Also features Meat Loaf, "I'd Do Anything for Love (But I Won't Do That)," George Strait, "I'd Like to Have That One Back," Aerosmith, "Amazing," Diane Schurr, "I'll Be Home for Christmas," Michelle Nicastro, "When You Wish Upon a Star," Elton John and KiKi Dee, "True Love," Reba McEntire, "Does He Love You," Robben Ford, "He Don't Play Nothing but the Blues," Mark Chestnutt, "Almost Goodbye," David Lanz and Paul Speer, "Bridge of Dreams," Aerosmith, "Shut Up and Dance," Vince Gill, "Have Yourself a Merry Little Christmas," Tom Petty and the Heartbreakers, "Mary Jane's Last Dance," Wynonna, "Is It Over Yet," and Best Kissers in the World, "Miss Teen USA."

Splunge: New Music a Little on the Warped Side   Geffen/DGC PRO-CD-4507
1993

Contains "Sliver." Also features Sonic Youth, "Sugar Kane," Sloan, "I Am the Cancer," Urge Overkill, "Woman 2 Woman," My Little Funhouse, "Wishing Well," The Candyskins, "Wembley," Murray Att Away, "No Tears Tonight," White Zombie, "Thunderkiss '65," Galactic Cowboy, "Circles in the Fields," Izzy Stradlin and the JuJu Hounds, "Bucket O' Trouble," The Posies, "Silver Sister," Cell, "Stratosphere," and Half Way Home, "You're So Essential."

Fender 50th Anniversary Guitar Legends   Point Blank/Virgin 7243 8 42088 2 0
1996

Contains "Come as You Are." Features Buddy Holly and the Crickets, "That'll Be the Day," Dire Straits, "Sultans of Swing," The Vaughn Brothers, "The Telephone Song," Eric Clapton, "Let It Rain," Bonnie Raitt, "Some Thing to Talk About," Jimi Hendrix, "Spanish Castle Magic," Buddy Guy, "Damn Right, I've Got the Blues," Deep Purple, "Smoke on the Water," Keith Richards and the Expensive Winos, "Take It So Hard" (live), Dick Dale, "Misirlou," Waylon Jennings, "Rainy Day Women," Jeff Beck with Terry Bozzic and Tony Hyman, "Where Were You," Richie Sambora, "Stranger in this Town," Beach Boys, "Surfin' U.S.A.," Kenny Wayne Shepard, "While We Cry," and Albert Collins and the Icebreakers, "Frost."

Saturday Night Live The Musical Performances   Dreamworks 0044-50206-2
Volume 2
1999

Contains "Rape Me." Also features Hole, "Doll Parts," Beastie Boys, "Sabotage," Green Day, "When I Come Around," Beck, "Nobody's Fault but My Own," and R.E.M., "Losing My Religion."

VINYL PICTURE DISC

Smells Like Teen Spirit / Drain You / Aneurysm   DGC/Sub Pop GET21712
1991

German picture disc. "Smells Like Teen Spirit" A side has the cover of *Nevermind*; the B side has a picture of the water.

Smells Like Teen Spirit / Drain You / Aneurysm   DGC/Sub Pop DGCTP 5 UK
1991

"Smells Like Teen Spirit" A-side has the water image in vinyl but a blurred picture of the band from the *Nevermind* cover in the middle circle. The B side has the water image on the entire side. Says on cover "Special Limited Edition."

Come as You Are / Endless Nameless / School   DGC/Sub Pop DGCTP7 UK
1992

"Come as You Are," LP version; "Endless Nameless," LP version; "School" recorded live at the October 31, 1991, Seattle gig. The A side features a bluish background with swimming sperm and a blurred picture of the band in the middle; the B side is black. Says on the cover, "Special Limited Edition 12" picture disc."

Come as You Are / Endless Nameless / Drain You   DGC/Sub Pop GET#21714
                                                        (German)
1992

Picture disc has "Come as You Are" A side with "Endless Nameless" and "Drain You" (live).

In Bloom   Geffen/Sub Pop GFSTP 34 UK
1992

"In Bloom," LP version; "Sliver" (live); and "Polly" (live). The A side has a flower picture on it; the B side has daisies-cloth pattern with a rip covering a knee. Live versions recorded at Del Mar, California, on December 28, 1991. Says on cover, "Strictly Limited Edition 12" Picture Disc."

Live at the Paradiso Club, Amsterdam   BBC/TS In Concert Show #666i
1991

Recorded live at the Paradiso Club, Amsterdam, Holland, on November 25, 1991. This show was recorded by the Fudge Mobile for the BBC. Some of the footage from this gig would end up in the video *Nirvana Live! Tonight! Sold Out!* The versions of "Lithium," "School," "Been a Son," and "Blew" would all eventually end up on *From the Muddy Banks of the Wishkah.*

RADIO SHOWS

In Concert Led Zeppelin/Nirvana   **Westwood One Show #92-12**
1992

This is a live concert recorded at the Del Mar Fairgrounds, Del Mar California, on December 28, 1991. This is a two-disc set. It features 11 songs: "Drain You," "Aneurysm," "School," "Smells Like Teen Spirit," "About a Girl," "Polly," "Sliver," "Breed," "Come as You Are," "Lithium," and "Territorial Pissings."

On the Edge   **Westwood One Show #94-19**

Nationally distributed radio show for week of May 2, 1994.

The show is hosted by Tom Calderone. It features interviews with Lisa Germano, Elvis Costello, and Perry Farrell, and four unreleased Nirvana tracks. The songs were borrowed from the BBC session in 1989. It features "Love Buzz," "About a Girl," "Spank Thru," and "Polly." It is a killer recording. Chad Channing is the drummer. The version of "Polly" is a little faster and more electric, but not as fast or hard as "New Wave Polly."

GUEST APPEARANCES BY BAND MEMBERS

Mark Lanegan: The Winding Sheet (album)   **Sub Pop Sp 61**
1990

Kurt and Krist appear on the track "Where Did You Sleep Last Night?" from this solo album by the Screaming Trees' Mark Lanegan. The first 1,000 copies were on red vinyl; the CD and cassette contain an extra track.

Tad: Salt Lick / God Balls (album)   **Sub Pop SP0049**
1990

Krist Novoselic is credited with "global coldcocking" on the album.

Screaming Trees: Down in the Dark /   **Glitterhouse GR0101**
I Love You Little Girl (single)
1990

Mark Lanegan from the Screaming Trees, solo 7-inch. There are two songs. "Down in the Dark" is the A side, and "I Love You Little Girl" is the B side. Kurt makes a guest appearance on the A side. The lineup is Mark Lanegan, vocals; Mike Johnson, electric guitar; Jack Endino, bass/second electric guitar; Mark Pickeral, drums; Kurdt Kobain, background vocals. The song was recorded in December 1989 at Reciprocal Studios in Seattle. Produced by Endino, Johnson, and Lanegan.

Earth: Bureaucratic Desire for Revenge (EP)   **Sup Pop SP 123**
1991

Kurt makes a guest appearance.

William Burroughs: The Priest They Called Him (EP)   **Tim Kerr TK 9210044**
1993

Kurt plays "noise guitar" backing behind William Burroughs's spoken-word rendition of a story written by himself; the B side of the vinyl version has no grooves, just both artists' autographs inscribed on vinyl. Kurt spells his name Curtis Donald Cobain here; Krist Novoselic appears on the cover in a priest outfit. On 10-inch vinyl EP. CD single numbered 92CD044.

The Melvins: Houdini   Amphetamine Reptile Records AMREP-532-1
1993
12-inch black vinyl version. Kurt is the producer on the songs "Hooch," "Joan of Arc," and "Set Me Straight." He also gets mixing credits with the Melvins.

VIDEO RELEASES

Live! Tonight! Sold Out!!   Geffen/DGC DGCV 3954
1994
"Aneurysm" recorded live in Amsterdam, Holland, in 1991 and in Sao Paulo, Brazil, in 1993. "About a Girl" recorded live in Seattle, Washington, in 1992. "Dive" recorded live in São Paulo, Brazil, in 1993. "Love Buzz" recorded live in Dallas, Texas, in 1991, and in Amsterdam, Holland, in 1991. "Breed" recorded live in Seattle, Washington, in 1992. "Smells Like Teen Spirit" recorded in London, England, at the *Top of The Tops* in 1991 and recorded live in Amsterdam, Holland, in 1991. "Negative Creep" recorded live in Honolulu, Hawaii, in 1992. "Come as You Are" recorded live in Amsterdam, Holland, in 1991. "Territorial Pissings" recorded live in London, England, on *The Jonathon Ross Show* in 1991 and in Amsterdam, Holland, in 1991. "Something in the Way" recorded live in Tokyo in 1991. "Lithium" recorded live in Reading, England, at the Reading Festival in 1992. "Drain You" recorded live in Amsterdam in 1991. "Polly" recorded live in Seattle, Washington, in 1992. "Silver" recorded live in Amsterdam in 1991. "On a Plain" recorded live in Roskilde, Denmark, at the Roskilde Festival in 1992. "Noise" recorded live in Seattle, Washington, in 1992. Reading, England, at the Reading Festival, 1992; New York, New York, on *Saturday Night Live* in 1992; Honolulu, Hawaii, in 1992; London, England, on *The Johnathon Ross Show* in 1991; Portland, Oregon, at "No on 9" in 1992; Brussels, Belgium, in 1991; and Tacoma, Washington, in 1992.

Sonic Youth in 1991: The Year Punk Broke   Geffen/DGC DGCV-39518
1993
Featuring Sonic Youth, Nirvana, Dinosaur Jr, Babes in Toyland, Gumball, and the Ramones. Directed by Dave Markey. Approximate running time 95 minutes. Includes "Negative Creep," "School," "Endless Nameless," "Smells Like Teen Spirit," and "Polly."

Sub Pop Video Network Program 1   Sub Pop SP 0627
1991
Contains the original video for "In Bloom," with Chad Channing in the video and playing on drums. The audio was recorded at the Smart Sessions in 1990. The Video was made after the lousy gig at the Pyramid Club in New York, New York.

Hype!   **6700**
1996

Features the first performance of "Smells Like Teen Spirit," taken from the O.K. Hotel in Seattle, Washington, on April 17, 1991. Directed by Doug Pray. A documentary of the Seattle scene.

Song by Song A–Z

The following list includes only songs that were officially released. Compilations have been omitted from this section unless the song appeared only on a compilation.

1. ABOUT A GIRL
Written by Kurt Cobain
Studio version
From the CD *Bleach* (1989) and the CD *Nirvana* (2002).
Recorded by Jack Endino at Reciprocal Recording, Seattle, Washington, December 1988
Kurt Cobain—vocals and guitar
Krist Novoselic—bass
Chad Channing—drums
Live version
From the "Sliver" CD single (1990)
Recorded at the Pine Street Theater, Portland, Oregon, February, 9, 1990
Kurt Cobain—vocals and guitar
Krist Novoselic—bass
Chad Channing—drums
Unplugged version
From *MTV Unplugged in New York* (1993)
Recorded by Scott Litt at the Sony Studios in New York, New York, November 1993
Produced by Nirvana and Scott Litt
Kurt Cobain—vocals and guitar
Krist Novoselic—bass

Dave Grohl—drums
Pat Smear—guitar

2. AERO ZEPPELIN
Written by Kurt Cobain and Krist Novoselic
Studio version
From the CD *Incesticide* (1992)
Produced by Jack Endino
Recorded by Jack Endino at Reciprocal Recording, Seattle, Washington, January 1988
One of the few previously unreleased songs that was featured on *Insecticide*.
Kurt Cobain—vocal and guitar
Krist Novoselic—bass
Dale Crover—drums

3. ALL APOLOGIES
Written by Kurt Cobain
Studio version
From the CD *In Utero* (1993)
Recorded by Steve Albini at Pachyderm Studios in Cannon Falls, Minnesota, February 1993
Technician: Bob Weston; additional mixing by Scott Litt with second engineer Adam Kasper
Kurt Cobain—vocal and guitar
Krist Novoselic—bass
Dave Grohl—drums
Kera Schaley—cello
Unplugged version
From the CD *MTV Unplugged in New York* (1993) and the CD *Nirvana* (2002)
Produced by Nirvana and Scott Litt
Recorded by Scott Litt at the Sony Studios in New York, New York, November 1993
Kurt Cobain—vocal and guitar
Krist Novoselic—bass
Dave Grohl—drums
Pat Smear—guitar
Lori Goldston—cello

4. ANEURYSM
Written by Kurt Cobain, Krist Novoselic, and Dave Grohl
Studio version
From the B side of the "Smells Like Teen Spirit" CD single (1991) and the CD *Hormoaning* (1991)
Produced by Craig Montgomery
Recorded by Craig Montgomery at the Music Source in Seattle, Washington, January 1991
Mixed by Andy Wallace
Kurt Cobain—vocals and guitar
Krist Novoselic—bass
Dave Grohl—drums

Alternate studio version
From the CD *Incesticide* (1992)
Produced by Miti Adhikari
Recorded and engineered by John Taylor at Maida Vale Studios, London, England, November 1991
Taken from the Mark Goodier Session on the BBC
Kurt Cobain—vocals and guitar
Krist Novoselic—bass
Dave Grohl—drums
Live version
From the CD *From the Muddy Banks of the Wishkah* (1996)
Recorded by Andy Wallace at the Del Mar Fairgrounds, Del Mar, California, December 1991
Mixed by Andy Wallace
Kurt Cobain—vocals and guitar
Krist Novoselic—bass
Dave Grohl—drums

5. BEEN A SON
Written by Kurt Cobain and Krist Novoselic
Studio version
From the *Blew* EP (1989) and the CD *Nirvana* (2002)
Recorded by Steve Fisk at the Music Source, Seattle, Washington, September 1989
Kurt Cobain—vocals and guitar
Krist Novoselic—bass
Chad Channing—drums
Alternate studio version
From the CD *Incesticide* (1992)
Produced by Miti Adhikari
Recorded and engineered by John Taylor at Maida Vale Studios, London, England, November 1991
Taken from the Mark Goodier Session on the BBC
Kurt Cobain—vocals and guitar
Krist Novoselic—bass
Dave Grohl—drums
Live version
From the "Lithium" CD single (1991)
Produced by Andy Wallace
Recorded and mixed by Andy Wallace at the Paramount Theater, Seattle, Washington, October 1991
Kurt Cobain—vocals and guitar
Krist Novoselic—bass
Dave Grohl—drums
Alternate live version
From the CD *From the Muddy Banks of the Wishkah* (1996)

Recorded by VPRO-TV at the Paradiso, Amsterdam, Holland, November 1991
Kurt Cobain—vocals and guitar
Krist Novoselic—bass
Dave Grohl—drums

6. BEESWAX
Written by Kurt Cobain
Studio version
From the K Records compilation CD *Kill Rock Stars* (1991) and the CD *Incesticide* (1992)
Produced by Jack Endino
Recorded by Jack Endino at Reciprocal Recording, Seattle, Washington, January 1988
Kurt Cobain—vocals and guitar
Krist Novoselic—bass
Dale Crover—drums

7. BIG CHEESE
Written by Kurt Cobain
Studio version
From the "Love Buzz" 7-inch single (1988) and the CD *Bleach* rerelease (1992)
Recorded by Jack Endino at Reciprocal Recording, Seattle, Washington, June 1988
Kurt Cobain—vocals and guitar
Krist Novoselic—bass
Chad Channing—drums

8. BIG LONG NOW
Written by Kurt Cobain and Krist Novoselic
Studio version
From the CD *Bleach* rerelease (1992) and the CD *Incesticide* (1992)
Recorded by Jack Endino at Reciprocal Recording, Seattle, Washington, December 1989 for
Bleach, but did not make the album. It was one of three unreleased songs on the CD *Incesticide*.
Kurt Cobain—vocals and guitar
Krist Novoselic—bass
Chad Channing—drums

9. BLEW
Written by Kurt Cobain
Studio version
From the CD *Bleach* (1989) and the CD *Blew* (1989)
Recorded by Jack Endino at Reciprocal Recording, Seattle, Washington, December 1988
Kurt Cobain—vocals and guitar
Krist Novoselic—bass
Chad Channing—drums
Live version
From the CD *From the Muddy Banks of the Wishkah* (1996)

Recorded by VPRO-TV at the Paradiso, Amsterdam, Holland, November 1991
Kurt Cobain—vocals and guitar
Krist Novoselic—bass
Dave Grohl—drums

10. BREED
Lyrics written by Kurt Cobain, music written by Nirvana
Studio version
From the CD *Nevermind* (1991)
Produced and engineered by Butch Vig and Nirvana; assistant engineer Jeff Sheehan
Recorded at Sound City Studios in Van Nuys, California, May 1991
Mixed by Andy Wallace at Scream, Studio City, California; assistant engineer Craig Doubet
Kurt Cobain—vocals and guitar
Krist Novoselic—bass
Dave Grohl—drums
Live version
From the CD *From the Muddy Banks of the Wishkah* (1996)
Recorded by Craig Montgomery at the Astoria Theater in London, England, December 1989
Kurt Cobain—vocals and guitar
Krist Novoselic—bass
Dave Grohl—drums

11. COME AS YOU ARE
Lyrics written by Kurt Cobain, music written by Nirvana
Studio version
Produced and engineered by Butch Vig and Nirvana; assistant engineer Jeff Sheehan
Recorded at Sound City Studios in Van Nuys, California, May 1991
From the CD *Nevermind* (1991) and the CD *Nirvana* (2002)
Mixed by Andy Wallace at Scream, Studio City, California; assistant engineer Craig Doubet
Kurt Cobain—vocals and guitar
Krist Novoselic—bass
Dave Grohl—drums
Second single released from the LP; also released as a 12-inch picture disc.
Unplugged version
From the CD *MTV Unplugged in New York* (1993)
Produced by Nirvana and Scott Litt
Recorded by Scott Litt at the Sony Studios in New York, New York, November 1993
Kurt Cobain—vocals and guitar
Krist Novoselic—bass
Dave Grohl—drums
Pat Smear—guitar

12. CURMUDGEON
Written by Kurt Cobain
Studio version
From the CD single "Lithium" (1992)
Produced and engineered by Barrett Jones and Nirvana at Laundry Room Studios, Seattle, Washington, April 1992
Kurt Cobain—vocals and guitar
Krist Novoselic—bass
Dave Grohl—drums

13. D-7
Written by Greg Sage
Studio version
From the CD *Hormoaning* (1991)
Produced by Dale Griffin, engineered by M. Engles and F. Kay
Recorded at Maida Vale Studios, London, England, October 1990
Taken from the John Peel Session
Kurt Cobain—vocals and guitar
Krist Novoselic—bass
Dave Grohl—drums

14. DIVE
Written by Kurt Cobain and Krist Novoselic
Studio version
From the CD single "Sliver" (1990), the CD *The Grunge Years* (1991), and the CD *Incesticide* (1992)
Produced by Butch Vig
Recorded by Butch Vig at Smart Studios, Madison, Wisconsin, April 1990
Kurt Cobain—vocals and guitar
Krist Novoselic—bass
Chad Channing—drums

15. DO YOU LOVE ME?
Written by Kim Fowley, Bob Ezrin, and Paul Stanley
Studio Version
From the LP *Hard to Believe* (1990)
The original was released on the KISS Version *Destroyer* album.
Hard to Believe is a KISS tribute record that was released before the *Kiss My Ass* tribute record. It is the only recorded performance from Jason Everman, even though he is listed as playing guitar on *Bleach*.
Kurt Cobain—vocals and guitar
Krist Novoselic—bass
Jason Everman—guitar
Chad Channing—drums

16. DOWNER
Written by Kurt Cobain and Krist Novoselic
Studio version
From the CD *Bleach* rerelease (1992) and the CD *Incesticide* (1992)
Produced by Jack Endino
Recorded by Jack Endino at Reciprocal Recording, Seattle, Washington, January 1988
Kurt Cobain—vocals and guitar
Krist Novoselic—bass
Dale Crover—drums

17. DRAIN YOU
Lyrics written by Kurt Cobain, music written by Nirvana
Studio version
From the CD *Nevermind* (1991) and the UK single "Smells Like Teen Spirit" (1991)
Produced and engineered by Butch Vig and Nirvana; assistant engineer Jeff Sheehan
Recorded at Sound City Studios in Van Nuys, California, May 1991
Mixed by Andy Wallace at Scream, Studio City, California; assistant engineer Craig Doubet
Kurt Cobain—vocals and guitar
Krist Novoselic—bass
Dave Grohl—drums
Live version
From the CD single "Come as You Are" (1991)
Recorded on the Dogfish mobile truck at the Paramount Theater, Seattle, Washington, October 1991
Engineered and mixed by Andy Wallace
Kurt Cobain—vocals and guitar
Krist Novoselic—bass
Dave Grohl—drums
Alternate live version
From the CD *From the Muddy Banks of the Wishkah* (1996)
Recorded by Westwood One at the Del Mar Fairgrounds, Del Mar, California, December 1991
Kurt Cobain—vocals and guitar
Krist Novoselic—bass
Dave Grohl—drums

18. DUMB
Written by Kurt Cobain
Studio version
From the CD *In Utero* (1993) and the CD *Nirvana* (2002)
Recorded by Steve Albini at Pachyderm Studios in Cannon Falls, Minnesota, February 1993
Technician: Bob Weston
Kurt Cobain—vocals and guitar
Krist Novoselic—bass
Dave Grohl—drums

Unplugged version
From the CD *MTV Unplugged in New York* (1993)
Produced by Nirvana and Scott Litt
Recorded by Scott Litt at the Sony Studios in New York, New York, November 1993
Kurt Cobain—vocals and guitar
Krist Novoselic—bass
Dave Grohl—drums
Pat Smear—guitar
Lori Goldston—cello

19. ENDLESS NAMELESS
Lyrics written by Kurt Cobain, music written by Nirvana
Studio version
From the CD *Nevermind* (1991)
Produced and engineered by Butch Vig and Nirvana; assistant engineer Jeff Sheehan
Recorded at Sound City Studios in Van Nuys, California, May 1991
Mixed by Andy Wallace at Scream, Studio City, California; assistant engineer Craig Doubet
Bonus track on *Nevermind*. The song pops up ten minutes and six seconds after last song ends. Was also a B side to the import copy (German, English, and Japanese) of the single "Come as You Are." Go to the end of cut 12 and fast-forward from 3:45 to 13:51 (still says track 12).
Kurt Cobain—vocals and guitar
Krist Novoselic—bass
Dave Grohl—drums

20. EVEN IN HIS YOUTH
Lyrics written by Kurt Cobain, music written by Nirvana
Studio version
From the CD *Hormoaning* (1991) and the CD single "Smells Like Teen Spirit" (1991)
Produced by Craig Montgomery
Recorded by Craig Montgomery at the Music Source in Seattle, Washington, January 1991
Mixed by Andy Wallace
Kurt Cobain—vocals and guitar
Krist Novoselic—bass
Dave Grohl—drums

21. FLOYD THE BARBER
Written by Kurt Cobain
Studio version
From the CD *Bleach* (1989)
Recorded by Jack Endino at Reciprocal Recording Seattle, Washington, January 1988
Kurt Cobain—vocals and guitar
Krist Novoselic—bass
Dale Crover—drums

22. FRANCES FARMER WILL HAVE HER REVENGE ON SEATTLE

Written by Kurt Cobain
Studio version
From the CD *In Utero* (1993)
Recorded by Steve Albini at Pachyderm Studios in Cannon Falls, Minnesota, February 1993
Technician: Bob Weston
Kurt Cobain—vocals and guitar
Krist Novoselic—bass
Dave Grohl—drums

23. GALLONS OF RUBBING ALCOHOL FLOW THROUGH THE STRIP

Written by Kurt Cobain, Krist Novoselic, and Dave Grohl
Studio version
Previously unreleased, found only on the B side of the promo 12-inch of "Heart-Shaped Box"; also found on the import full-length copy of *In Utero*
Recorded by Steve Albini at Pachyderm Studios in Cannon Falls, Minnesota, February 1993
Technician: Bob Weston
Kurt Cobain—vocals and guitar
Krist Novoselic—bass
Dave Grohl—drums

24. HAIRSPRAY QUEEN

Written by Kurt Cobain
Studio version
From the CD *Incesticide* (1992)
Produced by Jack Endino
Recorded by Jack Endino at Reciprocal Recording in Seattle, Washington, January 1988
One of the few unreleased songs on *Incesticide*.
Kurt Cobain—vocals and guitar
Krist Novoselic—bass
Dale Crover—drums

25. HEART-SHAPED BOX

Written by Kurt Cobain
Studio version
From the CD *In Utero* (1993)
Recorded by Steve Albini at Pachyderm Studios in Cannon Falls, Minnesota, February 1993
Technician: Bob Weston
This was the first single released from the album.
Kurt Cobain—vocals and guitar
Krist Novoselic—bass
Dave Grohl—drums
Live version
From the CD *From the Muddy Banks of the Wishkah* (1996)

Recorded by Craig Overbay on December 30, 1993, at the Great Western Forum, Inglewood, California
Kurt Cobain—vocals and guitar
Krist Novoselic—bass
Dave Grohl—drums

26. HERE SHE COMES NOW

Lyrics written by Lou Reed, music written by Sterling Morrison, John Cale, Maureen Tucker, and Lou Reed
Studio version
From the compilation *Heaven and Hell (1991)*, a tribute to the Velvet Underground—Volume One, also featuring Chapterhouse, The Telescopes, The Wedding Present, Buffalo Tom, James, Screaming Trees, Motorcycle Boy, Terry Bickers/Bradleigh Smith, and Ride
Also released as a 7-inch split single backed with the Melvins covering the Velvet Underground's "Venus in Furs" even though the Melvins song did not appear on this compilation.
Produced by Butch Vig
Recorded by Butch Vig at Smart Studios, Madison, Wisconsin, April 1990
Kurt Cobain—vocals and guitar
Krist Novoselic—bass
Chad Channing—drums

27. I HATE MYSELF AND I WANT TO DIE

Written by Kurt Cobain
Studio version
From the CD *The Beavis and Butt-Head Experience* (1993)
Recorded by Steve Albini at Pachyderm Studios in Cannon Falls, Minnesota, February 1993
Technician: Bob Weston
This song was supposed to be on *In Utero* and actually was supposed to be the title cut as well. It was pulled off the album at the eleventh hour, and the album title was changed. Creepy, but it is the last song released before Kurt's suicide. The compilation also features performances by the Red Hot Chili Peppers, White Zombie, Aerosmith, Anthrax, and more.
Kurt Cobain—vocals and guitar
Krist Novoselic—bass
Dave Grohl—drums

28. IN BLOOM

Lyrics written by Kurt Cobain, music written by Nirvana
Studio version
From the CD *Nevermind* (1991)
Produced and engineered by Butch Vig and Nirvana; assistant engineer Jeff Sheehan
Recorded at Sound City Studios in Van Nuys, California, May 1991
Mixed by Andy Wallace at Scream, Studio City, California; assistant engineer Craig Doubet
Fourth single from the album, also featured on a 12-inch picture disc.
Kurt Cobain—vocals and guitar

Krist Novoselic—bass
Dave Grohl—drums
Alternate studio version
Demo version available on *Sub Pop Video Network Program 1* (1991)
Produced by Butch Vig
Recorded by Butch Vig at Smart Studios, Madison, Wisconsin, April 1990
Kurt Cobain—vocals and guitar
Krist Novoselic—bass
Chad Channing—drums

29. JESUS DOESN'T WANT ME FOR A SUNBEAM
Written by Eugene Kelly and Francis McKee
Studio version
From the CD *MTV Unplugged in New York* (1993)
Produced by Nirvana and Scott Litt
Recorded by Scott Litt at the Sony Studios, New York, New York, November 18, 1993
Kurt Cobain—vocals and guitar
Krist Novoselic—accordion
Dave Grohl—drums with his feet and bass with his hands
Pat Smear—guitar
Lori Goldston—cello

30. LAKE OF FIRE
Written by Curt Kirkwood
Unplugged version
From the CD *MTV Unplugged in New York* (1993)
Produced by Nirvana and Scott Litt
Recorded by Scott Litt at the Sony Studios in New York, New York, November 18, 1993
Kurt Cobain—vocal
Krist Novoselic—guitar
Dave Grohl—drums
Pat Smear—guitar
Curt Kirkwood—guitar
Cris Kirkwood—bass and backup vocals

31. LITHIUM
Lyrics written by Kurt Cobain, music written by Nirvana
Studio version
From the CD *Nevermind* (1991)
Produced and engineered by Butch Vig and Nirvana; assistant engineer Jeff Sheehan
Recorded at Sound City Studios in Van Nuys, California, May 1991
Mixed by Andy Wallace at Scream, Studio City, California; assistant engineer Craig Doubet
Third single from the LP, also released as a 12-inch picture disc.
Kurt Cobain—vocals and guitar
Krist Novoselic—bass

Dave Grohl—drums
Live version
From the CD *From the Muddy Banks of the Wishkah* (1996)
Recorded by VPRO-TV at the Paradiso, Amsterdam, Holland, November 25, 1991
Kurt Cobain—vocals and guitar
Krist Novoselic—bass
Dave Grohl—drums

32. LOUNGE ACT
Lyrics written by Kurt Cobain, music written by Nirvana
Studio version
From the CD *Nevermind* (1991)
Produced and engineered by Butch Vig and Nirvana; assistant engineer Jeff Sheehan
Recorded at Sound City Studios, Van Nuys, California, May 1991
Mixed by Andy Wallace at Scream, Studio City, California; assistant engineer Craig Doubet
Kurt Cobain—vocals and guitar
Krist Novoselic—bass
Dave Grohl—drums

33. LOVE BUZZ
Written by Robby Van Leeuwen
Studio version
From the CD *Bleach* (1989)
Recorded by Jack Endino at Reciprocal Recording, Seattle, Washington, June 11 or June 30, 1988
The Shocking Blue were best known for their 1970 number-one hit "Venus." A popular remake of that song also became a number-one hit with Banarama's 1986 version. Nirvana's version is slightly different than the original. Oddly enough, one of the best songwriters of the 1990s would release a cover as the first single. It was originally released in 1988. One of the rarest Nirvana collectibles, it was also the very first single from Sub Pop's "Singles Club," which ended in December 1993. Only 1,000 copies were printed. The 7-inch version also contains an intro that has some cartoon voices.
Kurt Cobain—vocals and guitar
Krist Novoselic—bass
Chad Channing—drums

34. MARIGOLD
Written by Dave Grohl
Studio version
From the import CD single "Heart-Shaped Box"
Previously unreleased, a B side to "Heart-Shaped Box," UK CD single only
Recorded by Steve Albini at Pachyderm Studios in Cannon Falls, Minnesota, February 1993
Technician: Bob Weston
The only solo song written and sung by Dave Grohl released by Nirvana.
Dave Grohl—drums and lead vocal

Kurt Cobain—guitar and backing vocal
Krist Novoselic—bass

35. MEXICAN SEAFOOD
Written by Kurt Cobain
Studio version
From the Teriyaki Asthma compilations (1989) and the CD *Incesticide* (1992), a compilation of underground indie bands on the CZ label. It was first released as a compilation featuring five 7-inch singles (Volumes 1–5). Nirvana were featured on the first volume, originally released in 1989. It features two bands per side, with the 7-inch running at 33^1/$_3$ rpm. Nirvana and Helios Creed are on one side, Coffin Break and Yeast on the other. All of the bands from Volumes 1–5 were all eventually put on one CD entitled *Teriyaki Asthma EP Volumes 1–5*.
Produced and engineered by Jack Endino
Recorded by Jack Endino at Reciprocal Recording, Seattle, Washington, January 23, 1988
Kurt Cobain—vocals and guitar
Krist Novoselic—bass
Dale Crover—drums

36. MILK IT
Written by Kurt Cobain
Studio version
From the CD *In Utero* (1993)
Recorded by Steve Albini at Pachyderm Studios, Cannon Falls, Minnesota, February 1993
Technician: Bob Weston
Also featured as a B side to "Heart-Shaped Box"
Live version
From the CD *From the Muddy Banks of the Wishkah* (1996)
Recorded by Craig Overbay at the Seattle Center Arena, Seattle, Washington, January 1994
Kurt Cobain—vocals and guitar
Krist Novoselic—bass
Dave Grohl—drums
Pat Smear—guitar

37. MOLLY'S LIPS
Written by Eugene Kelly and Frances McKee
Studio version
A cover of the Vaselines song. Originally released as a 7-inch split single (this was a live version recorded in Portland, Oregon) on Sub Pop (their last single for Sub Pop). The single was backed with the song "Candy" by the Fluid (1990). From the CD *Hormoaning* (1991) and the CD *Incesticide* (1992)
Produced by Dale Griffin, engineered by M. Engles and F. Kay. Taken from the John Peel Session. Recorded at Maida Vale Studios, London, England, October 21, 1990
Kurt's favorite Vaselines song. Kurt left out some of the lyrics because he was too lazy to write them down.

Kurt Cobain—vocals and guitar
Krist Novoselic—bass
Dave Grohl—drums

38. MR. MOUSTACHE
Written by Kurt Cobain
Studio version
From the CD *Bleach* (1989)
Recorded by Jack Endino at Reciprocal Recording, Seattle, Washington, sometime in December 1988
Kurt Cobain—vocals and guitar
Krist Novoselic—bass
Chad Channing—drums

39. MV, OR MOIST VAGINA
Written by Kurt Cobain
Studio version
Recorded by Steve Albini at Pachyderm Studios, Cannon Falls, Minnesota, February 1993
Technician: Bob Weston
The song was credited as "MV" or "Moist Vagina," depending on if you have the English or the German import, respectively.
Kurt Cobain—vocals and guitar
Krist Novoselic—bass
Dave Grohl—drums

40. NEGATIVE CREEP
Written by Kurt Cobain
Studio version
From the CD *Bleach* (1989)
Recorded by Jack Endino at Reciprocal Recording, Seattle, Washington, sometime in December 1988
Also appears on *Hype! The Motion Picture Soundtrack* (1996)
Kurt Cobain—vocals and guitar
Krist Novoselic—bass
Chad Channing—drums
Live version
From the CD *From the Muddy Banks of the Wishkah* (1996)
Recorded by Andy Wallace at the Paramount
Theater, Seattle, Washington, October 31, 1991
Kurt Cobain—vocals and guitar
Krist Novoselic—bass
Dave Grohl—drums

41. (NEW WAVE) POLLY
Written by Kurt Cobain, Krist Novoselic, and Dave Grohl
Studio version
From the CD *Incesticide* (1992)
Produced by Miti Adhikari
Recorded and engineered by John Taylor at Maida Vale Studios, London, England, November 9, 1991
Taken from *The Mark Goodier Session* on the BBC
This is a more upbeat version than the original. It is a rerecording of the original featured on *Nevermind*.
Kurt Cobain—vocals and guitar
Krist Novoselic—bass
Dave Grohl—drums

42. OH ME
Written by Curt Kirkwood
Studio version
From the CD *MTV Unplugged in New York* (1993)
Produced by Nirvana and Scott Litt
Recorded by Scott Litt at the Sony Studios, New York, New York, November 18, 1993
Kurt Cobain—vocals and guitar
Krist Novoselic—bass
Dave Grohl—drums
Pat Smear—guitar
Curt Kirkwood—guitar
Cris Kirkwood—guitar

43. OH THE GUILT
Written by Kurt Cobain and Nirvana
Studio version
From the CD single and 7-inch split single with Jesus Lizard's "Puss" (1993); was released on the indie label Touch and Go even though Nirvana were signed with Geffen
Recorded by Nirvana and Barrett Jones at Laundry Room Studios, Seattle, Washington, April 1992
Kurt Cobain—vocals and guitar
Krist Novoselic—bass
Dave Grohl—drums

44. ON A PLAIN
Lyrics written by Kurt Cobain, music written by Nirvana
Studio version
From the CD *Nevermind* (1991)
Produced and engineered by Butch Vig and Nirvana; assistant engineer Jeff Sheehan
Recorded at Sound City Studios in Van Nuys, California, May 1991
Mixed by Andy Wallace at Scream, Studio City, California; assistant engineer Craig Doubet

Kurt Cobain—vocals and guitar
Krist Novoselic—bass
Dave Grohl—drums
Unplugged version
From the CD *MTV Unplugged in New York* (1993)
Produced by Nirvana and Scott Litt
Recorded by Scott Litt at the Sony Studios in New York, New York, November 1993
Kurt Cobain—vocals and guitar
Krist Novoselic—bass
Dave Grohl—drums
Pat Smear—guitar

45. PAPER CUTS
Written by Kurdt Kobain
Studio version
From the CD *Bleach* (1989)
Recorded by Jack Endino at Reciprocal Recording, Seattle, Washington, January 23, 1988
Kurt Cobain—vocals and guitar
Krist Novoselic—bass
Dale Crover—drums

46. PAY TO PLAY
Written by Kurt Cobain
Studio version
From *DGC Rarities Vol. 1*; (1994) also features Hole, Sonic Youth, Teenage
Fanclub, Beck, Weezer, and more
Recorded by Butch Vig at Smart Studios, Madison, Wisconsin, August 1990
This was the demo version of "Stay Away" that appeared on *Nevermind*. The structure of the song is the same, but the lyrics are slightly different, including the change from "Pay to Play" to "Stay Away." Some of the lines in the verses are also different. See "Stay Away."
Kurt Cobain—vocals and guitar
Krist Novoselic—bass
Chad Channing—drums

47. PENNYROYAL TEA
Written by Kurt Cobain
Studio version
From the CD *In Utero* (1993)
Recorded by Steve Albini at Pachyderm Studios in Cannon Falls, Minnesota, February 1993
Technician: Bob Weston
Kurt Cobain—vocal and guitar
Krist Novoselic—bass
Dave Grohl—drums
Unplugged version
From the CD *MTV Unplugged in New York* (1993)

Produced by Nirvana and Scott Litt
Recorded by Scott Litt at the Sony Studios in New York, New York, November 1993
Kurt Cobain—vocal and guitar

48. PLATEAU
Written by Curt Kirkwood
Unplugged version
From the CD *MTV Unplugged in New York* (1993)
Recorded by Scott Litt at the Sony Studios in New York, New York, November 1993
Kurt Cobain—vocal
Krist Novoselic—guitar
Dave Grohl—drums
Pat Smear—guitar
Curt Kirkwood—guitar
Cris Kirkwood—bass and backup vocals

49. POLLY
Lyrics written by Kurt Cobain, music written by Nirvana
Studio version
From the CD *Nevermind* (1991)
Produced and engineered by Butch Vig and Nirvana
Recorded at Smart Studios, Madison, Wisconsin, April 1990, and Sound City Studios in Van Nuys, California, May 1991
Assistant engineer: Jeff Sheehan
Mixed by Andy Wallace at Scream, Studio City, California; assistant engineer Craig Doubet
Recorded by Butch Vig in 1990, the master tape got some overdubs in 1990 and was used for the version on *Nevermind*. This would mean Chad Channing is actually the drummer.
Kurt Cobain—vocals and guitar
Krist Novoselic—bass
Chad Channing—drums (uncredited)
Live version
From the CD single "In Bloom"
Recorded by Andy Wallace at the O'Brien Pavillion, Del Mar, California, December 28, 1991
Produced by Andy Wallace
Kurt Cobain—vocals and guitar
Krist Novoselic—bass
Dave Grohl—drums
Unplugged version
From the CD *MTV Unplugged in New York* (1993)
Produced by Nirvana and Scott Litt
Recorded by Scott Litt at the Sony Studios, New York, New York, November 1993
Kurt Cobain—vocals and guitar
Krist Novoselic—bass
Dave Grohl—drums

Pat Smear—guitar
Lori Goldston—cello
Live version
From the CD *From the Muddy Banks of the Wishkah* (1996)
Recorded by Craig Montgomery at the Astoria Theater, London, England, December 5, 1989
Kurt Cobain—vocals and guitar
Krist Novoselic—bass
Dave Grohl—drums

50. RADIO FRIENDLY UNIT SHIFTER
Written by Kurt Cobain
Studio version
From the CD *In Utero* (1993)
Recorded by Steve Albini at Pachyderm Studios, Cannon Falls, Minnesota, February 1993
Technician: Bob Weston
Kurt Cobain—vocals and guitar
Krist Novoselic—bass
Dave Grohl—drums
Live version
From the compilation album *Home Alive, The Art of Self Defense*
Recorded by Craig Overbay at Le Summer, Grenoble, France, February 18, 1994
Kurt Cobain—vocals and guitar
Krist Novoselic—bass
Dave Grohl—drums
Pat Smear—guitar

51. RAPE ME
Written by Kurt Cobain
Studio version
From the CD *In Utero* (1993)
Recorded by Steve Albini at Pachyderm Studios in Cannon Falls, Minnesota, February 1993
Technician: Bob Weston
Kurt Cobain—vocals and guitar
Krist Novoselic—bass
Dave Grohl—drums

52. RETURN OF THE RAT
Written by Greg Sage
Studio version
Recorded by Barrett Jones at Laundry Room Studios, in Seattle, Washington, April 1992
From the 7-inch singles box set of Wipers covers called *Eight Songs for Greg Sage and the Wipers*. The original version is from the Wipers album *Is This Real?* (later available on CD).
Kurt Cobain—vocals and guitar

Krist Novoselic—bass
Dave Grohl—drums

53. SCENTLESS APPRENTICE
Lyrics written by Kurt Cobain, music written by Kurt Cobain, Krist Novoselic, and Dave Grohl
Studio version
From the CD *In Utero* (1993)
Recorded by Steve Albini at Pachyderm Studios in Cannon Falls, Minnesota, February 1993
Technician: Bob Weston
This song appeared on a promotional cassette as part of *Concrete Foundations* magazine's September 1993 issue (released before *In Utero*).
Live version
From the CD *From the Muddy Banks of the Wishkan* (1996)
Recorded by Scott Litt for *MTV Live and Loud* at Pier 48, Seattle, Washington, December 13, 1993
Kurt Cobain—vocals and guitar
Krist Novoselic—bass
Dave Grohl—drums
Pat Smear—guitar

54. SCHOOL
Written by Kurdt Kobain
Studio version
From the CD *Bleach* (1989)
Recorded by Jack Endino at Reciprocal Recording, Seattle, Washington, sometime in December 1988
Kurt Cobain—vocals and guitar
Krist Novoselic—bass
Chad Channing—drums
Live version
From the CD single "Come as You Are"
Recorded on the Dogfish mobile truck at the Paramount Theatre, Seattle, Washington, October 31, 1991
Engineered and mixed by Andy Wallace
Kurt Cobain—vocals and guitar
Krist Novoselic—bass
Dave Grohl—drums
Alternate live version
From the CD *From the Muddy Banks of the Wishkah* (1996)
Recorded by VPRO-TV at the Paradiso, Amsterdam, Holland, November 25, 1991
Kurt Cobain—vocals and guitar
Krist Novoselic—bass
Dave Grohl—drums

55. SCOFF

Written by Kurdt Kobain
Studio version
From the CD *Bleach* (1989)
Recorded by Jack Endino at Reciprocal Recording, Seattle, Washington sometime in December 1988
Kurt Cobain—vocals and guitar
Krist Novoselic—bass
Chad Channing—drums

56. SERVE THE SERVANTS

Written by Kurt Cobain
Studio version
From the CD *In Utero* (1993)
Recorded by Steve Albini at Pachyderm Studios in Cannon Falls, Minnesota, February 1993
Technician: Bob Weston
Kurt Cobain—vocals and guitar
Krist Novoselic—bass
Dave Grohl—drums

57. SIFTING

Written by Kurt Cobain
Studio version
From the CD *Bleach* (1989)
Recorded by Jack Endino at Reciprocal Recording, Seattle, Washington, sometime in December 1988
Kurt Cobain—vocals and guitar
Krist Novoselic—bass
Chad Channing—drums

58. SLIVER

Written by Kurt Cobain and Krist Novoselic
Studio version
From the CD single "Sliver" (1990)
Produced by Jack Endino
Recorded by Jack Endino
The 12-inch version contains a phone call by Sub Pop head honcho Jon Poneman. The same version can be found on the CD *Incesticide* (1992). There was a video made for the release of *Incesticide* with Dave Grohl on drums, but the song actually features the only recorded appearance by Mudhoney drummer Dan Peters.
Kurt Cobain—vocals and guitar
Krist Novoselic—bass
Dan Peters—drums
Live version
From the CD single "In Bloom" (1992)

Recorded by Andy Wallace at the O'Brien Pavillion, Del Mar, California, December 28, 1991
Produced by Andy Wallace
Kurt Cobain—vocals and guitar
Krist Novoselic—bass
Dave Grohl—drums
Alternative live version
From the CD *From the Muddy Banks of the Wishkah* (1996)
Recorded by Craig Overbay at the Springfield Civic Center, Springfield, Massachusetts, November 10, 1993
Kurt Cobain—vocals and guitar
Krist Novoselic—bass
Dave Grohl—drums

59. SMELLS LIKE TEEN SPIRIT
Lyrics written by Kurt Cobain, music written by Nirvana
Studio version
From the CD *Nevermind* (1991)
Produced and engineered by Butch Vig and Nirvana; assistant engineer Jeff Sheehan
Recorded at Sound City Studios, Van Nuys, California, May 1991
Mixed by Andy Wallace at Scream, Studio City, California; assistant engineer Craig Doubet
Kurt Cobain—vocals and guitar
Krist Novoselic—bass
Dave Grohl—drums
Live version
From the CD *From the Muddy Banks of the Wishkah* (1996)
Recorded by Andy Wallace at the Del Mar Fairgrounds, Del Mar, California, December 28, 1991
Mixed by Andy Wallace
Kurt Cobain—vocals and guitar
Krist Novoselic—bass
Dave Grohl—drums

60. SOMETHING IN THE WAY
Lyrics written by Kurt Cobain, music written by Nirvana
Studio version
From the CD *Nevermind* (1991)
Produced and engineered by Butch Vig and Nirvana; assistant engineer Jeff Sheehan
Recorded at Sound City Studios, Van Nuys, California, May 1991
Mixed by Andy Wallace at Scream, Studio City, California; assistant engineer Craig Doubet
Kurt Cobain—vocals and guitar
Krist Novoselic—bass
Dave Grohl—drums
Kirk Canning—cello

Unplugged version
From the CD *MTV Unplugged in New York* (1993)
Produced by Nirvana and Scott Litt
Recorded by Scott Litt at the Sony Studios, New York, New York, November 1993
Kurt Cobain—vocals and guitar
Krist Novoselic—bass
Dave Grohl—drums
Pat Smear—guitar

61. SON OF A GUN
Written by Eugene Kelly and Frances McKee
Studio version
From the CD *Hormoaning* (1991) and the CD *Incesticide* (1992)
Produced by Dale Griffin, engineered by M. Engles and F. Kay
Taken from the John Peel Session recorded at Maida Vale Studios, London, England, October 21, 1990
Kurt Cobain—vocals and guitar
Krist Novoselic—bass
Dave Grohl—drums

62. SPANK THRU
Written by Nirvana
Studio version
From the CD *Sub Pop 200* (1988)
Recorded by Jack Endino at Reciprocal Recording, Seattle, Washington, June 1988
Kurt Cobain—vocals and guitar
Krist Novoselic—bass
Chad Channing—drums
Jack Endino—backing vocals
Live version
From the CD single "Sliver" (1990)
Recorded at the Pine Street Theater, Portland, Oregon, February 1990
Kurt Cobain—guitar and vocals
Krist Novoselic—bass
Chad Channing—drums
Alternate live version
From the CD *From the Muddy Banks of the Wishkah* (1996)
Recorded by Stereoral at Il Castello Vi De Porta, Rome, Italy, November 19, 1991
Kurt Cobain—vocals and guitar
Krist Novoselic—bass
Dave Grohl—drums

63. STAIN
Written by Kurt Cobain and Krist Novoselic

Studio version
From the CD *Blew* (1989) and the CD *Incesticide* (1992)
Produced by Steve Fisk
Recorded by Steve Fisk at the Music Source, Seattle, Washington, September 1989
Kurt Cobain—vocals and guitar
Krist Novoselic—bass
Chad Channing—drums

64. STAY AWAY
Lyrics written by Kurt Cobain, music written by Nirvana
Studio version
From the CD *Nevermind* (1991)
Produced and engineered by Butch Vig and Nirvana; assistant engineer Jeff Sheehan
Recorded at Sound City Studios, Van Nuys, California, May 1991
Mixed by Andy Wallace at Scream, Studio City, California; assistant engineer Craig Doubet
Kurt Cobain—vocals and guitar
Krist Novoselic—bass
Dave Grohl—drums

65. SWAP MEET
Written by Kurdt Kobain
Studio version
From the CD *Bleach* (1989)
Recorded by Jack Endino at Reciprocal Recording, Seattle, Washington, sometime in December 1988
Kurt Cobain—vocals, guitar
Krist Novoselic—bass
Chad Channing—drums

66. TERRITORIAL PISSINGS
Lyrics written by Kurt Cobain, music written by Nirvana
Studio version
From the CD *Nevermind* (1991)
Produced and engineered by Butch Vig and Nirvana; assistant engineer Jeff Sheehan
Recorded at Sound City Studios, Van Nuys, California, May 1991
Mixed by Andy Wallace at Scream, Studio City, California; assistant engineer Craig Doubet
Kurt Cobain—vocals and guitar
Krist Novoselic—bass, and vocal intro
Dave Grohl—drums

67. THE MAN WHO SOLD THE WORLD
Written by David Bowie
Unplugged version
From the CD *MTV Unplugged in New York* (1993)
Produced by Nirvana and Scott Litt

Recorded by Scott Litt at the Sony Studios, New York, New York, November 1993
Kurt Cobain—vocals and guitar
Krist Novoselic—bass
Dave Grohl—drums
Pat Smear—guitar

68. TOURETTE'S
Written by Kurt Cobain
From the CD *In Utero* (1993)
Recorded by Steve Albini at Pachyderm Studios, Cannon Falls, Minnesota, February 1993
Technician: Bob Weston
Kurt Cobain—vocals and guitar
Krist Novoselic—bass
Dave Grohl—drums
Live version
From the CD *From the Muddy Banks of the Wishkah* (1996)
Recorded by Fujisankei Communications International Incorporated at the Reading Festival, Reading, England, August 1992
Kurt Cobain—vocals and guitar
Krist Novoselic—bass
Dave Grohl—drums

69. TURNAROUND
Written by M. Mothersbaugh and G. Casale
The Devo version originally appeared as the B side to the New Wave cult classic "Whipit"
Studio version
From the EP *Hormoaning* (1992) and from the CD *Incesticide* (1992)
Taken from the John Peel Session
Produced by Dale Griffin
Recorded by Mike Engles and Fred Kay at Maida Vale Studios, London England, October 1990
Kurt Cobain—vocals and guitar
Krist Novoselic—bass
Dave Grohl—drums

70. VERSE CHORUS VERSE
Written by Kurt Cobain
Studio version
From the compilation album *No Alternative* (1993), the sequel to *Red Hot and Blue*. The album benefits AIDS charities. The song is not listed anywhere on the CD, but it is the secret surprise bonus track at cut 19.
Recorded by Steve Albini at Pachyderm Studios in Cannon Falls, Minnesota, February 1993
Kurt Cobain—vocals and guitar
Krist Novoselic—bass
Dave Grohl—drums

71. VERY APE
Written by Kurt Cobain
Studio version
From the CD *In Utero* (1993)
Recorded by Steve Albini at Pachyderm Studios in Cannon Falls, Minnesota, February 1993
Technician: Bob Weston
Kurt Cobain—vocals and guitar
Krist Novoselic—bass
Dave Grohl—drums

72. WHERE DID YOU SLEEP LAST NIGHT
Written by Huddie Ledbetter, aka Leadbelly
Unplugged version
From the CD MTV *Unplugged in New York* (1993)
Produced by Nirvana and Scott Litt
Recorded by Scott Litt at the Sony Studios in New York, New York, November 1993
Kurt Cobain—vocals and guitar
Krist Novoselic—bass
Dave Grohl—drums
Pat Smear—guitar

73. YOU KNOW YOU'RE RIGHT
Written by Kurt Cobain
Studio version
From the CD *Nirvana* (2002)
Recorded by Adam Kapser at Robert Lang Studio in Seattle Washington, January 1994
Mixed by Adam Kaspar
Kurt Cobain—vocals and guitar
Krist Novoselic—bass
Dave Grohl—drums

Source Notes

Page v.

"We were the chosen": *Nirvana Live! Tonight! Sold Out!!*

One

"We don't like to": Author, *Nevermind It's an Interview*, January 1992.

Two

"Leave it to Beaver": Author, *Nevermind It's an Interview*, January 1992.

"It's totally secluded from": ibid.

"My mother was a": Steffan Chirazi, "Lounge Act," *Kerrang*, November 29, 1993.

"My mom was always": Michael Azerrad, *Come as You Are: The Story of Nirvana* (Doubleday, 1993), p. 13.

"There's nothing like your": ibid.

"He wanted me to": ibid.

"Oh heck yeah . . . Evel": ibid.

"After a while . . . every": Azerrad, *Come as You Are*, p. 15.

"Ever since I can": ibid., p. 16.

"When I was . . . around": ibid., p. 24.

"I just remember all": ibid., p. 17.

"Now that I look": ibid., p. 21.

"I do probably blow": ibid., p. 20.

"I felt alienated. Right": Jerry McCulley, "Spontaneous Combustion," *BAM*, January 10, 1992.

"My mom thought that": Azerrad, *Come as You Are*, p. 16.

"I never had a": Mike Gitter, "A Steady Current of Mistrust and Contempt for the 'Average American,'" *East Coast Rocker,* October 9, 1991.

"He played drums, and": Ralph Heibutski, "The Last Word on Kurt Cobain," *Discoveries for Record Collectors,* June 1994.

"I was chased around": Mike Gitter, "Anarchy in the UK," *RIP,* 1992.

"I don't feel sorry": Gitter, "A Steady Current of Mistrust and Contempt for the 'Average American,'" *East Coast Rocker,* October 9, 1991.

"[In Aberdeen] there was": Carl Williams, "Good Clean Fun," *The London Student,* November 19, 1999.

"I became antisocial": Jon Savage, "Sounds Dirty," *The Observer,* August 15, 1993.

"See, I've always wanted": Kevin Allman, "The Dark Side of Kurt Cobain," *The Advocate,* February 9, 1993.

"Women are totally oppressed": Savage, "Sounds Dirty," *The Observer,* August 15, 1993.

"We called it 'witch'": Heibutski, "The Last Word on Kurt Cobain," *Discoveries for Record Collectors,* June 1994.

"One of his ideas": ibid.

"That was a lot": ibid.

"My dad thought [Kurt]": ibid.

"I used to pretend": Allman, "The Dark Side of Kurt Cobain," *The Advocate,* February 9, 1993.

"felt threatened because they": Azerrad, *Come as You Are,* p. 33.

"My mother wouldn't allow": Savage, "Sounds Dirty," *The Observer,* August 15, 1993.

"The biggest reason I": Azerrad, *Come as You Are,* p. 33.

"When I did, he . . .": Jon Pareles, "The Band That Hates To Be Loved," *New York Times,* November 14, 1993.

"I was fifteen when": Author, *Nevermind It's an Interview,* January 1992.

"When I first started": Katherine Turman, "Smells Like Nirvana," *RIP,* 1992.

"We never even got": Heibutski, "The Last Word on Kurt Cobain," *Discoveries for Record Collectors,* June 1994.

"I don't understand anything": Seana Baruth, *The Northern Editor,* October 18, 1991.

"He was from a": Heibutski, "The Last Word on Kurt Cobain," *Discoveries for Record Collectors,* June 1994.

"He was washing dishes": ibid.

"I started watching the": Author, *Nevermind It's an Interview,* January 1992.

"It was like listening": Azerrad, *Come as You Are,* p. 31.

"The Sex Pistols, the": Jessica Adams, "Corporate Rock Whores?," *Select,* April 1992.

"It was definitely a": Azerrad, *Come as You Are,* p. 23.

"That was the day": Adams, "Corporate Rock Whores?," *Select,* April 1992.

"I used to see": Shaun Phillips, "Teenage Rampage," *Vox* (magazine), January 1992.

"He just had a": Azerrad, *Come as You Are,* p. 32.

"Becoming a punk rocker": ibid., p. 32.

"I knew I was": Amy Raphael, "In the Court of King Kurt," *The Face,* September 1993.

Three

"People think that you": Author, *Nevermind It's an Interview,* January 1992.

"Both my parents were": Krist Novoselic, "Masters of War," *Spin,* May 1993.

"It's isolated. It's a": Chris Morris, "The Year's Hottest New Band Can't Stand Still," *Musician,* January 1992.

"It was a big": McCulley, "Spontaneous Combustion," *BAM,* January 10, 1992.

"I looked like Jay": Azerrad, *Come as You Are,* p. 53.

"He'd go out and": ibid., p. 53.

"I've always been a": ibid., p. 51.

"You'd go to parties": bid., p. 51.

"He was a hilarious": ibid., p. 29.

"I think [we were]": Author, *Nevermind It's an Interview,* January 1992.

"I was a KISS": McCulley, "Spontaneous Combustion," *BAM,* January 10, 1992.

"I remember meeting Buzz": Author, *Nevermind It's an Interview,* January 1992.

Four

"The Melvins are really": Author, *Nevermind It's an Interview,* January 1992.

"We were like, 'Wow,' ": Heibutski, "The Last Word on Kurt Cobain," *Discoveries for Record Collectors,* June 1994.

"We just started accepting": Greg Kott, "Now that they've been found, Seattle bands fight for their independence," *Chicago Tribune,* October 20, 1991.

"They were just some": Azerrad, *Come as You Are,* p. 31.

"One of the songs": Author, *Nevermind It's an Interview,* January 1992.

"Krist and Kurt automatically": Heibutski, "The Last Word on Kurt Cobain," *Discoveries for Record Collectors,* June 1994.

"I played guitar": Author, *Nevermind It's an Interview,* January 1992.

"Fuck, she hated my": Azerrad, *Come as You Are,* p. 59.

"We all used to": Heibutski, "The Last Word on Kurt Cobain," *Discoveries for Record Collectors,* June 1994.

"I had the apartment": Azerrad, *Come as You Are,* p. 36.

"There really wasn't much": Heibutski, "The Last Word on Kurt Cobain," *Discoveries for Record Collectors,* June 1994.

"I'd get all pissed": Raphael, "In the Court of King Kurt," *The Face,* September 1993.

"We were out there": Heibutski, "The Last Word on Kurt Cobain," *Discoveries for Record Collectors,* June 1994.

"We had everyone so": Azerrad, *Come as You Are,* p. 59.

"Living [in Olympia] taught": AL, "Nirvana," *Flipside,* Fall 1989.

"I'm a good chef": ibid.

"We'll all vouch for": ibid.

"[When] I went to": Helbutski, "The Last Word on Kurt Cobain," *Discoveries for Record Collectors,* June 1994.

"He also had a": Azerrad, *Come as You Are,* p. 76.

"I think they were": ibid., p. 76.

"I wanted a name": ibid., p. 62.

Five

"The way I see": Author, *Nevermind It's an Interview*, January 1992.

"Music is most interesting": Untitled, *The Stony Brook Press* 13, no. 5, November 11, 1991.

"Kurt was pretty laid": "When They Were Crap," *Q Monthly*, June 1996.

"Five of these songs": Jack Endino, "The Ever-Popular Nirvana FAQ," www.jackendino.com.

"Jack was totally blown": "When They Were Crap," *Q Monthly*, June 1996.

"This guy's got a": Azerrad, *Come as You Are*, p. 70.

"It had this bridge": "When They Were Crap," *Q Monthly*, June 1996.

"We didn't really fuck": Charles R. Cross, *Heavier Than Heaven* (Hyperion, 2001).

"I was so fucking": Azerrad, *Come as You Are*, p. 77.

"They wanted to practice": ibid., p. 67.

"Seattle was, for a": "When They Were Crap," *Q Monthly*, June 1996.

"We started playing around": Andrew Perry, "Bleaching sartori," *The London Student*, November 23, 1989.

"And we were lucky": Raphael, "In the Court of King Kurt," *The Face*, September 1993.

"I remember Kurt telling": Azerrad, *Come as You Are*, p. 79.

"I think we all": AL, "Nirvana," *Flipside*, Fall 1989.

"in this shitty old": Morris, "The year's Hottest New Band Can't Stand Still," *Musician*, January 1992.

"Our [family] motto was": Azerrad, *Come as You Are*, p. 78.

"Those were magical times": Jim DeRogatis, "Smells Like A Nirvana Article," *Request*, November 1993.

"Blandest didn't come out": Endino, "The Ever-Popular Nirvana FAQ," www.jackendino.com.

"I collect children's records": Edwin Pouncey, "Kills All Known Germs," *NME*, September 2, 1989.

"The 'Love Buzz' single": Endino, "The Ever-Popular Nirvana FAQ," www.jackendino.com.

"Another difference between the": ibid.

"have recorded it a": Pouncey, "Kills All Known Germs," *NME*, September 2, 1989.

Six

"The problem with independent": Author, *Nevermind It's an Interview*, January 1992.

"We just recorded it": Perry, "Bleaching sartori," *The London Student*, November 23, 1989.

"About a week before": Mike Gitter, "Revenge of the Nerds," *Kerrang*, August 24, 1991.

"How could we deny": ibid.

"The only finished outtake": Endino, "The Ever-Popular Nirvana FAQ," www.jackendino.com.

"The band came in": Gillian G. Gaar, "Verse Chorus Verse," *Goldmine*, February 14, 1997.

"On the first day": Cayo and Claire, "Down to Earth Guys But Their Music's Red Hot!," *Metal Force*, November 19, 1989.

"A lot of people": Williams, "Good Clean Fun," *The London Student*, November 19, 1989.

"Bleach just seemed to": Author, *Nevermind It's an Interview*, January 1992.

"[It's] like what you": AL, "Nirvana," *Flipside*, Fall 1989.

"I write most of": ibid.

"At the same time": Arthur, *Nevermind It's an Interview*, January 1992.

"I wish we'd have": Azerrad, *Come as You Are*, p. 82.

"For me, recording always": Ibid., p. 82.

"We wrote down the": AL, "Nirvana," *Flipside*, Fall 1989.

"We basically were ready": Azerrad, *Come as You Are*, p. 91.

"I remember years ago": ibid., p. 103.

"antique craftsmanship, something that": Everett True, "Tad and Nirvana—The Larder They Come," *Melody Maker*, March 17, 1990.

"I was trying to be": Azerrad, *Come as You Are*, p. 102.

"We were all sick": ibid., p. 91.

"There were a lot": ibid., p. 87.

"I've never had any": ibid., p. 98.

"It was amazing,": ibid., p. 87.

"[To] be able to": ibid., p. 87.

"They were just constantly": ibid., p. 84.

"they can say whatever": "Nirvana," *Birmingham Sun*, November 9, 1989.

"People ask when the": True, "Tad and Nirvana—The Larder They Come," *Melody Maker*, March 17, 1990.

"For a few years": David Fricke, "Success Doesn't Suck," *Rolling Stone*, January 27, 1994.

Seven

"Basically this is the":Everett True, "Sub Pop Seattle: Rock City," *Melody Maker*, March 18, 1989.

"In the spring of": "A Fan's Notes," *Spin*, April 1995.

"I hated them, The": Azerrad, *Come as You Are*, p. 97.

"We played this tiny": "A Fan's Notes," *Spin*, April 1995.

"The first time I": ibid.

"It's one of my": True, "Tad and Nirvana—The Larder They Come," *Melody Maker*, March 17, 1990.

"We stayed at this": Morris, "The Year's Hottest New Band Can't Stand Still," *Musician*, January 1992.

"We hacked up a": ibid.

"We played in San": True, "Tad and Nirvana—The Larder They Come," *Melody Maker*, March 17, 1990.

"We've got this stupid": ibid.

"We were totally poor": Azerrad, *Come as You Are*, p. 115.

"He was like a": ibid., p. 117.

"Traveling is fun, and": True, "Tad and Nirvana—The Larder They Come," *Melody Maker*, March 17, 1990.

"Why do I do": ibid.

"It seemed like you": Azerrad, *Come as You Are*, p. 117.

"When we started smashing": Author, *Nevermind It's an Interview*, January 1992.

"No one said a": Cross, *Heavier Than Heaven*, page 134.

"We were just too": Azerrad, *Come as You Are*, p. 120.

"was very mutual. I": "Nirvana Nirvana Nirvana," *Zip Code*, October 29, 1989.

"I always felt kind": Azerrad, *Come as You Are*, p. 120.

"It's so raw and": ibid., p. 121.

"Ha! We didn't even": Williams, "Good Clean Fun," *The London Student*, November 19, 1989.

"England is very Americanized": Sam King, "Down the bleach," *Sounds*, June 9, 1990.

"Most Americans are drunk": ibid.

"I like the isolation": True, "Tad and Nirvana—The Larder They Come," *Melody Maker*, March 17, 1990.

"That was definitely my": "Nirvana Nirvana Nirvana," *Zip Code*, October 29, 1989.

"had a nervous breakdown": Azerrad, *Come as You Are*, p. 127.

"I was walking around": ibid., p. 128.

"Well, now that you're": ibid., p. 128.

Eight

"This was going to": Author, *Nevermind It's an Interview*, January 1992.

"pretty much sucked and": Endino, "The Ever-Popular Nirvana FAQ," www.jackendino.com.

"He's so easy to": Ned Hammad, "About a Band," *Pulse*, October 1991.

"If you took all": "Nirvana Nirvana," *Zip Code*, October 29, 1989.

"We're definitely not": ibid.

"It was hard to hear": "A Fan's Notes," *Spin*, April 1995.

"We knew Iggy Pop": Author, *Nevermind It's an Interview*, January 1992.

"Seven weeks, fucking seven": King, "Down the bleach," *Sounds*, June 9, 1990.

"But nothing is better": ibid.

'Chad wanted to express": Author, *Nevermind It's an Interview*, January 1992.

"I was really hoping": Azerrad, *Come as You Are*, p. 138.

"[But] it wasn't like": ibid., p. 139.

"I'd spent the last": Cross, *Heavier Than Heaven*.

"Overall, I have massive": Azerrad, *Come as You Are*, p. 141.

"So I got a": Keith Cameron, "If they could remember to . . . Breathe," *Mojo*, January, 2003.

"Jonathan [Poneman] called up": Gaar, "Verse Chorus Verse," *Goldmine*, February 14, 1997.

"There were two takes": ibid.

"If we wanted to": Author, *Nevermind It's an Interview*, January 1992.

"Yeah, it looked like": ibid.

"I was totally made": Cameron, "If they could remember to . . . Breathe", *Mojo*, January, 2003.

"He's a baby Dale": Interview with Calvin Johnson, KAOS-FM, Olympia, Washington, September 25, 1990.

Nine

"I dropped out of": Author, *Nevermind It's an Interview*, January 1992.

"I never got around": Foo Fighters biography, Capitol Records press release.

"I was always really": ibid.

"Tracy was two or": ibid.

"After I had been": Maureen Odell, "Nirvana, Fishin' with Winona," *B-Side*, December 1991/January 1992.

"The way America's money": Author, *Nevermind It's an Interview*, January 1992.

"Over the course of": Foo Fighters biography, Capitol Records press release.

"In 1987, I saw": ibid.

"I called Franz and": ibid.

"I was 18 years": ibid.

"I realized that if": ibid.

"The Melvins were playing": Phillips, "Teenage Rampage," *Vox* (magazine), January 1992.

"They were real rocker": Azerrad, *Come as You Are*, p. 153.

"I'd been a Scream": Author, *Nevermind It's an Interview*, January 1992.

Ten

"Corporate music has been": Author, *Nevermind It's an Interview*, January 1992.

"I was greeted at": Foo Fighters biography, Capitol Records press release.

"We were just amazed": Azerrad, *Come as You Are*, p. 150.

"If he ever leaves": Kristen Carney, "Nirvana," *Rockpool* (magazine), November 1, 1991.

"He just writes really": Gary Graff, "Nirvana can be found not just in Seattle anymore," *Detroit Free Press*, October 11, 1991.

"[The Nirvana/Vaselines relationship]": John Robinson, " 'I think I just saw God,' "*NME*, November 5, 1994.

"We heard a tape": Author, *Nevermind It's an Interview*, January 1992.

"I told [Kurt] he": Azerrad, *Come as You Are*, p. 184.

"We like to delve": Peter Atkinson, "Nirvana's Earthly Goal: To Be Wildly Successful," *Meriden (Conn.) Record Journal*, September 20, 1991.

"We were practicing": Author, *Nevermind It's an Interview*, January 1992.

'I really had no": Graff, "Nirvana can be found not just in Seattle anymore," *Detroit Free Press*, October 11, 1991.

"We wouldn't return their": Azerrad, *Come as You Are*, p. 136.

"was just something we": Gitter, "Revenge of the Nerds," *Kerrang*, August 24, 1991.

"I felt really bad": Azerrad, *Come as You Are*, p. 136.

"I think it's inevitable": Cameron, "If they could remember to . . . Breathe," *Mojo*, January, 2003.

"It was just obvious": Azerrad, *Come as You Are*, p. 130.

"They were all asking": Author, *Nevermind It's an Interview*, January 1992.

"Yeah, we knew Sonic": ibid.

"This whole business is": Odell, "Nirvana, Fishin' with Winona," *B-Side*, December 1991/January 1992.

"There were a lot": Author, *Nevermind It's an Interview*, January 1992.

"[We] are proud to": Medwin Pregill, "Pus Free Pop," *Columbia Daily Spectator*, September 26, 1991.

"Thirty-three percent of it": Brian Rainville, "Nirvana sells out the Paramount," *The Olympian*, October 25, 1991.

"It's nicer [being on]": Hammad, "About a Band," *Pulse*, October 1991.

"There were all these": Author, *Nevermind It's an Interview*, January 1992.

"The opportunity came and": Michael Deeds, "Nirvana," *New Route*, December 1991.

"Most mainstream music is": Crusty Muncher, "A New Dosage of Nirvana," *The Michigan Review*, September 25, 1991.

Eleven

"Someone at MTV says": Author, *Nevermind It's an Interview,* January 1992.

"We were afraid to": Kott, "Now that they've been found, Seattle bands fight for their independence," *Chicago Tribune,* October 20, 1991.

"We didn't want to": Author, *Nevermind It's an Interview,* January 1992.

"It was like a": Chris Mundy, "Nirvana Spill Blood in Europe," *Rolling Stone,* January 23, 1992.
    "It hadn't been touched": Odell, "Nirvana, Fishin' with Winona," *B-Side,* December 1991/January 1992.

"We really weren't thinking": Author, *Nevermind It's an Interview,* January 1992.

"I very rarely write": Patrick McDonald, "Smells like . . . a raging success," *Seattle Times,* October 25, 1991.

"It's just thumbing though": Pareles, "The Band That Hates to Be Loved," *New York Times,* November 14, 1993.

'Kurt is the meister": Muncher, "A New Dosage of Nirvana," *The Michigan Review,* September 25, 1991.

"He was just easy": Author, *Nevermind It's an Interview,* January 1992.

"It took about three": Odell, "Nirvana, Fishin' with Winona," *B-Side,* December 1991/January 1992.

"We'd been practicing for": Fricke, "Success Doesn't Suck," *Rolling Stone,* January 27, 1994.

"The Pixies. We saw": Azerrad, *Come as You Are,* p. 176.

"I don't know, everybody": Author, *Nevermind It's an Interview,* January 1992.

"Well, this friend of": ibid.

"Smells Like Teen Spirit": Hammad, "About a Band," *Pulse,* October 1991.

"It's about 'hey brother": Keith Cameron, "Nirvana Be in My Gang," *NME,* September 21, 1991.

"No one, especially people": Fricke, "Success Doesn't Suck," *Rolling Stone,* January 27, 1994.

"Just seeing Kurt write": Azerrad, *Come as You Are,* p. 214.

"Every once in awhile": ibid., p. 227.

"Football players who become": Phillips, "Teenage Rampage," *Vox* (magazine), January 1992.

"Yeah. I suppose it": Author, *Nevermind It's an Interview,* January 1992.

"I really don't know": ibid.

"People who are secluded": *Nevermind* bio, Geffen Records, 1991.

"About 400 lucky souls": "A Fan's Notes," *Spin,* April 1995.

"After I called her": Craig Marks, "Confessions of a Diva, the Untold Story," *Spin,* February 1995.

"I think the main": ibid.

"I saw him play": Christina Kelly, "Kurt and Courtney/Ain't Love Grand," *Sassy,* April 1992.

"I wasn't ignoring her": ibid.

"I really pursued him": ibid.

"I couldn't decide if": Azerrad, *Come as You Are,* p. 172.

"The production is obviously": Author, *Nevermind It's an Interview,* January 1992.

"It's fine, because we": True, "Tad and Nirvana—The Larder They Come," *Melody Maker,* March 17, 1990.

"Punk is musical freedom": *Nevermind* bio, Geffen Records, 1991.

"On one hand, we're": ibid.

"It's definitely an anti-rape": Turman, "Smells Like Nirvana," *RIP*, 1992.

"Just because I say": Author, *Nevermind It's an Interview*, January 1992.

"I think the reason": Morris, "The Year's Hottest New Band Can't Stand Still," *Musician*, January 1992.

"That's a 20-dollar junk": Jeff Gilbert, "Cool Hand Puke," *Guitar World*, January 1992.

"They just said 'sing' ": Azerrad, *Come as You Are*, p. 175.

"It's an amusing little": Author, *Nevermind It's an Interview*, January 1992.

"[Solanas] was a militant": Hammad, "About a Band," *Pulse*, October 1991.

"I guess you could": Author, *Nevermind It's an Interview*, January 1992.

"Come to think of": *Nevermind* bio, Geffen Records, 1991.

"That song is mostly": Author, *Nevermind It's an Interview*, January 1992.

"There are also some": ibid.

"There's so many bands": "Nirvana," *Birmingham Sun*, November 9, 1989.

"That song really wasn't": Author, *Nevermind It's an Interview*, January 1992.

"My favorite song on": ibid.

"It got screwed up": ibid.

" 'Something in the Way' ": ibid.

"We made the record": ibid.

"It's not like we": Randy Hawkins, untitled, *Arizona State University State Press*, October 23, 1991.

"I just thought [Nevermind]": Morris, "The Year's Hottest New Band Can't Stand Still," *Musician*, January 1992.

"What we've turned into": Hammad, "About a Band," *Pulse*, October 1991.

"It's just really heavy": Hawkins, untitled, *Arizona State University State Press*, October 23, 1991.

"Dave, Krist and I": Author, *Nevermind It's an Interview*, January 1992.

"I was in a": ibid.

"Yeah, I realized that": ibid.

"I think I wanted": Azerrad, *Come as You Are*, p. 108.

"And now we're snubbed": Lauren Spencer, "Heaven Can't Wait," *Spin*, January 1992.

"We're guaranteed two albums": Hammad, "About a Band," *Pulse*, October 1991.

"It's becoming a bit": Turman, "Smells Like Nirvana," *RIP*, 1992.

Twelve

"Eugene [Kelly] was in": Author, *Nevermind It's an Interview*, January 1992.

"On my [previous] trips": Foo Fighters biography, Capitol Records press release.

"We will tour until": Muncher, "A New Dosage of Nirvana," *The Michigan Review*, September 25, 1991.

"Medea would speak": Neal Karlen, "Love Among The Ruins," *US*, August 1994.

"a pep rally from": Azerrad, *Come as You Are*, p. 190.

"He's got a little": ibid., p. 190.

"It was just like": ibid., p. 190.

"It's sort of funny": Morris, "The Year's Hottest New Band Can't Stand Still," *Musician*, January 1992.

"That's a hell of": Gilbert, "Cool Hand Puke," *Guitar World*, January 1992.

"MTV is a really": David Schwartz, "Heaven on Earth," *Paper*, November 1991.

"Actually, MTV really does": Cameron, "Nirvana Be in My Gang," *NME*, September 21, 1991.

"I expected our core": Morris, "The Year's Hottest New Band Can't Stand Still," *Musician*, January 1992.

"Toward the end of": "A Fan's Notes," *Spin*, April 1995.

"Personally, I don't really": Odell, "Nirvana, Fishin' with Winona," *B-Side*, December 1991/ January 1992.

"You can do it": Spencer, "Heaven Can't Wait," *Spin*, January 1992.

"When I did it": ibid.

"My favorite memory of": "A Fan's Notes," *Spin*, April 1995.

"[We want] to play": Gina Bittner, "Blissful Band Burns on the Mind," *Temple News*, September 27, 1991.

"We're as exciting as": ibid.

"We're not like some": Cayo and Claire, "Down to Earth Guys But Their Music's Red Hot." *Metal Force*, November 19, 1989.

"Can you imagine us": ibid.

"Last night we played": Rainville, "Nirvana sells out the Paramount," *The Olympian*, October 25, 1991.

"The hooky, awesomely catchy": Johanthan Gold, "Power Trio, Pop Craft," *Los Angeles Times*, October 6, 1991.

"[*Nevermind* is] more hump": "On The Cover Jackpot!" (editorial), *CMJ*, September 20, 1991.

"So he got on": Kelly, "Kurt & Courtney/Ain't Love Grand," *Sassy*, April 1992.

"We didn't have an": Lynn Hirschberg, "Strange Love," *Vanity Fair*, September 1992.

"I mean, what does": Cameron, "Nirvana Be in My Gang," *NME*, September 21, 1991.

"The whole day there": "A Fan's Notes," *Spin*, April 1995.

"The police showed up": ibid.

"I have to practically": Author, *Nevermind It's an Interview*, January 1992.

"I started drinking and": Azerrad, *Come as You Are*, p. 200.

"I started to get": Phillips, "Teenage Rampage," *Vox* (magazine), January 1992.

"So I get pretty": ibid.

"I decided to get": Azerrad, *Come as You Are*, p. 201.

"They all happened to": ibid., p. 201.

"I've smashed three Mustangs": Author, *Nevermind It's an Interview*, January 1992.

"There were these very": Turman, "Smells Like Nirvana," *RIP*, 1992.

"There are also a": Schwartz, "Heaven on Earth," *Paper*, November 1991.

"The only way I": Morris, "The Year's Hottest New Band Can't Stand Still," *Musician*, January 1992.

"Is Nirvana a heavy": Gilbert, "Cool Hand Puke," *Guitar World*, January 1992.

"Most of the new": Morris, "The Year's Hottest New Band Can't Stand Still," *Musician*, January 1992.

"We really dig Nirvana": Phillips, "Teenage Rampage," *Vox* (magazine), January 1992.

"We'll rub elbows with": Spencer, "Heaven Can't Wait," *Spin*, January 1992.

"You know what I": ibid.

"It wasn't rock star": Mundy, "Nirvana Spill Blood in Europe," *Rolling Stone*, January 23, 1992.

"You know, if people": Odell, "Nirvana, Fishin' with Winona," *B-Side*, December 1991/ January 1992.

"We wanted to do": Mundy, "Nirvana Spill Blood in Europe," *Rolling Stone*, January 23, 1992.

"Everyone is always asking": Ibid.

"Nirvana possesses an intriguing": Alexandria Saperstein, "Guns and Roses, Nirvana—Must Buys," *Mills College Weekly*, October 18, 1991.

"Between the first Edinburgh": Robinson, " 'I think I just saw God,' " *NME*, November 5, 1994.

"Kim Gordon": David Frickle, "Life After Death," *Rolling Stone*, December 15, 1994.

"I wasn't hoping for": Jen Plantz, untitled, *The Sliding Edge Music Journal*, Fall Issue, 1991.

"Things are just getting": Schwartz, "Heaven on Earth," *Paper*, November 1991.

"We still feel as": McDonald, "Smells like . . . a raging success," *Seattle Times*, October 25, 1991.

"Do you think that": DeRogatis, "Smells Like A Nirvana Article," *Request*, November 1993.

Thirteen

"I'm not doing any": Author, *Nevermind It's an Interview*, January 1992.

"There's definitely going to": Odell, "Nirvana, Fishin' with Winona," *B-Side*, December 1991/January 1992.

"Kurt soldiers gamely on": McCulley, "Spontaneous Combustion," *BAM*, January 10, 1992.

"Nirvana is that rare": Paul Grein, *Billboard*, January 11, 1992.

"I punctured every speaker": Author, *Nevermind It's an Interview*, January 1992.

"For me, the point": Phil Sutcliffe, "King of Pain," Q (magazine), October 1993.

"Oh, geez. The autographs": Author, *Nevermind It's an Interview*, January 1992.

"I kinda felt like": Ibid.

"We were on tour": Allman, "The Dark Side of Kurt Cobain," *The Advocate*, February 9, 1993.

"On my way there": Ibid.

"They [Dave Grohl's few guests, . . .]": Michael Azerrad, "Territorial Pissings: The Battles Behind Nirvana's New Album," *Musician*, October 1993.

"That was fucked up": Spencer, "Heaven Can't Wait," *Spin*, January 1992.

"I wasn't very high": Azerrad, "Territorial Pissings: The Battles Behind Nirvana's New Album," *Musician*, October 1993.

"I didn't want Kurt": Ibid.

"I hate L.A.": Allman, "The Dark Side of Kurt Cobain," *The Advocate*, February 9, 1993.

"I didn't find myself": Azerrad, "Territorial Pissings: The Battles Behind Nirvana's New Album," *Musician*, October 1993.

"Life is like a": Hirschberg, "Strange Love," *Vanity Fair*, September 1992.

"Kurt's a fucking junkie": Azerrad, "Territorial Pissings: The Battles Behind Nirvana's New Album," *Musician*, October 1993.

"I felt like he": Ibid.

"The explosion of my": Foo Fighters biography, Capitol Records press release.

"I needed time to": Fricke, "Success Doesn't Suck," *Rolling Stone,* January 27, 1994.

"On average it's a": Adams, "Corporate Rock Whores?," *Select,* April 1992.

"I had one A&R": John Leland and Marc Peyser, "Searching for Nirvana," *Newsweek,* March 30, 1992.

"I got excellent, excellent": Hirschberg, "Strange Love," *Vanity Fair,* September 1992.

"If those sexist assholes": ibid.

"It's gonna be a": Adams, "Corporate Rock Whores?," *Select,* April 1992.

"I think that after": Chirazi, "Lounge Act," *Kerrang,* November 29, 1993.

"In the last couple": Kelly, "Kurt & Courtney/Ain't Love Grand," *Sassy,* April, 1992.

"We get attention for": ibid.

"It's really beautiful, it's": ibid.

"I just think that": Bill Flanagan, "Shadow Boxing With Axl Rose," *Musician,* June 1992.

"With little action on": Foo Fighters biography, Capitol Records press release.

"dancing with Mr. Brownstone": *Hits,* June 1, 1992.

Fourteen

"My father said this": Author, *Nevermind It's an Interview,* January 1992.

"Oh god, it was": Azerrad, "Territorial Pissings: The Battles behind Nirvana's New Album," *Musician,* October 1993.

"It's just amazing that": Allman, "The Dark Side of Kurt Cobain," *The Advocate,* February 9, 1993.

"We went on a": Hirschberg, "Strange Love," *Vanity Fair,* September 1992.

"I didn't have a": Azerrad, "Territorial Pissings: The Battles behind Nirvana's New Album," *Musician,* October 1993.

"Courtney was honest about": Allman, "The Dark Side of Kurt Cobain," *The Advocate,* February 9, 1993.

"I wouldn't have thought": Azerrad, "Territorial Pissings: The Battles behind Nirvana's New Album," *Musician,* October 1993.

"Everybody was blaming Courtney": Azerrad, *Come as You Are,* p. 237.

"Let's start saying, 'yes' ": Jonathan Poneman, "Family Values," *Spin,* December 1992.

"I'm having the baby": Azerrad, "Territorial Pissings: The Battles behind Nirvana's New Album," *Musician,* October 1993.

"I was so fucking": ibid.

"The day Frances was": Marks, "Confessions Of A Diva, The Untold Story," *Spin,* February 1995.

"Although I was doing": Chirazi, "Lounge Act," *Kerrang,* November 29, 1993.

"It was all a": Azerrad, "Territorial Pissings: The Battles behind Nirvana's New Album," *Musician,* October 1993.

"I just decided, 'Fuck": ibid.

"I was like 'I'll' ": Fricke, "Life After Death," *Rolling Stone,* December 15, 1994.

"[Eric] totally saved our": Azerrad, *Come as You Are,* p. 163.

"When we played that": Azerrad, "Territorial Pissings: The Battles behind Nirvana's New Album," *Musician,* October 1993.

"We were the foundation": Pleasant Gehman, "Artist of the Year," *Spin*, December 1992.

"[Danny] was the only": Ann Hornaday, "The Goldberg Variations," *New York*, October 3, 1994.

"I wanted it to": Azerrad, "Territorial Pissings: The Battles behind Nirvana's New Album," *Musician*, October 1993.

"I was just kind": ibid.

"They actually tried to": Allman, "The Dark Side of Kurt Cobain," *The Advocate*, February 9, 1993.

"I don't feel like": ibid.

"I stared into his": ibid.

"It's a part of": Raphael, "In the Court of King Kurt," *The Face*, September 1993.

"I'm afraid of dying": ibid.

"Fatherhood has completely changed": ibid.

"When we played Buenos": DeRogatis, "Smells Like A Nirvana Article," *Request*, November 1993.

"See, this thing is": Odell, "Nirvana, Fishin' with Winona," *B-Side*, December 1991/January 1992.

"I get recognized every": Gehman, "Artist of the Year," *Spin*, December 1992.

"I'll never get used": ibid.

"*Nevermind* goes platinum and": Azerrad, *Come as You Are*, p. 205.

"That's what I'm not": McCulley, "Spontaneous Combustion," *BAM*, January 10, 1992.

"We'd like to buy": Adams, "Corporate Rock Whores?," *Select*, April 1992.

"I guess the best part": Author, *Nevermind It's an Interview*, 1992.

"I wanted to at least": McCulley, "Spontaneous Combustion," *BAM*, January 10, 1992.

"I don't want to": Pareles, "The Band That Hates to Be Loved," *New York Times*, November 14, 1993.

Fifteen

"I really don't have": Author, *Nevermind It's an Interview*, January 1992.

"When they were planning": Endino, "The Ever-Popular Nirvana FAQ," www.jackendino.com.

"Hmm . . . I think I've": *Incesticide* press release, Geffen Records, 1992.

"Christ! Let's just throw": ibid.

"That's been the biggest": Allman, "The Dark Side of Kurt Cobain," *The Advocate*, February 9, 1993.

"There is a war": ibid.

"I just went into": Azerrad, *Come as You Are*, p. 295.

"I don't feel the": Liner notes, *Incesticide*, Geffen Records, 1992.

Sixteen

"Start a band . . . Especially": Author, *Nevermind It's an Interview*, January 1992.

"My attitudes and opinions": Sutcliffe, "King of Pain," Q (magazine), October 1993.

"Two years ago I": The Stud Brothers, "The Darkside of the Womb: Part 1," *Melody Maker*, August 21, 1993.

"We wanted to have": ibid.

"Kurt's the right person": Hirschberg, "Strange Love," *Vanity Fair*, September 1992.

"Oh yeah, embarrassingly so": The Stud Brothers, "The Darkside of the Womb: Part 1," *Melody Maker*, August 21, 1993.

"The biggest impact of": Chirazi, "Lounge Act," *Kerrang*, November 29, 1993.

"It's a whirling dervish": Gavin Edwards, "Heaven Can Wait," *Details*, November 1993.

"God! I don't want": Allman, "The Dark Side of Kurt Cobain," *The Advocate*, February 9, 1993.

"When I first met": Edwards, "Heaven Can Wait," *Details*, November 1993.

"Courtney's had misconceptions about": Allman, "The Dark Side of Kurt Cobain," *The Advocate*, February 9, 1993.

"Krist and Dave liked": ibid.

"he knew he was": Kurt Loder, MTV, September 8, 1994.

"Kurt would carry his": ibid.

"I don't know who": Odell, "Nirvana, Fishin' with Winona," *B-Side*, December 1991/January 1992.

"It's the attitude that": Mundy, "Nirvana Spill Blood in Blood in Europe," *Rolling Stone*, January 23, 1992.

"A lot of heavy": ibid.

"We've been wanting to": Robert Hilburn, "Cobain to Fans: Just Say No; Nirvana's New Father Addresses Drug Use," *Los Angeles Times*, September 21, 1992.

"I have been prescribed": ibid.

"I haven't written any": Allman, "The Dark Side of Kurk Cobain," *The Advocate*, February 9, 1993.

"I don't favor them": Gilbert, "Cool Hand Puke," *Guitar World*, January 1992.

"I own a '66 Jaguar": ibid.

"That's a thought, I": "Nirvana Nirvana Nirvana," *Zip Code*, October 29, 1989.

"from hearing the way": Jeremy Sheaffe, "Smells Like Platinum," *Metal CD* (magazine), 1993.

"When we went into": Erik Van den Berg, "Ready for the Next Round," *OOR*, September 4, 1993.

"That makes sense": ibid.

"Every recording we've done": Jennie Punter, "That's Grudge Rock," *Impact*, October 1993.

"If you put a": ibid.

"We were in this": ibid.

"Ugh. I'll never do": Pareles, "The Band That Hates to Be Loved," *New York Times*, November 14, 1993.

"The pressure is on": Van den Berg, "Ready For The Next Round," *OOR*, September 4, 1993.

"Lou Reed once made": ibid.

"It's up to [Geffen]": ibid.

Seventeen

"The only reason I": Ben Mothersole, "Nirvana's Kurt Cobain: Getting To Know Utero," *Circus*, November 30, 1993.

"I just like the": Azerrad, "Territorial Pissings: The Battles behind Nirvana's New Album," *Musician*, October 1993.

"The album's back cover": Pareles, "The Band That Hates to Be Loved," *New York Times,* November 14, 1993.

"I'm always the last": Azerrad, "Territorial Pissings: The Battles behind Nirvana's New Album," *Musician,* October 1993.

"But I'm getting so": Fricke, "Success Doesn't Suck," *Rolling Stone,* January 27, 1994.

"If it wasn't for": DeRogatis, "Smells Like A Nirvana Article," *Request,* November 1993.

"The label's all freaked": Azerrad, *Come as You Are,* p. 333.

"I would've done it": Raphael, "In the Court of King Kurt," *The Face,* September 1993.

"Almost all my lyrics": The Stud Brothers, "The Darkside of the Womb: Part 1," *Melody Maker,* August 21, 1993.

"I've always painted abstracts": Sutcliffe, "King of Pain," Q (magazine), October 1993.

"I was trying to": ibid.

"I've gone back and": Fricke, "Success Doesn't Suck," *Rolling Stone,* January 27, 1994.

"The song is so feminine": Brian Willis, "Domicile on Cobain St.," *NME,* July 24, 1994.

"['Dumb'] is just about": The Stud Brothers, "The Darkside of the Womb: Part 1," *Melody Maker,* August 21, 1993.

"I wish we could": Fricke, "Success Doesn't Suck," *Rolling Stone,* January 27, 1994.

"I just thought it": The Stud Brothers, "The Darkside of the Womb: Part 1," *Melody Maker,* August 21, 1993.

"Yeah, that kind of": Chirazi, "Lounge Act," *Kerrang,* November 29, 1993.

"At the time, I": "Interview from The Omni in Atlanta," *Kerrang,* November 29, 1993.

"That was another line": DeRogatis, "Smells Like A Nirvana Article," *Request,* November 1993.

"As literal as a": Fricke, "Success Doesn't Suck," *Rolling Stone,* January 27, 1994.

"It was made really": ibid.

"The first time I": Mothersole, "Nirvana's Kurt Cobain: Getting To Know Utero," *Circus,* November 30, 1993.

"I couldn't really say": ibid.

"We finally came to": Fricke, "Success Doesn't Suck," *Rolling Stone,* January 27, 1994.

"We thought it was": The Stud Brothers, "The Darkside of the Womb: Part 1," *Melody Maker,* August 21, 1993.

"The mixing we'd done": Sutcliffe, "King of Pain," Q (magazine), October 1993.

"He just remixed a": Mothersole, "Nirvana's Kurt Cobain: Getting To Know Utero," *Circus,* November 30, 1993.

"To remix any more": ibid.

"Our A&R man at": Sutcliffe, "King of Pain," Q (magazine), October 1993.

"You could put that": Azerrad, *Come as You Are,* p. 334.

"If they do, they": Azerrad, "Territorial Pissings: The Battles behind Nirvana's New Album," *Musician,* October 1993.

"The whole thing was": The Stud Brothers, "The Darkside of the Womb: Part 1," *Melody Maker,* August 21, 1993.

"I found him to": ibid.

"I happen to love": Sutcliffe, "King of Pain," Q (magazine), October 1993.

"I really liked the": "Interview from the Omni in Atlanta," *Kerrang,* November 29, 1993.

"It introduced a whole": Chirazi, "Lounge Act," *Kerrang,* November 29, 1993.

'That was hilarious!": "Interview from the Omni in Atlanta," *Kerrang*, November 29, 1993.

"I really want people": ibid.

"We think *In Utero*": Van den Berg, "Ready For The Next Round," *OOR*, September 4, 1993.

"We are going to": Sheaffe, "Smells Like Platinum," *Metal CD* (magazine), 1993.

"Cobain was conscious and": Seattle Police report.

"Once the cops explained": DeRogatis, "Smells Like A Nirvana Article," *Request*, November 1993.

"I have to admit I": Raphael, "In the Court of King Kurt," *The Face*, September 1993.

"Around the summer of": Foo Fighters biography, Capitol Records press release.

"Kurt totally died. His": Marks, "Confessions of a Diva, the Untold Story," *Spin*, February 1995.

"Well, here we are": Raphael, "In the Court of King Kurt," *The Face*, September 1993.

"John played on four": Sheaffe, "Smells Like Platinum," *Metal CD* (magazine), 1993.

"I'm glad to have": Sutcliffe, "King of Pain," Q (magazine), October 1993.

"The acoustic set was": ibid.

"He just kept to": Neal Strauss, "The Downward Spiral," *Cobain*, edited by the Editors of *Rolling Stone* (Rolling Stone Press, 1994), p. 87.

"Ever since *Nevermind* came": Punter, "That's Grudge Rock," *Impact*, October 1993.

"I was racking my": Steffan Chirazi, "Growing Pains," *RIP*, May 1994.

"I don't know, we": ibid.

"He's got this great": Punter, "That's Grudge Rock," *Impact*, October 1993.

"[Having another guitarist] gives": ibid.

"I'm caught. So I": Azerrad, "Territorial Pissings: The Battles behind Nirvana's New Album," *Musician*, October 1993.

"At the time, when": The Stud Brothers, "The Darkside of the Womb: Part 1," *Melody Maker*, August 21, 1993.

"Krist and I [thought]": Azerrad, "Territorial Pissings: The Battles behind Nirvana's New Album," *Musician*, October 1993.

"At the time, I": ibid.

"I have to deal": ibid.

"We're always doing benefits": Punter, "That's Grudge Rock," *Impact*, October 1993.

"I'll be taking [Frances]": ibid.

"I used to read [fan]": Fricke, "Success Doesn't Suck," *Rolling Stone*, January 27, 1994.

"I got used to": Gaar, "Verse Chorus Verse," *Goldmine*, February 14, 1997.

"I got a ducking": ibid.

"would have been the": Fricke, "Success Doesn't Suck," *Rolling Stone*, January 27, 1994.

"I heard he really": Grahamn, Caveny, Little, Brown, "Gentleman Junkie," *The Face*, September 1993.

"There was something boyish": ibid.

"We've been touring since": Chirazi, "Lounge Act," *Kerrang*, November 29, 1993.

"Before we were just": Azerrad, "Territorial Pissings: The Battles behind Nirvana's New Album." *Musician*, October 1993.

"I know this sounds": Edwards, "Heaven Can Wait," *Details*, November 1993.

"About halfway through our": "A Fan's Notes," *Spin*, April 1995.

"I'm looking forward to": Edwards, "Heaven Can Wait," *Details*, November 1993.

"I was sorry to": Gaar, "Verse Chorus Verse," *Goldmine*, February 14, 1997.

"Why not? We weren't": Official *Unplugged* biography, Geffen Records, 1994.

"I don't have high": Pareles, "The Band That Hates to Be Loved," *New York Times*, November 14, 1993.

"Doing *MTV Unplugged* was": Official *Unplugged* biography, Geffen Records, 1994.

"It was a step": ibid.

"I didn't expect it": ibid.

"We didn't want to": ibid.

"We knew we didn't": ibid.

"I was simply blown": "A Fan's Notes," *Spin*, April 1995.

"I was always comfortable": Chirazi, "Lounge Act," *Kerrang*, November 29, 1993.

"It's really hard to": "Interview from The Omni in Atlanta," *Kerrang*, November 29, 1993.

"Kurt came in on": David Fricke, "The Tenth Anniversary of Nirvana's *Nevermind*," *Rolling Stone*, September 13, 2001.

"With *Nevermind*, we wanted": ibid.

"Kurt didn't have any": Fricke, "Life After Death," *Rolling Stone*, December 15, 1994.

"You shouldn't be singing": Strauss, "The Downward Spiral," *Cobain*, p. 87.

"[Kurt] was told to": ibid, p. 87.

"He said he was": Steve Dougherty, "Kurt Cobain," *People*, April 25, 1994.

Eighteen

"Let's keep the music": Krist, from Kurt's memorial service.

"the longest we'd gone": Marks, "Confessions of a Diva, The Untold Story," *Spin*, February, 1995.

"He knew how obsessed": ibid.

"The rejection he must": Fricke, "Life After Death," *Rolling Stone*, December 15, 1994.

"Even If I wasn't": ibid.

"I woke up to": Marks, "Confessions of a Diva, The Untold Story," *Spin*, February, 1995.

"There's blood coming out!": ibid.

"A note was found": Fricke, "Life After Death," *Rolling Stone*, December 15, 1994.

"I don't know if": Strauss, "The Downward Spiral," *Cobain*.

"I was hysterical throughout": Andrew Harrison, "Love and Death," *Select*, May 1994.

"had suffered a complete": Geffen Records press release.

"I didn't find this": Marks, "Confessions of a Diva, The Untold Story," *Spin*, February, 1995.

"And there were the": ibid.

"Due to the volatile": Seattle Police report.

"The reason I flipped": Fricke, "Life After Death," *Rolling Stone*, December 15, 1994.

"They called me to": Strauss, "The Downward Spiral," *Cobain*, p. 82.

"I was not supportive": ibid, p. 83.

"These things are so": Hornaday, "The Goldberg Variations," *New York*, October 3, 1994.

"He said, 'Courtney, no": Strauss, "The Downward Spiral," *Cobain*, p. 83.

"[Kurt] seemed normal": ibid.

"I was ready to": ibid.

"When I went to": ibid.

"We watch our patients": ibid.

"Where are my friends": ibid.

"I talked to Cali": ibid.

"After Kurt left Exodus": ibid.

"miserable, self-destructive": Kurt Cobain's suicide letter, April 1994.

"a goddess of a": ibid.

"please keep going": ibid.

"That last week was": Karlen, "Love Among The Ruins," US, August 1994.

"Although we had been": Gold Mountain Management press release.

"At first I thought": Strauss, "The Downward Spiral," Cobain, p. 82.

"The scoop of the": Ibid, p. 90.

"Broadcasting this information was": ibid.

"Now's he gone and,": Jeff Giles, "The Poet of Alienation," Newsweek, April 18, 1994.

"It's better to burn": Kurt Cobain's suicide letter, April 1994.

"I have a daughter": ibid.

"I believe [Kurt] lived": Karlen, "Love Among The Ruins," US, August 1994.

"I certainly don't feel": New York, October 3, 1994.

"On behalf of Dave": Gillian G. Gaar, "Kurt Cobain: The Death of a Reluctant Icon," Goldmine, May 13, 1994.

"I don't know what": Courtney Love's audio statement played at Kurt's vigil, Seattle, Washington, April 1994.

"All the warnings from": Kurt Cobain's suicide letter, April 1994.

"And there is some": Courtney Love's audio statement played at Kurt's vigil, Seattle, Washington, April 1994.

"He wrote me a": Strauss, "The Downward Spiral," Cobain, p. 87.

Nineteen

"For a long time": Keith Cameron, "Seconds Out . . . Round 2," Q (magazine), October 2002.

"It's not a crime": Arf Rock fax.

"Imagine this": Marks, "Confessions Of A Diva, The Untold Story," Spin, February, 1995.

"Michael [Stipe was] so": Loder, MTV, September 8, 1994.

"I think we all": Barbara A. Serrano, "Cobain Statue criticized," Seattle Times, July 8, 1994.

"Thank you all for": Krist's e-mail to fans.

"It's tragic, that we": Dougherty, "Kurt Cobain," People, April 25, 1994.

"For five years during": Fricke, "Success Doesn't Suck," Rolling Stone, January 27, 1994.

"That pretty much defines": ibid.

"Look, I lived with": Fricke, "Life After Death," Rolling Stone, December 15, 1994.

"I've always been a": Chirazi, "Growing Pains," RIP, May 1994.

"feel like a completely": ibid.

"pig-headed enough to": ibid.

"Kurt and I used": Karlen, "Love Among The Ruins," US, August 1994.

"It's hard to watch": Official Unplugged biography, Geffen Records, 1994.

"I looked at the": Peter Blackstock, "Minor Threat," Rolling Stone, March 23, 1994.

"After Kurt's death I": Foo Fighters biography, Capitol Records press release.

"I decided to do": ibid.

"The first four hours": ibid.

"I wanted to see": ibid.

"My next mistake was": ibid.

"I jammed around with": ibid.

"Not long after meeting": ibid.

"I saw them play": ibid.

"I didn't want this": ibid.

"You have to let": Chris Mundy, "The Man Who Fell to Earth," *Select,* February 1996.

"We FedExed a": Anthony DeCurtis, untitled, *Rolling Stone,* October 20, 1994.

"I wanted to get": ibid.

"I feel so much": ibid.

"Punk rock should mean": David Geffen Company press release for *Nirvana Live! Tonight! Sold Out!!,* October 27, 1994.

"This is a celebration": ibid.

"Great care was taken": ibid.

"It was Krist and Dave's": ibid.

"I washed the blood": Fricke, "Life After Death," *Rolling Stone,* December 15, 1994.

"I used to be": ibid.

"No, *[Vitalogy]* was written": Robert Hilburn, "All Revved Up (As Usual)," *Los Angeles Times,* November 20, 1994.

"In presenting this record": Liner notes, *From the Muddy Banks of the Wishkah,* Geffen Records, 1994.

"The culture of the ": Steve Morse, "Corgan Blasts 'Culture of the Dead,' " *Boston Globe,* July 31, 1998.

"There's millions and millions": Kim Neely, "Into the Unknown," *Rolling Stone,* June 16, 1994.

"Everything's great, I'm happy": Paul Stokes, "Cash for Questions," (magazine), March 2003.

"We bombed it together": Cross, *Heavier Than Heaven,* page 306.

"It's great to be": Stokes, "Cash for Questions," Q (magazine), March 2003.

"You know, people find": Hugo Lindren, "Love of His Life," *New York Times Sunday Magazine,* October, 20, 2002.

ACKNOWLEDGMENTS

My first and foremost to the band Nirvana for daily inspiration since 1989.

The friends and Nirvana fans whose contributions to this book are too numerous to list.

To my coauthor, Troy Smith, I owe a deep debt. When it was almost over you brought it back to life. I am truly grateful for our friendship. Here comes the tidal wave.

Grateful acknowledgement is made to Megan Rawa and Angie Creeden for their endless hours of transcribing and editing. Other help came from John Wallace, who has the best and most detailed Nirvana collection in the world.

My thanks to Amy Davis, Anthony Holland, Authors and Artists Group, Ben Semerdjian, Beth Keifitz, BG Dilworth, Bill Carroll, Bonnie Drucken-miller, Brad Wood, Bruce McDonald, Butch Vig, Calvert Morgan, Capacitor Network, Chad Channing, Charles R. Cross, Colleen Rawa, Courtney Love, Craig Montgomery, Dale Crover, Dan Peters, Dana Albarella, Dave Grohl, Dave Rosencrantz, David Beiber, David Fisher, David Fricke, Dean Williamson, Dudley, Eleanor Thomas, Elizabeth Bewley, Ethan Gussow, Gary Spivack, George Witte, Greg Wymer, Henry Santoro, Ian Clark, Jack Endino,

Jason Markey, Jeff Sodikoff, Jim Fitzgerald, Jim Merlis, Jon Cohen, Jon Leshay, Jon Rosenfelder, Jon Silva, Jonathan Ehrlich, Josh Brown, Julie Kramer, Karen Appuzo, Karen Glauber, Krist Novoselic, Kurt Cobain, Laurie Gail, Leon Femino, Lisa Berg, Margaret Rawa, Mark Kates, Max Tolkoff, Michael Azerrad, Michelle Munz, Mike Gioscia, Monica Mylod, Myles, Patty Jones, Paul Brown, Paul Buckley, Paul Langton, Paul Sleven, Rasmus Holden, Ross Zapien, Sandro Pugliese, Spencer Albee, Steve Ralbovsky, Surie Rudoff, Susie Tennant, Ted Volk, Todd Nichols, Tom Druckenmiller, Tom Gates, Tracy Leshay, Walter McDonough, WFNX staff 1987–1995.

Troy would like to give a very special thank you with heartfelt love and appreciation to Beth, Julian, and Simon for their never-ending support and encouragement and for allowing me to steal precious time from them to complete this project. From my heart, thank you so much for helping me realize a lifelong dream. And thank you to Nelly Asselta, who taught me how to take passion from my heart, pass it through to my hand, and inscribe it for all to read and see when the moment was just right.

Thank you to my mother and father and my entire family for all of the love and support.

Without the friendship and love of my wife, Megan, and the patience she endured during the project, the book could not have been completed. This book is for you.

Index

birth of, 7
Bleach album, 38–42
Channing, Chad and, 63
childhood of, 6–14
DGC Records, 82
diaries of, published, 228
disappearance of, 204–205
estate of, 218
fans of, 127, 180, 185, 192, 211–212, 213, 215–216, 227–228
From the Muddy Banks of the Wishkah, 226–227
funeral and memorial services for, 210–213
Grohl, Dave and, 75–76
guitars, 14–15, 162, 190–191
health of, 8, 57, 128, 161, 170, 182, 187–188, 195–196, 198–200
heroin use, 78, 124, 130, 133, 134–135, 136–137, 138, 139–140, 146–147, 177, 179, 181–182, 188, 195, 196, 197, 198–200, 205, 208
heroin use intervention attempts, 201–202
heroin use treatment, 203–204
house purchases, 193–194, 206
Insecticide, 154–155
instrument/equipment smashing, 36, 52–53, 58, 113, 117, 126, 127, 144
In Utero, 162–164, 165–168, 172–173, 175–176
The Jury, 54
Love, Courtney marital relationship, 133–134, 147, 156–159, 177–178, 180, 195, 197–198, 200–201, 203, 206
Love, Courtney marries, 129–130
Love, Courtney meets, 93
Love, Courtney relationship, 111, 118, 120–121
mourning for, 214–215
MTV network, 105
MTV Video Music Awards (TV program), 142, 143–146
musical influences on, 22
Nevermind album, 88, 91, 94–95, 99–101
Nirvana Live! Tonight! Sold Out! (video), 224
Novoselic, Krist and, 20, 23–25, 34, 130, 144
personality of, 5, 15–16, 17, 27, 60, 62
Peters, Dan and, 73–74
punk music, 16–17
quoted, 1, 6, 38, 75, 102

rehearsals, 25, 33, 79
Rolling Stone magazine, 128–129
royalty-sharing arrangement, 182–183
Saturday Night Live appearance, 124–127
sexuality of, 11–12, 13
Smear, Pat and, 180–181
"Smells Like Teen Spirit," 89–90, 103–104, 137–138
songwriting, 3, 42–43, 64, 76, 79, 87, 91, 95–98, 120, 132, 153, 157, 159, 161–162, 165–171, 180, 183
Stipe, Michael and, 222–223
Sub Pop Records, 46, 80–81, 83
suicidal ideation, 11, 15, 141–142, 170, 188, 216–218
suicide discovered, 207–208
suicide note, 206, 209–210, 212–213
suicide of, 170, 171, 194, 205–210
tours, 50–53, 55–58, 60, 61, 103, 105–112, 119, 129, 131–132, 185–196
Vail, Tobi and, 77–78
Vig, Butch and, 87
Cobain, Wendy Elizabeth Fradenburg (mother), 7, 8, 9, 10, 13, 14, 15, 76, 177, 179, 205, 208–209, 216, 217–218
cocaine abuse, 60
codeine, 45
Cokeley, Scott, 10
The College Media Journal's New Music Report, 109
Columbia Records, 81, 225
Come, 185
"Come as You Are," 90, 91, 118, 126, 127–128, 132, 134, 149
Come as You Are (book, Azerrad), 7, 139
"Come as You Are" video, 127–128, 148
Communion label, 109
Cope, Julian, 92
Corbijn, Anton, 172, 222
Corgan, Billy, 227
Cornell, Chris, 29, 60
Cox, Alex, 92
Creem magazine, 16
Croatia, Novoselic, Krist and, 159, 177, 178
Crover, Dale, 20, 23, 24, 31, 32, 36, 38, 44, 45, 56, 65, 66, 73, 105, 108, 153
Cult, 120
Cure, 143
"Curmudgeon," 132, 138
A Current Affair (TV program), 210
Cypress Hill, 192
C/Z Records, 41, 56, 153

Porno for Pyros, 225
Posies, 108
Postmyr, Line, 184
Power, Katherine Ann, 92
Premiere magazine, 92
prenuptial agreement, Cobain/Love, 130
Pretty on the Inside (Hole), 103
"The Priest They Called Him," 186
punk music. *See also* alternative music; grunge
   music
  Cobain, Kurt and, 16, 22, 155
  Grohl, Dave, 68–69
  Nirvana, 94
  Novoselic, Krist and, 20–21
"Puss," 132, 161

Q: Are We Not Men? A: We Are Devo (Devo),
  68

Rachtman, Rikki, 116
Radding, Reuben, 70
"Radio Friendly Unit Shifter," 170, 184, 192
The Raincoats, 200
"Rain Song," 69
The Ramones, 21, 103, 107
Ranaldo, Lee, 225
rape, 95, 168–169
"Rape Me," 103, 143, 144, 168–169, 184,
  192, 194, 204
Raphael, Amy, 146
Ras Records, 71
Rat Club (Boston, Massachusetts), 4
"Raunchola," 25
Reciprocal Recording, 31, 36
Reckoning (R.E.M.), 223
Red Hot Chili Peppers, 121, 143, 160
Red Kross, 91
Reed, Jesse, 12–13, 14, 15, 22, 23, 25, 27
Reed, Lou, 39–40, 164
Reimer, Marty, 208
R.E.M., 29, 45, 75, 169, 173, 184, 210, 222–
  223
Renaldo, Lee, 106, 179
The Replacements, 120
"Return of the Rat," 117, 133
Rimbaud, Arthur, 211
Riot Grrrl, 206
RIP magazine, 15, 217
Ritalin, 8
Rock 'n' Roll High School (Ramones), 103
Roeser, "Eddie" King, 179

Rolling Stone magazine, 128–129, 213, 222,
  225
Rolling Stones, 68, 222
Rollins, Henry, 225
Rooney, Andy, 213
"The Rose," 143
Rose, Axl, 112, 134, 142, 145–146
Rosenblatt, Ed, 208
Rosenfelder, John, 3
royalty-sharing arrangement, Nirvana, 182–
  183

Sage, Greg, 117, 133
Salt-n-Pepa, 222
Saperstein, Alexandra, 120
"Sappy" ("Verse Chorus Verse"), 57, 59–60,
  61
Sargent, Stephanie, 210, 219
Sassy magazine, 125, 133
Saturday Night Live (TV program), 4, 124–
  127, 128, 138, 154, 184, 224
"Scentless Apprentice," 167, 192
Schemps, 29
"School," 37, 43, 50, 107, 118, 119
"Scoff," 44, 136
Scratch Acid, 161
Scream, 71–73, 75
The Screaming Life/Fopp (Soundgarden),
  30
Screaming Trees, 35, 49, 54, 83, 143, 213
The Scum Manifesto, 96, 97
Seattle Sound, 29–31, 33–35. *See also*
  alternative music; grunge music; punk
  music
Seattle Times (newspaper), 205, 208
Select magazine, 132, 137
Seliger, Mark, 128, 129
"Serve the Servants," 192, 195
7 Year Bitch, 105, 210, 219
"Sex Bomb," 26
The Sex Pistols, 16, 21, 162
Sgt. Pepper's Lonely Hearts Club Band
  (Beatles), 85
Shelley, Steve, 225
Shocking Blue, 25, 43
Shonen Knife, 150, 185
Showbox Club (Seattle), 29
Sid and Nancy (film), 92
"Sifting," 37, 44
Silva, John, 84, 107, 202
Silver, Susan, 81
Simple Machines, 102